People, Power, Places

People, Power, Places

PERSPECTIVES IN VERNACULAR ARCHITECTURE, VIII

Edited by

Sally McMurry

and Annmarie Adams

THE UNIVERSITY OF TENNESSEE PRESS / KNOXVILLE

First Edition.

The paper used in this book meets the minimum requirements of ANSI/NISO Z39.48-1992 (R 1997) (Permanence of Paper). The binding materials have been chosen for strength and durability. Printed on recycled paper.

Library of Congress Cataloging in Publication Data (Revised for volume 8)

People, Power, Places/edited by Sally McMurry and Annmarie Adams.—1st ed.
p. cm.—(Perspectives in vernacular architecture; 8)
Includes bibliographical references and index.
ISBN 1-57233-075-9 (pbk.: alk. paper)
1. Vernacular architecture—United States.
2. Architecture and society—United States.
I. McMurry, Sally. II. Adams, Annmarie.
III. Series: Perspectives in vernacular architecture (Knoxville, Tenn.); 8.

for the preservation community worldwide
—S. M.

to Katie
—A. A.

Contents

Part II. Space and Power

Part III. The Interpenetration of Private and Public

Illustrations

Acknowledgments

We would like to express our thanks to the many people who have given generously of their time and expertise in the shaping of this volume. The University of Tennessee Press staff and editors have patiently answered our queries along the way, and to them we extend our thanks. In addition, we especially would like to thank others who have contributed from their fund of advice, expertise, and experience: Anne Allen, Peter Boag, Jim Buckley, Betsy Cromley, David Danbom, Pete Daniel, Dennis Domer, Amy Greenberg, Paul Groth, Richard Harris, Greg Hise, David Hounshell, Thomas Hubka, Tera W. Hunter, Joyce Ice, David Jaffee, Berkeley Kaite, Neil Larson, Carol Lee, J. N. Lightstone, Richard Longstreth, Carl Lounsbury, James Merrell, Joanne Meyerowitz, Gulsum Nalbantoglu, Gerald Pocius, Mark Reinberger, Adam Rome, Susan Shirk, Pamela H. Simpson, Billy Smith, Daphne Spain, Myron O. Stachiw, Paul Touart, Laurel Ulrich, Ellen Weiss, Camille Wells, Richard Guy Wilson, David Vanderburgh, R. J. Van Pelt, and Abby Van Slyck. Annmarie Adams thanks the School of Architecture, McGill University, and Sally McMurry thanks Penn State's history department office staff, especially Karen Ebeling.

People, Power, Places: An Introduction

The essays in *People, Power, Places* represent a continuing effort to define and explore important issues in vernacular architecture studies. These essays were originally papers presented at the annual meetings of the Vernacular Architecture Forum (VAF) held in Lawrence, Kansas (1996), and Portland, Oregon (1997). Since the VAF's formation in 1980, the organization's annual meetings have attracted scholars active in a wide range of enterprises. Some are public historians, activists, or preservationists. Others are academics representing many disciplines, including geography, American studies, architectural history, and folklore, to name just a few. All share a commitment to understanding and protecting the vernacular built environment. Over time, the VAF and its major publication, *Perspectives in Vernacular Architecture*, have contributed mightily to this understanding, and even to redefining the scope of "vernacular" itself. Originally tending to focus on the old, the rural, and the handmade, vernacular architecture studies has in more recent years remade itself into a far more wide-ranging inquiry that stresses a set of questions rather than a particular type of building. As it is currently evolving, vernacular architecture studies endeavors to fashion a "new architectural history"—a phrase Bernard Herman and Thomas Carter introduced when they edited *Perspectives in Vernacular Architecture, IV*—which will exploit the power of interdisciplinary thinking to analyze buildings within a social, cultural, historical, and aesthetic context. *Perspectives in Vernacular Architecture*, the series of which this volume is the eighth, collectively trace the evolution of vernacular architecture scholarship. The essays in this volume—papers first given at the VAF meetings, then selected on the basis of specialist reader reports, and then revised—offer fine examples of the insights that have resulted as investigators turn their attention to modern buildings or examine afresh issues that present continuing challenges.

Whether explicitly or implicitly, all of the essays address questions of how people, power, and places intersect. A basic premise of vernacular architecture studies is that in order to explain the built environment we must analyze how the culture, social structure, and values of people—whether designers or users—shape the landscape. People and places are inextricably linked. The first section of the book, "Vernacular Building as Process," offers varied examples of how people in particular places interpreted and reinterpreted vernacular structures in response to shifting cultural, economic, and political currents. The next two sections, "Space and Power" and "The Interpenetration of Private and Public," explicitly examine how power relationships enter the equation, showing how spatial organization sometimes codifies power relationships and at other times challenges the existing power structure. The relationship between private and public, too, can be an issue of power, since the very definition of *public* has historically excluded whole categories of people based on divisions by race and gender.

Part I: Vernacular Building as Process

Every building begins to undergo a process of change almost the minute the last nail is hammered down. Indeed, at the heart of the study of vernacular buildings is the relationship between people and buildings over time. Thus some of the most fertile work in the field has concerned the process whereby the built environment is adapted over time as societies change. In the mute testimony of framing members, nails, hinges, and moldings, we may read the story of changes to individual buildings, and from there we may move toward an understanding of important historical changes. Cloverfields Plantation on Maryland's Eastern Shore, for example, originally faced the river; late-colonial additions were oriented to the road—one indication of shifts in transportation patterns and even of the source of information and social contacts. When the study is extended to groups of buildings, the insights become still richer and more complex. One need only think of the work of Thomas Hubka, who discovered that the connected New England farm originally consisted of scattered, separate buildings, or Cary Carson and his associates, who marked out the momentous transition from earthfast to permanent structures in the colonial Chesapeake. The new essays in this collection contribute further to our understanding of the patterns of process in vernacular architecture.

One clear characteristic of vernacular process is that it is the product of thousands of individual decisions, which when taken collectively produce change on the landscape. Fred Peterson examines one of the most enduring subjects of interest in the history of construction technology—the emergence of the balloon frame. This American innovation forms the basis of much residential construction even today. Peterson shows that the technique evolved over a period of half a century, as artisans all over the nation experimented with different types and configurations of framing members. This happened in tandem with the rise of milling machinery for mass producing lumber, and with the steady extension of transportation systems. Peterson's painstakingly analyzed frames call into question any notion of "standardization" for the nineteenth and early twentieth centuries. His careful study lays to rest, once and for all, any notion that the balloon frame was a single individual's "invention." The evidence amassed from building after building conclusively refutes the interpretations of well-known scholars such as Sigfried Giedion.

Other essays presented here also challenge the

scholarship of Giedion and his generation. If the balloon frame was not the epitome of the new machine age, neither were all Americans comfortable or enthusiastic about the rise of industrial civilization. Indeed, antimodernism surfaced in unlikely spots; as the machine age bumped up against nostalgia for old times, strange and ambiguous hybrids appeared on the vernacular landscape. These idiosyncratic buildings speak to Americans' deep ambivalence about modernity. William Rhoads's analysis of the "trolley car cottage" is a case in point. In the early twentieth century, as electric streetcars replaced their horse-drawn predecessors, a few were reclaimed for beach cabins, residences, shops, summer homes, or country camps. These unconventional buildings were often portrayed in romantic, nostalgic terms and associated with supposedly traditional values of self-sufficiency, rural life, or idyllic pastoralism. Thus their "machine" qualities were either downplayed or denied outright. Sometimes they embodied subtle resistance to the often rigid middle-class strictures which accompanied modernity. Yet at the same time, trolley cottages could also affirm modernity as "machines for living," made of modern materials (iron and steel, containing electric motors). The process of turning old trolleys into buildings never became widespread, but it did reveal fractures in the response to modernization. The trolley car, then, embodies in material culture the antimodernist strains examined by such scholars as Jackson Lears. It offers concrete evidence of how an ambivalent antimodernism extended beyond the American intellectual elite and upper class.

During the same years as balloon-framing experimentation and trolley cottage nostalgia, the United States experienced one of its biggest waves of immigration. Immigrants from eastern and southern Europe encountered an unfamiliar environment, and in turn contributed much to reshaping the landscape. This encounter, too, shaped vernacular building process. Thomas Hubka and Judith Kenny offer a fascinating view of the "Polish cottage" in Milwaukee's immigrant neighborhoods. This form (a four-room frame dwelling with various modifications, such as roof, basement, front, rear, or middle additions) was so ubiquitous among the city's Poles that it acquired the sobriquet "Polish cottage." Operating here was a complex process of assimilation in which immigrants showed great facility in mastering the new Anglo-American world of construction, standardized technology, innovative financing, and contracting—not building themselves, as in other urban areas such as Flint and Milwaukee (see *PVA, VII*), but entering the conventional system by which so much of the American urban fabric was constructed and financed. Immigrant homebuilders modified the "workers' cottage" for heavily populated centers. Yet they injected a distinctive twist into this system, too, for the houses they bought allowed for a vibrantly syncretistic mix of cultural elements. For one thing, they could be adapted to accommodate tenants. Often this served as a means of allowing immigrants to afford to buy a house, but it also promoted immigrant adjustment. Scholars have noted that boarding served an important purpose in many immigrant communities, perpetuating kinship and Old World geographical ties and offering a place in which new immigrants could find familiar surroundings but also learn the English language and American work mores. As Polish families grew more prosperous in Milwaukee, the Polish cottage was often reconverted to single-family housing. Over time, they also adopted American-style spatial patterns by incorporating separate dining rooms, individualized children's sleeping space, and including plumbing. Thus the presence on the landscape of this distinctive building type is evidence of the cultural mixing that took place over half a century.

Milwaukee's Poles enjoyed a degree of success, but migrants moving from the Midwest's "Cutover" region (Michigan's Upper Peninsula, northern Wisconsin, and Minnesota) to Alaska during the Great Depression were not so fortunate. Under a Federal Emergency Relief Administration (FERA) sponsored resettlement program, nine hundred people moved to Alaska's Matanuska valley to homestead. Government officials reasoned that these migrants, accustomed as they were to harsh conditions in the upper Midwest, would be ideally suited to adapt successfully and farm in the fabled Matanuska valley. However, the venture foundered. Fewer than half the original families remained after four years. Many factors contributed, but Arnold Alanen argues that inappropriate building should take a large share of the blame. The FERA-designated architects had little Alaska experience, and the log and frame farmhouses and barns they insisted on were woefully unsuited to farming purposes, not to mention incapable of withstanding Alaska winters. Settlers rightfully protested, but to no avail. Those few who did stick it out managed to do so because they adapted and upgraded their buildings.

In this case, the process of planning and building on the land resulted in failure. The Alaska case study raises interesting questions about the vernacular as process, especially with regard to why some building processes flourish and others struggle or decline altogether. It surely illustrates the problems that can result when the links among sponsor, user, designer, and builder are attenuated or even at cross-purposes. In this case, different constituencies had conflicting agendas; within the New Deal, for example, conservative and left-leaning approaches to problems of depression and poverty vied for preeminence, and resettlement programs eventually lost out. The state was also trying to achieve too many different goals in the Alaska resettlement experiment—both sending a message to the Soviet Union and solving "overpopulation" problems in the Lower 48, for example. Whatever the goal, funding was clearly inadequate, and the consulting architects for the job were chosen for political rather than professional reasons. Meanwhile, the settlers wanted a legitimate chance to farm successfully, but were not supplied with the means to do so.

Part II: Space and Power

The story of the unsuccessful state-sponsored building program in Alaska points to the critical role that power relationships play in any analysis of vernacular landscapes. These relationships become more visible, and sometimes more potent, when formal governmental institutions are involved, but they exist in all landscapes. In the colonial era landscapes of Charleston, Virginia, or Maryland, for example, the white elite sought to reinforce its own dominance. As Dell Upton showed in *Holy Things and Profane,* in Anglican parish churches, architectural finishes, sculpture, wall ornament, and spatial layout all communicated the message that the earthly hierarchy mirrored a heavenly order. Similarly, Bernard Herman argued in *Exploring Everyday Landscapes: Perspectives in Vernacular Architecture, VII*, that the Charleston single house employed spatial signals to convey messages about status and power. Like many other places along the Atlantic seaboard, Charleston merchants arranged their entertaining rooms with the intention of impressing and competing with their peers. The quality of finishes diminished with distance away from the social center, until finally at the rear of the site, steps down physically reinforced the position of slaves, at the bottom of the social hierarchy. In Tidewater Maryland, plantation houses occupied high terrain overseeing slave work areas and living quarters.

Within these landscapes of power, subordinated people often contested these messages and created spaces for themselves, however tenuous and insecure. In Charleston, slaves congregated in back alleyways; in the Virginia countryside, they created intricate networks of paths in the wooded areas; in Tidewater Maryland, they invested the northeast corners of buildings with religious significance and secretly carried on spiritual practices representing a syncretistic blend of African and European elements.

Four of the essays in *Perspectives in Vernacular Architecture, VIII*, concern themselves explicitly with these sorts of relationships of space and power. Systems of racial segregation exemplify some of the most brutal ways in which white elites have used state power to enforce white dominance. Under both apartheid in South Africa and Jim Crow laws in the American South, legal, spatial regulation was one of the key elements in a vast system of oppression that systematically denied people basic civil and economic freedoms on the basis of race. In these instances, space was one of the most effective means of communicating power —simply by dictating where certain individuals could live and move, and by keeping races physically apart, segregation assured white dominance.

In her essay "'Come in the Dark': Domestic Workers and Their Rooms in Apartheid-Era Johannesburg, South Africa," Rebecca Ginsburg takes a close look at how African women contested the strict spatial regulations placed on their behavior under apartheid in the 1960s and 1970s. As domestic servants to white families, black women inhabited two distinct forms of housing in Johannesburg: the so-called back room, a separate structure built in the rear yard of suburban houses, and the skylight location, the uppermost floor of apartment buildings. These rudimentary dwellings were places in which African women housed family members, sexual partners, and even complete strangers, unbeknownst to their employers. According to Ginsburg, the complex system of observation and concealing that she uncovers with her interviewees went far beyond satisfying their need for companionship; it provided a means by which this oppressed group mitigated the harshness of their lives. Ginsburg also effectively shows how Africans created a different mental urban geography than did whites. In analyzing vernacular space from the perspective of the powerless, Ginsburg's essay contributes to the rewriting of South African history now under way as black-majority rule has replaced the old regime. It also makes a methodological contribution in vernacular architecture studies more generally by reconstructing the mental geography of an entire class of people.

Zeynep Kezer's essay examines another sinister case in which state power was communicated through spaces and artifacts: republican Turkey used a museum to create a modern national landscape. In the early twentieth century, during the rise of Kemal Atatürk, the founder of modern Turkey, "traditional" Turkish customs and groups were regarded as inimical to modernization. One such group was the Sufi order known as *tarikats*. As it consolidated its power, the Turkish state in 1925 closed all the sacred sites used by tarikats, identifying them as sites of subversive political activities. Officials inventoried and looted the contents of these places. In addition, small mosques were shut down by the state in an attempt to undermine the constitutive role of Islam in everyday life.

At the same time, in the newly established Ethnography Museum in Ankara, sited on Namazgah Hill between the new national capital and the old town and citadel, artifacts from the sect were assembled into an exhibit which portrayed them as the innocuous remnants of a bygone Turkish folklife. Here, the state engaged in a powerful manipulation of both space and facts to distort history and to assert a specific vision of secularization.

In nineteenth-century America, by contrast, the state was less successful in imposing spatial discipline. Elaine Jackson-Retondo examines the Massachusetts State Prison, opened in 1805. By midcentury, the prison fabric had been extended and altered many times. Jackson-Retondo takes issue with the pioneering interpretations of scholars such as David Rothman and Michel Foucault, who stress the punitive intent behind the two primary prison plans of the nineteenth century: the spoke/hub of the Eastern States Penitentiary in Philadelphia and the solitary confinement cells of Auburn Penitentiary in New York State. These analyses, while they did place the penal reform movement into broader context, "sidelined everyday realities" of how the prisons actually operated. In Massachusetts, a large percentage of the prison's physical environment consisted of work spaces. The extensive manufacturing activities that went on inside the prison took place in shops, which offered prisoners a chance to make weapons, keys, and tools. Officials responded in various ways—for example, by adding an open workshop where workers could be easily observed—but eventually accreted many specialized work buildings onto the original prison block. The Massachusetts State Prison eventually became a "hybrid" of the Eastern and Auburn systems, overlaid—indeed overshadowed—by the work buildings.

Here, officials' eagerness to profit from inmates' labor prompted deviation from strict adherence to moral reform through spatial discipline. Perhaps this history is best seen as an aspect of the stage in which state government stood at midcentury. Governments reached into far fewer aspects of people's lives and had not consolidated their power to the same extent as they would by the twentieth century. The liberal state, too, was consistent with encouraging capitalistic endeavors such as the profit-making inmate work programs. Both the essays by Kezer and Jackson-Retondo represent a new generation of scholarship in which the "old" political history and the "new" social history are merged in provocative ways. In this rich analysis, the state is considered in a complex relationship with social groups and forces, and the interaction between the two creates a new perspective on both. Such a perspective calls into question monolithic views of the early state's power and show how much stronger the twentieth-century state was than its predecessor. It also reconfirms the power of buildings and spatial analysis to contribute to the reshaping of historical discussion.

Another key element in Foucault's analysis of penal institutions was what he called the "gaze" of surveillance: the "process of vision involving a sustained and purposeful look that has as its intent processes of transformation and the power to affect behavior through the very act of gazing." While in Foucault's analysis the "gaze" went in one direction, from overseers to the punished, Anna Vemer Andrzejewski's analysis of camp meetings suggests that lines of vision were constructed so as to permit reciprocity. In the context of the revivalistic camp-meeting landscape, the "gaze" operated to construct new social hierarchies—for example, by dividing people according to whether or not they were saved. Not only "divisive" hierarchies developed but also "affirmative" ones based on such actions as spectatorship.

Part III: The Interpenetration of Private and Public

Andrzejewski's reexamination of camp meetings as arenas where complex power relations were played out contributes equally to recent research on the interpenetration of the so-called private and public spheres. While the model of the "separate spheres" acted as a useful paradigm for many pioneering women historians of the 1970s, who mostly employed it to illuminate the systematic oppression of women in (sometimes) spatial terms, scholars of the 1990s have devoted considerable attention to the dismantling of the separate spheres idea, arguing instead for an understanding of industrial society which saw a considerable overlap in public and private aspirations.

In the field of vernacular architecture studies, this shift in outlook has mostly affected our understanding of the middle-class home. Whereas historians of the 1970s typically argued the home was an isolated, feminized, and thus protective space, more recent scholarship on domestic architecture of all classes has revealed the home to be a realm occupied and affected by women and men, connected in complex ways to the broader domain of the unpredictable, industrialized city.

Five papers in *PVA, VIII*, deal directly with this interpenetration of private and public. None of them deals with the architecture of the traditional, middle-class home, and yet they all attempt to recast the place of home, in different ways, as essentially public.

Two essays, one by Larry Morrisey and Michael Ann Williams and another by Travis McDonald Jr., explore this intersection of public and private by examining how well-known "public" figures have provided insight into their private lives through architectural form. Morrisey and Williams look at the relationships of country music stars—John Lair and Dolly Parton—to the tourist sites they helped create. Just as Lair's Renfro Valley, a popular attraction in the 1940s and 1950s, was a fascinating mix of his own rural roots and modern consumer culture, Dollywood of the 1980s combined aspects of Parton's poor childhood and her shrewd business sense. Both sites acted as expressions of self-documentation or auto-ethnography and, as public places, came to occupy this ambiguous zone between the private and the public.

Countless other places like Renfro Valley and Dollywood dot the North American tourist agenda: Graceland, Hearst Castle, Monticello, to name a few. Presumably, they reveal *something* of their famous inhabitants' real experiences, no doubt tempered by pressures to turn a profit as tourist sites in the twentieth century. At Elvis's Memphis mansion, for example, many of the King's personal effects, including his clothes and guitars, are displayed museum-style in glass cases.

At Hearst Castle, visitors delight at the chance to see William Randolph Hearst's dining table set for company, including his beloved bottle of ketchup. Monticello, of course, reveals much about its chief occupant, Thomas Jefferson, as well as his employees, their families, his relatives, frequent visitors, and the numerous African American slaves who lived there with him.

In his essay "Constructing Optimism: Thomas Jefferson's Poplar Forest," McDonald casts new light on the third president of the United States by looking at a less famous home than Monticello, Poplar Forest, and by documenting the role played by Jefferson in the construction rather than the design per se of this private retreat. Since Poplar Forest was destroyed by a devastating fire in 1845, McDonald reconstructs Jefferson's efforts largely through his correspondence and argues, like Morrisey and Williams, that buildings are hard evidence of an individual's inner soul. In Jefferson's case, McDonald reads certain instances of architectural compromise (poor brickwork, etc.) as exemplary of the sorts of contradictions that plagued the president. In general, however, as his title attests, McDonald sees Jefferson's concern for details as a form of optimism typical of the American Enlightenment Jefferson helped design and construct.

McDonald's paper, in addition, illuminates the names and contributions of the workers who labored on Poplar Forest. A significant aspect of vernacular architecture studies over the past few decades has involved uncovering the roles of individuals who inhabited, constructed, altered, and demolished buildings, yet whose presence is typically overshadowed by the grandeur of a more famous designer or occupant. This is particularly true of construction workers, whose efforts have been completely neglected in the historical record. McDonald's paper is a reminder, like Peterson's, of how buildings are collaborative efforts among many individuals, rather than simply the products of individual architects.

Ann Smart Martin's essay "Commercial Space as Consumption Arena: Retail Stores in Early Virginia" argues the interpenetration of private and public from outside the home. By exploring the spatial arrangements of eighteenth-century shops in Virginia, Martin shows that these commercial establishments were significant sites of inclusion for blacks, whites, women, men, poor, and rich. In addition, these shops, which at first glance had rather simple massing, were complex diagrams of social relations in terms of their planning; merchants and their spaces had to woo customers and control their movements simultaneously, which they accomplished through the careful placement of windows, counters, offices, and storage.

The relationship of house to shop was sophisticated too. Despite their growing identity as specialized commercial establishments, eighteenth-century shops in Virginia retained significant aspects of domestic ideology, perhaps as an expression of their rather unique positions as privately owned establishments that were open to the public.

This tension between public institutions and their overtly domestic roots is also a central theme in the two papers included in *PVA, VIII*, that deal with Progressive reform: "Chicago's Eleanor Clubs: Housing Working Women in the Early Twentieth Century" by Jeanne Catherine Lawrence and Marta Gutman's "Inside the Institution: The Art and Craft of Settlement Work at the Oakland New Century Club, 1895–1923." Both these studies deal with change over time as new building types moved from occupying "borrowed buildings," in this case houses, to inhabiting purpose-built, large-scale spaces. In this way both Lawrence and Gutman show how temporary accommodations (much neglected in the scholarship) hold significant information for the observer of vernacular architecture.

Lawrence's essay is a case study of a housing type, the Eleanor Club, which offered accommodation to unmarried, working women in early-twentieth-century Chicago. Her analysis of the plans of these buildings (like Martin's interpretation of the shops' plan) underlines the fine line between the freedom and security that Eleanor Clubs extended its young inhabitants.

Gutman's paper, on the other hand, looks at the public side of private life, as the settlement house offered instruction in domestic service, among other skills, to the working-class inhabitants of West Oakland, California. As she shows, the Oakland New Century Club occupied a Janus-like position at the turn of this century, seeking to reconcile older ideas about charity, reform, identity, and domesticity with more modern approaches and conceptions. In Gutman's essay, the analysis of building interiors is a means to explore how the institution bridged these traditional and modern ideals.

The range of questions asked in the thirteen essays included in *Perspectives in Vernacular Architecture, VIII*, then, make substantial contributions to our understanding of how people, power, and places have shaped each other in a variety of time periods and geographical areas. What the authors share is a scholarly curiosity about ordinary places and what buildings might reveal about their makers, users, and even interpreters. The authors' differences, of course, are what make the field of vernacular architecture studies the rich, interdisciplinary domain that it has become over the past two decades.

PART I

VERNACULAR BUILDING AS PROCESS

CHAPTER 1

Fred W. Peterson

Anglo-American Wooden Frame Farmhouses in the Midwest, 1830–1900: Origins of Balloon Frame Construction

Four major factors contributed to the origin of balloon frame construction in the midwestern United States from the 1830s through the 1890s. First, steam-powered saws milled standardized dimension lumber from an abundant supply of timber in the pineries of Wisconsin, Michigan, and Minnesota. Second, industries in the eastern states supplied kegs of cut iron nails at reasonable costs. Third, water and overland transportation systems enabled shipment of these essential materials to places in the region where the building of commercial and domestic structures proceeded at a rapid pace. Finally, local carpenters, already familiar with labor saving approaches to building with wood, nailed together standard-sized members of structures to assemble sturdy lightweight frames. By the mid-1840s the varied results of their labors became identified as balloon frame construction.[1]

Before scholarship in vernacular architectural studies informed discussions of the development of balloon frame construction, Sigfried Giedion traced the origins of the building method to the work of one man, George Washington Snow.[2] In the 1941 edition of *Space, Time, and Architecture*, Giedion claimed that Snow's invention "must have seemed utterly revolutionary to carpenters."[3] He traced his inventor-hero's pedigree to the *Mayflower*, described him as "a rather restless spirit" with a "pioneer temperament," a "jack-of-all-trades," and added that a portrait of the man from a family album revealed "a face at once full of puritan energy and of human sensitivity."[4]

Walker Field reexamined the origins of balloon frame construction in 1965 and concluded that a practical carpenter, Augustine Deodat Taylor, was the inventor of the framing system, evaluating it as "so new as to be startling."[5] In the 1983 Paul Sprague "Chicago Balloon Frame" study, the origin of the method returned to G. W. Snow. Sprague conjectured that the idea for wooden framing came to Snow "in a flash of genius."[6]

These searches for and discoveries of inventors of balloon frame construction are based on assumptions that revolutionary theories and startlingly new practices originate from creative, virtuous individuals. Innovators whom historians have recognized are almost always white males to whom are attributed qualities of extraordinary theoretical and practical knowledge, profound insight, pioneering spirit, and competitive edge to know and develop a good thing when they see it.[7]

Examination of the literature about balloon frame construction from the mid-1840s to the 1890s indicates that if Snow or Taylor had actually invented something, no one knew exactly what it was. Descriptions and illustrations of balloon frame construction varied considerably from one author to another. Further, few architects or engineers recommended the materials and technique, and those that did eventually changed their minds and advised against what they claimed was a flimsy way to build.[8]

George Woodward published a series of articles in *The Cultivator* from 1860 to 1861 in which he explained balloon frame construction in the most positive terms. Woodward's series and essays written by other planners and engineers no doubt had an effect on readers of the agricultural journals and architectural stylebooks; but one cannot imagine that local carpenters, who learned from concrete experience and tended to distrust abstract theory, readily put aside their acquired ways of building to fully comprehend and utilize a new method of construction that was neither clearly defined nor consistently applied. Practical carpenters seemed to have formed an operational definition of balloon frame construction as a general approach to building that was not rigidly fixed into a system that strictly defined the kind, size, and placement of members of the frame.

Anglo-American carpenters and farmers in the Midwest performed variations of the framing technique according to local building practices and consonant with their own skills. These builders had already learned from previous generations of Yankee craftsmanship ways to save time, energy, and materials in building wooden frame structures. From the seventeenth through the eighteenth centuries carpenters in New England introduced labor saving modifications to traditional timber framing methods and materials by simplifying mortise and tenon joints, reducing the scale of frame members, or eliminating studs when heavy boards were vertically nailed to the frame to stiffen the structure in plank frame construction.[9] Changes in wooden frame construction in the Chesapeake region during the seventeenth century also revealed patterns of change guided by economies achieved through reducing the dimensions of structural members and standardizing processes of building.[10]

From the early 1830s to the 1860s, Anglo-Americans were the first to migrate to new areas of settlement in the Midwest from New England, New York, Pennsylvania, Ohio, Indiana, and Illinois. Yankee builders brought "the old ways" of doing things with them from their place of origin in the East or the lower Midwest. The first permanent houses they built in every new area of settlement in the region were traditional heavy-frame upright and wing or I-houses. During the second generation of building in these areas, farmers and carpenters constructed varieties of lightweight balloon frame dwellings of the same house types.[11] Documentation and analysis of forty of these farm homes built from the mid-1830s to about 1900

Fig. 1.1a. Timber frame/balloon frame farmhouse, Dane County, Wisconsin, c. 1850–70. Photograph by the author.

provides material evidence that Anglo-American carpenters and farmers experimented with the means and methods of building economically and efficiently that developed from traditional timber frame construction to versions of braced frame building, and eventually resulted in balloon frame construction.[12]

The upright section of a farmhouse built in Dane County, Wisconsin, about 1840 was framed with four-by-four inch studs spaced at about twenty-inch intervals and mortised into both sill and plate (fig. 1.1). The frame was securely braced at top and bottom corners and filled with chunks of limestone between external sheathing and inner lath and plaster. Eight rough-hewn eight-by-twelve-inch log joists mortised into the sill and spaced thirty-

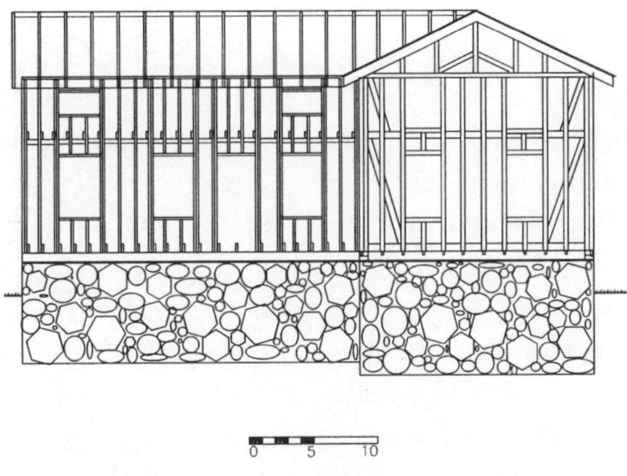

Fig. 1.1b. Timber frame/balloon frame farmhouse, Dane County, Wisconsin, c. 1850–70, framing system.

Fig. 1.2a. Balloon frame farmhouse, Columbia County, Wisconsin, c. 1865–70. Photograph by the author.

six inches on center supported the first-floor parlor and dining room. The wing added to the upright section about 1870 is a sturdy version of balloon frame construction. This structure is typical of the earliest frame dwellings built in rural areas of the region. The two units document a change from heavy construction that is neither timber nor braced frame to a local version of a balloon frame while preserving a traditional house type in elevation and floor plan.[13]

A farmhouse constructed in two phases from about 1865 to 1890 in Columbia County, Wisconsin, represents the next generation of upright and wing house types in that state (fig. 1.2). Although

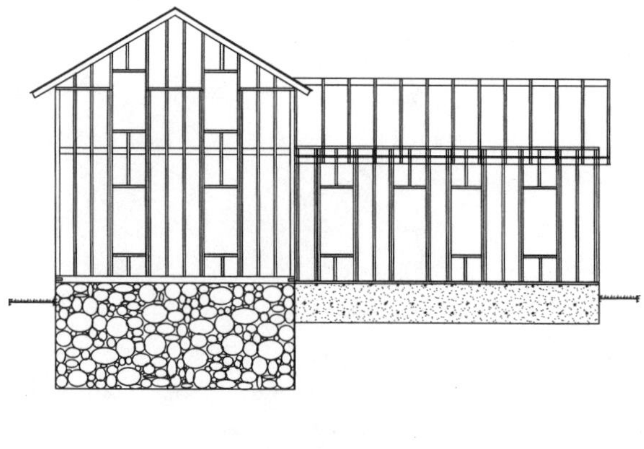

Fig. 1.2b. Balloon frame farmhouse, Columbia County, Wisconsin, c. 1865–70, framing system.

Fig. 1.3a. Balloon frame farmhouse, Waupaca County, Wisconsin, 1904. Photograph by the author.

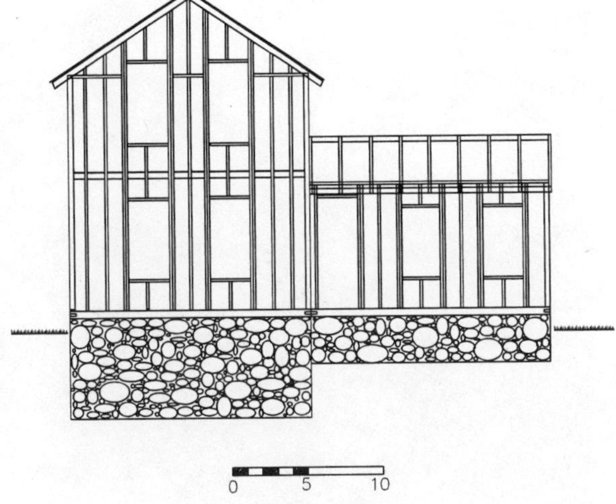

Fig. 1.3b. Balloon frame farmhouse, Waupaca County, Wisconsin, 1904, framing system.

the carpenter joined corners of the sill by an open mortise cut and mortised the joists into the sill and a central first-floor beam, he nailed together the studs, plate, and rafters. More compact than the Dane County dwelling, this farmhouse maintained a traditional layout of rooms.

Farther north, in Waupaca County, an inscription on the sill of the house dates a later example of a Wisconsin upright and wing in 1904 (fig. 1.3). A two-foot-wide stone foundation supported an eight-by-eight-inch sill that was mortised at each corner. The builder also mortised floor joists into the sill as well as a central basement beam. He nailed two-by-four studs to the sill sixteen inches on center then sheathed them with rough boards and clapboard siding. An extra layer of thin sheathing boards fastened to the interior surface of the studs provided the surface for lath and plaster on chamber walls and ceilings. The completed structure has the characteristic thin, crisp appearance of a balloon frame structure while incorporating some conservative construction features of its traditional ancestors.

A similar pattern of change in adapting traditional house types to new construction techniques was evident on Iowa frontiers. The first unit of an I-house built on a Muscatine County farm about 1840 was a lightweight timber frame made of a four-by-eight sill and four-by-four-inch corner posts, studs, and plate (fig. 1.4). The carpenter used both mortise and tenon joints and nails to assemble members of the frame. Brick chimneys at each gable end of the one-and-one-half-story structure served traditional hall and parlor spaces divided by a staircase. Carpenters built balloon frame additions to the core of the house in the 1880s. Similar to the Dane County, Wisconsin, farmhouse, the structure of this I-house developed from a heavy frame using locally available materials for balloon frame construction while preserving a traditional house type in elevation and floor plan.

A framing technique that developed from lightweight timber construction is represented in a braced frame I-house built about 1850 in Keokuk County, Iowa, by a Yankee farmer/carpenter from

Fig. 1.4a. Timber frame/balloon frame farmhouse, Muscatine County, Iowa, c. 1840–80. Photograph by the author.

Pennsylvania (fig. 1.5).[14] He used locally milled lumber to construct a frame of six-by-six-inch corner posts and two-by-six-inch studs mortised into a ten-by-ten-inch hand-hewn oak sill.[15] Two-by-ten-inch joists supported first- and second-story floors. Securely fastening all members of the frame with an abundance of iron nails, he also braced the frame at each corner on both stories.

By the 1870s, when railroad lines shipped industrially milled lumber and iron nails to established farming communities in the state, carpenters initiated experiments with the basic components of what was to become balloon frame construction.[16] By the mid-1870s a farmer used the lighter weight

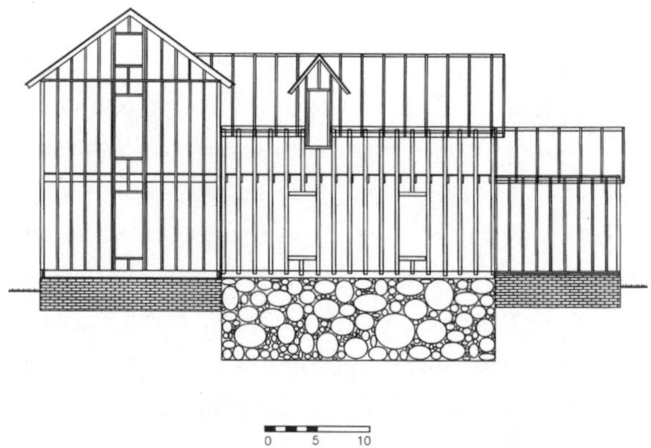

Fig. 1.4b. Timber frame/balloon frame farmhouse, Muscatine County, Iowa, c. 1840–80, framing system.

Fig. 1.5a. Braced frame farmhouse, Keokuk County, Iowa, c. 1850. Photograph by the author.

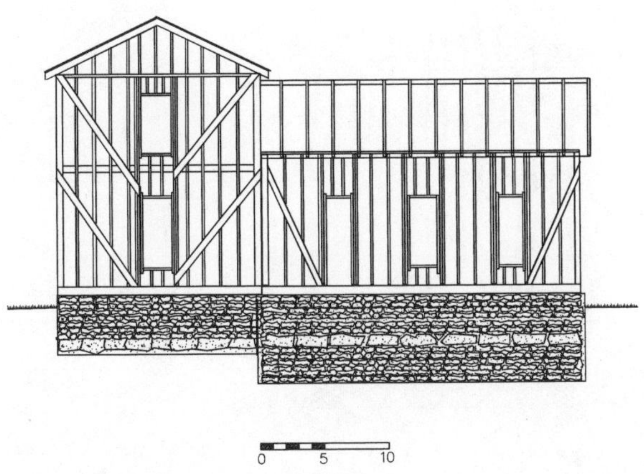

Fig. 1.5b. Braced frame farmhouse, Keokuk County, Iowa, c. 1850, framing system.

materials to assemble a two-story I-house in Muscatine County in which he nailed together all members of the frame with a consistent spacing of studs and joists at sixteen inches on center and roof rafters at twenty-four inches on center (fig. 1.6). Window and door openings were scaled to fit thirty-two-inch intervals between two studs. Although this structure does not exhibit the typical tall narrow I of the house type, the consistent measurements and proportions of the structure indicate that the carpenter had a clear, practical conception of balloon frame construction.

During the 1860s to the early 1900s, as the frontier moved westward into Nebraska and northward

Fig. 1.6a. Balloon Frame Farmhouse, Muscatine County, Iowa, c. 1880. Photograph by the author.

into South Dakota, similar transitions from heavy framing techniques to local versions of balloon frame construction appeared as local craftsmen experimented with the new materials to build in a way that suited their own sense of structure and satisfied their clients' desire for a good product at a low cost. An analysis of some of the structural details of these wooden frame farmhouses illustrates the variety of building techniques used with the new materials. From the 1840s to the 1890s no general consensus prevailed on what constituted the proper way to assemble a frame structure composed of standardized milled lumber, cut iron nails, or wire steel nails.[17]

Sill construction ranged from solid members

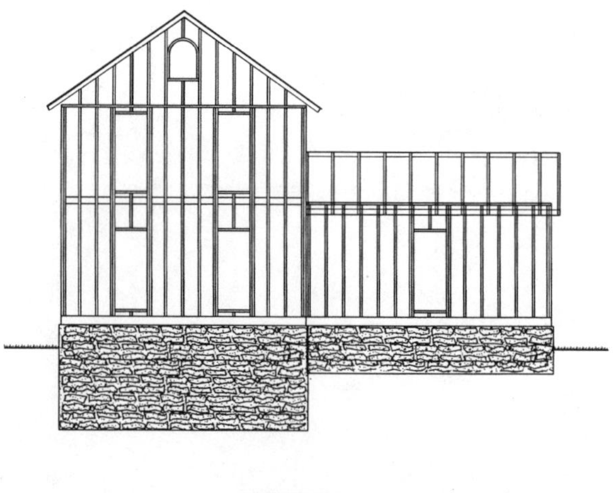

Fig. 1.6b. Balloon Frame Farmhouse, Muscatine County, Iowa, c. 1880, framing system.

Fig. 1.7. Variations of sill construction.

measuring from eight-by-twelve inches, six-by-six inches, to configurations of two-by-eights and two-by-sixes in L or box shapes. Studs were mortised and/or nailed directly to the sill, nestled in the L or box of the sill, or let-in to the vertical section of the L- or box-shaped sill (fig. 1.7).[18] Two-by-eight first-floor joists were sometimes mortised into the sill, positioned on top of the sill and nailed to studs, or framed and nailed within a box sill. Two-by-eight or two-by-six-inch second-floor joists rested on a ledger let-in and/or were nailed to the studs. In one instance, a builder used two-by-four members to span the ceiling of the first floor and another series of two-by-fours positioned only four inches above, nailed and braced to the first series. This trusslike assemblage acted as the second-floor joists.

The length of the studs determined the elevation of the larger unit of an upright and wing or I-house. The requisite eight-foot ceiling more or less set the height for kitchen wings. Builders calculated the length and width of structures according to their skill and experience as well as ability to conceive of the structure as a whole. A builder then could predetermine a regular placement of studs and calculate window and door openings that would create formal symmetry of facade and also functional alignments with interior spaces. For instance, a carpenter could run a continuous series of studs at sixteen inches on center for a wall twenty-four feet long. For an extension of twenty-eight feet, he had to begin and end the sequence with a twelve-inch interval before the studs created an uninterrupted sixteen inches on center sequence. Some builders appeared to have calculated these measurements before construction; others seemed to have learned the logic of balloon construction through experience. Builders with less foresight or experience syncopated the rhythm of studs throughout the frame at irregular intervals. When a carpenter doubted the strength of the wall, he nailed horizontal or diagonal one-by-four or two-by-four-inch braces between studs to stiffen the slender two-by-four-inch members.

The unbroken rise of studs from sill to plate in one-story, one-and-one-half-story, and two-story structures is a distinguishing feature of balloon frame construction. In rare instances, carpenters built the first story of a house as a platform for the second, cutting studs to the height of each story. Rather than being early examples of platform frames, these structures seem to reflect aspects of timber frame construction in which studs did not rise from sill to plate.

In balloon frame construction the plate functioned to cap the studs, stiffen the top of the frame, and act as a platform for an integrated roof structure. Before the plate became a standard two-by-four-inch member nailed to the top of studs, carpenters made plates ranging from four-by-six inches, four-by-four inches, or two two-by-four boards nailed together. Heavier plates were mortised to studs. Two-by-six or two-by-four roof rafters spaced at either eighteen, twenty-four, or thirty inches on center were properly mitered at top and bottom and notched at the place where each was nailed to the plate. Some early farmhouses like the Dane County, Wisconsin, dwelling had closed eaves with a neoclassical return. Consistent with economies of balloon frame construction, carpenters finished eaves in a simple fashion by nailing a fascia board to the end of the rafters and either nailing a board to the underside of the rafter or leaving the rafters and roof boards exposed (fig. 1.8).

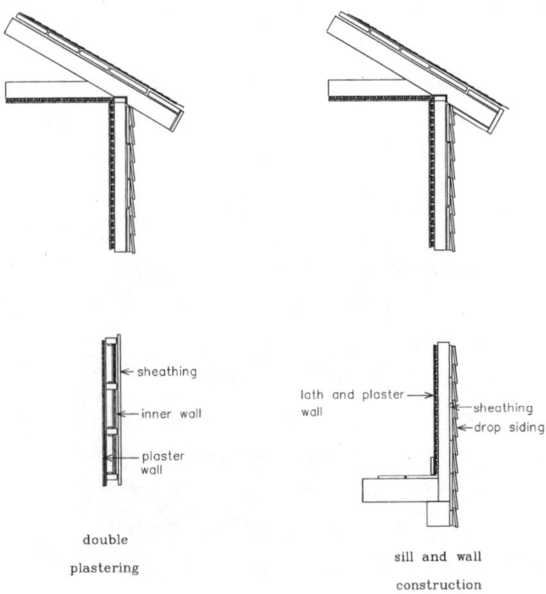

Fig. 1.8. Balloon frame construction details.

Builders enclosed and strengthened the balloon frame by nailing sheathing boards to the exterior of the studs. These one-inch boards varied in width from six to twelve inches. Most carpenters applied these boards at right angles to the studs, but some builders set them at a forty-five-degree angle, believing this pattern would add strength to the frame. A layer of insulation paper was customarily tacked onto the sheathing before clapboard siding finished the exterior wall.

Local carpenters nailed lath to studs to support an application of plaster that formed a continuous interior wall and ceiling surface. Some builders nailed sheathing to both the exterior and interior of the studs before adding the appropriate finish to each surface. Other builders "double plastered" the walls by nailing lath to strips attached to the inside surfaces of studs then applied a rough coat of plaster before they covered inner walls with lath and plaster (fig. 1.8). The double-plaster technique was one of many ways used to insulate the thin walls of balloon frame houses.

Builders fashioned economical interior floors with a single layer of one-by-six-inch tongue-and-groove boards nailed at right angles to the floor joists. A firmer, finer surface included a second layer of narrow hardwood flooring applied at right angles to the subfloor. Some builders believed that the ninety-degree angle of application caused the floor joist to warp along the length of a large chamber. In order to prevent this structural defect, carpenters nailed the subfloor to joists at a forty-five degree angle. They then nailed hardwood boards at a ninety-degree angle to the side wall. Builders also nailed one-by-three-inch bridging between each joist to stiffen these horizontal members.

The number and nature of these variations in

balloon frame construction practiced by local midwestern carpenters paralleled the debate of the pros and cons of the framing method that took place in stylebooks and agricultural journals during the second half of the nineteenth century. As architects and professionals used rhetorical persuasion, Anglo-American carpenters developed a mixed architectural language that retained some grammatical features of traditional folk building while acquiring a new vernacular syntax of industrially produced parts. This was a viable synthesis in so far as the new vernacular expression did not become static or fixed. That kind of definitive statement about balloon frame construction was made seventy years after its supposed invention. By the early 1900s, when architects and engineers employed by Aladdin Homes, Sears & Roebuck, Montgomery Wards, and Gordon Van Tine defined the framing method as a *system* of building. These large corporations controlled stands of timber, transportation systems, lumber mills, and factories filled with laborers who mass produced precut balloon frame houses for a competitive market. Professional designers dressed up traditional and popular house types for an urban environment and prepackaged them for moderate-income families. Sears & Roebuck's No. 105 from *Modern Homes* of 1908 offered a modern version of an I-house type (fig. 1.9). The dimensions and location of every member of the frame remained consistent throughout the structure. Each window and door in the structure was proportioned to fit into the frame at regular intervals. Designed by a committee, processed by machines, and assembled according to plan, No. 105 represents balloon frame construction in its most mechanical level of application.

The logical reduction of the parts and process of balloon frame construction to assembly-line production of "readi-made" houses became possible because practical carpenters had already subjected the building technique to rational analysis. The balloon frame I-house in Muscatine County, Iowa, is a vernacular counterpart to the Sears & Roebuck No. 105 (fig. 1.6). The Yankee carpenter assembled the frame of that house approximately forty years before a corporate committee produced designs for *Modern Homes* of 1908. The Iowa structure is representative of many second- and third-generation wooden frame farmhouses in Nebraska and South Dakota built from the 1880s to 1900. Anglo-American settlers in every area of the region individually and collectively utilized the new industrially produced building materials in

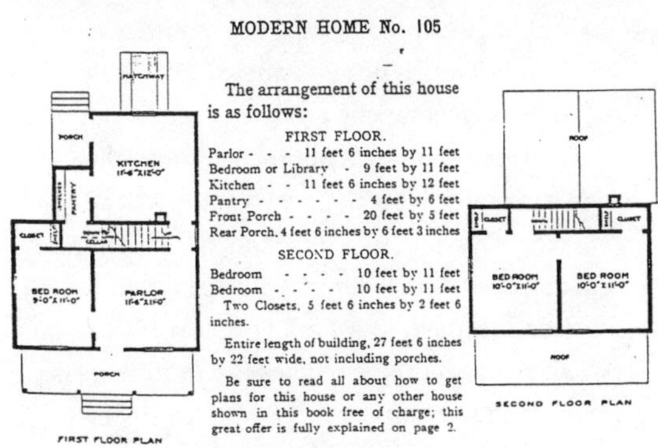

MODERN HOME No. 105

The arrangement of this house is as follows:

FIRST FLOOR.

Parlor - - - 11 feet 6 inches by 11 feet
Bedroom or Library - 9 feet by 11 feet
Kitchen - - 11 feet 6 inches by 12 feet
Pantry - - - - - - 4 feet by 6 feet
Front Porch - - - - 20 feet by 5 feet
Rear Porch, 4 feet 6 inches by 6 feet 3 inches

SECOND FLOOR.

Bedroom - - - - 10 feet by 11 feet
Bedroom - - - - 10 feet by 11 feet
Two Closets, 5 feet 6 inches by 2 feet 6 inches.

Entire length of building, 27 feet 6 inches by 22 feet wide, not including porches.

Be sure to read all about how to get plans for this house or any other house shown in this book free of charge; this great offer is fully explained on page 2.

SEE ABOUT OUR FREE SPECIAL CATALOGUE OF MILL WORK AND OTHER CATALOGUES ON LAST PAGE.

Fig. 1.9. Sears "Modern Home no. 105," 1908.

ways to conserve time, energy, materials, and money. The "invention" of balloon frame construction was not the work of an individual but the outcome of many creative craftsmen expediently doing more with less.

Notes

1. Solon Robinson, "A Cheap Farmhouse," *American Agriculture* 5 (Feb. 1846): 57.
2. As early as 1860, George E. Woodward presented the pre-Giedion source of balloon frame construction, claiming that "The balloon frame belongs to no one person, nobody claims it as an invention." See George E. Woodward, "Balloon Frames—IVth Article," *Cultivator* 8 (Aug. 1860): 249.
3. Sigfried Giedion, *Space, Time and Architecture* (Cambridge: Harvard Univ. Press, 1941), 281–89.

The accounts of the appearance of wooden frame construction in Chicago during the early 1830s were published as reminiscences in the *Chicago Tribune* during 1876. Charles Cleaver, who had arrived in Chicago in 1833, recalled that a small sawmill run by water from the North Branch of the Chicago River "sawed out such timber that grew in the woods adjoining, consisting of oak, elm, poplar, white ash, etc. Of such lumber most houses were built, and any carpenter that has ever been compelled to use it, particularly in its green state, will appreciate its quality. In drying it will shrink, warp, and twist in every way, drawing out nails, and, after a summer has passed, the siding will gape open, letting wind through every joint." Cleaver did explain that pine lumber supplies began to increase during the summer of 1834, but timber remained scarce until 1837. He continued to say that "heavy timber for frame buildings soon after that came into disuse, as it was found the present way of putting up frame buildings was much stronger and better. It used to be then called balloon framing. G. W. Snow, an old settler, had the credit of first originating the idea." "Charles Cleaver, " *Reminiscences of Chicago during the Forties and the Fifties* (Chicago: Lake Side Press, 1913), 54–55.

William Bross arrived in Chicago in 1846. In 1876 he recalled Chicago buildings at the time of his arrival. "Stores and dwellings were, with few exceptions, built in the balloon fashion. . . . Posts were placed in the ground at corners, and at proper distances between them blocks were laid down singly or in cobble house fashion. On these foundations were laid, and to these were spiked, standing on end, 3" x 4" scantling. On these sheathboards were nailed, and weatherboards on the outside of them; and lath and plaster inside, with the roof completed the dwelling or store. This cheap, but for a new town, excellent, mode of building, it is claimed, was first introduced, or if you please, invented, in Chicago, and I believe the claim to be true." See "William Bross," *Reminiscences of Chicago during the Forties and the Fifties* (Chicago: Lake Side Press, 1913), 4.

Cleaver and Bross recalled a complex, rapidly changing environment that existed thirty years ago. Although these accounts of Chicago in the 1830s and 1840s refer to balloon construction and allude to G. W. Snow as the first to use it, the recall of the past was likely informed by assertions and stories that appeared after the fact but did not prove or explain the fact. Given the nature of the materials available and the number of new structures being built in the city, it seems it would be difficult for anyone to accurately remember that builders exclusively used what was later called balloon construction or a variety of similar techniques to frame structures.

4. Giedion, Space, *Time and Architecture*, 347–53.
5. Walker Field, "A Reexamination into the Invention of the Balloon Frame," *Journal of the Society of Architectural Historians* (Oct. 1942): 3–29.
6. Paul E. Sprague, "Chicago Balloon Frames," *Technology of Historic American Buildings*, ed. H. Ward Jandl (Washington, D.C.: Foundation for Preservation of Technology and the Association for Preservation Technology, 1983), 35–53. The author of a less central work maintains that Snow was the first to "use" balloon frame construction in 1832 and Taylor followed in 1833. See Gordon A. Jelley, "The Balloon Frame" (master's thesis, California State Univ., 1985), 51. "The Balloon-Frame House" chapter in Daniel Boorstin's *The Americans* of 1965 acknowledged Snow as the inventor. In 1968, architectural historian Carl W. Condit claimed George W. Snow as inventor but acknowledged Taylor's role as following up on Snow's "technique." See Daniel Boorstin, *The Americans: The National Experience* (New York: Vintage Books, 1965), 148–52, and Carl W. Condit, *American Building: Materials and Techniques from the First Colonial Settlement to the Present* (Chicago: Univ. of Chicago Press, 1968), 43.
7. Historical investigation of this kind moves from effect to cause with the assumption that significant change in history is brought about by so-called great men. These arguments are counter to our understanding of the processes leading to inventions in nineteenth-century America. In many instances it is impossible to attribute important developments to any one cause or to an individual person. Confusion and controversy surround the advent of standard items such as the sewing machine, the cotton gin, or the railroad locomotive. On the one hand, persons have been accused of practicing skullduggery by stealing or plagiarizing others' ideas and methods, making it difficult to impossible to identify who accomplished what. On the other hand, persons might be said to have shared ideas and methods in a democratic way, assuming that it was everybody's right to know and utilize new techniques and materials. In this kind of free and free-wheeling environment, it is difficult to find individuals solely responsible for particular inventions. See David Freeman Hawke, *Nuts and Bolts of the Past: A History of American Technology, 1776–1860* (New York: Harper & Row, 1988). Removed from the context of a heroic inventor role, all we know of George Washington Snow is that he was Chicago's first assessor and surveyor after an 1849 appointment, became involved in lumber trade, worked as a building contractor, and was active in the real estate business.
8. See Fred W. Peterson, *Homes in the Heartland: Balloon Frame Farmhouses of the Upper Midwest, 1850–1920* (Lawrence: Univ. Press of Kansas, 1992), 5–24.
9. Dell Upton, "Traditional Timber Framing," *Material Culture of the Wooden Age*, ed. Brooke Hindle (Tarrytown, N.Y.: Sleepy Hollow Press, 1981), 43–44.
10. Cary Carson, et al., "Impermanent Architecture in the Southern American Colonies," *Winterthur Portfolio* 16, no. 2/3 (summer/autumn): 135–60.
11. Dates of structures are approximated as closely as possible according to various kinds of information. County and township histories provide dates of incorporation as well as chronologies of development in addition to biographies of some settlers. Records in State Historical Preservation Offices and other archival materials frequently give dates in which one can frame the time when a farm family built their house. Construction of railroad lines to areas within the region

document when and where building materials became available to build a house. Interviews of farm family members still living on the homestead offer fairly accurate recalls of the year the farmhouse was built.

12. The timber, braced, and balloon frames illustrated here are generic and do not reflect the regional and historical variations of these techniques of wooden frame construction.

    This study of wooden frame farmhouses is based on surveys of rural Wisconsin and Iowa that I accomplished in 1980–81, 1984–85, 1985–86, and 1991–92. I did the Nebraska and South Dakota phases of fieldwork during 1994–95 and 1995–96. I located about 60 upright and wing farmhouses in Wisconsin and more than 800 I-houses and variations of the type in Iowa, Nebraska, and South Dakota. I photographed approximately 150 structures and thoroughly documented 40 farmhouses.

13. Terminology identifying kinds of framing techniques is not uniform. For the purposes of this study a timber frame designates a frame of heavy members joined by mortise and tenon. A braced frame is composed of milled lumber joined by nails, using two-by-six-inch studs sometimes mortised into the sill and diagonally braced at each corner of the frame. See figure 1.5. Balloon frame construction fastens lighter weight two-by-four-inch studs and all other members of the frame with nails. See figure 1.6.

14. This house was built in section 29 of English River Township in Keokuk County, Iowa. Records indicate that of the eight persons owning land there, two were carpenters who had learned the trade in Pennsylvania. One of them probably built this house for S. H. Seaman. See "South English Township," *Atlas of Keokuk County, Iowa* (Clinton, Iowa, 1874), 21; *The History of Keokuk County, Iowa* (Des Moines, 1880), 788, 793–96; and *A Genealogical and Biographical History of Keokuk County, Iowa* (Chicago, 1903), 298–300.

15. For information on early local sawmills in Iowa, see Jacob A. Swisher, "Sawmills on the Frontier," *Land of Many Mills* (Iowa City: Historical Society of Iowa, 1940), 65–73.

16. The development of the lumber market in Iowa is discussed in George W. Siber, "Railroads and Lumber Marketing 1858–78: The Relationship between an Iowa Sawmill Firm and the Chicago & Northwestern Railroad," *Annals of Iowa* 39, no. 1 (summer 1967): 33–46.

17. Wire nails were available in the United States as early as 1850, but they were not readily used by carpenters because they doubted their holding power. These early versions of the wire nail apparently did not have ridges on the shaft near the head of the nail in order to securely hold them in the fiber of the wood. See John I. Rempel, *Building with Wood and Other Aspects of Nineteenth Century Building in Central Canada* (Toronto: Univ. of Toronto Press, 1980), 99–102.

18. For professional models of sill construction, see *Audel's Carpenter's and Builder's Guide* (New York: Theo Audel & Co., 1939), 881–88.

CHAPTER 2

William B. Rhoads

The Machine in the Garden: The Trolley Cottage as Romantic Artifact

Cottages formed from discarded trolley cars placed in picturesque settings—abandoned machines in the garden[1]—have been a common but arresting sight across America in the twentieth century. Electric-powered trolleys or streetcars early in the century routinely carried billions of passengers annually: 11 billion carried by 80,000 cars in 1917.[2] But the idea of turning obsolete cars into housing was a little strange: the cast-off bodies of San Francisco's horse-drawn streetcars (replaced by cable cars and electric trolleys) formed a village named Cartown or Carville "on the shifting sands of the beach of San Francisco Bay" (fig. 2.1). In 1901 a London magazine proclaimed Cartown "the most remarkable settlement in the world," or at least "one of the queerest towns" in the United States.[3]

The trolley cottage was strange enough to attract the attention of journalists, but it was also appealing, especially when pleasantly landscaped and occupied by congenial people. The trolley home of John and Carrie Burns, an impoverished couple with two children, was written up by the *Philadelphia Inquirer* in 1935, because the Burns family offered proof that it was possible to experience "love in a trolley car—even as in a cottage . . . especially when the car is surrounded by a nice vegetable garden" and the end of the trolley is covered "with pink climbing roses that promise literally . . . to transform the old car into the proverbial 'rose-covered cottage.'" The Burns trolley cottage, once a well-engineered vehicle, had become an approximation of Andrew Jackson Downing's picturesque cottage for the working class. Downing had discovered "the presence of heart" in

Fig. 2.1. Former horse-drawn streetcars at Carville on San Francisco Bay, c. 1900. California Historical Society, FN-229I6.

the bay window and vine-covered walls of the cottage; similar sentiments clung to the rose-bedecked trolley whose curved and glazed ends resembled Downing's bay windows.[4]

The electric trolley car had multiple meanings for Americans around 1900.[5] On the one hand, electric traction, made practical as a mover of the urban masses by Frank Sprague in the late 1880s, was a technological triumph and an important factor in the growth of cities, yet the cars accidentally killed hundreds of persons each year.[6] Powered by electric motors and efficiently assembled of wood and steel in large plants like J. G. Brill's in Philadelphia, the trolley still related easily to the rural landscape when its tracks and cars, lighter and smaller than those of steam railroads, wandered beyond the city into fields and woods.[7] Leisurely, cooling country excursions became popular with city people who came to associate the trolley with good times. Norman Rockwell fondly recalled boyhood evening and Sunday excursions taken by families from Manhattan to countrified parts of the Bronx: "trolley riding was a popular entertainment, almost an institution."[8] The author William Dean Howells thought "all trolley-lines are pleasant," but most pleasant was a rural New England route "through lush meadowlands and among rich fields of wheat and corn and under the lee of orchards, that almost kiss the car-roofs with their blossoms in spring and with their down-streaming strands of apples in autumn."[9] Open-sided summer trolleys allowed the most direct experience of trackside nature and provided the strongest breezes, but closed cars could also admit refreshing air through rows of opened windows. The stationary trolley cottage might lie as lightly in the landscape as it had when operating along grassy roadsides, and whether used as a part-time retreat or full-time residence, it still might connote the shedding of workaday cares.

Trolleys in their prime had human qualities making their cottage transformation appealing for adults and children. Artists manipulated their fronts into faces: a particularly handsome private interurban car, the *Mabel*, when a cottage in Maryland, was drawn as aging but still pertly flirtatious (fig. 2.2).[10] Diminutive and amiable, trolleys were more often considered feminine than masculine, although there was a strong masculine presence in the one- or two-man crew of motorman and conductor. Moving trolleys, like steam locomotives, seemed alive, thanks to breathing air compressors and warm, well-lighted interiors.

Usually operating as a single car with motorman and conductor constantly in view of passengers, trolleys had a more intimate, personal feeling than trains. Often passengers and crew were on

Fig. 2.2. "A Streetcar Named Mabel," once a luxuriously appointed interurban car, transformed into a cottage near the Chesapeake Bay. *Railroad Magazine*, Aug. 1951.

friendly terms. "Trolley friendliness" made Howells prefer the trolley to the automobile. Not only was the landscape better appreciated from a trolley car, but the car itself was "the kindly, the neighborly, the brotherly trolley," since the crew was generous and helpful, and passengers mixed easily with each other and the motorman and conductor, even when of differing social classes.[11] An affable motorman familiar with the people along his route in Pelham, New York, was a model for the Skipper, the motorman in Fontaine Fox's cartoon, Toonerville, whose ramshackle trolley amused millions of newspaper readers from 1916 until 1956.[12] The Toonerville trolley, a tiny four-wheeler, was also marketed as a popular toy and was featured in a series of film comedies. Several trolley cottages were named "Toonerville," as was a men's club established in two cars outside Lewistown, Pennsylvania. The Toonerville Club's entrance sported a sign depicting Fox's "quaint little, lop-sided . . . four wheel conveyance." Cottages and clubs were named Toonerville not so much because they were rickety but to allude to their quaintness and friendliness.[13]

The trolley breakdown was humanized in an instruction manual for Philadelphia trolley crews: a "dead car" was drawn belly-up with attending physician.[14] When trolley routes were abandoned or converted to bus operation, "last-run" ceremonies typically had a festive side, celebrating the triumph of the modern bus and the end of the old, noisy (rattling and grinding) trolleys whose rails and slow speed impeded auto traffic.[15] But there was also a funereal element in many last runs, the car operated by a saddened, veteran motorman. The car might be draped in black bunting or hung with funeral wreaths, even artistically transmogrified into an aged person or attended with pall bearers.[16] These were mock funerals, but the playful was tinged with sadness, a lament for the passing of an era, if not of a faithful friend.[17] Dead trolleys were described as awaiting the "funeral pyre" while stored in the melancholy "boneyard."[18] However, the bodies of some cars, after being stripped of seats, trucks, and most mechanical and electrical parts, lived on (after a fashion) as diners, chicken coops, storage sheds, offices, and various sorts of housing.[19] The Burns' home, "Toonerville," was said to be "human," and Philadelphians were told how fortunate the car was to have an attractive young family as "company" during "its declining years."[20]

A drawing in a 1930s newspaper depicts the ideal trolley cottage (fig. 2.3).[21] Set in a picturesque landscape, the wheelless car body is small enough (perhaps thirty feet long) to look like a cozy cottage, although many car bodies were longer (about forty-five feet). Decks or porches were often added, leading one into the adjoining flower or vegetable garden, or more distant landscape vista. Each window is curtained, and the current-gathering trolley pole has been removed in favor of a domestic-looking chimney. Internally, one of the motorman's platforms would become the kitchen, with or without running water and electricity. The passenger seats would all or mostly be removed, and living, sleeping, and dining areas minimally defined by simple partitions or curtains. Similar trolley cottages were set up from coast to coast, often sited to take advantage of landscape, river, or ocean views.[22]

Trolley cottages proliferated in the 1890s as large numbers of horse-drawn streetcars were replaced by electric trolleys. Ex-horsecars were spotted along the coast from Rhode Island to suburban New York, "perched up on top of some breezy bluff on the sandy shore, or in some quiet, shaded nook, affording temporary habitation for families, fishermen, hunters, etc."[23] Obsolete San Francisco horsecars entered new lives as "economical and highly picturesque" beach cabins, clubhouses, and permanent residences—as well as shops, restaurants, and an Episcopalian church—at Cartown, or Carville (fig. 2.1), south of Golden Gate Park.[24] By 1900 there were more than one hundred cars, some set in the hollows of dunes and surrounded by nasturtiums, while others were stacked atop buildings as "skyscrapers" for the ocean view through broad bands of windows. The commu-

Fig. 2.3. "Street Car Mountain Homes," the ideal of the cozy trolley cottage in a picturesque landscape. Unidentified Pennsylvania newspaper (1930s). Ben Hershey scrapbook.

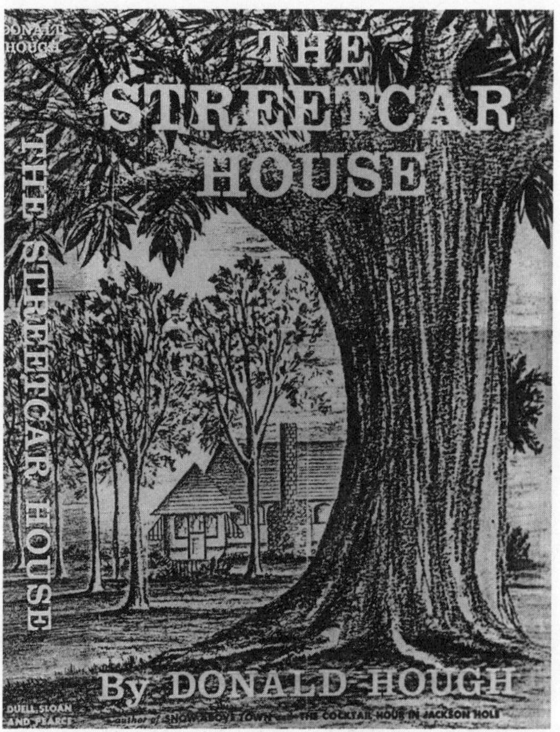

Fig. 2.4. *The Streetcar House* (New York: Duell, Sloan and Pearce, 1960), dust jacket of Donald Hough's recollections of the gradual transformation of five trolleys into a residence as permanent as the sturdy tree in the foreground.

nity's peculiar appearance seemed just right for San Francisco's bohemian society, whose "facetious idiosyncrasies" led them to give their "car-palaces" such names as Villa Miramar and Chateau Navarre.[25] Interiors ranged from the shabby and makeshift to tasteful examples of the aesthetic movement. Some had sleeping compartments whose efficient use of space reminded visitors of railroad sleeping cars, houseboats, or ship cabins.

A Carville house often comprised three car bodies. Donald Hough's boyhood home outside St. Paul, Minnesota, began in 1905 as a grouping of five cars: kitchen, dining room, living room, and two bedrooms. The Hough trolleys, like others that have survived as permanent residences, were much altered (fig. 2.4). More durable roofs were added over the wood and canvas originals; walls were resurfaced outside and in; a substantial fieldstone fireplace built; a cellar dug; and rooms tacked on that were not trolley based. Hough's father envisioned through watercolors various trolley cottage schemes. Invariably the "naked cars" were enveloped within lovely vegetation that softened their intrusion into the landscape.[26] The cover illustration of the son's book captures the much-altered cars at rest in the well-tended yard. The stability of the formerly mobile components is assured by the stone fireplace and chimney, a rootedness echoed in the sturdy tree trunk.

Car bodies intended primarily for daytime use needed little alteration. The body of a small, Reading, Pennsylvania, Birney car (a lightweight trolley produced in large numbers in the teens and twenties) was acquired by James Boltz, a carpenter employed by the Reading traction company. In 1947 he had it hauled to five acres of rural land he owned near his residence. Boltz regularly drove his Buick to the country place to work in his truck patch and orchard, or preside over family picnics at the outdoor fireplace near the trolley. His wife, Jean, tended the flowers. A son created a family pet cemetery across the road.[27]

The trolley acquired curtains, stove and stovepipe, entrance porch with vine-covered lattice, as well as a screened porch (fig. 2.5). It rested on firm foundations incorporating a basement. Inside, the seats and motorman's controls were removed and replaced with simple furnishings allowing eating and sleeping; one end became a workshop. But remarkably, many of the details that signaled "trolley"—such as headlights and destination signs—were preserved.

Here the desire for inexpensive shelter was clearly joined with affection for the vanishing trolley.

In 1924 employees of the Brooklyn-Manhattan Transit Corporation were offered old trolley bodies for twenty-five dollars apiece, along with suggestions on how to make the body into a "cozy" summer home.[28] After the 1927 abandonment of the Centre and Clearfield (Pennsylvania) Street Railway, James Walter Lamb, a former relief motorman, brought a car body he had purchased to a wooded site near Lewistown. Lamb and his wife, Ada, first made it a curtained but little-altered "camp in the country." As it became a full-time residence, extensive alterations and additions were made, including a monumental, anchoring fireplace (c. 1934–38), said to incorporate stones from the state's sixty-seven counties.[29]

During the Great Depression, trolley bodies were pressed into service as cheap housing for the unemployed. Four members of the Mellinger family occupied a former Lancaster, Pennsylvania, trolley sited along an abandoned trolley line that had attracted sightseers, thanks to its "tortuous pathway through forest primeval and dreamy dell." Photographs published in the Lancaster newspaper show Mrs. Mellinger at her cookstove and play-

Fig. 2.5. Marguerite Boltz and grandson amid her flowers at the Boltz family trolley cottage near Centerport, Pennsylvania, c. 1951. Courtesy of Donald Borkey.

ing an upright piano (fig. 2.6): conventional middle-class life was difficult in such emergency housing with poor heat, little or no plumbing, and few partitions for privacy.[30] Later, about 1952 to 1965, "dirt poor farmers"—a hard-working wife, alcoholic husband, six daughters, and a son—occupied a once-imposing Southern New York Railway car in rural Laurens. The interior was not cozy but barracks-like and so damp that a daughter remembers being hospitalized as a consequence:

LANCASTER, PA., APRIL 29, 1934

Here's New Design For Living

Trolley Car Houses Family of Four With Innovations

Fig. 2.6. "Here's New Design for Living," Mellinger residence in former Conestoga Traction trolley at Chiques, Pennsylvania. *Lancaster Sunday News*, Apr. 29, 1934.

"The memories of that place and time are not happy for us."[31]

By contrast, the Smail "retirement cottage" in Jeannette, Pennsylvania, a former West Penn Railway car, achieved something like middle-class comfort and respectability with awnings and shrubs outside, curtains and Colonial Revival butterfly table within (fig. 2.7).[32] Highly respectable and very picturesque in its wooded setting at Inspiration Point on Lake Ontario's Irondequoit Bay was Msgr. Louis W. Edelman's ex-Rochester and Eastern interurban-turned-summer cottage.[33] Lewistown's Toonerville Club, for the enjoyment of "a select little coterie of business and professional men," was sited with a "grand view" of the Juniata River. The club erected a foot bridge over an abandoned canal bed paralleling the river "so members could walk down to the towpath . . . when they wished to take a stroll over their little 'estate.' "[34] Also far removed from squalor, Mr. and Mrs. E. W. Perrott III were handsomely set up in their converted Denver Tramways trolley home about 1950. The venetian blinds, porch, and skirting around the foundation that appear in a photo (fig. 2.8) published in Denver Tramways's magazine suggest an above-average budget for the conversion. This is confirmed by the stylish garden furniture and well-dressed party of occupants.[35] No sordid junkyard fate for the Perrott's car, which did enter a trolley heaven.

Still, many trolley residences were not well maintained and neatly landscaped. A run-down trolley house was a sign of an undesirable neighborhood. Readers of *American Home* in 1949 would instantly recognize in a photo of a rusting trolley body a "perfect example of why zoning laws are necessary."[36] In fact, some traction companies, like Halifax's, refused to sell car bodies in the belief that the cars, "after a long and faithful service," should not be degraded as tourist cabins and hotdog stands

Home in a Trolley

ONE of the more unusual homes in Jeannette, Pa., is owned by the James Smails. The house once was a streetcar. Smail, who had purchased a narrow strip of land in the area, paid $250 for the car in 1953. It was one of 67 which had been auctioned to a junk dealer by the West Penn Railway Co. Supervising the construction work himself, Smail installed a concrete foundation, refurbished the inside and put on a new roof to cover the original top, which leaked. Mrs. Smail decorated the interior of the 9-by-60-foot car. It has three rooms.

Mrs. Smail relaxes in parlor while her granddaughter, Jill Sutherland, plays near the double folding doors.

THE PHILADELPHIA INQUIRER MAGAZINE, NOVEMBER 2, 1958

Fig. 2.7. "Home in a Trolley," the Smail residence, Jeannette, Pennsylvania. *Philadelphia Inquirer Magazine*, Nov. 2, 1958.

Fig. 2.8. "Is Heaven Really Like This?" Former Denver Tramway streetcar converted to the Mr. and Mrs. E. W. Perrott III residence. *Tram Topics*, May 1950. Colorado Railroad Museum.

—"eyesores" reflecting badly on the company. Responsible suburban property owners feared for their investment if any sort of trolley residence (or later a trailer) appeared nearby.[37]

Unkempt trolley bodies were repulsive to the eye and also were associated with moral corruption. After 1900, bohemian Carville's motley collection of horsecar houses (some being love nests with beer buried in the sand) was endangered by the progressive, improving efforts of those who wanted to "burn . . . the Car out of Carville" and make it into something more respectable.[38] The Hough family—father a telephone company clerk, mother a housewife—found themselves "quarantine[d]" by their prosperous middle-class neighbors, who, when the cars first were set up, predicted the opening of a brothel. A stuffy neighbor erected a fence to shield herself from the offensive cars.[39] And however distinguished was the membership of the Toonerville Club, a raffish aura clung to the trolley clubhouse where men had jolly parties and played pinochle and hausenpeffer.[40]

Vanquished by the auto as a popular mode of transport, some trolley carcasses were pressed into service as tourist cabins for motorists: several were found along U.S. 40 in Kansas, and in Oregon brightly painted trolley cabins were reported to be appealing to motorists drawn by the "novelty" of sleeping in a trolley.[41] A Pennsylvania example published in *Popular Science* in 1932 was typical in lacking running water, heat, and window screens.[42] Near Kingston, New York, motorists were lured to camp in car bodies, essentially spacious tents, with lake view and canopy of shade trees. The camp's eccentric proprietor, John D. Propheter, placed open trolleys along the heavily trafficked highway to serve as stationary "observation cars for those who on holidays wish to see the world 'roll' by them while they are seated comfortably in a safe place."[43] Better designed and executed was Happy Acres (fig. 2.9) in rural Middlefield, Connecticut, which billed itself as a "popular priced lake-in-the-mountains resort." There a dozen overage Connecticut Company trolleys were made over into tree-shaded bungalows, lounge, and laundromat.[44] At another lakeside camp, Barnard's, at Lamoka Lake, New York, old Birney cars (fig. 2.10) have long poked their faces over the water.[45]

Fig. 2.9. Former Connecticut Co. streetcar at Happy Acres, Middlefield, Connecticut. Probably in use as a cottage or Laundromat, c. 1941. Courtesy of John H. Koella.

Young working women from New York escaped the hot city streets by coming to refreshing Moodna Creek in upstate Orange County beginning in 1907. Sponsored by the Ethical Culture Society, Camp Moodna set up twenty former New York horsecars side by side like tents at an unshaded camp meeting (fig. 2.11).[46] Sanita Hills, a much larger summer camp, opened in 1941 for New York City Sanitation Department employees and their families. The camp, on a grassy Dutchess County hillside, occupied dozens of former Sixth Avenue elevated railway cars transformed into comfortable, well-appointed "bungalows" and "pullmanettes."[47]

Fig. 2.10. Disheveled Birney cars overlooking Lamoka Lake, New York, Spring 1995. Photograph by the author.

A boys' camp occupied simply furnished cars in one section of Sanita Hills. Trolleys from horsecars to streamliners of the 1930s were sometimes made into children's playhouses, as stagecoaches had been in the 1870s.[48] Children have been entertained for decades by the car body lettered "Toonerville" at Knoebels Grove (Pennsylvania) amusement park. By 1959 the modern, streamlined PCC car of the 1930s was thought outmoded, and so six were lined up at a children's day camp in Brooklyn—wheelless on the ground, beached like the nearby rowboat (fig. 2.12).[49] The trolley cottage had overtones of the childish, the world of fantasy and make believe: a journalist touring the Mellinger trolley cottage was reminded of the Old Woman Who Lived in a Shoe.[50]

Fig. 2.11. Former New York City horsecars at Camp Moodna, Orange County, New York. Early-twentieth-century postcard.

The Trolley Car Family (fig. 2.13) was an enormously popular story written for children by Eleanor Clymer. First published in 1947 and often reprinted, it credits a young girl with suggesting a trolley home for her family after the father, a motorman who loves his trolley "like one of his own children" and refuses to become a bus driver, is given the old car as severance pay. The trolley is taken on abandoned tracks to an abandoned farm, and there, for a time, the family lives idyllically, growing their own food and living simply in the trolley.[51]

Clymer avoided the realm of fantasy, but other writers followed Oliver Wendell Holmes, who explained poetically the mysteries of streetcar propulsion: trolley poles were witches' broomsticks and purring motors their cats.[52] A trolley which had become a house struck some as more than curious. Carville, as has been noted, was about as queer a place as existed anywhere. One visitor to the Mellinger home found it "odd, but . . . true" that the dinner bell had originally served "to warn people to get out of the way so Mellinger's house wouldn't run over them." He looked out to find "another trolley car looming just ahead as if for a head-on crash," but it turned out to be just "the house next door." It was even "a little uncanny . . . to see a kitchen stove . . . or a piano . . . in a trolley car." Realities strangely, sometimes menacingly, juxtaposed, as in a dream, but this was not a dream. It was emergency shelter from a harsh winter during the Depression. The writer concluded that the Mellingers "are householders like everyone else, . . . even if it does look more romantic."[53]

Donald Hough, his parents, and their friends also struggled with the confusion resulting from

Fig. 2.12. Former Brooklyn PCC car at Day Camp, Brooklyn, c. 1961. Courtesy of Everett A. White.

Fig. 2.13. *The Trolley Car Family* by Eleanor Clymer. Front cover (by Ursula Koering) of the Scholastic Book Services edition (fifth printing, 1962). While reminiscent of the ideal trolley cottage in fig. 2.3, the windows and trucks resemble those of a caboose.

the conflicting identities of trolley and house. Guests entertained in the living-room trolley, seated face to face in the original longitudinal seats had "the set and expressionless countenances of the short-haul public-conveyance traveler" and were "automatically wait[ing] for the thing to stop." When the trolley seating was replaced with standard furniture and the stabilizing fireplace and chimney added, the sense of motion was supplanted with "Gibralter-like immutability." Even so, the potential for imagined movement never quite left the cars: Hough envisioned a future owner of the house, unaware of its genesis, descending to the basement and looking up to discover the underframe of a trolley running over him.[54]

John Stilgoe has described converted horsecars as the "nation's first modular housing."[55] The architectural profession took little notice of trolley housing. The *American Architect* in 1922 did observe that "discarded" streetcars were "helping to relieve the housing shortage in Salem, Mass."[56] In 1944 *Architectural Forum* compared the resourcefulness and imagination that went into the transformed El cars at Sanita Hills to that of housing for war workers. Many of these workers were quartered in demountable houses hauled by trailer trucks, but builders of the arsenal in Milan, Tennessee, occupied Street Car City, some fifty Nashville car bodies.[57]

The Mellinger house was obviously a faded, obsolete trolley, but to one reporter it also seemed "a new design for living" and "a steel house," a product of the 1930s when steel houses were among the "greater wonders of the age."[58] In 1932 Henry Russell Hitchcock identified an architectural project as adhering to the principles of "modern architecture," or the International Style. The project was composed of prefabricated units with standard window frames and metal spandrels in horizontal bands.[59] The trolley house typically shared these characteristics and was raised on posts (*pilotis*-like), with neither cellar nor attic nor many partitions.

So, was the trolley house "a machine for living in" (Le Corbusier)?[60] In part, but it was a machine so overlaid with domestic additions, picturesque landscaping, and family life as to become a romantic cottage. Moreover, in contrast to the combination of auto and trailer (also a machine-age product that might rest in the garden[61]), the trolley cottage was both antiquated and stationary. Donald Hough looked back upon his boyhood home as "a blessed sanctuary" which "seemed to have grown from the soil itself."[62] The James Boltz trolley cottage and its parklike landscape, after almost fifty years of recreational use by Boltz and his offspring, are being preserved, in effect, as a family shrine. The Cali family's cottage (fig. 2.14) in Elverson, Pennsylvania, is more worn, but this old Reading trolley also rests happily amid grass, trees, and picnic paraphernalia.

The trolley with up-to-date electric motors by General Electric or Westinghouse moved city workers from home to factory. It was the product of industrial technology that inspired modern designers and architects. Discarded trolleys offered scrap metal for new machines, but newspapers and children's books reflected and encouraged the popular conception of the ideal (but also paradoxical) reuse, the trolley cottage in the bucolic landscape, where the trolley was not a cold industrial object but warmly human, still linked with happy times on pleasure rides into the country. Yet for the bohemians of Carville and for Hough's quarantined father, to occupy a streetcar was surely a gentle reproof of middle-class standards of taste and propriety. All who became trolley dwellers by choice apparently were willing to make a mild gesture of idiosyncrasy in a convention-ridden society.[63]

Fig. 2.14. Former Reading, Pennsylvania, trolley at Elverson occupied by the Cali family (1998 photo).

Sadly, trolley cottages with roofs of canvas and wood resemble the human body in their aging, rot, and decay. Some declining examples have taken on third lives, spruced up as nostalgic commercial attractions (for example, the Spaghetti Warehouse restaurant chain[64]) or thoroughly rebuilt as resurrected trolleys. The body of a splendid interurban, Lehigh Valley Transit's 801, was carried in 1938 to farmland in Neola, Pennsylvania, where it was set upon stone pedestals. There it became "a fine summer residence . . . with a beautiful view of the wooded hills and rolling fields." It seemed to have "taken root . . . upon its rocky pedestal, there to spend its remaining days."[65] However, in 1967 Edward H. Blossom removed the car and began painstakingly restoring it to operating condition.[66] Most trolley cottages, like the Mellingers', have perished. Among the survivors, many, including several at Lamoka Lake, remain as disintegrating bodies or picturesque ruins.

Notes

My research has been generously assisted by trolley enthusiasts across the country—especially Ben Hershey, Edward H. Blossom, Bob Janssen, John Koella, and Joel Salomon.

1. For the machine (particularly the railway) in the garden, see Leo Marx, *The Machine in the*

Garden: Technology and the Pastoral Ideal in America (New York: Oxford Univ. Press, 1964); John Stilgoe, *Metropolitan Corridor: Railroads and the American Scene* (New Haven: Yale Univ. Press, 1983); Susan Danly Walther, ed., *The Railroad in the American Landscape* (Wellesley: Wellesley College Museum, 1981), with essays by Leo Marx and Kenneth W. Maddox.

2. Frank Rowsome Jr., *Trolley Car Treasury* (New York: McGraw-Hill, 1956), 170. Other popular histories of street and interurban railways are William D. Middleton, *The Interurban Era* (Milwaukee: Kalmbach, 1961), and William D. Middleton, *The Time of the Trolley* (Milwaukee: Kalmbach, 1975); more academic is George W. Hilton and John F. Due, *The Electric Interurban Railways in America* (Stanford: Stanford Univ. Press, 1964). While a trolley car is narrowly defined as an electric-powered railcar with current brought from overhead wire to car motors through a pole above the roof, horse-drawn streetcars or horsecars are sometimes called trolleys. In fact, some horsecars were converted into electric trolleys. Also, while trolley cars usually ran in cities and suburbs and were of modest size and speed, larger and faster interurbans that sped through the countryside have also been called trolleys. Subway and elevated railway cars drawing their power from third rails are usually distinguished from trolleys.
3. Leslie E. Gilliams, "Cartown," *Strand Magazine* 22, no. 131 (Dec. 1901): 574.
4. John A. Lieper, "Family of 4 Lives in Old Trolley Car," *Philadelphia Inquirer*, July 28, 1935; A. J. Downing, *The Architecture of Country Houses* (New York: D. Appleton, 1851), 78–79.
5. David E. Nye, *Electrifying America: Social Meanings of a New Technology, 1880–1940* (Cambridge: MIT Press, 1990), 85–137.
6. Kenneth T. Jackson, *Crabgrass Frontier: The Suburbanization of the United States* (New York: Oxford Univ. Press, 1985), 103, 115, 117; Nye, *Electrifying*, 93–96, 102.
7. Stilgoe, *Metropolitan*, 297–99; William Dean Howells, *Literature and Life* (New York: Harper and Brothers, 1902), 238–39.
8. Norman Rockwell, *Reminiscences of My Life as an Illustrator* (Garden City: Doubleday, 1960), 40. See also John H. White Jr., "Party-Time Trolleys," *Timeline* 6 (1989): 44–53.
9. W. D. Howells, "Editor's Easy Chair," *Harper's Monthly* 137, no. 821 (Oct. 1918): 735.
10. Horace S. Thorne, "A Streetcar Named Mabel," *Railroad Magazine* 55, no. 3 (Aug. 1951): 84–85.
11. Howells, "Editor's Easy Chair," 734–36.
12. Joseph P. Hunt, "A Few Notes on a Famous Trolley," *American Book Collector* 7 (June 1957): 7.
13. Joseph P. Eckhardt, "Clatter, Sproing, Clunk Went the Trolley," *Pennsylvania Heritage* 18, no. 3 (summer 1992): 24–31; Ben Meyers, "We Notice That," *Lewistown Sentinel*, Apr. 9, 1962. A former Sunbury and Selinsgrove Railway car sported a sign identifying it as "Tooner villa" in the 1950s when it was a cottage along Penns Creek near New Berlin, Pennsylvania. Gene D. Gordon photo with letter to author, Feb. 20, 1996.

    Fox's last Toonerville trolley cartoon (1955 or 1956) showed the car leaving the tracks and rolling into a field where one could imagine it found contented retirement, as did some trolley cottages. Shore Line Trolley Museum, East Haven, Conn., exhibition label.
14. Philadelphia Transportation Co., "Trouble Shooting Sequence," 1949. Author's collection.
15. "Swift Buses Oust Madison Trolleys. Quiet Vehicles Open Service as Cars of Century-Old Line Rattle into Limbo. 500 Celebrate Demise," *New York Times*, Feb. 1, 1935.

16. "Car Named Expire Makes Last Trip. Pallbearers and Crape Signify New Rochelle's Sorrow as Old Line Becomes Bus Route," *New York Times*, Dec. 17, 1950.
17. Hortense Calisher's novelette, *The Last Trolley Ride*, employs the last run as a metaphor for life's transitional events, such as weddings and funerals. Calisher, *The Railway Police and the Last Trolley Ride* (Boston: Little, Brown, 1966), 192–93.
18. *New York Times*, Aug. 13, 1929; *Lancaster Sunday News*, Jan. 19, 1947.
19. "Trolley Car Hen House," Lancaster, Pa., newspaper, c. 1934. Ben Hershey scrapbook, Manheim, Pa. Retired cabooses also were put to a variety of uses—summer cottage, clubhouse, playhouse, motel. While their interiors were not so familiar to the public as were trolleys', they were already fitted for sleeping and eating. William F. Knapke with Freeman Hubbard, *The Railroad Caboose* (San Marino: Golden West, 1968), 19, 180–84; Stilgoe, Metropolitan, 212.
20. *Philadelphia Inquirer*, July 28, 1935.
21. "Street Car Mountain Homes," unidentified Pennsylvania newspaper (1930s). Hershey scrapbook.
22. "Street Cars Converted into Summer Homes," *Popular Mechanics* 20 (Sept. 1913): 381.
23. "New Uses for Old Horse Cars," *Scientific American* 75 (Sept. 12, 1896): 216.
24. "Method of Utilizing Old Street Cars," *Scientific American* 84 (June 29, 1901): 409; Natalie Jahraus Cowan, "Carville: San Francisco's Oceanside Bohemia," *California History* 57 (1978): 308–19; Jennifer Reese, "Streetcar Suburb," *Preservation* 51 (Jan.–Feb. 1999): 52–57.
25. Gibbs Adams, "A City of Cars," *Overland Monthly* 52, no. 5 (Nov. 1908): 402; Gilliams, "Cartown," 575–76.
26. Donald Hough, *The Streetcar House* (New York: Duell, Sloan and Pearce, 1960), 13, 17, 18, 25, 27, 45, 79, 83, 133–35.
27. Conversation with Donald Borkey, a grandson of James Boltz, Aug. 15, 1994; letter from Borkey to author, May 1, 1996.
28. "Cars as Summer Homes," *New York Times*, Apr. 20, 1924.
29. Letters from Walt Lamb to author, Jan. 15 and Feb. 2, 1995; "House Has Fireplace Built of Stones from 67 Counties," unidentified newspaper (probably Harrisburg, Pa., ca. 1960), author's scrapbook. In addition to the trolley occupied by the Lambs, James Walter Lamb bought six other Centre and Clearfield car bodies which were converted to diners and residences.
30. "Here's New Design for Living," *Sunday News* (Lancaster, Pa.), Apr. 29, 1934; *Seeing Lancaster through a Trolley Window* (Lititz, Pa.: Express Printing, 1910), 12.
31. Barbara B. Brooks to author, Aug. 1994; author's telephone conversation with Brooks, Sept. 23, 1994. Harry R. Van Dyck, "A Bethel College Memoir," *Mennonite Life* (Sept. 1994): 13, describes the lack of privacy and the cold endured sleeping on a cot in an interurban-turned-dormitory at Bethel College, North Newton, Kansas, in 1940. Four car bodies were arranged to form U-shaped "Pullman Court," although the cars lacked the amenities of actual Pullman sleeping cars. Malcolm D. Isely, *Arkansas Valley Interurban* (Glendale, Calif.: Interurbans, 1977), 23.
32. "A Streetcar Named Home," Pittsburgh Press, Oct. 26, 1958; "Home in a Trolley," *Philadelphia Inquirer Magazine*, Nov. 2, 1958. This trolley home has been acquired by the Pennsylvania Trolley Museum, Washington, Pennsylvania, for restoration as a trolley.
33. William Reed Gordon, *The Story of the Canandaigua Street Railway* (Rochester, N.Y.: author, 1953), 42. At his funeral mass, February 22, 1964, Monsignor Edelman was called an "inveterate traveler"—hence, presumably, the appeal of his interurban cottage. Information

provided by Audrey Johnson, Pittsford, New York, historian, July 25, 1996.

34. *Lewistown Sentinel*, Apr. 9, 1962. At Carville, among the women's clubhouses was one, "A Haunt of Bohemia," for seven young literary women, and another for the Falcons, a group of "brilliant" women bicyclists. Gilliams, "Cartown," 576; Cowan, "Carville," 310. Trolley cottages and clubhouses appealed to women, men, and children.
35. "Is Heaven Really Like This?" *Tram Topics* 5, no. 11 (May 1950): 1–2. The Perrott home exists, enclosed on three sides within an immaculate contemporary house. E. W. Perrott III to author, July 28, 1996.
36. Robert H. Williams, "How to Stretch Your Land Money," *American Home* 41, no. 3 (Feb. 1949): 39.
37. Allan D. Wallis, *Wheel Estate: The Rise and Decline of Mobile Homes* (New York: Oxford Univ. Press, 1991), 22, 71, 73, 178.
38. Cowan, "Carville," 312, 316, 318.
39. Hough, *Streetcar House*, 34–35.
40. Conversations with residents of Lewistown, Pa., 1995.
41. "Trolley Camps for Tourists," *New York Times*, June 6, 1937.
42. "Trolley Cars Now Tourist Cabins," *Popular Science* 121 (Oct. 1932): 45.
43. "Old Trolley Cars Will Grace Mr. Propheter's New Amusement Park," *Kingston Daily Freeman*, Oct. 1, 1930; Joe Easley, "Along the Iron Pike," *Railroad Magazine* 24, no. 4 (Sept. 1938): 107. Easley's drawing overstates the site's idyllic qualities.
44. John Koella to author, Mar. 5, 1996; Pamela K. Sibley to author, Aug. 13, 1996.
45. William R. Gordon, *Elmira and Chemung Valley Trolleys* (Rochester, N.Y.: author, 1970), 19, 121–22.
46. Janet Dempsey to author, Mar. 20, 1996; "Tram-Car Town," *Collier's* 45 (Aug. 27, 1910): 14.
47. "'El' Cars Rise Anew as Sanita Retreat," *New York Times*, July 13, 1941; William B. Rhoads, "The Great Saga of Sanita," New York History, forthcoming.
48. See Eastman Johnson's painting, *The Old Stage Coach* (1871), with frolicking children. Patricia Hills, *The Genre Paintings of Eastman Johnson* (New York: Garland, 1977), 127–29.
49. Gene D. Gordon, *Shamokin & Mount Carmel Transit Co.* (West Chester, Pa.: Ben Rohrbeck Traction Publications, 1994), 77; letter from Everett White to author, May 24, 1995. A wingless airplane, like a truckless trolley, could serve as home for youthful adventures in the imagination: after World War II, a naval transport plane became a "romantic home" for Boy Scouts in Armonk, N.Y. *New Yorker* 22, no. 47 (Jan. 4, 1947): 19–20.
50. "Here's New Design," *Sunday News*, Apr. 29, 1934.
51. Eleanor Clymer, *The Trolley Car Family* (New York: David McKay, 1970), 31, 32, 60, 61, 64, 160, 164.
52. Oliver Wendell Holmes, *The One Hoss Shay . . . & the Broomstick Train* (Boston: Houghton, Mifflin, 1892), 59–80. Influenced by Holmes, Theodore Pratt recounted the wondrous adventures of Betsy, a retired trolley that can be moved without electricity thanks to "sorcery" and "witchcraft." It (she) finally became a residence in a Los Angeles orange grove trailer camp. Pratt, *Mr. Thurtle's Trolley: A Novel* (New York: Duell, Sloan and Pearce, 1941).
53. "Here's New Design," *Sunday News*, Apr. 29, 1934.
54. Hough, *Streetcar House*, 48, 143, 167. In 1996 one window of the immobile Perrott trolley house is filled with a poster of a San Francisco cable car negotiating a hill. Comparable issues of mobility and permanence in regard to trailers are discussed by Charles W. Moore, "Trailers," in *Home Sweet Home:*

American Vernacular Architecture (Los Angeles: Craft and Folk Art Museum, 1983), 49–50.

55. Stilgoe, *Metropolitan*, 308. Earlier, Cowan, "Carville," 309, compared its housing to "ready-made modular units" of the 1970s.
56. "Street Cars Used as Houses," *American Architect* 122 (Sept. 20, 1922): 16.
57. "Wreck in Dutchess County" and "Demountable Dither," *Architectural Forum* 80, no. 1 (Jan. 1944): 48; (Milan, Tenn.) *Mirror-Exchange*, Feb. 13, 1991.
58. "Here's New Design," *Sunday News*, Apr. 29, 1934.
59. Henry-Russell Hitchcock in *Modern Architecture* (New York: Museum of Modern Art, 1932), 172–77.
60. Le Corbusier, *Towards a New Architecture* (London: Architectural Press, 1952), 10.
61. Wallis, *Wheel Estate*, 47–48.
62. Hough, *Streetcar House*, 143, 166.
63. Comments by Chris Wilson at Vernacular Architecture Forum, Lawrence, Kansas, May 25, 1996.
64. Dieter Esch to author, Dec. 20, 1994.
65. "Trolley Car Becomes Summer Home on Neola Farm," (Allentown, Pa.) *Morning Call*, Mar. 1938.
66. Edward H. Blossom to author, Mar. 2, 1995. For a description of the retrieval of car bodies for restoration, see Ben Minnich, "Chicken Coops of Colorado," *Timepoints: The Southern California Traction Review* 86, nos. 1–3 (July–Sept. 1994): 1–13.

CHAPTER 3

Thomas C. Hubka and Judith T. Kenny

The Workers' Cottage in Milwaukee's Polish Community: Housing and the Process of Americanization, 1870–1920

Few observers of the American urban environment at the beginning of the twentieth century could find anything positive to say about the housing of Polish Americans.[1] It is surprising, therefore, to find in Karl Harriman's 1903 short story, "The Homebuilders," a sympathetic account of a young immigrant's progress toward acquiring a home which suggests the importance of homeownership for members of Detroit's turn-of-the-century Polish community.[2] As the story unfolds, young Henry Brosczki has already purchased land when he visits a lot filled with houses to be auctioned for removal to new sites. He considers his prospects: "There stood the houses, quite as though they were waiting for him. All were of wood, a story and a half in height, small, compact, without foundation, but with little porches at the front and sides . . . The advertisement had said that fences and sidewalks were to be sold with the houses. [He planned to return the next day to bid on a house.] Satisfied immeasurably . . . Henry Brosczki slept brokenly that night, and dreamed that he owned a great brick home on Jefferson Avenue [a fashionable Detroit street]."[3] Whether a Polish resident of Chicago, Buffalo, Milwaukee, or Detroit, a member of America's *Polonia* would surely have recognized the ubiquitous wooden, story-and-a-half cottages (fig. 3.1).[4] And while their own process of acquiring homeownership may have been different, they would have well understood the sentiment represented in this story of an immigrant homebuilder as similar to their own.[5]

Harriman's sympathetic depiction of the quality of life within an immigrant neighborhood, how-

Fig. 3.1. 1899 photograph of the Mazur cottage on old south Tenth Avenue, Milwaukee, Wisconsin. Courtesy of Bernice Mazur.

ever, contrasts significantly with the accounts of contemporary social scientists and urban reformers who wrote of social deterioration and slum conditions. Instead, the standard reform text equated Henry Brosczki's new house with overcrowding, disease, and despair. As the 1911 *Report of the Immigration Commission* stated, immigration was a "problem" that took its form in the "congestion of immigrants in the cities."[6] Drawing primarily on examples of some of the worst tenements and slums from the largest cities, these reformers' image of immigrant housing supported the public's "frightened fascination" with Manhattan's Lower East Side and Chicago's Near West Side.[7] And when distinctions were drawn among the various ethnic groups, even the most supportive social reformers left the impression that the Poles "merited liberal sympathy and efforts in large part because they were unable to change the intolerable living conditions by themselves."[8] Stories of Polish homebuilders like Henry Brosczki were rarely told outside the ethnic neighborhoods and have only begun to emerge in recent studies of the immigrant experience.

The historical record of American urban housing continues to be incomplete if not actually skewed because of the Progressive Era reformers' focus on the problems of the tenement apartment house in the largest urban centers.[9] Paradoxically, the idealized accounts of middle-class suburban housing traditionally provide the only significant complement to the record of the era's housing conditions. In the new industrial cities of the Midwest, the wooden houses of Henry Brosczki's Detroit, or the "typical" cottages of Milwaukee (fig. 3.2 and 3.3) warrant greater attention since densely clustered one- and two-family housing was far more representative of the typical immigrant experience. Recent studies by researchers such as Roger Simon, Craig Reisser, Olivier Zunz, Richard Harris, Anne Mosher, and Deryck Holdsworth begin to correct this deficiency by exploring the significance of such structures in the housing supply and, thus, they contribute to our understanding of working-class housing history.[10] We seek to further remedy this oversight in the knowledge of urban housing conditions by focusing on the Polish immigrant neighborhoods of Milwaukee.

These basic wooden buildings, consisting of several distinct house types, were neither new urban building types nor imported ethnic creations, but

Fig. 3.2. This unidentified Milwaukee block was labeled "typical housing of German laborers" in a 1905 study of Milwaukee housing conditions. *Source*: "The Housing Problems of Milwaukee," *Wisconsin Bureau of Labor and Industrial Statistics*, 12th Biennial Report, 1905 (Madison, 1906), 315.

Fig. 3.3. A southside Milwaukee real estate firm advertised this structure as "For Two Families." From *Kruyer Polski* (1918). State of Wisconsin Historical Society Collection, Madison, Wisconsin.

reflected preexisting American house forms and technology modified for dense urban environments during the second half of the nineteenth and early twentieth century.[11] Furthermore, these modifications to the existing housing forms can be attributed to the needs of the immigrant "homebuilder." The term homebuilder is used here in the same sense that it was employed in Karl Harriman's story—not to imply actual involvement in construction on the part of the immigrant but, instead, to acknowledge the active role of immigrants in providing for the needs and values of their families.[12]

Although the structures themselves were not the result of traditional building techniques, the houses built in Milwaukee reflect cultural values of Polish Americans.

Immigrants adapted and expanded a standard type of post–Civil War cottage. The immigrant worker's cottage was not a uniform building type but existed in several regional and local variations.[13] One of these regional types (fig. 3.4), the Polish workers' cottage of Milwaukee, forms the principal unit of this investigation. Milwaukee's Polish homebuilders became agents of landscape change through their *reconfiguration* of the workers' cottage in a process of Americanization. If not restricted to the limited perspective of most urban reform literature, the term *Americanization* acknowledges a complex process by which Polish immigrants created their residences in America, selectively adopting American cultural elements.[14] This transformation process produced various forms of the expanded cottage, including the "rear" or "alley-house," the distinctive form of the raised cottage—known in Milwaukee as the "Polish flat" —and culminated in the ideal of the American bungalow.

The Workers' Cottage

Although the word cottage was used in the nineteenth century to describe small, one-story workers' housing, the term was also applied to many

Fig. 3.4. Labeled "Typical Homes of Polish Working Men," this unidentified block on Milwaukee's south side served as an example of the city's Polish neighborhood. From "The Housing Problems of Milwaukee," *Wisconsin Bureau of Labor and Industrial Statistics*, 12th Biennial Report, 1905 (Madison, 1906), 315.

kinds of buildings both real and idealized, including the rural vacation retreats of wealthy Americans. The label "workers' cottage" is, therefore, particularly important so as not to confuse this modest structure with "cottages" of the rural, romantic movements.[15] While there are local and regional studies of workers' cottages, there are, as yet, no commonly agreed upon building terminology and classification systems. Furthermore, the problem of whether to even classify the housing types of European immigrants separately from other, similar forms of housing for all urban or semi-urban Americans of limited economic status is a complex issue and awaits further demographic study.[16]

Despite the lack of detailed architectural studies, many types of late-nineteenth-century urban workers' cottages appear to share a group of similar building characteristics. The typical workers' cottage of midwestern cities might be described as a one-story (or story and one-half) wood frame structure with its gable and offset front door facing the street. The successful Chicago real estate developer S. E. Gross sold many such structures in the working-class neighborhood known as the Back-of-the-Yards.[17] Gross's advertisement, shown in figure 3.5, illustrates the features of these simple workers' cottages. In plan, it usually contained two major rooms along one side: a living room (also called a parlor) and a kitchen (fig. 3.5). Along the opposite side were two or more smaller rooms, usually used for bedrooms. This standard workers' cottage usually had two entries, one from a front porch opening to a small entry hall into the living room, and the other from the rear or side into the kitchen. In some cases, the cottage had a basement or minimum underground storage area. The upstairs or attic was almost always used for sleeping areas (often left unfinished) for children or boarders.

The post–Civil War workers' cottage is a significant house type not only because of its wide popularity in American urban and semi-urban areas during the second half of the nineteenth and early twentieth century, but also because it should be considered one of the first forms of fully industrialized housing for working-class Americans.[18] Although a modest structure, it united many of the most advanced technological and planning

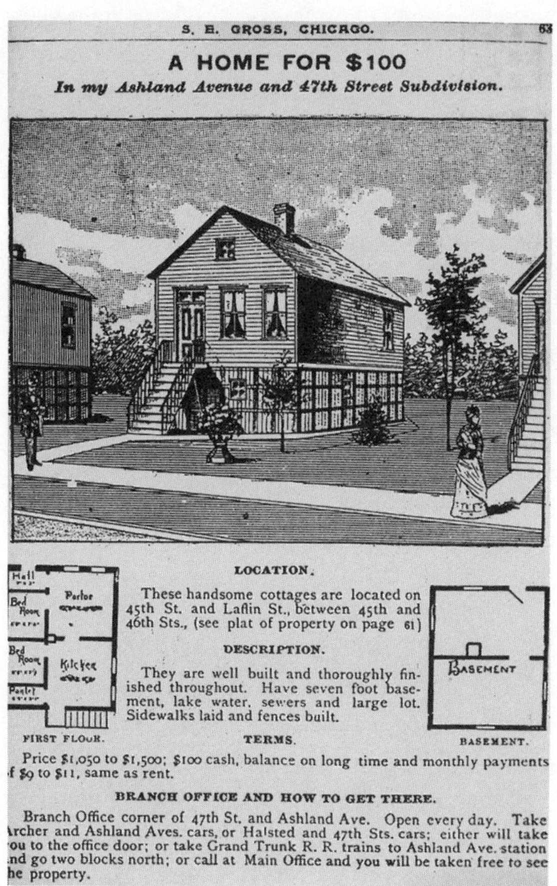

Fig. 3.5. Real estate developer S. E. Gross's cottage advertisement for Chicago's Back-of-the-Yards neighborhood, 1880s. Courtesy of the Chicago Historical Society.

ideas of its era. Its machined components included doors, windows, casings, hardware, and decorative detailing, as well as standardized components for the wood structural and material finish systems.[19] These materials were assembled following newly developed construction, merchandising, and distribution systems featuring the following: (1) standardized, interchangeable components, such as nails, studs, and casings, which were particularly adapted to the new balloon frame type of structural system; (2) a national production and distribution system for building materials, facilitated by the railroad; (3) contractor and speculator initiation of the house building process, with minimal owner contribution to the design or construction; and (4) modern land development practices such as lot standardization, financing, and marketing practices. As it was constructed in midwestern cities after 1880, this new type of cottage was specifically intended for a non-farm, industrial worker's family. It was mass-produced because it proved to be an efficient housing solution in an era of rapid industrial development and its flexibility and mobility permitted incremental expansion and improvement according to the needs and finances of the immigrant families.

Incremental Growth: From Cottage to Bungalow

Returning to figure 3.1, this picture exemplifies a typical turn-of-the-century workers' cottage. This particular building was constructed circa 1889 and was slightly smaller than the typical Milwaukee cottage with its kitchen in a shed at the rear of the house (see fig. 3.6).[20] Newly married Anton and Katarzyna Mazur bought this five-year-old cottage in 1894 for $800. An arranged marriage had brought together Anton, a twenty-six-year-old Austrian steelworker, and Katarzyna, a twenty-one-year-old recent arrival from the Poznan District of western Poland. The newlyweds moved into their new home along with Katarzyna's father, younger sister, and brother. When the photograph was taken in 1899, the family had already expanded to include Anton and Katarzyna's two children. By 1914, five more children joined the Mazur family, and ultimately the original three-room cottage would accommodate an extended family of twelve members. Additional sleeping space for the grandfather and boys was located in the unfinished basement. Windows in the cedar-post foundation gave some light to their basement room.

Establishing themselves in a new house in a new country, the Mazurs, like the majority of immigrants, raised children and accommodated family members in the typical multigenerational immigrant family. Children contributed to the family income by leaving school at thirteen or fourteen to begin work and, thus, their wages greatly contributed to the ability of an unskilled industrial worker's family to purchase a house.[21] Frequently, as in the case of the Mazur house, when the

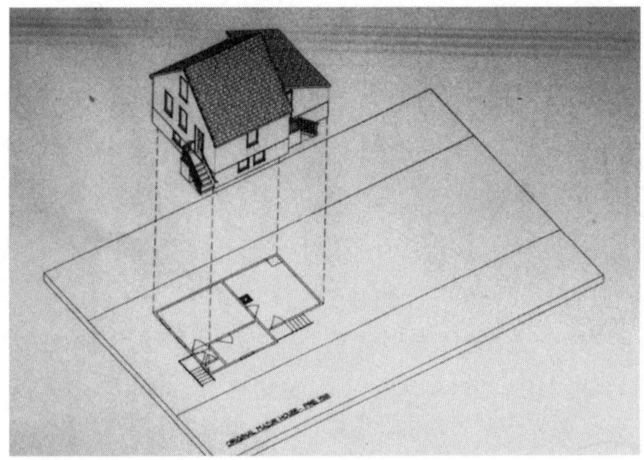

Fig. 3.6. Plan and elevation of the original Mazur cottage.

children's incomes began to supplement the family budget (along with the financial support of several extended-family members), improvements to the cottage could be considered. Such improvements reflect the conservative, additive approach to building more living space typical of many Milwaukee working-class homeowners.

In 1917, after twenty-three years of residence and the contribution of approximately six wage earners, the Mazurs transformed their cottage by conducting a series of ambitious building improvements as illustrated in figure 3.7. First they bought "Uncle" Joe Nisiewiecz's cottage, which was lifted off its foundation and rolled down the street from its site one block away. As one observer of Milwaukee's Polish business community noted, there was a "blooming business" for Polish American house movers by the turn of the century.[22] Indeed, to a certain degree, a separate Polish American economy operated within their neighborhoods, providing skilled contractors and architects.[23] The original Mazur cottage was then spun and moved toward the back of the site and attached to the newly relocated Nisiewiecz's cottage. The cedar-post foundation under the original cottage, typical of nineteenth-century, lower-income housing in Milwaukee, was replaced with concrete blocks underneath the entire expanded structure. The final product was an expanded, raised cottage remodeled into a version of the bungalow plan with a series of three major public rooms—the living room, dining room, and kitchen—along one side and smaller bedrooms along the other side. Although the converted Mazur cottage was not stylistically an American bungalow, this type of house remodeling was usually labeled a "bungalow" by Milwaukee's Polish inhabitants whose image of the American bungalow—suggesting relative spaciousness and social mobility—had become a popular goal for single-family housing.[24] When completed in 1918, the Mazurs' remodeled cottage represented a common sequence of incremental expansions conducted by Polish immigrants.[25]

Transforming the Cottage into the Polish Flat

Near the end of the nineteenth century, the numerical dominance of the workers' cottage in Milwaukee began to be challenged by a new, larger type of popular housing, the duplex. Described as the "rule"

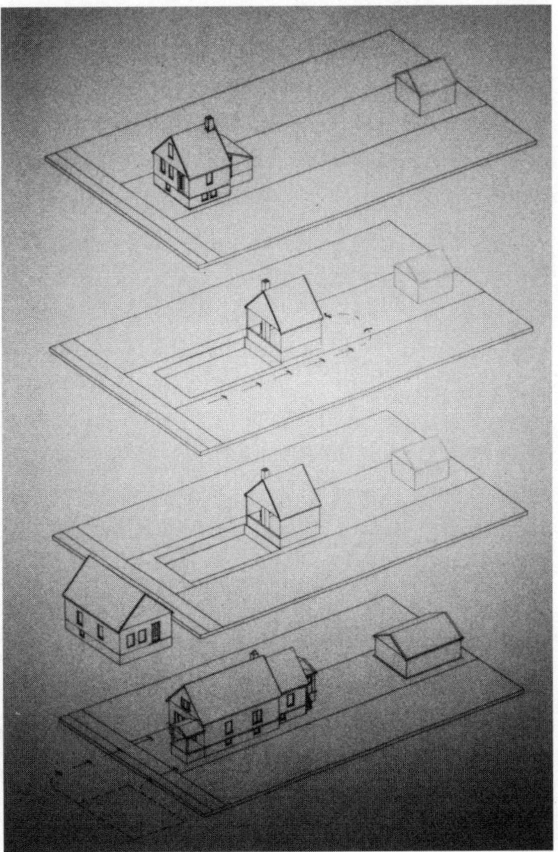

Fig. 3.7. Diagrams showing the expansion of the Mazur cottage, 1917.

in a 1911 housing study, this two-story, two-family duplex (with upper and lower flats) replaced the cottage as the dominant house type in many working-class neighborhoods of Milwaukee (fig. 3.8).[26] In Polish neighborhoods, however, this Milwaukee flat never achieved popularity because it was an expensive, larger structure, generally built at one time and thus beyond the means of most Poles. Despite their financial limitations, the Poles composed their own, less expensive version of the two-story, two-apartment flat as described in a 1911 Milwaukee housing study: "In the south side district, where a large class of the poorer section of the Poles live, the custom is to erect first a four-roomed frame dwelling (or cottage). When this has been paid for, it is raised on posts to allow a semi-basement dwelling to be constructed underneath, This basement, or the upstairs flat, is then let (rented) by the owner, who, as soon as his funds permit, substitutes brick walls for the timber of the basement."[27] Based on our preliminary estimates, in a fifty-year period (1870–1920), ten thousand Polish flats were constructed, representing approximately 5 to 10 percent of Milwaukee's total housing units. In the area known as the Polish south side, the house type constituted over 50 percent of the housing supply.

Fig. 3.8. A typical Milwaukee duplex. Photograph by the authors (1994).

Recently arrived immigrants created a market for rental housing for which the raised cottage was ideally suited. The raised cottage form appears in immigrant working-class areas of Chicago and other midwestern cities as well.[28] Apparently, because of its dominance in the Polish immigrant neighborhoods, the "raised cottage" earned the title "Polish flat" in Milwaukee—but only in Milwaukee. With the housing supply strained to accommodate the workers' demands, the Polish flat was an inexpensive solution that benefited both the small working-class landlord and their working-class tenant. Meeting this demand provided rental income that could be useful for paying off the mortgage. The particular advantage of the Polish flat was that once the mortgage was paid, the flat could be converted back to a single-family house, which consistently remained the goal of many Polish immigrants.

Changing family needs and values might also be factors in the construction of a Polish flat. Joseph and Josephine Potrykus provide such an example. They raised seven children in the original worker's cottage but when their oldest child married in 1914, they began a reconstruction of the house to provide a first-floor apartment for the new couple (fig. 3.9). The original structure was first raised to build a new brick-walled basement floor for an expanded basement living area. The roof was raised to obtain bedroom space, and the house was expanded on both floors to the rear. In one of the most significant functional changes, the Potrykuses moved their cooking and laundry activities downstairs into a large kitchen that concentrated the major domestic chores of both families in the basement unit. The extended family gathered in the large basement kitchen for shared meals and evening gatherings, thus preserving the upstairs and its kitchen and dining room for special occasions. The completed house (fig. 3.9) was a hybrid adaptation reflecting both the assimilation of American middle-class, domestic reform ideas—particularly by the adoption of the dining room—and the reinterpretation of these ideas within the shared environment of an extended family of Polish Americans.[29]

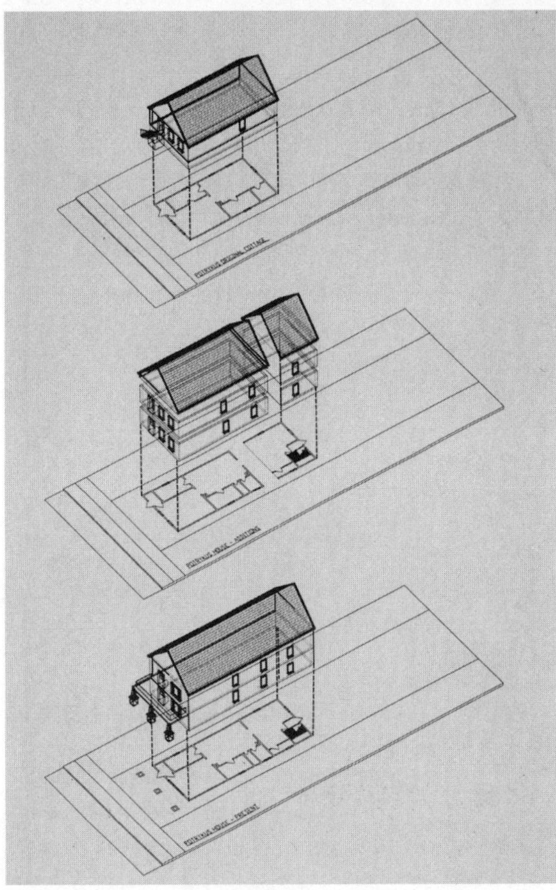

Fig. 3.9. Diagrams showing the expansion of the Potrykus cottage to create a Polish flat, 1914.

As this "poor man's" duplex became a common house form in the *Polish* neighborhoods, many began to build these structures as full two-story Polish flats rather than as adaptations of the single-story cottage.[30] The application of the popular term Polish to the typical raised basement cottage (or this less expensive duplex) in Milwaukee reflects both the density of this house type in the city's *Polonia* and the public consciousness of this phenomena. A reading of early-twentieth-century texts reveals contrasting views of the Polish community that are reflected in the discussion of the Polish flat. One social worker spoke of the Polish wards as "the regions of the modern cave dweller," where "the basements are occupied from choice and long fixed habit."[31] In contrast, a friend of the Polish community wrote of the same neighborhoods as "an area of cottages with high basements" and of the Polish residents as pioneers of the city's southern frontier.[32] There are those among Milwaukee's older Polish Americans who still remember the sting attached to the label "Polish flat" and prefer to call this adaptation of the cottage a one-and-a-half-story flat.[33] With regard to the basement quality of the Polish flat, it must be emphasized that in most cases this area was sunk only three to four feet into the ground in order to allow for standard residential windows of three to four feet in height. Therefore, the negative image of "basement dwellers" in unlighted, fully submerged basements must be adjusted to accept a modified basement with lower unit just a few feet below grade.

The Rear House

Another building strategy typically employed by Milwaukee's immigrant Poles to expand their housing opportunities was the alley house or rear house. This house was typically constructed on the rear portions of the site, usually next to an alley. Often, an alley house was an earlier, original cottage that had been moved to the back of the site and placed upon a new raised foundation while a new house was built on the front of the lot. An advertisement from the building trade's newspaper, *The Daily Reporter*, in April 12, 1914, records this common practice: "Architect A. Michalak is taking bids for the erection of a 2-family flat for John Novakowski at 442 5th Ave. The old cottage is to be moved to the rear."[34] There were also cases where a small original house was built on the back of the site in anticipation of the construction of a later, larger house in front.

House movement and rear house development were almost certainly the case in the expansion process of the Weisniewski House, whose original cottage now stands at the rear of the site with a raised basement living space (fig. 3.10). The original cottage appears to have been moved to make way for the building of a larger two-story flat on the front of the lot. Following the completion of the project in 1919, the two buildings housed four families, providing income for the Weisniewski family to pay off their mortgage. Until enforcement of building codes eliminated the rear house (following World War I), immigrants actively pursued this practice of adding a second house to long, narrow city lots.[35]

Urban reformers interpreted the rear house and the raised cottage as introducing an unsanitary, unhealthy, and possibly immoral degree of population density into ethnic neighborhoods. While many health concerns were justified, such analyses frequently overlooked the economic benefits of home expansion projects to the residents. The expansions to the Glazewski property demonstrate the variety of needs met by such arrangements (fig. 3.11). After obtaining a mortgage on two cottages on a single lot, Helen Glazewski contracted to have the rear cottage raised and transformed into a two-family flat in 1912. Her husband's death had left her as the sole support for her children, and rental income from tenants and boarders provided for them. Eight years later, she sold the property to her brother-in-law Vincent Glazewski. Helen's reasons for the sale were not recorded, but the chil-

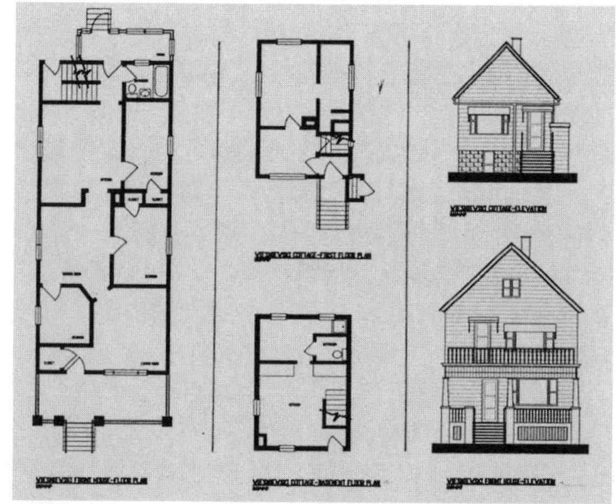

Fig. 3.10. Plans and elevations of the Weisniewskis' front and rear houses on South 14th Street, Milwaukee.

dren of Vincent and Lucia Glazewski recall that their parents lived in the upstairs rear house while the front house and other rear unit earned income for the mortgage. By 1923, they could afford to assume the front house for the family while continuing to rent the rear house. Earning between eight and ten dollars a month, the rental property provided financial and social stability—with one tenant occupying the rear house for twenty-five years (fig. 3.12). In the Polish community, this widely recognized strategy for increasing family income is clearly stated by a Pole writing home to a friend and prospective immigrant. Here he wrote about the wisdom of bringing a wife to provide for boarders: "come with your wife because . . . some of the men are in America with their wives and have already made a lot of money . . . they [husband and wife] can live quite well if they have six men na borcie [boarding] with them for which they charge each of them $15 a month."[36]

These examples of house adaptation demonstrate combinations of the most typical expansion and remodeling strategies of the standard cottage employed in the Polish community between the 1870s and the 1920s. Summarized, these strategies include (1) inserting a basement under the cottage to produce a raised cottage, or Polish flat; (2) raising the roof to make a heightened attic, or a full second floor above the cottage; (3) additions to front, middle, or rear of existing cottage; (4) moving the original cottage to the rear and building a new house or cottage (or constructing the original structure at the rear of the lot in anticipation of building a finer, larger house at the front of the lot); (5) remodeling the cottage floor plan to produce a flat or bungalow plan; and (6) removing the entire cottage and building a new flat or bungalow. Although uniformly condemned by reformers as disorderly, unsightly, and overcrowded, these incremental projects provided an accessible strategy to both accommodate

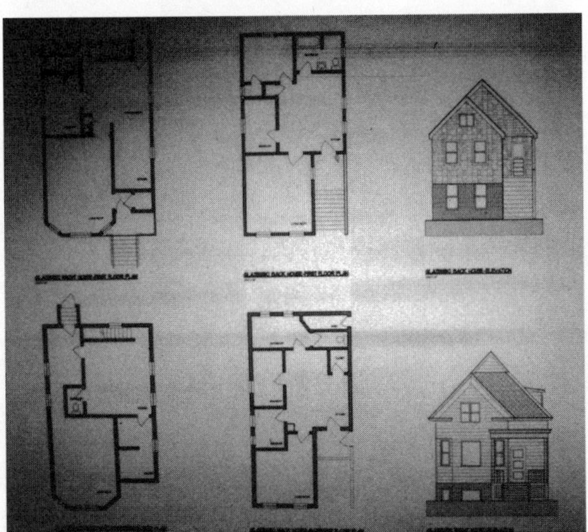

Fig. 3.11. Plans and elevations of the Glazewskis' front and rear houses on South 15th Street, Milwaukee.

Fig. 3.12. Glazewski rear house. Photograph by the authors (1994).

relatives and newcomers and to obtain scarce income critical to improving the quality of domestic life and achieving the widely shared goal of homeownership. In the immigrants' eyes, meeting the demand for shelter and obtaining the stability of homeownership compensated for the crowded conditions.[37] Each of these incremental home-expansion projects occurred thousands of times in Milwaukee's Polish community and constituted an evolving, critical mass of new urban house forms. One of Milwaukee's prominent citizens provided the following image of the Polish and their neighborhoods: "they looked toward the wooded lands south of Greenfield Avenue, which they later transformed into a vast area of cottages with high basements, each accommodating two families, with gardens in the rear and some shrubbery and a rest bench in the front."[38] As the immigrants transformed the basic workers' cottage, they created a distinctive new landscape of homeownership.

Enculturation and Assimilation

To evaluate the role of "the home" in the enculturation process, attention must be paid to questions of homeownership and house form. In doing so, it is clear that strongly held ethnic values as well as newly acquired American building technologies helped the Poles negotiate their transition to American life. The greater difficulty is to disentangle the complex motivations that might distinguish the influence of ethnic values as opposed to "American" values.[39] This is particularly evident in regard to issues of homeownership. It is often taken for granted that the United States has a national culture of homeownership—that homeownership represents a "socially compulsive ideal."[40] But it is also assumed in the historical analysis of Poles that Polish "land hunger" drove their behavior.[41] This suggests that a complex analysis of class, ethnicity, and cultural differences must be employed when considering homeownership and the experience of members of Milwaukee's Polish community.

Although contemporary critics condemned the outcome of the Poles' incremental building efforts, they applauded the high rate of homeownership among the Poles. Expressing civic boosterism, one late-nineteenth-century Milwaukee resident argued that despite the city's large immigrant population, "there is not of its size in all America a city that contains a population more self-respecting, more law-abiding, more cheerful and content than Milwaukee."[42] He concluded his praise with the observation that homeownership was a virtue and that "no matter how humble it may be, it is the home that makes the citizen who has the public interests at heart."[43]

The Poles shared this high value placed on ownership. One Polish American expressed the lesson learned by the landless Polish peasant by stating: "A man without land is like a man without legs; he crawls about but never gets anywhere."[44] Polish immigrants began translating their land hunger into the goal of homeownership upon their arrival in American cities. This is clearly reflected in a Milwaukee Polish language newspaper advertisement for new housing, where it is stated, "Only the homeowner is truly independent."[45] Such Polish publications emphasized that homeownership provided a source of security as well as autonomy and a stake in their adopted country.

The Poles' low position in the Milwaukee labor hierarchy made ownership all the more desirable—and difficult. A 1911 study conducted by the British Board of Trade outlined the relationship between ethnicity and occupation by ranking the various groups within Milwaukee.[46] American-born employees engaged in "mercantile pursuits, office work and positions of trust." The Germans occupied skilled positions while the Poles and other recent immigrants, including Russian Poles, Austrian Slavs, and Italians, were associated with unskilled work. The British study made a particular point that Poles were well suited to occupations "requiring a considerable amount of physical strength."[47] Built into the labor hierarchy, such assumptions significantly limited occupational mobility. Consequently, some scholars argue that the Poles turned to home ownership as a means of solidifying their precarious economic strategy.[48]

Yet, Milwaukee Poles surmounted limitations on their opportunities for homeownership in several ways. As cited previously, family strategies for increasing income relied on taking in boarders and increasing the number of wage earners within the household, including relatives and older children. The widespread desire for ownership in the Polish community was further facilitated with the advent of Polish American building and loan associations. These Polish loan associations, called "skarbi" (treasury), facilitated a family's initial purchase and development of property, allowing even poor families to participate in the process of acquiring and remodeling a home.[49]

Their high rate of homeownership allowed the Milwaukee Poles a remarkable ability to manipulate the environment to meet their immediate housing needs.[50] Consequently, one might expect that the housing or environment characteristics in the dominantly Polish districts might reflect indigenous Polish domestic spatial and cultural patterns imported to the New World. This, however, was not the case despite an extensive and well-documented tradition of Polish ethnic cohesiveness. Old World Polish cultural values and traditions persisted, for example, in the spheres of language, food, and religion.[51] In the physical spheres of the dwelling, cultural retention seems to have a less significant impact. Perhaps urban America's dramatically different environmental context accounts for this selectivity.

Space limitations prevent a detailed analysis of these Old World domestic environment and cultural traditions of the Milwaukee's pre-1900 Polish immigrants who largely came from the small towns and agricultural regions of western Poland. Here the common housing traditions were based on late-medieval agrarian precedents related to one-room deep, side-entry house types. These dwellings were typical of the rural villages, even in the Germanized regions of western Poland, into the twentieth century.[52] For example, in the region surrounding Plock, Poland—in over twenty-five agricultural villages sending immigrants to America—the typical rural house types were single-pile farmhouses dominated by masonry-stove, kitchen-dominant room arrangements.[53] These buildings and traditions of usage had few direct parallels to the methods of America's commercial/industrial economy where a dramatically different urban American environment context imposed severe constraints.[54]

In reiterating that there was nothing uniquely Polish about the Polish flat, it should be noted that people of different European origins—but similar economic status—developed this house form as well. The American urban/industrial workers' cottage was the basic housing unit of material culture that rural immigrant Poles first encountered and then reconfigured in the evolving process of incorporating American cultural values into their domestic environment (see fig. 3.13). To a large extent, immigrant Poles consistently modeled and then remodeled their dwelling after the housing examples of the dominant American middle-class culture. For example, the Polish flat in Milwaukee was loosely modeled after the common Milwaukee flat.

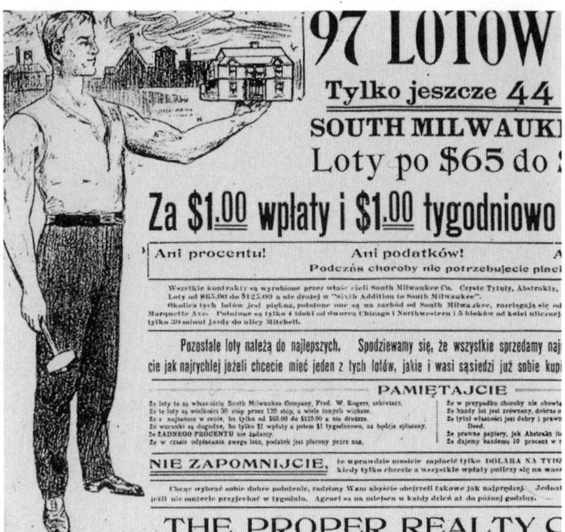

Fig. 3.13. An advertisement in a Polish-language newspaper for the sale of lots in South Milwaukee. From *Kruyer Polski* (1919). State of Wisconsin Historical Society Collection, Madison, Wisconsin.

These immigrant families, however, were never passive receptors of middle-class culture or its domestic reform ideology, but, as this chapter has demonstrated, they reinterpreted and reformulated ideas and examples from American popular culture within the framework of their Old World cultural traditions and their New World cultural context (for example, the prevalence of the extended family in the house). Polish America's most famous historian, Waclaw Kruszka, suggested in 1908 that: "Like a tree transplanted onto foreign soil, we assimilated the lifeblood of this land and those of American customs that suited our Polish nature."[55]

To a certain extent we might endorse this Polish nationalist's assessment of the complex blending and interaction of a domestic reform ideology with the remodeling of the immigrant cottage over a period of time, dating from the late nineteenth century through the early twentieth century. The principal physical results of this process of assimilation are clear. These include (1) the separation of food preparation and dining activities with the eventual adoption of the dining room; (2) the individualization of sleeping spaces for children, or at least their separation by sex into bedrooms; (3) the incorporation of more and larger windows throughout the entire dwelling, and especially in the basement units; (4) an increased emphasis on plumbing and sanitation facilities, especially in the adoption of kitchen plumbing and interior bathrooms for each family unit; and (5) the conformity of exterior building aesthetics and yard maintenance practices and the elimination of agrarian-influenced practices (or at least confining them to the private backyard).[56] If there is one practice that most fully symbolizes the adoption of middle-class domestic values and the abandonment of Old World cultural values for the immigrant family, it is the addition of the dining room with its attendant demand for the separation of food preparation and consumption—and the implied prestige of upward social and economic mobility. This practice was not fully realized for the majority of Polish flat users until the 1930s, often in the form of a remodeled bungalow.

The reconfigured workers' cottage should be seen as an evolving physical and cultural setting in which immigrant Poles adjusted, altered, and finally incorporated an Americanized vocabulary of house forms and patterns of living guided, in part, by an ideology of domestic reform and their own predilection for homeownership. As demonstrated from advertising in numerous Polish language newspapers, homeownership supported the goal of independence and economic security. For its Polish immigrant occupants, largely from an agrarian background, the industrially formulated cottage was certainly not a neutral object in this process. It was a culturally encoded artifact providing its occupants with embedded suggestions sanctioning both the domestic values of the dominant American culture and fostering an experimental attitude toward change, particularly in the flexibility of the lightwood construction system and the traditions of change and transformation long associated in American development with these systems. In this interpretation, the standard, preexisting cottage was the setting for an enculturation and assimilation process in which the immigrants transformed their lives from being influenced primarily by agrarian, preindustrial ways to becoming (materially) modern Americans.

Conclusion: Modernization and Americanization

We began our discussion with Henry Brosczki—a representative of Polonia. He purchased a small wooden house that could be relocated to his own land in a Polish neighborhood of Detroit and, thus, became a "homebuilder." We would like to conclude with an observation about the Polish workers' cottage in relation to the processes of modernization and Americanization, and especially the problem of cultural loss and cultural gain within immigrant ethnic groups. This was an issue of particular urgency for working-class Poles, and perhaps for most immigrant groups to America, where the contrasts and struggles between the extremes of Old World cultural retention and New World cultural adaptation were, and still are, played out with intensity.

The broad issues related to the modernization process are challenging for American vernacular architectural historians, particularly because considerable research has been influenced by intellectual models emphasizing the retention and persistence of Old World, preindustrial patterns of building and living.[57] But, if we are to account for the transformation of structures like the Polish workers' cottage, then we must find new and inventive ways to account for the unparalleled reconfiguration of Old World traditions and the adoption of new ideas through processes many have labeled either Americanization or modernization. Such an accounting is not a nostalgic review of Old World vernacular heritage but must tell the story of the immigrants' adaptation of traditional cultural values and assimilation of modern American ones in the late nineteenth and early twentieth century. Tracing the transformation of these values may be most easily assessed in built forms, but their influences extend to all realms of cultural endeavor. And it is these values coiled within the twin concepts of Americanization and modernization which seem to summarize the profound ways immigrant Poles transformed their domestic environments and, in the process, transformed themselves.

This Americanization process also had, and still has, negative effects resulting in considerable cultural loss. There were Poles disillusioned with the American enculturation process who returned to Poland.[58] Others simply ended their lives in sadness and bitterness as they watched their Polish cultural values disintegrate under a barrage of foreign, American cultural values. For the vast majority, however, these wrenching losses of cultural identity were offset by the clearly chosen gains of accommodating and adapting to the dominant American culture. It is important to emphasize that the reformulated Polish workers' cottage was initiated from within the Polish community and largely by the owners of their own housing. The evidence of this powerful transformation process is, however, only vaguely recognizable today. So complete was the Americanization process for most later generations of Polish Americans that there is not even significant cultural memory to recall the loss of a former culture. That is why the story of the transformation of the cottage/flat/bungalow is such an important example and paradigm for understanding the immigrant enculturation process for Polish Americans, and perhaps, for Americans of other ethnic backgrounds. It is a story that externalizes, in architectural form, the often hidden complexities of a process which assimilated one immigrant group into the mainstream of popular American culture.

Notes

We wish to acknowledge the Urban Research Initiatives Program, operated by the University of Wisconsin–Milwaukee Center for Urban Initiatives and Research, which funded the majority of this study. Jason Nyberg and Paula Oeler assisted in the fieldwork and figure preparation. Translations from the Polish newspapers were provided by Michael Mikos, professor of Slavic languages at the University of Wisconsin–Milwaukee.

Other individuals advanced the study through their contribution of time and information. We wish to acknowledge them by outlining our methodology. Information was collected on twenty-five households with architectural drawings completed on seventeen structures. These records complemented contemporary inventories and descriptions of the housing stock reported in State of Wisconsin Public Documents. Oral histories with current and former residents of the study area assisted in compiling building case studies and enriched our findings on the physical and social history of the Polish neighborhoods.

1. Through an analysis of a vast literature, David Ward examines the central position that the immigrants held in urban reform discussion of poverty and urban problems during this period in *Poverty, Ethnicity, and the American City, 1840–1925: Changing Conceptions of the Slum and the Ghetto* (Cambridge: Cambridge Univ. Press, 1989). Studies concerned with the assimilation process, such as W. Thomas and F. Znaniecki's *The Polish Peasant in Europe and America* (Chicago: Univ. of Chicago Press, 1927), gave particular attention to the social deterioration experienced by immigrant groups. The serious attention given to *The Polish Peasant* offended Polish Americans who thought the study biased in its representation of the community.
2. Karl Harriman, "The Homebuilders," in his short-story collection *The Homebuilders* (Freeport, N.Y.: Books for Libraries Press, 1903; reprinted, 1969), 9–65. Harriman's attitude toward the Polish "homebuilder" was overwhelmingly positive and sympathetic relative to other period authors. His stories provide a fairly extensive description of Detroit's Polish community. See Robin Elliot, "The Eastern European Immigrant in American Literature: The View of the Host Culture, 1900–1930," *Polish American Studies* 17, no. 2 (autumn 1985): 25–45, for a discussion of the prevalent treatment of Slavic immigrants in the American literature of the period.
3. Harriman, "The Homebuilders," 28–29.
4. As described in Waclaw Kruszka's *A History of the Poles in America to 1908* (Washington, D.C.: Catholic Univ. of America Press, 1993), these four cities contained major Polish settlements with populations of approximately 250,000, 70,000, 65,000, and 50,000 respectively.
5. For discussions of Polish homeownership, see references such as John Bodnar, "Immigration and Modernization: The Case of the Slavic Peasants in Industrial America," *Journal of Social History* 10, no. 1 (fall 1976): 44–71, and Roger Simon, "Housing and Services in an

Immigrant Neighborhood: Milwaukee's Ward 14," *Journal of Urban History* 2 (1976).

6. Sen. William Dillingham, Report of the Immigration Commission, vol. 26., 61st Cong., 2d sess., 1911, S. Doc. 338. (Reprint, New York: Arno & *New York Times*, 1970).
7. Gwendolyn Wright, *Building the Dream: A Social History of Housing in America* (New York: Pantheon Books, 1981), 114–34.
8. This quotation represents historian Victor Greene's summary of the Polish worker's image as stated in his article—"The Polish American Worker to 1930: The 'Hunky' Image in Transition," *Polish Review* 21, no. 3 (1976): 66.
9. In "Beyond the Tenement: Patterns of American Urban Housing, 1870–1930," *Journal of Urban History* 9, no. 4 (Aug. 1983): 395–420, Robert Barrows calls for further study, noting that the focus on the largest cities made it difficult to see "the housing for the tenements."
10. For research conducted on the meaning and form of immigrant, working-class housing in North America at the turn of the century, see such examples as Simon, "Housing and Services"; Craig Reisser, "Immigrants and House Form in Northeast Milwaukee" (master's thesis, Univ. of Wisconsin–Milwaukee, 1977); Olivier Zunz, *The Changing Face of Inequality: Urbanization, Industrial Development, and Immigrants in Detroit, 1880–1920* (Chicago: Univ. of Chicago Press, 1982); Richard Harris, "Working-Class Homeownership in the American Metropolis," *Journal of Urban History* 17, no. 1 (Nov. 1990); and Anne Mosher and Deryck Holdsworth, "The Meaning of Alley-Housing," *Journal of Historical Geography* 18, no. 2 (1992).
11. The cottage was associated with the provision of housing for workers' families in the earliest of America's new industrial centers. See James Vance's "Housing the Worker: The Employment Linkage as a Force in Urban Structure," *Annals of the Association of American Geographers 1966*, for a discussion of cottage design in the "Arkwright villages" of Rhode Island, circa 1810. See also Wright, Building the Dream.
12. In making this distinction, we dispute Richard Harris's interpretation of Milwaukee's Polish flats as evidence of the role of the "homebuilder." See Richard Harris, "Reading Sanborns for the Spoor of the Owner-Builder, 1890s–1950s," *Perspectives in Vernacular Architecture, VII* (Knoxville: Univ. of Tennessee Press, 1997), 251–68. Although homeowners often describe work done to their homes in terms of personal action, this language generally reflects their role in the decision-making process. From numerous interviews, the review of building permits, and evidence of Polish American construction firms, we conclude that contractors (rather than homeowner/builders) completed the actual construction tasks. It should be noted that remodeling projects (such as digging the basement beneath a raised cottage) may have involved a degree of owner participation, but the evidence indicates that professionals assumed primary responsibility in the process.
13. See, for example, Virginia and Lee McAlester, *A Field Guide to American Houses* (New York: Alfred Knopf, 1992), 24–31, 309–20, and Sally McMurry, *Families and Farmhouses in Nineteenth Century America* (New York: Oxford Univ. Press, 1988), 106–28, 209–19.
14. Americanization is a problematic term given its association with late-nineteenth and early-twentieth-century urban reformers' use of it when prescribing behavioral changes for immigrants.
15. John E. Crowley, "'In Happier Mansions, Warm, and Dry': The Invention of the Cottage

as the Comfortable Anglo-American House," *Winterthur Portfolio* 32, no. 2/3 (1997): 169–72, 182–88.

16. See Herbert Gottfried, "The Machine and the Cottage: Building, Technology and the Single-Family House, 1870–1910," *Journal of the Society for Industrial Archaeology* 21, no. 2 (1995), and Fred W. Peterson, *Homes in the Heartland* (Lawrence: Univ. Press of Kansas, 1992), 25–60.
17. See Wright, *Building the Dream.*
18. Gottfried, "The Machine and the Cottage," 47–68.
19. Ibid.
20. Interview with Bernice Mazur, Milwaukee, Wis. (Apr. 18, 1994), and review of title papers for the property.
21. Urban reform literature criticized this common practice of ending their children's education as soon as permissible so that the Polish immigrant children might contribute to the family's income.
22. Waclaw Kruszka, *A History of the Poles to 1908* (Washington, D.C.: Catholic Univ. of America Press, 1993), 189.
23. See Bayrd Still, *Milwaukee: The History of a City* (Madison: State Historical Society of Wisconsin, 1948), 273.
24. Interviews with Polish Americans, for example, Bernice Mazur (Apr. 18, 1994) and Henry Wojcik of Wojcik Realty Company, Milwaukee, Wis. (June 1994).
25. Similar incremental building practices have been documented for the Polish residential areas of Winona, Minnesota. For further information consult the City of Winona, Minnesota, historic building inventory (unpublished city document, 1992).
26. United Kingdom Board of Trade, *Cost of Living in American Towns* (London: His Majesty's Stationery Office, 1911), 266.
27. Ibid.
28. There were contextual factors that contributed to the development of the Polish flat which suggest a link to Chicago where a simultaneous development of "raised cottages" can be identified. After the fire of 1871, many frugal builders raised cottages and built a new brick first story to conform to the new fire code elimination of ground-level wood construction in the central city. See Harold Mayer and Richard Wade, *Chicago: Growth of a Metropolis* (Chicago: Univ. of Chicago, 1969), 152–55, 262–63.
29. Interview with Leonard Zurkowski, Milwaukee, Wis. (June 16, 1994).
30. Additional study is required to determine the number of original structures built as Polish flats rather than adapted incrementally to this use. Preliminary inventories provide examples of houses that conform to this neighborhood style from their initial construction. The brick duplex of the Domagalski family represents an exceptional example since it conforms to neighborhood style but represents a higher status in its choice of building materials. See *Milwaukee: Ethnic Houses Tour* (City of Milwaukee, Dept. of City Development, 1994).
31. Wisconsin Public Documents, "Basement Tenements in Milwaukee," *Fifteenth Biennial Report* (Madison, 1912), 5:381.
32. W. George Bruce, "Contacts with the Polish-American Element," in *I Was Born in America* (Milwaukee: Bruce Publishing, 1937), 322.
33. Interviews with Henry Wojcik, Wojcik Realty Company, Milwaukee, Wis. (June 1994).
34. (Milwaukee, Wis.) *Daily Reporter*, Apr. 12, 1914.
35. Judith Kenny, "Americanizing Milwaukee's Polish South Side, 1900–1925," *Wisconsin Geographer* 10 (1994): 41–50.
36. Witold Kula, Nina Assorodobraj-Kula, and Marcin Kula, *Writing Home: Immigrants in*

Brazil and the United States, 1890–1891 (New York: Columbia Univ. Press, 1986), 414, 493–94. The advice was given by Simon Sosienski (Allegheny County, Pa.) in a letter to his brother Adam.

37. For a discussion of declining densities in Polish neighborhoods over time, see Judith Kenny, "Americanizing Milwaukee's Polish South Side," 45–50.
38. Bruce, *I Was Born in America*, 322.
39. Lizabeth Cohen suggests the difficulty of disentangling ethnic values/identity and the influence of mass or popular culture during the early part of the twentieth century in her monograph *Making a New Deal: Industrial Workers in Chicago, 1919–1939* (New York: Cambridge Univ. Press, 1990). Such an effort requires a sensitive analysis of a variety of aspects of material culture and the influence of ethnicity, "mass" culture, and middle-class American values.
40. Richard Harris reviews the diversity of scholarly views regarding the meaning of homeownership in "Working-Class Home Ownership in the American Metropolis," *Journal of Urban History* 17, no. 1 (Nov. 1990): 46–69.
41. Thomas's and Znaniecki's major study of the assimilation of immigrants, *The Polish Peasant in Europe and America*, devotes considerable attention to what is described as the "land hunger" of the Poles and its influence on their social and economic motivations.
42. Charles King cited in George Lankevich, *Milwaukee: A Chronological and Documentary History* (Dobbs Ferry, N.Y.: Oceana Publishers), 119.
43. Ibid.
44. Wladislaw Reymont cited in Caroline Golab, *Immigrant Destinations* (Philadelphia: Temple Univ. Press, 1977), 67.
45. Fons & Company's advertising in Kruyer Polski, 1919. Fons & Company was a leading real estate firm in the south side Polish community.
46. United Kingdom Board of Trade, *Cost of Living in American Towns* (London: His Majesty's Stationery Office, 1911), 260.
47. Ibid.
48. John Bodnar, "Immigration and Modernization: The Case of the Slavic Peasants in Industrial America," *Journal of Social History* 10, no. 1 (fall 1976): 44–71.
49. Kruszka, *A History of the Poles to 1908*, 21.
50. Roger Simon notes in his study of Milwaukee's Polish community that the Poles held the highest percentage of homeownership among ethnic groups in the city. See Simon, "Housing and Services," 448–50.
51. Maria Anna Knothe, "Land and Loyalties" and "Recent Arrivals" in *Peasant Maids/City Women*, ed. Christiane Harzig (Ithaca: Cornell Univ. Press, 1997), 144–76, 327–38.
52. Adam Milobedzki, *Zarys dziejow architektury w polsce* (Warszawa: Wiedza Powszechna, 1988), 239–43, 285–89.
53. See "Album of Villages" (unpublished portfolios, 1930), Warsaw: Library of Warsaw Polytechnic Institute, and Adam Milobezki, "Architecture in Wood," *Artibus et Historiae* 19 (1989): 180–96.
54. We acknowledge that there might be similarities of use and form between the Old and New World. See endnote 56 below for an example of ethnic practices transferred to the American urban context. Other practices have been identified in certain oral histories that suggest a transfer of Polish customary uses—as when an individual recalled his grandmother's "summer kitchen" in the basement. (For further discussion see Judith T. Kenny, "Polish Routes to Americanization: House Form and Landscape on Milwaukee's Polish South Side," in *Wisconsin Land and Life*, ed. R. Ostergren

and T. Vale [Madison: Univ. of Wisconsin Press, 1997], 263–81.) Polish farmhouses, however, do not have basements. Further study will be pursued to define the extent to which various ethnic uses and/or forms may have been transferred intact or adapted to a new physical environment.

55. Kruszka, *History of the Poles to 1908*, 21.
56. For a discussion of conformity of exterior building aesthetics and yard maintenance practices to dominant American practices, see Craig Reisser, "Immigrants and House Form in Northeast Milwaukee" (master's thesis, Univ. of Wisconsin–Milwaukee, 1977). He suggests that the greatest distinction between Polish immigrant neighborhoods and middle-class aesthetics involved the retention of certain agricultural uses.
57. Thomas C. Hubka, "American Vernacular Architecture," in *Advances in Environment, Behavior and Design*, ed. E. H. Zube and G. T. Moore (New York: Plenum Press, 1990), 3:161–64, 166–67.
58. Ewa Morawska gives particular attention to strategies of adaptation and the proportion of "persisters" and "returnees" in her study of Johnstown, Pennsylvania, in *For Bread with Butter: The Life-Worlds of East Central Europeans in Johnstown, Pennsylvania, 1890–1940* (New York: Cambridge Univ. Press, 1985).

CHAPTER 4

Arnold R. Alanen

Midwesterners in the Matanuska Valley: Colonizing Rural Alaska during the 1930s

This is a strange land.

—*David Williams to Lylita Williams, July 17, 1935*

In 1931 George and Edith Connors and their two young children moved from Milwaukee to a seven-acre parcel of land near South Range, Wisconsin. A World War I veteran, Conners had lost his job as a carpenter and was unable to find further work in Milwaukee. By moving to a northern area of the state, the family hoped to establish a small truck farm. But the Conners's plans to sell garden produce and secure employment in the nearby city of Superior came to naught when neither a market for produce nor a job materialized. Four years later, and after the addition of two more children to the family, the Conners had acquired a small house, two outbuildings, two acres of cultivated land, one truck, one cow, twenty-five chickens—and significant debt. They were able to survive only by requesting relief assistance from Douglas County.[1]

The Conners's situation was indicative of the destitution experienced by many rural and mining town residents of northern Michigan, Wisconsin, and Minnesota during the Great Depression. In fact, federal investigators identified the northern Great Lakes region as "one of the nation's critical social and economic problems." The majority of the vast coniferous forests that once covered much of the district had already been depleted by the early twentieth century, and many of the region's copper and iron ore mines were shut down for lengthy periods throughout the 1930s. In the copper mining county of Keweenaw, situated at the tip of Michigan's Upper Peninsula, 70 percent of the population in 1935 was on relief—the highest rate for any county in the nation. Also in 1935, more than 18 percent of the region's farmers were receiving some form of relief or rehabilitation aid, a figure that exceeded the national average by more than two times.[2]

As one means of addressing the regional economic crisis, officials in President Franklin Delano Roosevelt's New Deal administration forwarded a plan in early 1935 to resettle two hundred families —including the Conners—from northern Michigan, Minnesota, and Wisconsin to a new agricultural colony in Alaska's Matanuska valley. Plans for the colony were based on several principles. One objective was to transplant to Alaskan soil the form and function of a small midwestern agricultural community, including its building types, spatial arrangements, and farming practices. Other objectives, however, were more experimental, especially those that envisioned a community based upon "voluntary disciplined cooperation," including agreements among members to raise similar crops and to engage in group purchasing and selling. The Matanuska project, these promoters reasoned, would serve as "an attempt to leave an instructive and permanent demonstration of what American life might produce."[3]

The 917 midwestern adults and children who arrived in Alaska in May 1935 represented one of the largest and most expensive rural resettlement projects of the New Deal era. When compared to other similar efforts undertaken throughout the nation, the initial planning, development, and settlement of the Matanuska valley was also noted as "the most exciting to the press and popular imagination."[4] However, only four years later, close to one-half of the original colonists had departed the valley, with most returning to the lower United States. Today, remnants of the project still endure as elements of the local landscape, including the community of Palmer, and nearby fields, roads, houses, and, most distinctively, several small barns that look as if they could have been transplanted from the Midwest. These physical remains represent the colonists' attempts to reconcile their own earlier midwestern experiences with the idealism and rigidity of New Deal policy makers, and the harsh realities of a new and different land.

What follows is an account of the Alaskan resettlement program, with an emphasis on the built environment of the Matanuska farm colony during its early period of development. The sources used in developing this account include the original plans and records of the Federal Emergency Relief Administration, the project's sponsoring agency; early personal accounts; newspaper reports; studies made by colonists, administrators, scholars, and other early onlookers; and fieldwork conducted by the author from 1992 to 1997.

Colony Origins

As one way of alleviating some Depression-era problems, New Deal officials proposed the development of new communities in suburban and rural areas of the nation. The best known of several community-development initiatives was the Greenbelt Towns program of the Resettlement Administration, one of many New Deal agencies that emerged during the 1930s. Started in 1935 under the auspices of charismatic economist Rexford Tugwell, who once hoped that the Resettlement Administration would sponsor suburbs in many metropolitan areas of the nation, only three greenbelt communities were actually developed: Greenbelt, Maryland; Greendale, Wisconsin; and Greenhills, Ohio.[5]

Close to one hundred much smaller resettlement communities were also planned by two U.S. Department of Interior agencies: the Subsistence Homesteads Division and the Federal Emergency Relief Administration (FERA). Formed in 1933, the Subsistence Homesteads Division was envisioned as a way to redistribute the "overbalance" of population in America's industrial centers by making loans to people who wished to move to the land and establish small farms. Alabama Sen. John Bankhead, a primary supporter of this back-to-the-land movement, claimed that such measures would result in "the restoration of that small yeoman class which has been the backbone of every great civilization." FERA's programs, on the other hand, were directed toward people already located on the land, with its major objective being one "of returning stranded agricultural workers to farms and of making special loans to those farmers who needed to replace work stock and equipment in order to become self-sustaining."[6]

Harry Hopkins, the chief administrator of FERA who later went on to head the Works Progress Administration (WPA), called upon Lawrence Westbrook, a Texas agriculturist, engineer, and politician, to develop the agency's rural rehabilitation program in 1933.[7] Assisting Westbrook was Dallas architect David R. Williams, a bon vivant and romantic idealist who, at the onset of the Depression, had prepared a proposal to relocate three million families from urban areas to rural utopias that he termed "our seven thousand cities of Cibola." Titling his plan "A New Declaration of Independence: Plan for Permanent Relief of the Unemployed," Williams actually designed one settlement in 1933, the Woodlake Cooperative Community, for the Texas Civil Works Organization. Located in the vicinity of Houston, Woodlake was a corporate farm jointly operated by one hundred former farmers and their families, who lived on private, three-acre holdings. The settlers constructed their own log and frame dwelling units, grew subsistence crops, and worked at cottage industries. Woodlake, which attracted the attention of Eleanor Roosevelt in 1934, served as a model for many FERA communities that emerged shortly thereafter. While working for FERA, Williams participated in the planning of several resettlement enclaves, including Cherry Lake, Florida; Pine Mountain Valley, Georgia; Dyess Colony, Arkansas; and the Matanuska settlement in south-central Alaska.[8]

Shortly after the organization of FERA, a few influential Alaskan officials and politicians began promoting the idea of government-sponsored colonization in the territory. As early as May 1934, President Roosevelt also expressed interest in the possibility of providing transportation for some five hundred families to Alaska, where they would be offered "appropriate land" and residences. From August 1934 to March 1935, Williams explored the possibility of sending settlers from drought- and poverty-stricken farming areas of the United States to Alaska. After word of the discussions appeared in newspapers throughout the nation, President Roosevelt and federal officials received the first of more than 26,000 desperate letters from destitute Americans who asked, and even pleaded, to be sent to the far North. The people of drought-ridden Jones County, Texas, requested that all of its citizens be sent to Alaska, while the president of the Cleveland-based "Alsakian [sic] Colonization Branch of the United Congo Improvement Association, Inc.," asked that seven of its African American members be granted passage to Alaska, where they would build roads and determine whether or not the territory could support colonization.[9] The following note sent to President Roosevelt by a down-and-out resident of Castlewood, South Dakota, is typical of the plight faced by many Americans during this period:

> I cannot live on $8.40 per week and pay my rent & clothe my family & feed them on that. Now Mr. President I know you are a very busy man & I suppose you get lots of letters from all over the country like this but I don't think the people in the east realize what us people here are up against in these small rural towns.
>
> Now Mr. President I am not complaining or anything like that about the relief set up or anything but thot [*sic*] if they were going to put people like us some where they could make themselves self sustaining. I would like to have a chance as I cannot see where we are going to do so here for some time to come.[10]

In late 1934, another South Dakotan, Rudolph V. Ruste of Verdun, proposed a group settlement for Alaska that would be organized around a town with a maximum population of one thousand people. Ruste, a high school principal, believed that close to 75 percent of all Americans eventually could live in such model settlements. These communities, he proclaimed, would "revolutionize" the nation's civilization and achieve a standard of living greater than anywhere in the world. "The ample leisure, the freedom from economic warfare, and the assurance of fundamental necessities of life should generate a culture equal to that of the Greek city states and their best," Ruste argued.[11]

President Roosevelt's New Deal administration certainly included its quota of dreamers and idealists, but Ruste's vision of classical cities, as well as several other projects proposed by individuals throughout the nation, were ignored by FERA officials. During late 1934, investigators in Alaska and Washington, D.C., made studies of the territory to locate areas where resettlement projects might be developed. Attention quickly focused upon the Matanuska valley, an area termed "something of an agricultural Utopia" by Williams, and the "California of Alaska" by other enthusiastic boosters. Situated about forty miles northeast of the railroad settlement of Anchorage, the Matanuska valley had already been the site of some limited homesteading and farming activity during the early twentieth century, and it was the site of an Alaskan agricultural experiment station. While some governmental officials envisioned the Matanuska settlement as a cooperative endeavor that would demonstrate "what American life might produce," other individuals, ranging from President Roosevelt and FERA bureaucrats to Alaskan politicians and businessmen, had more specific agendas and visions for the project. Included among them were assisting the Alaskan economy by producing locally grown food; directing federal funding to the nation's far northern outpost; determining whether or not Alaska was a settlement frontier that could absorb some of America's excess population; getting people off relief rolls elsewhere in the nation; and demonstrating that by building "strategic outposts on the Pacific frontier," the United States was prepared to defend Alaska from military aggression.[12]

There was, however, an important difference between two groups of individuals involved in promoting and planning the Matanuska settlement. One group, typified by Westbrook and M. D. Snodgrass, manager of the agricultural experiment station in Palmer, believed that Alaska's environmental and economic constraints never would allow the colonists' farms to proceed beyond a subsistence level; therefore, they felt that individuals with skills in fields such as carpentry and blacksmithing could pursue small-scale, part-time farming for supplementary income. On the other hand, architect Williams, the media, and some Alaskan officials and boosters claimed that the colonists could develop profitable dairy farms and sell their excess produce to the territory's future settlers and residents.[13]

Colonists from the Cutover

Despite the pleas they received from people located throughout the nation, Westbrook and FERA officials quickly decided to limit their Alaskan recruitment efforts to individuals then residing in northern Michigan, Minnesota, and Wisconsin—a section of the United States that began to be termed the "Cutover" region in the 1930s. (The word referred to the cutover appearance of the landscape after timber companies had removed much of the region's tree cover during the late nineteenth and early twentieth centuries. See fig. 4.1.) Since a relatively large number of farms within the region were isolated, the dispersed settlement pattern contributed to high service-delivery costs for many local governments. FERA and state governments provided grants to some farmers who resided on adequate land but needed monetary assistance to

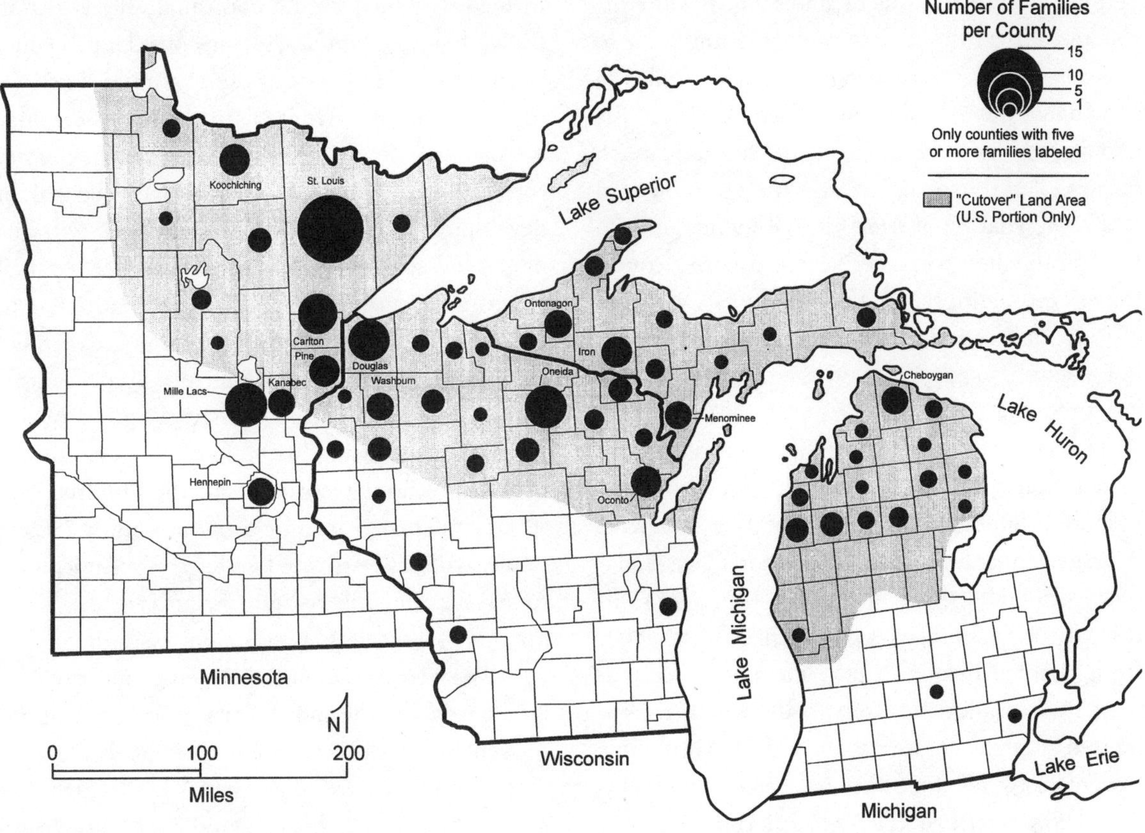

Fig. 4.1. County of origin in Minnesota, Wisconsin, and Michigan, of families selected for the Matanuska valley resettlement project in 1935. The vast majority of colonists came from the northern Cutover region of the three states. Derived from data in Lawrence Westbrook, "Alaska: Matanuska Valley Project, 1936," in Record Group 126 Office of the Territories Classified Files, 1907–1951, Alaska, Development of Resources, Matanuska Valley Farmers Co-op, National Archives and Records Administration, Suitland, Maryland. Cartography by Julie Goodman, 1998.

achieve self-sufficiency; other farmers were helped to relocate elsewhere if their individual situations proved especially onerous.[14] The Matanuska project represented another form of these resettlement efforts, albeit one that required the participants to move across the continent to another geographic region and an entirely different ecosystem.

Westbrook gave numerous explanations for the policy to restrict the search for Alaskan colonists to the Cutover region: "Limited funds and time for this migration influenced the decision to send families from relief rolls of states whose climatic, soil and agricultural conditions are comparable to those of the Matanuska Valley." Such people, he concluded, were "best fitted for such strenuous life and already have a knowledge of dairy and truck farming," and they also were "known to be used to a somewhat pioneering kind of living, and . . . were acclimated to rather severe weather conditions." Furthermore, the future colonists were envisioned as being "old enough to know depression but young enough to retain their hardihood for years to come."[15]

The Matanuska valley may have been Alaska's most productive agricultural area, but it also posed numerous limitations to the prospective agrarians. Average temperatures, as Hopkins noted, were relatively similar to those of Duluth, Minnesota, although the Matanuska winter generally stretches from October through April. There is no permafrost in the valley, but some soils, which receive limited sunlight because the Chugach Mountains tower nearby, remain frozen until May. The Matanuska was described in a 1946 federal report as a place where "the summer is cooler than in any agricultural section of the United States; the fall and winter are much warmer than in a large part of the Northern States; and the spring is very much colder than in any agriculturally settled part of the United States." Only some 59,000 acres of land, or 19 percent of the Matanuska's total area, were deemed suitable for cultivation in a comprehensive soil survey conducted in 1939–40, although the acreage figure increased somewhat when agricultural settlement extended farther west of Palmer at a later date.[16]

In March 1935, representatives from relief agencies in the three states were called to Washington, where they received information about the envisioned project from Westbrook and other FERA officials. The assembled representatives were informed that they should coordinate the selection of two hundred families, giving consideration only to "honest-to-God" farmers and "families who love the soil." Inquiries from "fly-by-nights, weaklings or curious folks" were to be discouraged. County social workers were then charged with the task of developing a pool of possible applicants, with the names being forwarded to the state office for final selection. Detailed procedures were adopted to judge the families "from the standpoint of relief eligibility, health, ability to fit into a cooperative enterprise of this nature, initiative and resourcefulness, credit rating of the family before the depression, school records of all the children and special talents of members of the family." Each family would be provided with free transportation to Alaska and the right to bring two thousand pounds of household goods along with them. The colonists were to establish themselves on forty-acre land parcels, with funds for the property, land improvement, buildings, and machinery being provided in the form of a 3 percent, $3,000, loan that did not have to begin to be paid back until 1940. The loans were administered by the Alaska Rural Rehabilitation Corporation (ARRC), a newly created organization that provided medical, educational, cultural, recreational, and supervisory services for the project.[17]

While Harry Hopkins stated that individuals

selected for the "pioneer development" represented a group of "young men and women who come from pioneering stock, [and] who are used to long, cold winters and hardships," most shared a common bond: impoverishment. "The hardiness of these depression victims," stated one account, "has been tested in the wastelands of the northern part of the state[s] where lean years, drought and individual misfortunes have meted out unhappy lots." Another report emphasized that the government had attempted to paint a realistic picture of Alaska so the selectees would not be disappointed in "believing themselves en route to a Garden of Eden." From Alaska, Don Irwin, the first general manager of the project, added a further cautionary note: "all is not going to be wild strawberries and cream for the Matanuska pioneers."[18]

Among the future colonists awaiting resettlement, the Conners reported from South Range, Wisconsin, that they had been provided with "little information on their prospective new homeland" in Alaska, but expressed "no fear of a venture they are sure will spell lasting security and happiness for them and their four small children." From Michigan's Upper Peninsula, future colonists reportedly were "leaving behind them disappoint-

Fig. 4.2. Photograph of a northern Wisconsin farmstead, probably that of colonists Martin and Genette Soyk of Minocqua, early 1930s. The conditions are illustrative of the situation experienced by many prospective colonists prior to their departure for Alaska. From Herbert H. Hilsher, "A Professional Scrap Book: A Record of the Matanuska Valley Settlement in 1935," B97.25.1148 (Anchorage Museum of History and Art, Anchorage, Alaska), 2.

ment and heart-breaks, and looking forward to independent livelihoods on farms in Alaska's Matanuska valley" (fig. 4.2). A member of the Michigan contingent stated that he and his colleagues had been "trying to make a living in farming and lumbering, and haven't been able to make a go of it. We're glad of this chance to start over and hope that Alaska will give us the opportunity to make good." Oscar Kerttula of Deer River, Minnesota, expressed both stoicism and hope as he, his wife, Elvi, and their son and daughter set off for Alaska: "Nothing can discourage us now," he wrote in his diary. "The worst has happened that could possibly happen to us. Cattle have died, farms are ruined, dust storms and blizzards have left us little in material wealth; all that is left to us is courage to try and carve new homes for ourselves in the North."[19]

The colonists started their journey from the Midwest to Alaska during April and May 1935, traveling by rail in two separate groups to the West Coast; the Minnesotans departed first and went to San Francisco, followed two weeks later by the families from Michigan and Wisconsin who left for Seattle. Both groups were then transported separately by an army motor ship, the *St. Mihiel*, to Seward, Alaska, followed by a rail trip to Anchorage and finally to Palmer and the Matanuska valley. As the colonists entered each city they were feted as modern-day pioneers and "triumphant personages." They were greeted and sent off by bands, given gifts and complimentary meals, and offered free access to local attractions. In addition, the midwesterners were followed by reporters from numerous newspaper, radio, and movie outlets throughout their journey, including photographer Dorothea Lange, whose camera artistry documented the Minnesotans as they boarded the *St. Mihiel* in San Francisco. The most extensive and accurate descriptions of the settlement's early evolution was reported by *Milwaukee Journal* reporter Arville Schaleben. The energetic and prolific Schaleben lived with the transplanted midwesterners from mid-May through August 1935, and over subsequent decades, generally at ten-year intervals, returned to the Matanuska valley to report on changes and current conditions.[20]

From Tents to Homes

When the colonists arrived at the project site in Palmer (fig. 4.3), they immediately encountered the realities of their new Alaskan living environment: rain, mud, wind, dust, mosquitoes, primitive accommodations, bureaucratic red tape, and what old-timers in the area identified as "work, damn hard work!" Some colonists were deeply disappointed

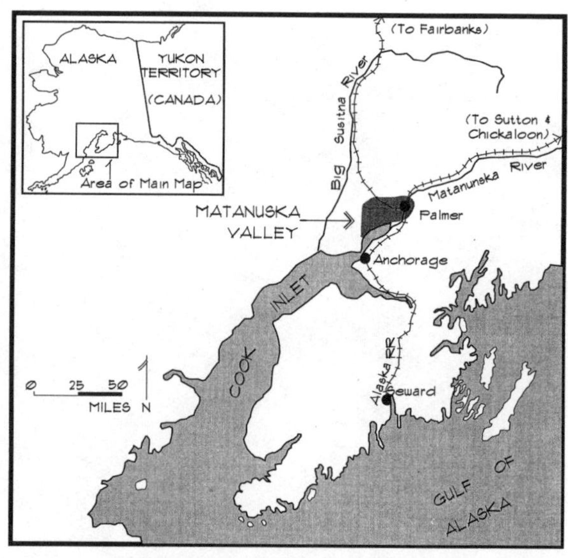

Fig. 4.3. The Matanuska valley and its environs in 1935. The midwestern colonists arrived by ship at Seward, and then went by rail to their destination, located some forty miles northeast of Anchorage. Cartography by Julie Goodman.

by the conditions they encountered, which included "angry wives, yelling, tired kids"; others, identified by Schaleben as "yowlers," complained that "their tent homes were not ready." However, at least a few, such as LeRoy Hamann from Wisconsin, saw opportunity: "Well heck," he commented, "this is a pretty good big place, so we ought to do OK." Minnesotan Hortense Carson also claimed that both the site and her early experiences in the Matanuska valley were "not bad at all." In fact, she remarked shortly after arriving at Palmer, "it is kind of fun."[21]

The Minnesota migrants, who disembarked from the train at the site of their future home on May 10, found a tent city under construction by four hundred young, male Civilian Conservation Corps (CCC) relief workers from California, a number of whom had arrived a few days earlier on the North Star, a Bureau of Indian Affairs ship loaded with food, stoves, cots, trucks, farm equipment, lumber, and other supplies for the new colony. Throughout the summer, these so-called transients assisted the colonists in constructing houses and farm buildings and in clearing land and harvesting crops.[22]

Journalist Schaleben described the tents as being "pitched in exact alignment, so that their lines make a geometrical design no matter from which point you look." Each tent was sixteen by twenty feet in plan; had five-foot-high walls made of twelve-ounce canvas stretched over a wooden frame; was constructed on a poorly fitted, rough plank floor; and was divided into partitions by wood, canvas, or cloth. A Montgomery Ward cookstove, a scuttle of coal, a washbasin, and two to six metal cots with mattresses were provided in each unit. The tents proved sufficient for families with five or fewer children but were "hardly adequate" for some people, such as the Bouwens from Rhinelander, Wisconsin, who had eleven offspring. Several families had to double up until additional tents were assembled. The tents could get "almost unbearably hot" during the long daylight hours of the summer, but then could be freezing cold by autumn. Some colonists piled dirt around the base of the units to curtail the winds that swept through the canvas and threatened to blow down stovepipes. The soil, described as "so fine[ly] textured any breeze gives it a ride," often covered the tent floors with dirt.[23]

On May 23, 1935, just one day after the *St. Mihiel* docked in Seward with the Michigan and Wisconsin colonists on board, all of the men assembled to draw lots for the forty-acre land parcels allocated to each family. For a month thereafter, trading was allowed among people who wished to settle near to friends and acquaintances. In addition, if a land parcel was deemed unsatisfactory because of poor soil conditions, the colonist could secure an additional forty-acre property. After the parcels had been allocated, the tents were moved to one of eight camps situated close to the individual land tracts. A ninth camp, the largest, remained at Palmer, where a new community center was under construction, while a tenth camp accommodated the transients. Because of the muddy conditions, some more distant camps were virtually inaccessible for a period of time, and administrative confusion initially relegated several settlers to the wrong locations. "There seems to be a lack of organization in getting things straightened out," stated Dorothy Bell, originally a school teacher from Kanabec County, Minnesota. "Everything has been done in a big hurry and of course much mismanagement and waste energy has resulted," she said.[24]

Once the Matanuska project received approval from federal officials in March 1935, David Williams and his staff of architects in Washington, D.C.,

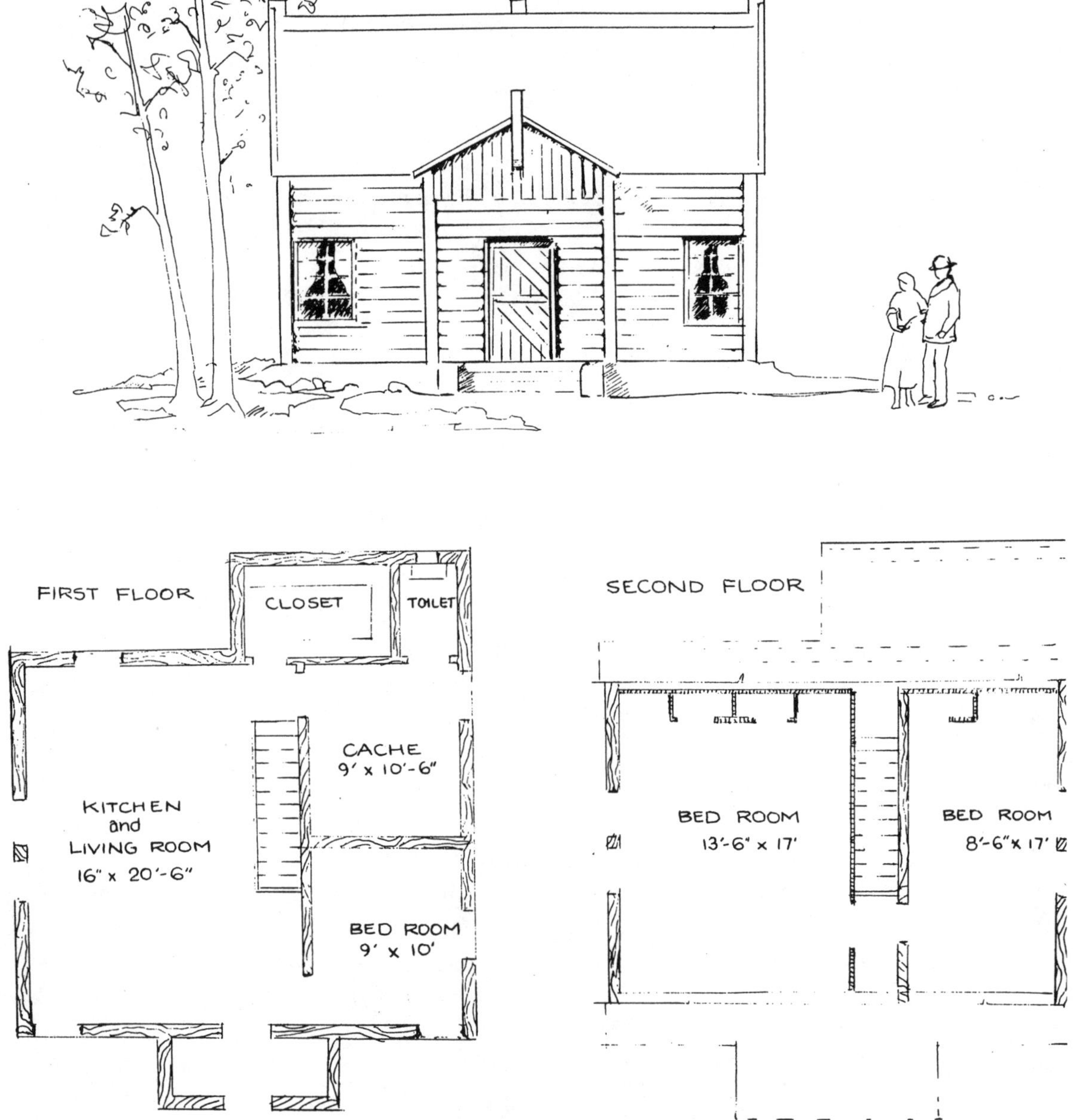

Fig. 4.4. Architects working for FERA in Washington, D.C., and on site in the Matanuska Valley, developed five "rustic cottage" house designs for the colonists in 1935. Simplified examples of the plans were distributed to the colonists for their selection shortly after they arrived in Alaska. This version offered 860 square feet of living space. Based upon drawings in the David Williams Papers, which were redrafted by Mary Simpson in 1985 and published in Vickie Cole, Pat O'Hara, Pandora Willingham, Ron Wendt, and Mary Simpson, *Knik, Matanuska, Susitana: A Visual History of the Valleys* (Palmer, Alaska: Matanuska-Sustina Borough, 1985), 175.

began to prepare designs for the single-family houses and farm buildings, as well as the structures that would be constructed in Palmer. The plans were then sent to the on-site architects, where the colonists reviewed and commented on them during long May and June evenings illuminated by the midnight sun (fig. 4.4). Initially, nine house plans were prepared for the colony, but the architects winnowed these down to five "rustic cottage" models. Four of the five prototypes had five rooms—a combination kitchen-living room, a cache (storage) room, and three bedrooms—while the six-room prototype had an additional bedroom. All of the houses were intended to include built-in features such as kitchen cabinets, linen cabinets, and, as Edith Conners excitedly observed, "even beds that look to be drawers in the wall, when put away." Alys Vickaryous, a recently married twenty-one-year-old woman, compared her living conditions in far northern Minnesota, where she had resided on an island close to the Canadian border, with the new house available to her in the Matanuska valley. In Koochiching County, Minnesota, she recalled, "we melted snow and ice for water in winter, packed water in and out, washed on a washboard and went out to a two-holer." Her new Alaskan house may still have had a "two-holer" outside, but it offered "a pump over the sink and . . . a sewing machine and washing machine."[25]

Prior to joining FERA, David Williams had achieved renown in the Southwest for his efforts to develop and advocate "indigenous architecture," a design style he defined as "a logical regional architecture [that] has for its origin the simple, early forms of building native to its own locale, and grows by purely functional methods into an indigenous form of art." Because of his interest in local and traditional architectural forms, Williams considered log buildings as typical examples of Alaskan vernacular. Some experienced local officials, such as Otto G. Ohlson, a Swedish immigrant, general manager of the Alaska Railroad, and an advocate of settlement in the territory, also advised the federal planners that log buildings could be constructed relatively quickly from the heavily timbered Matanuska valley. Initial estimates noted that an average house would require "125 logs with 12-inch butts and 7-inch heads."[26]

Only one of the FERA architects, N. Lester Troast, appears to have had any previous Alaskan experience, and Williams did not visit the project until mid-July. When touring the site, Williams wrote privately to his wife about the "strange country" of Alaska, and the "tough job" he faced. In his public pronouncements, however, Williams expressed effusive praise for the area: "I'm surprised to find the country looking as good as it does," he stated after arriving by train from Seward. "It looks much nicer than I imagined it would be and is much finer than the region of my boyhood [Texas]."[27]

The FERA architects' designs were criticized by many colonists upon first reviewing them on site. Dorothy Bell claimed that she did "not know who drew these plans, but whoever did never lived on a farm. They were all the most inconvenient plans I ever laid eyes on." The lack of a "barnyard view" caused another woman to conclude that "city people never do understand why farmers want their kitchens facing barns. Well we do most of our work in the kitchen and if any stock get loose, or anything like that, we can see them. My husband won't even let me have a wash line between the kitchen and the barn." Indeed, until they realized the need for a view of the barn, the architects could not understand why so many colonists chose the house plan that had the kitchen at the rear where it faced the farmstead buildings rather than the road. The colonists also could be somewhat coy with the architects, as evidenced by a Minnesota settler who, when writing to relatives, stated that he and his wife had just visited the architects' office where "they showed us a new type of house they had figured out and drawed [sic] the plans that morning. So we changed our plans as they wished us to do. Although this new plan we really liked better, but we didn't give them that satisfaction of them knowing it."[28]

One of the greatest points of dissension arose between several colonists and architect Troast when it was realized that the residences were to have small cellars rather than full basements, and were to be built on "mud sill" foundations—that is, by laying timbers directly on the earth and then constructing the walls upon them. Unlike inhabitants of many other areas of Alaska, the Matanuska colonists did not have to contend with the problem of permafrost; nevertheless, the new settlers contended that the proposed foundations may have been satisfactory for "temporary shacks" but not for permanent houses. "We resent it when we are told log houses built on the ground for other Alaskans are good enough for us," wrote Dorothy Bell," and we do not care to go into debt for something that will not last but a few years or be so warped by frost that it will be ruined." (The colonists' fears were well founded, for the sills and beams began to rot within three to five years.) In mid-June, Schaleben wrote in the *Milwaukee Journal* about another emerging problem when he noted that the "shortage of available house timber, which had been represented as so plentiful when the Matanuska valley colonization was undertaken, is causing project authorities to plumb the possibilities of constructing some frame houses." Since not even one house had been completed by this date, Schaleben claimed that conditions were "becoming alarming," and that the timber situation and a lack of construction tools and sawmills were prime examples of "mismanagement somewhere along the line."[29]

Because of the lack of progress, a number of colonists expressed their concerns in a June 17, 1935, telegram to President Roosevelt and to politicians in Alaska and their three home states. Soon thereafter, newspaper headlines and articles, many of which were sensationalized and greatly exaggerated, appeared throughout the nation, providing commentary on mismanagement and disgruntled colonists. Within a few days, Troast, on loan to FERA as an architect from the Bureau of Indian Affairs in Juneau, was removed from his position. Hopkins then appointed one of his troubleshooters, Eugene Carr, to the post of general manager.[30]

After Carr arrived at the site and inspected the log houses then under construction, he stopped the work, announcing that the structures needed to be supplied with better foundations: "they should be built from the bottom up," he commented, "not from the top down." Recognizing that the labor force—comprised of colonists and the young CCC men from California—was of insufficient size to finish the structures during Alaska's short building season, Carr sought to transfer six Alaskan construction foremen and 125 "genuine lumberjacks" from the Pacific Northwest to the project, and he imported additional sawmills and well-drilling machines. Carr's paternalistic management philosophy ("the people had to be told what to do and how to do it") ordered the colonists to follow his directives without question. "Individualistic ideas must die," he pronounced. "I want, I ask for, I demand co-operation of every man, of every woman in this colony!" The colonists quickly became hostile and antagonistic toward Carr, and he was soon removed from the post of general manager and reassigned to the more innocuous position of head of procurement and business administration.

Williams later summarized Carr's Matanuska career as "Czar-absolute for less than a week, and then quite suddenly reduced . . . to the warehouse."[31]

Although construction activity increased, the project officials and architects decided, in late July, that insufficient time remained to complete the houses as originally planned. Instead, they recommended that one new prototype unit, termed a "growing house," be substituted for all of the original five designs. The new proposal, which was little more than a ten-by-thirty-foot three-room rectilinear unit that, according to Schaleben's sardonic observations, could be added onto, "possibly with government assistance, when there's time this fall, next winter, next summer, in 1941, or whenever they get to think of it." Many colonists had been informed in their home states that they might initially live in very small residences, but after arriving in Alaska a number threatened to abandon the project if the government foisted such "sheep sheds" and "chicken houses" upon them. "I never lived in nothing but a regular house and I'm not going to start living in a sheep shed now," fumed one agitated colonist, while another lamented that she had been "planning a pretty house and now I'm getting a chicken house"; several irate women expressed further frustration, wondering how the furniture they had ordered for their envisioned residences could be arranged in such a "growing house." After hearing of threats to quit the project, the managers quickly decided to discard their new suggestions, choosing instead to hire experienced Alaskan carpenters and construction workers to augment the labor force. By early August, 750 men, including colonists and CCC employees, were organized into twenty-five construction crews scattered throughout the incipient settlement.[32]

Some seventy-five log and combination log-frame houses were distributed across the Matanuska valley landscape by late summer, followed by the completion, during the early weeks of autumn, of more than one hundred frame residences constructed of imported milled lumber (figs. 4.5, 4.6). Other than the sawmills, only hand tools were employed in constructing the buildings. Already in mid-August, Schaleben was commenting that

Fig. 4.5. An example of a single-story, five-room log dwelling (with attic), termed an "L-house," as it appeared shortly after being built in early autumn 1935. From National Archives and Records Administration, Suitland, Maryland.

Fig. 4.6. Because of a shortage of spruce logs suitable for construction purposes, several two-story houses were built of both logs and lumber. By late November 1935, a total of 75 log and combination log-frame dwellings and 125 residences built entirely of milled lumber accommodated all of the colony's new families. From National Archives and Records Administration, Suitland, Maryland.

despite "the rush for roofs," the settlement's "new houses stand out attractively in the woods. Tourists are constantly astonished at the beauty of both the frame and log dwellings." Edith Conners also wrote that the log houses gave the appearance of being "squatted . . . to stay, regardless of any and all the windstorms that may come this way." A few relatively minor design alterations the colonists requested were approved by FERA architects—as long as the budget allocated to each house was not exceeded—but the regimentation that characterized so much of the colony's initial history did not permit the desired features of two or more house designs to be combined. Most official changes involved modifications to the type and placement of windows and doors, the addition and treatment of dormers and porches, and occasional differences in roof forms.[33]

Nevertheless, several colonists did manage to circumvent the regulations by making certain, often major, changes without informing the architects. Leo Jacobs wrote to David Williams in Washington, lamenting over the colonists' actions. "We have everything from one-room log cabins housing large families to seven-room mansions housing a man, wife, and dog," he complained from Palmer. "Anything goes. We have Dutch gable roofs, and I am afraid that at least one modern flat roof design . . . Cabins are being constructed here on which a loan could not have been obtained even during those boom years prior to 1929. I hope that some of them don't fall down during the coming winter."[34] The cabins Jacobs described, termed "Alaskan houses" by those individuals who built them to their own plans, were intended to save money, a fact noted by colonist Harold Davis of Michigan in late July: "None of this fancy stuff for me. My wife and I laid out a three-room place and we're going to start it and be in it in a week. It'll be easier to heat and won't cost me over $300. I'm not even going to have an inside toilet. No, sir, not in Alaska. Those other places are costing about $900 with a well or a fence, so I'm going to have plenty of credit left over to buy socks with."[35]

When time permitted, the spruce logs used to construct the house walls were milled on three sides, with the round side exposed to the exterior. Many houses, however, used logs in a full round form or shaped on one or two sides. Either full dovetail, square, or saddle notches were used to lock the horizontally stacked logs together. In an effort to speed up construction during August, one architect was sent out to convince the colonists to employ "the butt [square] joint instead of the overlap [dovetail] joint for log house corners." In some cases, the first courses of logs on houses under construction by colonists were disassembled when the inspecting architect was able to fit his fist between the green, poorly fitted log members.[36]

Barn Business

Plans were also prepared for several types of outbuildings, including barns, poultry houses, feed storage buildings, pump houses, and privies, while many colonists constructed sheds and other structures that did not follow any formal plan, such as the saunas erected by Finnish American settlers. Of the designs developed for the colony, the most widely adopted was the barn plan (fig. 4.7). Given their gambrel roofs and squat dimensions (thirty-two by thirty-two by thirty-two feet), the barns represented the most distinctive and midwestern-like architectural forms on the Matanuska landscape. The lower stories of the barns were constructed of horizontal logs piled ten feet high, while the second story hay mow utilized a balloon frame structure. The lower story of the front and rear facades each featured large entry doors flanked by win-

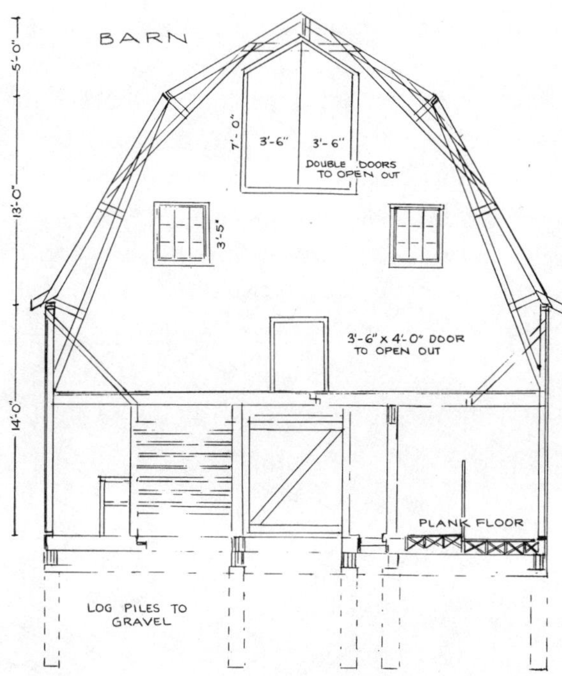

Fig. 4.7. Elevation of the barn plan that served as the most common building form in the Matanuska valley. The lower story, built of horizontal logs, was topped by a balloon-frame hay mow that included a verge. Based upon drawings in the David Williams Papers, which were redrafted by Mary Simpson in 1985 and published in Vickie Cole, Pat O'Hara, Pandora Willingham, Ron Wendt, and Mary Simpson, *Knik, Matanuska, Susitana: A Visual History of the Valleys* (Palmer, Alaska: Matanuska-Sustina Borough, 1985).

dows, while both side walls included four window openings. The upper story of the front facade displayed a small door, two square windows at midlevel, and a large door located under a projecting verge that accommodated the hay track. The interior was divided into five cow stalls, two horse stalls, another stall that could be used for a bull or an additional horse or cow, and a storage area. The barns were placed on six-foot-long spruce log posts driven into the ground. Though the colonists were allowed to make some small alterations to the plan, most changes were limited to doors, windows, and interior arrangements; the basic form and construction of the barns followed the single original plan almost entirely.[37]

With so much time and energy devoted to the construction of residences prior to the onset of winter in late 1935, most barn building was delayed until the subsequent spring; therefore, during the first winter the animals often were sheltered in the original tent homes, in buildings constructed by earlier settlers, or in small neighborhood sheds put up by the colonists themselves. After the barns had been constructed (almost 115 were completed by May 1936), and despite the fact that experts employed by the Alaska Agricultural Experiment Station at Palmer participated in their design, the colonists soon realized that the structures were inadequate for anything beyond subsistence farming purposes. The pilings shifted and often rotted away quickly, and the colonists voiced complaints "that the barns were too small, inefficiently partitioned, drafty and poorly built." Even with six cows and two horses, recalled a former Minnesotan, the barn interior was the "coldest darn place" during the long winter; when the manure froze into a solid mass, it could be chipped away only by employing a pickax. LeRoy Hamann, one of the project's strongest supporters throughout the more than sixty years (1935–96) he lived on the same Matanuska valley farm, could not find anything positive about his barn: "it's the most useless dad-blamed thing on the place," he exclaimed in 1970. "Thirty-two by thirty-two. You can't cut that up into useful parts no matter what." The barns may have been suitable for turn-of-the-century subsistence farming, claimed one settler, but they were entirely inadequate to meet the needs of the 1930s, much less those of later decades. Those colonists who eventually expanded their barns into Grade-A dairy operations so they could sell milk to the local Matanuska Maid Dairy Cooperative, were forced to spend large sums of money to make the structures usable. The two-inch plank floors were replaced with cement, permanent foundations took the place of the rotting log pilings, and milking machines and metal stanchions were purchased. Milk houses and silos were attached to the barns, and in some cases, two barns were joined together to create more space.[38] The failures of the initial building construction program were clearly summarized in a scholarly overview sponsored by the federal government fifteen years after the colony was established: "The farm building program was executed crudely. By the first winter, most of the colonists' dwellings were barely ready and housing for animals was inadequate. Houses and barns were erected inefficiently. Throughout the program haste and confusion so reigned that costs were higher than had been anticipated. The core of these difficulties was incomplete, and partly impractical, planning which was prompted by the speed required."[39]

Creating a Cultural Landscape

Once the tent camps were established, some nearby land that had been previously cleared was planted to gardens. The midwesterners felt encouraged to pursue gardening after hearing of the huge vegetables that old-time pioneers had grown in the Matanuska valley for many years.[40] Henry Lipke, when departing his home in Harrietta, Michigan, joked that the colonists would need to "handle those 30-pound cabbages with cant hooks." While still residing in their tents, each family drew a number to determine which portion of the gardens—whether peas, string beans, lettuce, parsnips, cabbages, radishes, and cauliflower—they were expected to cultivate and keep free of weeds. General Manager Irwin later recalled that a number of families gave their gardens "excellent care" (fig. 4.8), but a few believed the plots required "too much work to weed and cultivate." Arville Schaleben's August garden survey revealed that fully one-half of the plots had been "permitted by the colonists

Fig. 4.8. Shortly after arriving in Alaska, the colonists could observe the huge vegetables they previously had heard about in the Midwest. The photograph portrays early Matanuska valley homesteader Emil "Shorty" Kircher with three turnips he raised in 1935. From National Archives and Records Administration, Suitland, Maryland.

to grow up in weeds. Too many of the colonists have found it easier to buy whatever is wanted from the commissary on credit." Jack Allman, editor of the Matanuska Valley Pioneer, which began as a mimeographed newspaper shortly after the colonists arrived, noted the following in describing the garden at Camp 2: "A short time after planting the weeds started to grow but some of the boys couldn't find time to weed, their answer being that they could always get something to eat and a house came first—'and the stuff probably won't grow anyway.'" At Camp 8, on the other hand, where the garden was laid out in a long strip and divided into sections for each family, the colonists successfully raised a large crop of vegetables. The first animals, 50 horses and 70 cows, arrived from the state of Washington in May, and one month later a drawing was held for 30 pigs and an additional 150 cows. Eventually, however, it was determined that many of the cows had been selected too hastily, with little attention given to their potential as milk producers; therefore, for some time the colonists had to feed animals that proved excessively expensive for their modest incomes.[41]

At the end of June, the planting of field crops commenced, an activity that demanded rapid attention because of the late arrival of the colonists and the short growing season. To do so, the Alaska Rural Rehabilitation Corporation hired an experienced local farmer, Harry Sears, to supervise the planting of 210 acres of oats and Canadian field peas for hay and 35 acres of potatoes, carrots, turnips, and rutabagas. The crops, seeded on patches of land cleared by previous homesteaders and settlers, were scattered over an area of sixty square miles. The planting was done by employing shifts of men who toiled twenty-two hours each day. Explaining the haste, Sears reported that "when you got growing weather here you got to give it hell. You got to plant all hours of the day and night and you got to cultivate the same way, for this old sun doesn't wait for any man. It's got other stuff besides yours to tend to." Because of the pressing need to complete the residences and other buildings, most land-clearing activities were delayed until 1936; nevertheless, during the summer of 1935 some areas began to be cleared of brush and trees, with the suitably sized logs skidded off so they could be used for building construction purposes. Seventeen Caterpillar tractors supplied by the federal government proved "indispensable" in pulling out the stumps and arranging them into long windrows that later were burned. Large breaking plows and disks then prepared the ground for planting.[42]

By August 1935 some harvesting could begin, although it was well into the next month before most crops matured. Laurence Vasanoja from Cromwell, Minnesota, who was used to making hay during June and July at his former home, expressed amazement when writing to relatives in September: "Can you imagine the haying is at its height now and won't be done for a week yet?" Since hay and grain drying was often a vexing problem during the autumn of 1935, it was sometimes necessary to use what were termed "special methods" or the "Norwegian" technique: after cutting the hay or grain, it was lifted off the ground and placed on peeled stakes or staves so it could dry without rotting. This was a common practice in Alaska at the time, and at least some of the colonists were familiar with the Nordic technique in the Cutover region. By late October it was announced that the ARRC and Sears had been successful in harvesting 250 tons of potatoes and in putting up 350 tons of tame hay as well as 125 tons of wild hay from Cottonwood Flats. Once the colonists were able to experience a full growing season in subsequent years, however, haying could occur from June to September, or even as late as October during a good year.[43]

The more experienced and knowledgeable farmers in the group realized that the Matanuska's soil required fertilizers and special treatment to maintain its productivity. One veteran agrarian from Minnesota commented that since the soil was powderlike and did not cake, the removal of large areas of timber meant "the farms would be likely to blow into Cook Inlet." Windbreaks, he predicted, would need to be placed around the farms and buildings. In fact, general manager Irwin, on the day of the land drawing, made a prescient announcement to the colonists: "Leave windrows when you clear the land," he warned. "This land blew in and it'll blow out too." Only some years later was it realized that several homes and farmsteads, built on what proved to be unsheltered land tracts, were "locations that neither the colonists nor the administrators would have approved if precolonization studies of winds in the Valley had been made."[44]

The Matanuska settlement, with its display of modest farm buildings, cubelike barn forms, cattle grazing in woodland pastures, and grain and hay fields laid out in patchwork patterns, bore several similarities to the cultural landscape the colonists had departed in the Midwest. Nevertheless, the farmsteads in the Matanuska colony were spaced, on average, one-quarter to three-eighths of a mile apart. This created a denser settlement pattern than in the Cutover region, where average distances

Fig. 4.9. By spring 1936, the ensemble of structures that made up a typical Matanuska valley farmstead—a house, a barn, and a few outbuildings—were visible throughout the colony. From National Archives and Records Administration, Suitland, Maryland.

ranged from one-half to three-quarters of a mile. In addition, Williams and his staff concentrated the farmsteads at road intersections, which created barriers to contiguous land assembly when individual farmers sought to expand their operations during future years. What clearly differentiated the landscape of the Alaskan enclave from the Cutover region, however, were the snow-capped Chugach and Talkeetna mountains that bordered the Matanuska valley on three of its sides (fig. 4.9). Unlike early Great Plains pioneers, who often were overwhelmed by the vastness of the open spaces they encountered, some Matanuska settlers admitted that they felt claustrophobic in their more confined settings: "I just wanted to push the mountain away so I could see," recalled Lillian Eckert of Mille Lacs County, Minnesota. "It felt so far away from the rest of the world. I felt so hemmed in."[45]

Aftermath

Even before the first Alaskan summer was over, the government approved the requests of several families to be sent back to the lower forty-eight states. By August 1935, forty "malcontent" families had departed the Matanuska valley. The first group of families gave reasons for their departure that included illness, misrepresentation, disappointment in not finding steady colony employment, and even the claim of being "an office worker, not a farmer." Federal case workers who interviewed thirty of the families prior to January 1936 determined that sixteen left the colony for health reasons, ten for what they claimed was a misrepresentation of facts, and four because of what they termed "general dissatisfaction." Dorothy Bell agreed, in 1936, that some people exited because of illness, but also claimed, rather caustically, that others departed because the women couldn't get along without movies and bright lights, while "the greater majority left because they smelled work and decided that the vacation was over." Likewise, August Raschke of Wisconsin complained that a number of people "just came up for the trip and others to hunt and fish." Arville Schaleben made a similar observation to readers of the Milwaukee Journal in late May 1935, when he reported that some colonists believed the "hero stuff" they heard about themselves in their home states and were boasting about the "millionaire's vacation" to Alaska that Uncle Sam had provided them. The realities of pioneer life, however, quickly punctured their dreams: "Loud now is the wail of the deflated vacationists," Schaleben noted shortly after the colonists had received their land allocation.[46]

Several accounts have noted that several settlers simply could not contend with the collective and paternalistic nature of the project: "the very qualities for which the colonists were chosen to go to Alaska—independence, courage, self-sufficiency—proved to be stumbling blocks in the highly regimented and socially controlled regimes of some of the colony managers." Other colonists, however, were disappointed that the communitarian intentions of the project did not develop as planned. Matt Saarela of Swan River, Minnesota, complained that he "left home with the idea that the colony was a co-operative enterprise, but I find the type of people sent here are not co-operative minded. We Finns believe in co-operation with our whole heart and soul." Florence Hess, whose family stayed in the valley for only a year and a half, provided a more poignant, personal reason for their departure: "There was no way of making a living up there," she stated in 1995. "We were some of the unlucky ones. We never really got going." Some husbands and wives were not necessarily unanimous in their decision to depart the project. Ray and Ruth Wilkes and their family returned to Minnesota in

1937, not only because of concerns over the health of a young child, but also because of his disillusionment "over the communal-type system"; his wife, on the other hand, had positive memories of Alaska's beautiful mountains and the friendships that developed among women who shared ideas about food preservation and handiwork projects.[47]

Most assessments also have pointed out that due to haste and a lack of or inaccurate information about Alaska, the initial screening and selection of applicants was conducted poorly by local case workers. Colonist Frank Ring made such an observation already by early June 1935: "Get all these kickers together and load them on a train and then, back to the states, and discharge the case worker who ever dared recommend them," he wrote to the relief office in Marinette County, Wisconsin. "Don't send us pansys [*sic*] up here . . . it's wonderful for anyone who has ambition enough to work for himself and doesn't expect roses without thorns." U.S. Secretary of the Interior Harold L. Ickes made a similar comment when he visited the colony in 1938: "Apparently some communities saw a chance to get rid of their ne'er-do-wells and the sentimental social-service people in charge of selecting the settlers allowed their sentimentality to run away with their judgment." Greater efforts should have been devoted to the selection of more "Scandinavians and other hardy, industrious, and self-respecting people," claimed Ickes. Don Irwin expressed the frustrations of a general manager who dealt with the colonists and their problems on a day-to-day basis: "Believe me, I'd like to have hold of some of the social workers who made promises that men would get work in shops and things like that!" he grumbled in June 1935. "They have cost me a lot of sleep."[48]

Even George and Edith Conners, who had expressed such initial hope and enthusiasm over the project, departed the Matanuska valley for the Seattle area in early 1937.[49] After the first colonists left, new families were interviewed and selected to replace them. A few replacements already had Alaskan experience, and several were related to the initial colonists; most came from the midwestern and western United States. But even after the departure of the "malcontents" and the infusion of new residents, there still were complaints. In 1939, a small group of individuals rebelled against what they perceived was the excessive authority, power, and paternalism of the ARRC—their "source of credit, supervision, and nagging guidance." Calling themselves "Ice Worms," the semisecret organization gradually dispersed by 1942, when wartime conditions brought relative prosperity to the settlement.[50]

On the other hand, the settlers who stayed on for decades with rather little complaint about conditions or management shortcomings offered a host of reasons for their tenaciousness, ranging from the pragmatic to the humorous. "We were here to make our homes," Cora Hemmer of Wright, Minnesota, reminisced in 1974. "I think the real reason we stayed is that most of us hadn't left anything behind . . . just our families . . . . What would we have done if we'd stayed there?" When LeRoy Hamann and his family departed for Alaska in 1935, he expressed absolutely no qualms or reservations about leaving a hardscrabble existence in Wisconsin and making the Matanuska valley a permanent home: "When we're gone, we're gone," he retorted, "and we're going to stay gone!" Barney Anderson, who arrived in Palmer as a nine-year-old "colony kid," chose to move in with another colonist after his family departed the valley in 1937:

"I've been here 60 years," he joked shortly before his death in early 1996. "If I find something good I'll probably stay."[51]

Because of Alaska's natural and environmental constraints, the small size of the agricultural units, and a lack of adequate farm markets, the Matanuska valley settlement evolved slowly and under great duress until the end of the Depression decade. By early 1939, just over one-third (78) of the original 202 families still remained on their initial properties. The military buildup that began to impact the Anchorage area in 1940, however, presented the valley's residents with new agricultural marketing and employment opportunities. Between 1935 and 1953, cropland in the district increased from 600 acres to more than 10,000 acres, and the number of Grade-A dairy farms grew from none to thirty-nine. By 1957, some 75 percent of all milk produced and sold in Alaska came from farms in the Matanuska valley, as well as close to 70 percent of the state's field crops, and just under 50 percent of its vegetables.[52]

Agriculture reached its zenith in the Matanuska valley during the late 1960s. In 1967, when all but two of the state's forty Grade-A dairy farms were located in the valley, more than 90 percent of Alaska's milk production came from the district, as did more than 70 percent of its vegetables. However, construction of the Alaskan pipeline, which occurred during the late 1970s and early 1980s, brought a large influx of new people to Anchorage and other areas of the state; the Matanuska valley, located at the edge of the Anchorage metropolitan area, was affected very significantly by this expansion. The population of the valley, which had doubled from 900 to 1,800 residents when the midwestern colonists arrived in 1935, swelled to 43,000 people by 1980, and to some 50,000 by the mid-1990s. Land prices rose to more than $6,000 per acre during the 1980s boom period, and then settled back to a per-acre figure of $4,000 to $6,000 by 1995. Given the magnitude of these increases, many farmers chose to sell or develop their land for subdivisions, highway-oriented commercial enterprises, hobby farms, and even three attractions that now lure tourists to view reindeer, musk oxen, and wolves. As of 1997, only two of Alaska's eleven Grade-A dairy farms and less than one-third of the state's total cropland acreage were found in the Matanuska valley. However, the demand for fresh produce in the Anchorage area has contributed to an increase in truck farming activities: almost 85 percent of all vegetables grown in Alaska now come from producers scattered throughout the valley.[53]

Conclusion

The history of the Matanuska project is little known outside Alaska today, although for a brief period of time it was the most highly publicized of all the rural resettlement efforts undertaken by the federal government during the Depression. Unlike the three suburban greenbelt towns, which are among the best-known examples of planned communities in the United States, the legacy of Matanuska and the other New Deal rural experiments is "relatively small in terms of final accomplishments." Nonetheless, historian Paul Conkin has stated that the resettlement projects "remain vivid reminders of a time, not so long past, when Americans still could dream of a better, more perfect world and could so believe in that dream that they dared set forth to realize it, unashamed of their zeal." This same enthusiasm continued to be expressed by ninety-four-year-old LeRoy Hamann as late as 1996. When asked why he had never even returned to Wisconsin for a visit during the six decades he had resided on his Matanuska valley farm, Hamann snorted: "I left a gol-darn place and came to a good place! Why should I go back?"[54]

While all of the resettlement projects undertaken throughout the United States were characterized by unique situations and requirements, the problems encountered in the Matanuska valley were more complex than those faced elsewhere in the nation. Not only did typical community planning and development issues have to be faced in the Alaskan colony, but it also was necessary to accommodate the movement of people and goods over thousands of miles of land and sea, to undertake the program in great haste, and to do this with incomplete and imperfect information about Alaska's geography and natural conditions. A number of the social workers, federal bureaucrats, and architects possessed little more than a limited knowledge about either Alaska or farming. In addition, many prospective colonists simply were not prepared, by experience or temperament, to become successful farmers anywhere in the United States, much less in an environment as demanding as that posed by Alaska. There are some "sorry looking cowmen among these colonists," observed an experienced agrarian after the first cattle arrived in Palmer; they don't seem to know "the difference between a cow's teat and a garden hose."[55]

Despite its tenuous beginnings and limited successes, the Matanuska colony played an important role in Alaska's evolution from territory to statehood. Colonists who remained on the land showed prospective settlers that survival was indeed feasible above the 60th parallel. In addition, the colony formed the nucleus of a regional agricultural pro-

Fig. 4.10. In many areas of the Matanuska valley, new homes are now emerging in subdivisions platted on former agricultural land. Photograph by the author, November 1997.

duction system that helped to support the territory's population growth beginning in the 1940s.

Today, much of the physical evidence that remains of the district's early settlement history is threatened by new building development. The colony's midwestern origins can yet be seen in the barn forms, small fields, and pastures that still survive at a few points in the valley. However, just as in many areas of Michigan, Minnesota, and Wisconsin, subdivisions, strip malls, parking lots, and fast-food restaurants are overrunning the rural landscape, and as a result the material history of Alaska's most distinctive agricultural landscape is being lost (fig. 4.10).

Notes

I am especially indebted to Jim Fox, the acknowledged local historian of the Matanuska valley, for his numerous insights and suggestions. Other assistance was provided by Joanie Juster, Lynn Bjorkman, and the two anonymous reviewers who commented on the manuscript.

1. *Evening Telegram (Superior, Wis.)*, Apr. 23, 1935, 12.
2. Northern Lakes States Regional Committee, *Regional Planning: Part VIII—Northern Lakes States* (Washington, D.C.: U.S. Government Printing Office, 1939), viii; Orlando W. Miller, *The Frontier in Alaska and the Matanuska Colony* (New Haven, Conn.: Yale Univ. Press, 1975), 55; Rudolph A. Christiansen and Sydney D. Staniforth, *The Wisconsin Resettlement Program of the 1930's: Relocation to the Matanuska Valley in Alaska, Bulletin No. 50* (Madison: Dept. of Agricultural Economics, Univ. of Wisconsin, 1967), 11.
3. Letter from H. M. Colvin to Lawrence Westbrook, June 18, 1937, included in Miller, *The Frontier in Alaska*, 235.
4. Miller, *The Frontier in Alaska*, 62.
5. For background information on the Resettlement Administration and the three greenbelt communities, refer to the following: Joseph Arnold, *The New Deal in the Suburbs: A History of the Greenbelt Town Program, 1935–1954* (Columbus: Ohio State Univ. Press, 1971); Arnold R. Alanen and Joseph A. Eden, *Main Street Ready-Made: The New Deal Community of Greendale, Wisconsin* (Madison: State Historical Society of Wisconsin, 1987); and Mary Lou Williamson, ed., *Greenbelt: History of a New Town, 1937–1987* (Norfolk, Va.: Donning Co., 1987).
6. Paul K. Conkin, *Tomorrow a New World: The New Deal Community Program* (Ithaca, N.Y.: Cornell Univ. Press, 1959), 87, 88, 131–35; quotations on 87, 133.
7. In late 1935, FERA was absorbed by the WPA.
8. David R. Williams, "A New Declaration of Independence: Plan for Permanent Relief of the Unemployed," unpublished report in the David R. Williams Papers, May 23, 1934, Archives Department, Edith Garland Dupre Library, University of Southwestern Louisiana, Lafayette, Louisiana; Muriel Quest McCarthy, David R. Williams, Pioneer Architect (Dallas: Southern Methodist Univ. Press, 1984), 119–25.
9. David Williams, "Laymans Manual: Alaska—Progress of Project," 1934, handwritten memorandum in the David R. Williams Papers; Lawrence Westbrook, "Alaska: Matanuska Valley Project," 1936, memorandum in RG 126, Office of the Territories Classified Files, 1907–1951, Alaska, Development of Resources, Matanuska Valley Farmers Co-op, National Archives and Records Administration, Suitland, Md.; letters from Harry L. Hopkins to Alaskan Gov. John W. Troy (May 21, 1934) and President Franklin D. Roosevelt (Apr. 7, 1935), and from Joe T. Thomas to Congressman Charles V. Truax (Feb. 17, 1935), all on file in the Harry L. Hopkins Papers, Franklin D.

Roosevelt Library, Hyde Park, N.Y.; Evangeline Atwood, *We Shall Be Remembered* (Anchorage: Alaska Methodist Univ. Press, 1966), 22; *Anchorage Daily Times*, Jan. 10, 1935, 1.

10. Dick Beman to F. D. Roosevelt, Mar. 15, 1935, RG 126, National Archives and Records Administration.
11. Rudolph V. Ruste quoted in Miller, *The Frontier in Alaska*, 47.
12. David R. Williams, "Matanuska Valley: The Latest Frontier," unpublished manuscript in the David R. Williams Papers; Westbrook, "Alaska: Matanuska Valley Project"; Ernest Gruening, *The State of Alaska* (New York: Random House, 1954), 299; Miller, *The Frontier in Alaska*, 41–43.
13. Miller, *The Frontier in Alaska*, 69; Williams, "Matanuska Valley: The Latest Frontier"; Jim Fox to Arnold Alanen, June 8, 1998.
14. Miller, *The Frontier in Alaska*, 55, 60–61.
15. Lawrence Westbrook to Congressman John T. Buckabee, May 21, 1935, in "Correspondence Relating to Settlement at the Matanuska Valley Colony, 1934–39," RG 126, National Archives and Records Administration; Westbrook, "Alaska: Matanuska Valley Project"; Lawrence Westbrook quoted in Atwood, *We Shall Be Remembered*, 23; *(Marquette, Mich.) Daily Mining Journal*, Apr. 25, 1935, 1.
16. W. A. Rockie, *Physical Land Conditions in the Matanuska Valley, Alaska* (Washington, D.C.: U. S. Dept. of Agriculture, Soil Conservation Service, 1946), 9, 19, 20, 24.
17. Westbrook, "Alaska: Matanuska Valley Project"; Christiansen and Staniforth, "Wisconsin Resettlement Program," 5; Miller, *The Frontier in Alaska*, 76; *Daily Mining Journal*, Apr. 6, 1935, 7; Kirk H. Stone, *Alaskan Group Settlement: The Matanuska Valley Settlement* (Washington, D.C.: U. S. Dept. of the Interior, Bureau of Land Management, 1950), 26.
18. *Evening Telegram*, May 13, 1935, 3; Harry Hopkins cited by Schaleben, "Alaska Holds Great Hopes, Says Hopkins," *Milwaukee Journal*, May 12, 1935, 3; Don Irwin quoted in the *Rhinelander (Wisc.) Daily News*, May 13, 1935, 3.
19. *Evening Telegram*, Apr. 23, 1935, 12; May 14, 1935, 5; Oscar Kerttula cited in Atwood, *We Shall Be Remembered*, 40. The Kerttulas's son, Jalmar (Jay), later served as a highly regarded, long-term member of the Alaska legislature.
20. *Anchorage Daily News*, May 10, 1935, 1, 12; undated letter from Laurence (Sulo) Vasanoja to his brother and sister, reprinted in Brigitte Lively, *The Matanuska Valley: Fifty Years, 1935–1985* (Palmer, Alaska: Matanuska Impressions Printing, 1985), 19; Atwood, *We Shall Be Remembered*, 42–57; Don L. Irwin, *The Colorful Matanuska Valley* (privately printed), 90; and the following two articles by Schaleben in the *Milwaukee Journal*: "Alaska Perils Have Altered," May 26, 1935, 1; "Pioneers Steaming North to New Destiny in Alaska," May 19, 1935, 3.
21. Dorothy Newville Woods quoted in Lively, *Matanuska Valley*, 88; Schaleben, "Some Alaska 'Farmers' Now Don't Like Farming," *Milwaukee Journal*, June 2, 1935, 1; LeRoy Hamann quoted by Jim Stingl, "Home Away from Home," *Wisconsin Magazine (Milwaukee Journal Sentinel)*, Aug. 6, 1995, 10; Hortense Carson quoted in Atwood, *We Shall Be Remembered*, 60.
22. Miller, *The Frontier in Alaska*, 38; Irwin, *Colorful Matanuska Valley*, 54–56; Atwood, *We Shall Be Remembered*, 59.
23. Schaleben, "Tent Becomes Home, If There's a Housewife," *Milwaukee Journal*, June 17, 1935, 2; James H. Fox, *The First Summer: Photographs of the Matanuska Colony of 1935* (Palmer, Alaska: privately printed, 1980), 5–6, 19, 45; *Minneapolis Tribune*, May 14,

1935, 5; *Anchorage Daily Times*, July 11, 1935, 7; Dorothy Bell to *Kanabec County Times* (Mora, Minn.), July 4, 1935, 4, and July 25, 1935, 7; comments from Jim Fox to Arnold R. Alanen, May 18, 1998; interview with Dorothy Bouwen Onka, conducted by Arnold Alanen, Wasilla, Alaska, June 13, 1994.

24. Irwin, *The Colorful Matanuska Valley*, 57–58; Atwood, *We Shall Be Remembered*, 61–62; Dorothy Bell letter, July 4, 1935.
25. Edith Chambers to the *Evening Telegram*, June 17, 1935, 5; Stone, *Alaskan Group Settlement*, 55–56; Fox, *The First Summer*, 33; Alys Vickaryous quoted in Carol Murkowski, "The Last Colony," *Take Me Away* (Sept. 1981), 10. Of the five-room residences, only one was a single-story unit: a cross-gabled nineteen-by-thirty-one-foot structure with a ten-by-sixteen-foot front wing, which offered 750 square feet of living space. One of the five-room, one-and-one-half story examples included a twenty-one-by-twenty-three-foot footprint, a small, enclosed central entry porch, and a rear wing, all of which provided 860 square feet of space; both the main mass of the house and the entry porch were sheltered by gabled roofs, while the wing displayed a shed roof. A somewhat similar plan included 840 square feet of space, a twenty-by-twenty-six-foot plan, a side-gabled roof, and an enclosed central entry covered by a shed roof. Another five-room example, with a twenty-by-twenty-three-foot plan and a five-by-fifteen-foot front wing, both of which were covered by gabled roofs, provided 910 square feet of space; it was the largest prototype plan presented to the colonists. The only six-room house, with 840 square feet of space, had a twenty-by-twenty-six-foot plan and a gabled roof, one side of which was built to extend down over an enclosed central entry porch. These dimensions are for the log houses; the frame structures were somewhat larger. Many of the plans for the houses and other buildings, which may be found in the David R. Williams Papers, were redrawn by Mary Simpson and published in Vickie Cole, Pat O'Hara, Pandora Willingham, Ron Wendt, and Mary Simpson, *Knik, Matanuska, Susitna: A Visual History of the Valleys* (Palmer, Alaska: Matanuska-Susitna Borough, 1985), 170–77.
26. "Guide to the David R. Williams Papers"; David R. Williams, "Toward a Southwestern Architecture," *Southwest Review* 16 (Apr. 1931): 301; Miller, *The Frontier in Alaska*, 28–29, 37–38; Stone, *Alaskan Group Settlement*, 56. Schaleben, "Pioneer Life Full of Work," *Milwaukee Journal*, June 20, 1935, 6. In her recent review of Alaskan architecture, Alison Hoagland commented that log houses, built to a standardized plan on the northern frontier, "strike a faintly artificial note"; see Alison K. Hoagland, *Buildings of Alaska* (New York: Oxford Univ. Press, 1993), 133.
27. David R. Williams to Lylita Williams in the David R. Williams Papers; Schaleben, "Fever, Probers Hit Colonists," *Milwaukee Journal*, July 12, 1935, 1.
28. Dorothy Bell, July 4, 1935; Atwood, *We Shall Be Remembered*, 63; L. Vasanoja to his brother and sister, July 24, 1935, reprinted in Lively, *Matanuska Valley*, 33.
29. Dorothy Bell, July 4, 1935, and July 25, 1935; comments from Fox to Alanen; Schaleben, "Colony Faces Log Shortage," *Milwaukee Journal*, June 14, 1935, 1.
30. *Ashland (Wis.) Daily Press*, July 2, 1935, 1; Irwin, *The Colorful Matanuska Valley*, 70; Miller, *The Frontier in Alaska*, 85–86; and the following two articles by Schaleben, both of which appeared in the *Milwaukee Journal*: "Alaska Groups Asks Roosevelt for Help," June 18, 1935, 1; "One Alaska Thorn Gone,"

June 19, 1935, 3. In a memorandum from FBI director J. Edgar Hoover to Harry Hopkins, dated July 18, 1935 (on file in the Harry Hopkins Papers), Hoover inquired about "the possibility of trouble-making in the Alaska Colony on the part of the Japanese or Communist element."

31. Miller, *The Frontier in Alaska*, 85–86; Irwin, *The Colorful Matanuska Valley*, 70; memorandum to Col. Westbrook from David R. Williams in the David R. Williams Papers; and the following three articles by Schaleben, all of which appeared in the *Milwaukee Journal*, "Shelter First, Aim of Colony," July 3, 1935, 2; "100 More Transients Arrive," July 5, 1935, 2; "Carr Seeks Tract of 30 Square Miles," July 6, 1935, 2.
32. Miller, *The Alaskan Frontier*, 86; comments from Fox to Alanen; three articles by Schaleben, all published in the *Milwaukee Journal*: "Sheep Sheds? Colony Irked by House Idea," July 23, 1935, 1; "Real Houses or Back to the States! Makes Alaska Officials Shift Plan," July 25, 1935, 1; "750 Rushing Colony Work," Aug. 4, 1935, 1.
33. Schaleben, "Colony Future More Hopeful," Aug. 13, 1935, 1; *Milwaukee Journal*; Edith Conners letter (Aug. 14, 1935), printed in the *Evening Telegram*, Sept. 7, 1935, 3; Cole, et al., *Knik, Matanuska, Susitna*, 185, 187; Atwood, *We Shall Be Remembered*, 76.
34. Leo B. Jacobs to David R. Williams, Aug. 29, 1935, and Sept. 13, 1935, both in the David R. Williams Papers.
35. Schaleben, "50 Dwellings Rise in Alaskan Colony as Bickering Disappears," *Milwaukee Journal*, July 28, 1935, 2. Quite amazingly, the Davis "Alaskan house" still stands in the Matanuska valley.
36. Schaleben, "Colony Houses Rushed in Big Push by Officials," *Milwaukee Journal*, July 21, 1945, 1; "750 Rushing Colony Work"; Cole et al., *Knik, Matanuska, Susitna*, 170–77, 194, 198–99.
37. Letter from Helen Vasanoja to her sister-in-law and brother-in-law, Sept. 17, 1935, reprinted in Lively, *Matanuska Valley*, 36; Matanuska building plans in the David R. Williams Papers; Stone, *Alaskan Group Settlement*, 56; Cole et al., *Knik, Matanuska, Susitna*, 178–79; Hoagland, *Buildings of Alaska*, 134.
38. Hugh A. Johnson and Keith L. Stanton, *Matanuska Valley Memoir* (Palmer: Alaska Agricultural Experiment Station, Univ. of Alaska, 1955), 34; Fox comments to Alanen; interview with Laurence Vasanoja Jr., conducted by Arnold Alanen in Palmer, Alaska, July 30, 1996; LeRoy Hamann quoted in Diana VanHoesen, "First Barns of Matanuska Valley," *This Alaska* 11 (May–June 1970): 5; Stone, *Alaskan Group Settlement*, 56; Cole et al., *Knik, Matanuska, Susitna*, 182.
39. Stone, *Alaskan Group Settlement*, 55. Although it is beyond the scope of this discussion, it must be mentioned that the townsite of Palmer was also under construction from August 1935 to May 1936. The incipient community included a school, a hospital, a post office, a warehouse, a depot, a trading post, a barbershop, a water tower, a powerhouse, offices for the ARRC, and a teachers' dormitory.
40. Today, Matanuska gardeners continue to raise colossal vegetables, such as the ninety-eight-pound cabbage that set an Alaskan record at the 1983 state fair in Palmer. See Penny Rennick, ed., "Alaska's Farms and Gardens," *Alaska Geographic* 11, no. 2 (1984): 8.
41. *Daily Mining Journal*, May 14, 1935, 5; Dorothy Bell letters, July 4, 1935, and July 25, 1935; Conners letter; Irwin, *Colorful Matanuska Valley*, 77; Schaleben, "Colony Certain of Homes Now," *Milwaukee Journal*, Aug. 18, 1935, 3; Jack Allman, "Crops Silence

Colony Critics," *Milwaukee Journal*, Oct. 27, 1935, 6 (reprinted from the Matanuska Valley Pioneer).

42. Schaleben, "Crops Grow Fabulously in Alaska's Magic Soil," *Milwaukee Journal*, June 30, 1935, 14; Dorothy Bell letter, July 5, 1935; Atwood, *We Shall Be Remembered*, 64; Stone, *Alaskan Group Settlement*, 72; Fox comments to Alanen.
43. H. W. Alberts, *Bulletin No. 11, Forage Crops in the Matanuska Region, Alaska* (Juneau: Alaska Agricultural Experiment Stations, 1933), 3, 7; Herbert G. Hanson, "Agriculture in the Matanuska Valley, Alaska," typewritten manuscript in RG 126, Alaska Development of Resources, Matanuska Valley Farmers Co-op, National Archives and Records Center; Laurence Vasanoja to his brother and sister, Sept. 17, 1935, reprinted in Lively, *Matanuska Colony*, 36; Schaleben, "Crops Grow Fabulously"; Irwin, *Colorful Matanuska Valley*, 77; Allman, "Crops Silence Colony Critics"; Fox comments to Alanen.
44. Letter from Lloyd Bell to Kanabec County Times, Sept. 19, 1935, 2; Stone, *Alaskan Group Settlement*, 56; Donald Irwin quoted by Fox in letter to Alanen.
45. Stone, *Alaskan Group Settlement*, 58–59; Fox comments to Alanen; Lillian Eckert quoted in Cole, *Knik, Matanuska, Susitna*, 172.
46. Schaleben, "11 More Families to Leave Alaska Colony on Saturday," *Milwaukee Journal*, July 24, 1935, 1; "Some Alaska 'Farmers' Now Don't Like Farming"; Westbrook, "Alaska: Matanuska Valley Project"; Dorothy Bell to the *Kanabec County Times*, Mar. 19, 1936, 1, and Mar. 26, 1936, 7; August Raschke to the *Evening Telegram*, July 9, 1935, 3.
47. Atwood, *We Shall Be Remembered*, 151; Florence Hess quoted in Stingl, "Home Away from Home," 11; letter from Marjorie Wilkes McKinney to Arnold Alanen, Sept. 27, 1994; Matt Saarela quoted in the *Minneapolis Tribune*, July 5, 1935, 7. Saarela's observation about the Finns' passion for cooperative enterprise is confirmed by the more than 175 retail cooperative stores and scores of cooperative creameries, insurance companies, petroleum outlets, telephone associations, lending libraries, and burial societies that Finnish Americans organized in Michigan, Minnesota, and Wisconsin during the period from the early 1900s to World War II. See Arnold Alanen, "The Development and Distribution of Finnish Consumers' Cooperatives in Michigan, Minnesota, and Wisconsin, 1903–1973," in *The Finnish Experience in the Western Great Lakes Region: New Perspectives*, ed. M. G. Karni, M. E. Kaups, and D. J. Ollila (Turku, Finland: Institute for Migration, Univ. of Turku, 1975), 103–30.
48. Frank Ring to Marinette County Relief Unit, June 7, 1935, included in the "Wisconsin Report," files of the Wisconsin Emergency Relief Administration, RG 126, Alaska Development of Resources, National Archives and Records Administration; Harold L. Ickes, *The Secret Diary of Harold L. Ickes, vol. 2, The Inside Struggle, 1936–1939* (New York: Simon and Schuster, 1954), 442; Schaleben, "Plot to Wreck Alaska Colony Project, Charge," *Milwaukee Journal*, June 15, 1935, 1.
49. George Conners, who had numerous run-ins with ARRC officials during the less than two years he and his family resided in Alaska, complained that "colonists' wages were too low, seed too expensive, land costly to clear, his wells unproductive, and the ARRC unattentive to his troubles." The disillusioned Conners later wrote to Eleanor Roosevelt, requesting back pay for his work in developing Tract 132 (the ARRC quickly abandoned the property because of a lack of water), claiming

that "he had done his part, that the ARRC had failed him, that he was in dire need, and that something should be done to secure what he was owed." There is no further information on the outcome of his request. See Miller, *The Frontier in Alaska*, 108–9.

50. Memorandum from Stewart C. Campbell to Col. Lawrence Westbrook, "Status of Matanuska Valley Family Replacement as of October 15, 1936," David Williams Papers; Miller, *The Frontier in Alaska*, 113, 154.
51. Cora Hemmer quoted by Pat Monaghan, "Settling Alaska's Matanuska Valley: What Happened to the Minnesota Immigrants," *Preview: Minnesota Public Radio 8* (Nov. 1974), 9; Hamann interview; Barney Anderson quoted in Stingl, "Home Away from Home," 15. Because of the assistance the colonists received from the federal government, some commentators termed them "cream puff pioneers," while the communitarian nature of the project led others to identify them as "red-plush pioneers."
52. Johnson and Stanton, *Matanuska Valley Memoir*, 34; Richard A. Andrews and Hugh A. Johnson, *Farming in Alaska, Bulletin 20* (Palmer: Alaska Agricultural Experiment Station, 1956), 8; John R. Parks, H. P. Gazaway, and Allan H. Mick, eds., *Alaska Farm Facts: A Compilation of Agricultural Statistics for the Years 1953 through 1957, Bulletin 27* (Fairbanks: Agricultural Experiment Station, Univ. of Alaska, 1961), 5.
53. Clarence A. Moore, "Farming in the Matanuska and Tanana Valleys of Alaska," *Bulletin 14, Alaska Agricultural Experiment Station* (Palmer, Alaska: The Station, 1952); Alaska Division of Agriculture, *1967 Annual Report* (Palmer, Alaska: Division of Agriculture, 1967), 8, 18–19; Alaska Agricultural Statistics Service, U.S. Dept. of Agriculture, *Alaska Agricultural Statistics, 1998* (Palmer: Univ. of Alaska, Alaska Cooperative Extension, 1998), 14–22; Johnson and Stanton, *Matanuska Valley Memoir*, 34; Carolyn Cage, "'Red-Plush Pioneers': The 1935 Colonists and Agriculture in the Matanuska Valley," brochure prepared for an exhibit produced by the Anchorage Museum of History and Art, 1995; Stingl, "Home Away from Home," 16–17; Fox comments to Alanen.
54. Conkin, *Tomorrow a New World*, 331; Hamann interview.
55. Stewart Campbell quoted by Schaleben in "Some Alaska 'Farmers' Now Don't Like Farming."

PART II

SPACE AS POWER

CHAPTER 5

Rebecca Ginsburg

"Come in the Dark": Domestic Workers and Their Rooms in Apartheid-Era Johannesburg, South Africa

Apartheid was good for no one, but there was nobody it was worse for than African women. This was especially true with regard to housing. South Africa's vast collection of policies and regulations governing who could live in which areas under what conditions imposed more hardships upon African women than on any other group. Whether in rural African villages, white farms, or cities, they found themselves disadvantaged by discriminatory laws based on race and restricted because of their gender. Both legal and social structures assumed and demanded female dependence on men for housing and support. African women had few options and little autonomy in deciding where and how to live.

The quiet tree-lined streets of segregated white residential neighborhoods, miles from the areas where most Africans lived, were an unlikely setting for African women's challenges to this state of affairs. Nonetheless, it was here that significant numbers of them began to exercise control over the terms of their housing and to take charge of the conditions of their family life. Indeed, as apartheid became ever more repressive, with the government making even harsher attempts to squeeze Africans from the cities and into so-called homelands, women found themselves holding increasingly greater power over their domestic arrangements. This tension—between the oppression of apartheid and the opportunities it provided women to alter the conditions of home life—reached a peak during the height of apartheid, in the 1960s and 1970s. What happened during these years on the properties and in the homes of middle-class white families did not constitute an abrupt break from the past. Rather, those employed as full-time domestic workers in white households formed part of a growing swell of African women throughout the country who, under diverse circumstances, were challenging dominant gender relations. Even so, servants' activities were particularly noteworthy for at least two reasons. First, they posed an especially strong challenge to conventional African family roles, and, second, domestic servants' efforts to negotiate the terms of their relationships with their men had repercussions upon the very course of apartheid itself.

At the center of the story was a humble structure: the live-in domestic worker's quarter, commonly known as a "back room" (fig. 5.1). Every middle-class property contained one of these shelters, constructed at the same time as the main house and considered just as essential. These small detached buildings were where a household's live-in African servant retired after completing her day's work in the white house. Though she did not own this building, it was probably her most valuable asset. Back rooms, as simple and as crude as they were, represented a form of urban accommodation during a severe African housing shortage. It was because she had access to such a place that an African woman could shift the balance of power in her domestic arrangements. My account of how domestic workers exploited their control over these rooms and the implications of their activities there is based mainly on interviews I conducted between 1995 and 1998 with former domestic workers and their employers in Johannesburg, South Africa's largest city.

Fig. 5.1. Domestic worker's quarter, Florida, Johannesburg. Toilet entrance is located behind low wall to left.

The Call of the City

African men and women had worked in white people's homes—as paid employees, indentured servants, or slaves—since the earliest days of European colonization. The attraction of higher paying mine jobs and other considerations gradually pulled men away from such employment, until by the mid-twentieth century domestic service was almost entirely a female-only occupation.[1] Most domestic workers came from the ranks of rural migrants who, despite the government's vigorous attempts to curb black urbanization during this period, continued to leave the farms and countryside to work in the cities. Earning money to support their families was usually the first consideration of a woman who decided to pack her few belongings into a bag and head to Johannesburg.

"At home we were suffering, I want to tell you. Because we had nothing," Mabel T. said, describing her youth in the Standerton district.[2] In rural African communities throughout the countryside, women, children, and the elderly tried desperately to scrape by on subsistence farming and the meager allowances contributed by their menfolk employed as migrant laborers. Unfortunately, the redistribution of African lands under apartheid had reduced the amounts of land available for agriculture and grazing. Money sent home by husbands and fathers was not always enough to cover basic expenses. According to one woman's contemporary account, "Sometimes there is almost nothing. Only porridge. There are so many of us—five children—so I just mix the porridge with a lot of water".[3]

The situation was no better, and was often considerably worse, on white-owned farms, where entire families of Africans lived and worked in conditions similar to those of American plantation slavery. Children were sent to sleep with empty stomachs when the white farmer's rations were stingy and a household had no cash to spend on store-bought goods, even assuming shops existed within an easy day's walk. "We earned one rand a year and every year we received twenty bags of mealie [corn] meal," reported one survivor of such conditions. "At times we were also beaten."[4] Many women decided that the best chance for their families' survival lay in their seeking employment elsewhere. At the very least, their departure would mean one less mouth to feed.[5]

There were other reasons, as well, for a woman to leave her rural home. Since as early as the turn of the nineteenth century, African marriages had been subject to a series of profound stresses related to increased male migration to the mines and the cities. Men's long terms of absence and the personal and social affronts they endured while living in white society raised their interests in coming home to a family in which their roles as patriarchs and masters were respected. At the same time, the women they had left behind found themselves increasingly disinclined to submit to the authority of someone whom they only rarely saw and who provided little support toward the day-to-day maintenance of the household.[6]

This was especially true for those women who had converted to Christianity, attracted to and emboldened by its stress upon individual salvation and denunciation of polygamy. Western-style education, also introduced by the missionaries to the African countryside, encouraged similar ruminations by women on notions of and possibilities for personal autonomy. Women throughout rural South Africa found themselves readjusting their expectations of marriage, just as their husbands sought entrenchment of the reassuring status quo.[7] Many men continued to believe that "women . . . are like children. We keep them like pets." But fewer of their wives were willing to accept such "old school" attitudes.[8] Rates of adultery, divorce, desertion, and premarital pregnancy increased as women and men tried to work out new ways of relating to one another. Many women made the move to the city precisely to escape the increasingly stressed gender and familial relations of rural areas, and this exodus continued well into the 1960s and 1970s.[9]

Whatever combination of factors motivated a particular woman, her final decision to leave home was rarely painless. Children had to be left behind with grandparents or other kin, many of whom would disapprove of her unbecoming independence and grieve the loss of another loved one into the city's warren. The journey itself could be long and dangerous. Traveling through certain parts of the country, she would have to sleep in trees to avoid being eaten by lions.[10] Each woman realized that she faced an uncertain future in a strange and alien environment. Lacking proper documentation to be in the city, she would also risk arrest, fines, and deportation back to the countryside. Yet, thousands, borrowing money from relations and neighbors, for whom such a loan could be an investment, rode buses and trains, hitched rides, or simply walked to Johannesburg.

The rural women who reached the city understood that their employment options were effectively limited to domestic service. After all, most lacked education, proficiency in English or Afrikaans, and experience other than house or fieldwork—not to mention a valid work permit, which would have been required by any reputable corporate employer. They also recognized that their housing needs could most efficiently and easily be met by taking a back room on a white employer's property. For that reason, most found themselves heading directly to the white suburbs upon their arrival in the city.

Suburban Johannesburg

Johannesburg's white residents lived in comfortable, racially exclusive neighborhoods that, in the opinion of one American visitor in the mid-1960s, resembled nothing so much as Lawrence, Kansas.[11] On tree-lined streets sat mostly single-family residences, separated from the sidewalks and their neighbors by low fences or brick walls that sheltered fragrant front gardens and backyards with swimming pools and patios (fig. 5.2). Neighbors greeted each other when they passed while unloading groceries from their cars or spied one another

Fig. 5.2. House, Parkview, Johannesburg, with driveway leading to back yard and domestic worker's room.

gardening, and their children raced bicycles up and down the streets.

Johannesburg's several dozen suburbs were by no means interchangeable with one another: some suburbs were more prestigious; others had marked immigrant influences in shops and restaurants; others were known for their views or the reputations of their schools. But they did bear similarities. In accordance with apartheid planning principles, they lay close to the city's central business district. Other areas, known as "locations" or "townships," served each of the country's three nonwhite "population groups"—Indians, Coloureds, and Africans. These were separated by natural or man-made features like train tracks or industrial zones from what constituted, in effect, a core "white" city. For historical reasons, the southern areas of Johannesburg were mostly working-class Afrikaner. The middle-class suburbs that are the focus of my study lay north, northeast, and northwest of downtown. Bearing names like Parkview, Kensington, and Northcliff, they sheltered most of the city's English-speaking majority and shared common cultural, economic, and, especially, physical features.

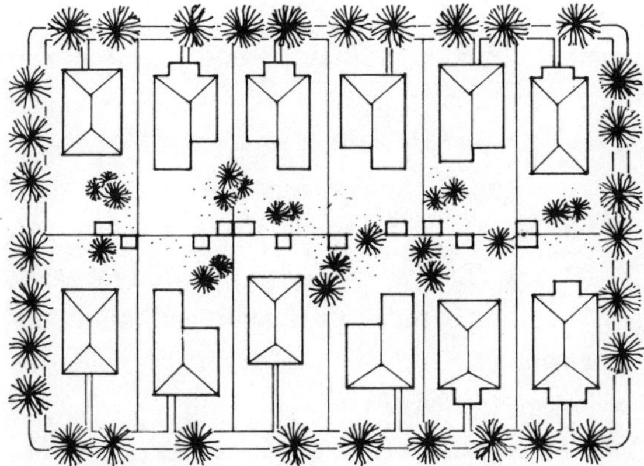

Fig. 5.3. Site plan, typical Johannesburg suburban block, showing relation of back rooms to main houses and avenues of exit from properties. Drawing by Sibel Zandi-Sayek.

Typically, a main house designed for nuclear family occupation by white residents sat facing the street (fig. 5.3). A driveway might lead to a garage and a walkway to the front door. In the backyard was a cluster of service buildings—toolshed, storage bin, a servant's back room or two, and a toilet and shower stall for African staff. Backrooms varied only slightly in size and plan, generally measuring about eight by ten feet, almost always constructed of brick, with concrete floors and no ceilings. They rarely had electricity. Furnishings consisted usually of the cast-offs of the employer. A twin bed, wardrobe, and small bench were standard. Not much more could fit inside. There was a single door that locked with a key, usually held by both the worker and her white employers, and, typically, a single, small window. One generally had to walk through the front gate of the property and along the side of the main house to reach the back room. Landscaping devices like tall shrubs or walls that partially blocked sights and sounds that would otherwise carry between the back room and main house were a common feature (fig. 5.4).

A minority of suburbs were high-density areas that contained large apartment buildings. Their modernist designs excited Nikolaus Pevsner when he visited Johannesburg in the 1950s, but for my purposes what distinguished these buildings were their roofs.[12] On the top of each apartment building—in a few cases, in their basements—was a dormitory for workers. Along narrow hallways open to the sky were rows of single rooms, communal toilets, and bathing facilities. Each room was owned or rented by the white resident for whom its occupant worked; servants' rooms were included in the purchase or lease of a flat. The quarters were about the same size as back rooms, each also with

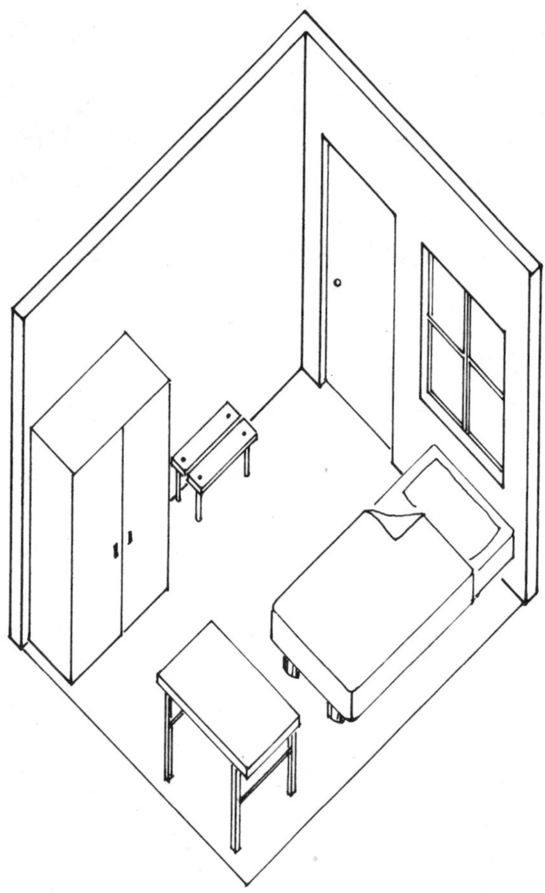

Fig. 5.4. Schematic sketch of a domestic worker's room illustrates size of rooms and the furnishings typically provided by an employer. Drawing by Sibel Zandi-Sayek.

a single door and window. The "skylight locations" were accessible from stairs that ascended from the top floor of the building. Elevators did not travel this high and were reserved anyway for white passengers only. Entry to the building itself was gained from a separate servants' entrance on the ground floor. Officially, about 100,000 African servants lived in Johannesburg during this period, about three-quarters of them in back rooms and the rest in skylight locations. By comparison, white Johannesburg had a population of about 400,000 and nearby Soweto of approximately 750,000.[13]

Domestic Service

Domestic work, by all accounts, was a miserable occupation.[14] A single servant could be responsible for preparing meals, serving them, baking, cleaning house, childcare, washing and ironing, tending pets, and sometimes caring for elderly parents as well. Days were long, often more than twelve hours, and many employers expected their workers to be "on call" during evening hours as well.

The conditions under which many African women performed this labor increased the weight of its load. In some households, white employers regularly slapped their servants. Yelling and harsh words, including racial slurs, were common. Domestic workers were pained also by the indignities of their position. Being forbidden to eat off their employers' plates humiliated them, as did being fed separate food that butchers sold as "dogs' meat." Some even had their consumption of tea rationed. Precious M. was allowed one bag every two days.[15] Most did not earn enough to afford decent clothing or, more importantly, to send sufficient money to support family back home. "It was terrible, I don't want to remember it. . . . Now I can talk about it, but at that time, really, it was terrible."[16]

By no means was domestic service an unmitigated evil. There did exist some decent labor conditions and affectionate, even loving, ties between employers and employees. More often, though, mutual dependencies and jealousies between white family members and the worker bred an uneasy and often fragile symbiosis that worked to the distinct disadvantage of the worker. Most appreciated the vulnerability of their positions. "[Your madam] can get up in the morning and say, 'I don't want to see you next to me today. You can get out of my yard.'"[17]

The ease with which they could be fired—expressed significantly in terms of an eviction—was only one problem faced by servants. They had to deal as well with financial worries, physical fatigue, and the preservation of their dignity in conditions that conspired to undermine it. Domestic workers' greatest concern, though, on a daily basis, was fighting loneliness. They spent most of their waking hours inside the white house. If the sole employee of a household, they passed much of this time in relative isolation. The habit of some employers of locking their workers in the house during the day to ensure they did not leave, in addition to being a dangerous practice, accentuated these women's feelings of being removed from others. If, on the other hand, "madam" was a housewife, workers had to become used to a pair of eyes following them around the house, checking on their work, and offering running commentaries on anything from the affairs of the neighbors to their own deficiencies as workers. "She [was] watching you . . . like a snake . . . You [couldn't] rest."[18] Such "companionship" tended to heighten rather than diminish their sense of being alone.

Nighttime could be even worse. For many, the communal life among strangers in the skylight location was alienating and frightening after the accustomed order of their rural communities. Many retreated to their rooms, though there was little to do there. The government did not introduce television to South Africa until 1976, and books were little companionship to the illiterate majority. Women from the northern Transvaal used to keep busy with fancy needlework, for which they were renown. Others might go "eye shopping" in town, often daydreaming about one day being able to purchase goods like those they encountered in their employers' homes. Alberta S. played her battery-operated hi-fi all night long, in part to keep herself company.[19] It was at such times that many workers' thoughts turned to those left behind. "I used to cry for my children," Linda S. said.[20] Many considered returning home. But, as Jacqueline M. explained, "You [would] think, 'if I go back, what can [they] eat, my kids? My kids, what can dress my kids?'"[21] Like Jacqueline, most decided to stay.

Under these conditions, any interpersonal relationship assumed great importance. The conversations they might strike with the next-door servant over the backyard fence, or friendships with other workers who congregated in neighborhood parks on their days off, helped considerably. Many women became active members of African church groups that proliferated largely in response to such need. Others used their off-days to visit relatives and "home girls" from their region who had also journeyed to town. Even these efforts, though, often did not go far enough. What women seemed to miss most of all were intimate and sustained relationships with men. Although it meant breaking the law and, usually, the explicit rules of their employers, and therefore risking their jobs, they arranged to sneak African men onto white properties and into their backrooms to stay with them there.[22]

There was no shortage of males looking desperately for lodging. African men had been making their ways to Johannesburg since the earliest days of European settlement in the region, following the discovery of gold in 1867. Some had city roots that stretched back for generations and, accordingly, well-established rights to live in government-provided township housing. Others were more recent arrivals. Under influx control laws that aimed to reduce the number of Africans in urban areas, they were "illegal" and ineligible for such housing.[23] Still others fell somewhere in between these two extremes. Perhaps they lived in one of the workers' hostels or industry compounds for single men that lay along the outskirts of the city. Whatever their situation, men had many motivations to seek a place in a domestic worker's room.

Men who arrived in the city without the proper documentation and without a job in hand were in the least favorable housing position. They qualified for none of the official African housing in townships or workers' hostels. Johannesburg's hotels and boarding residences were strictly "whites only." African newcomers to the area found themselves essentially homeless. Some found shelter in public spaces, for instance, on city streets, public toilets, parks, mine dumps, and train stations. The possibility of spending time in a servant's room while trying to secure one's own job and, possibly, independent accommodation offered a much more pleasant alternative.

Men housed in workers' hostels at least had a bunk to call their own, but such hostels were notoriously brutal environments. One Johannesburg-area mining hostel, the subject of a contemporary study, housed about 3,700 men who slept sixteen to twenty, on average, in each room. They worked, bathed, ate, and drank together. In the words of one resident, trying to describe the social atmosphere, "if you put a whole lot of cattle together in a kraal and overcrowd them, then they will stamp and horn each other." [24] Violence, including sexual violence, was common in these complexes.[25]

Disease was another hazard of hostel living. Beriberi, pellagra, and scurvy flourished, due to the poor diet. High blood pressure was also a serious problem. Many men tried to help themselves. Some turned to "witchdoctors," or *sangomas*, for help in treating their conditions.[26] One unknown resident of a city hostel painted a window at one end of his concrete bunk in a twenty-man room.[27] Others made literal escapes from these environments by moving in with domestic workers.

Even some men who had their own township houses—in nearby Soweto, for example (fig. 5.5)—preferred to stay instead in the back rooms with

Fig. 5.5. The barren landscape of Soweto, with its rows of identical "matchbox" houses.

their girlfriends.[28] One attraction was no doubt the lure of the mistress over the wife and children, but living with a domestic worker also offered material amenities. Far from the dirt roads of the townships or the noxious noises of industry, backrooms sat in green gardens in quiet neighborhoods. Birds nested in fruit trees and cats curled up in flower beds that were often meticulously maintained by gardening staff (fig. 5.6). Reaching overhead, one could pluck an apricot from a low-hanging bough or snap an apple from a twig. The setting was pleasant enough and, in some cases, the infrastructure sound enough, that some households chose to convert unused back rooms into working studios or teenagers' rooms. They were probably too rustic for guests' quarters. Compared to other housing alternatives, and even in its own right, the back room offered a pleasant spot to return to in the evenings.

The physical setting of the back room was matched favorably by its amenities. Beds, though often the rejects of the employers, were an improvement over the concrete slabs of the hostels. Some backyard bathrooms had hot and cold running water, unlike either township houses or the compounds. And the toilet and bathroom would be shared by only two instead of ten or two hundred. A few rooms even had electricity.

The domestic workers themselves were practiced in the arts of making a clean and comfortable home.[29] Many were accomplished cooks and bakers. They were valued as well for the access they had to the things of the white house, to valuable commodities like butter, white sugar, tasty jams, and biscuits, things too expensive for most Africans to purchase on a regular basis but that workers might, with a little skill, be able to convey secretly back to the room at night. Overall, these rooms were about as comfortable a home that a working-class African man could hope to secure in the city (fig. 5.7).

Fig. 5.6. Tree sheltering the entrance to a domestic worker's room, Germiston, Johannesburg.

Fig. 5.7. These backrooms sit behind the vegetable garden in Parkview, Johannesburg. Even in upper-middle-class homes, where more than one servant was expected to be employed, accommodation was in small, separate, single rooms, presumably to discourage the sharing that went on regardless.

Every domestic worker that I interviewed had engaged, at some point during this period, in the practice of secretly hiding people in the back room. Several of them seem to have run virtual boarding houses. "You [would] find that in the rooms, we [slept] like the sardines."[30] Though they also housed their children, friends and, sometimes, absolute strangers, the most common guests, by far, were male lovers. And while practical necessity and the pangs of loneliness were often the driving forces in bringing two people together, these relationships were by no means completely mercenary affairs.[31] Love did exist in the back rooms. However, the forms that it assumed were subject to change. In these settings that they controlled, women began to ask for new forms of attachment from their partners.

Hiding Guests

Women's positions for negotiating new terms of romantic relationships rested on the power they held over backroom arrangements. The extent to which they were in charge becomes clear upon closer examination of what was actually involved in keeping secret visitors. Deciding to harbor an undocumented houseguest, whether for a long weekend or on a semipermanent basis, was only the first step. Once she chose to break her employer's rules and the government's law by bringing an additional person onto the property, a domestic worker faced a host of practical challenges. How could her guest avoid detection by unsympathetic white employers, apartment managers, and "concerned" citizens? And how could they evade the police during the municipality's frequent raids for illegal Africans during this period? The solutions to these problems lay in clever and judicious use of suburbia's built environment. The domestic worker's abilities to hide her movements and camouflage her activities depended on her knowledge of and control over the spatial and temporal orders of white neighborhoods.

The first task faced by the domestic worker who sought to shelter a guest was getting the unauthorized tenant onto the property without alerting the police or her employers. Each household had its own set of rules. Although some white householders might grant permission for certain types of visitors—for example, allowing close family of the domestic, daytime guests, or sleepovers during the weekend only—most workers found even these sorts of arrangements, where they existed, too restrictive. Even women who worked for relatively liberal families found themselves eventually secretly bringing people back into their rooms. Accomplishing this was largely a matter of timing. Her knowledge of the family's comings and goings, combined with an intimate acquaintance with the layout of the house, guided the worker's judgment of when in the day her employers were more or less likely to be alert to activity outside.

Mealtimes often presented opportunity. I was told, "when the employers are busy eating at suppertime, then you'll run and open the gate for [your friend] to go in."[32] If the dining room overlooked the driveway, though, it might make more sense to wait until they had retired for the night. Nancy M., for instance, knew that whenever her madam was settled in the living room, it was safe to move her friends.[33] For Jacqueline M., the best time was when her madam was setting the dining table.[34]

My own position as a researcher, some twenty years later, echoed that of earlier illicit guests, and the scheduling of my interviews was often regulated in the same way. I was told by one worker to show up at 2:00, since madam returned from work at 3:00; by another to arrive in the morning so we could talk before the children, who presumably would tell their parents of my unauthorized visit, came home for lunch. While influx control no longer pertains in South Africa, employers still have control over their properties and many workers continue to time carefully the comings and goings of their visitors.

Dogs always posed a problem. Even if friendly, they were likely to bark and alert their owners. Workers developed a wide range of ruses to assure the safety of their guests. Sally V.'s boyfriend used to approach her back room by walking onto the premises backwards. If detected, he would claim to be leaving anyway.[35] Sophia B., whose employer allowed female but not male visitors, had her gentleman lover wear a dress when he came visiting.[36]

Until the hour it was safe to enter the property, a guest had to wait. Sometimes it was possible to linger inconspicuously on the street outside the house, but after the 9:00 P.M. curfew for Africans, this carried substantial risks. Then men were better off hiding in a nearby park or sheltering themselves in bushes where they could not be seen. Knowledge of the hours "madam" and "master" rose in the morning, when and for how long they were in the bath, the time they left for work, when the children came home from school, the schedule of regular shopping trips, and bedtime hours allowed a worker to make informed choices about the timing of her own activities. The white family's movements formed the basis of her guest's, in a shadowed or inverse way, and it was the domestic's strategic position as overseer of the one that allowed her to plan the other.

In an apartment building, white employers did not control entry, the superintendent or watchman did, patrolling even the servants' entrance. Sometimes they could be bribed, as could the police on occasion. But, as Molly T. told me, "the watchmen were not the same."[37] Some were more sympathetic, others more greedy. A servant had to learn who worked the various shifts and make her plans accordingly. Sometimes, none of the guards could be trusted and then she would have to sneak the visitor into the building after dark. If the circumstances were such that the risk of detection ran very high—perhaps the guards were particularly hostile or nearby white neighbors overly nosy—the worker would confine her visitor to her room for the entire duration of his visit, not allowing him to leave until the final departure date. It helped that other workers could usually be counted on to assist with one's guests—cooperation in these matters was great—but such arrangements were generally stressful for all the parties involved.

Getting their guests inside was not the end of the challenge. Domestic workers had also to plan for the eventuality of a police raid or surprise visit by their employers. The question was how to hide both their visitor and his personal effects in such an event. The fact that employers often provided their workers with crude and cheap pieces of furniture worked to their advantage here. At any given time, domestic workers were forced anyway to pile, stack, and squeeze their belongings into overly small spaces. Their rooms were often crowded with garments hanging from nails, bags jammed under stools, and pillows stuffed with personal effects. An extra person's things were often difficult to identify in such a clutter. Linda M., for instance, kept her boyfriend's clothes in a box that she kept covered with cushions. Though it was large, it did not attract attention in her crowded room.[38]

These circumstances also made it easier to hide people themselves (fig. 5.8). In a raid they could crawl into wardrobes and hampers and under tables. Bed legs were raised on bricks or empty paint tins. The dominant white view of the practice was that superstitious Africans did this in fear of the dreaded *tokoloshes*, mythical creatures that attacked unsuspecting humans in their sleep. Several of my informants chuckled at this idea. On the contrary, they said, not only did this arrangement increase their storage space, it also created room for hiding a guest's things and, if need be, the guest him- or herself. Emily M. told me it was her preferred hiding spot for her friends. She would pull boxes and blankets in front of them. As long as the police didn't pull the blankets, she explained, you were safe.[39] The semidarkness of these rooms lit only by candles or paraffin lamps also served as an advantage. Lydia M.'s aunt hurriedly directed her to the cupboard one night when the police paid a surprise call during her own visit to the city. It was so crowded with things, the officers couldn't see her even after they had opened the door and looked inside. She managed to evade arrest, but only at the expense of her heart, as she told me, dropping to her feet. She never visited her aunt again.[40]

Significance

The practice of hiding people carried multiple significance for domestic workers. At the most basic level, it provided warm human contact. These women were often miserably lonely. Many were ill-treated. Their rooms were cold and dark. Having a roommate offered assurance that at the end of a long day, there was, in the words of Flora M., "somebody to talk to."[41] As Candy M. put it, it meant "somebody . . . to sleep by you at night."[42]

Clearly, though, once a person made a commitment to hiding someone, for a weekend or for months at a time, she found that the comforts of companionship carried a whole host of problems. Would the dogs bark? Was the new watchman bribable? When would the police next raid? Thoughts like these seem to have occupied many a servant during her working hours. Anita S. explained, "You'd be working in the daytime, being happy. But [then] you'd [stop to] think, what's going to happen in the night? My man is going to come and wait for me outside. Sometimes it's cold. . . . Sometimes he doesn't come. You don't know where he is."[43] A range of possibilities could present themselves to the worried mind: arrested and jailed by the police, threatened away by a passing white neighbor, in the arms of another woman. The workers I interviewed spoke often of their fear. Many seem to have lived with omnipresent stress and tension over their arrangements. "We didn't sleep that time," Amy K. said of those days.[44]

Nonetheless, it was partly just because there were so many pressures associated with hiding others that the practice provided meaning on a second level. It gave these women the satisfaction of

Fig. 5.8. Beds were often made unstable by being raised off the ground. Occupants sometimes found themselves thrown to the ground when energetic bedtime activity knocked it off its stands. The noise of such a crash could bring white employers running to investigate.

taking control of their lives and making bearable hard conditions. As Elizabeth M. explained, with a hint of pride in her voice, "If you suffer, you must have a lot of plans."[45] There was pleasure in designing a room to accommodate secret visitors, plotting escape routes, and devising schedules of entry and egress. To successfully hide a guest, workers needed to establish and then implement a series of steps, from collecting empty paint tins to saving money for bribes, that required short- and long-range planning. Part of the delight of engaging in this activity may have been the intellectual satisfaction it provided. Many workers were frustrated by their employers' typically heavy-handed supervision. They resented not being able to decide for themselves how best to perform their various tasks and in what order. The challenge of keeping secret visitors could compensate somewhat for the often mundane routine employment of domestic workers.

In addition, these schemes allowed servants to put one over on their employers. Whites had a habit of saying their domestic workers were part of the family. Workers usually experienced their relations very differently. Breaking the explicit rules of the household, lying to "madam's" face about whether one had guests, and then stealing food from the kitchen to feed an extra mouth, could provide a pleasing sense of undermining unjust authority. These practices allowed domestic workers a means of resisting individually and privately what they saw as unfair labor practices, at the same time their menfolk were organizing into trade unions and engaging in collective action to assert themselves within their own employment spheres.

"Come in the Dark"

What most distinguished the use of domestic workers' quarters from other historical examples of surreptitious use of space—for example, from the hiding of black slaves in the United States or Jews during the Holocaust—was that women controlled these places and set the terms for their use. It was the meaning that the practice held for domestic workers *as women* that was ultimately most significant. Many domestic workers, as we have seen, sought what some called "modern" relationships, unions that offered fewer restrictions and, as they saw it, greater personal dignity. City life offered many favorable conditions for achieving this. Women's potential for financial independence there and their release from the controls of authoritative family members made it easier for them to negotiate domestic relations on terms that suited their interests.

However, at the same time, women in the city encountered a significant new obstacle. An African woman needed a man to register for a township house. This requirement, first introduced in the 1930s and strongly reinforced by the apartheid regime in the 1960s, often cut against women's efforts to establish themselves independently. Indeed, many women tolerated severe marital hardships rather than risk losing their rights to urban residence. "Women did everything to save their houses. They . . . married their own cousins or relatives, or even men they did not like."[46]

The alternative to township living, squatting, or homelessness was, of course, domestic service. And while township women needed men to secure housing, servants did not. Indeed, in the suburbs a woman's best strategy for obtaining a position and a place to live was to present herself as unattached.

Domestic workers had another advantage over their township and country sisters in their shared efforts to create personally satisfying relationships. Their direct and intimate exposure to white families helped broaden their vision of what marriage could be. It encouraged them to consider new options for themselves and, perhaps most importantly, provided them a model to assert against their partners for negotiating purposes.[47] Their impressions of white marriage may have sometimes been rose-hued—"I have worked in town and in my experience the white marriages are always happy and lead a better life than the black marriages"—but it was not as important that African women were accurate in their perceptions of white marriage, sometimes confusing the privileges of class with those of race, as that they were moved and empowered by them.[48]

The consequences of this could be profound. For what were often the first times in their lives, many workers began to explicitly challenge the assumptions of their most intimate relationships and to redefine their terms. Linda M. was one such woman. Her boyfriend, hired by one of many city employers who hired "illegal" Africans without bothering to regularize their status, had no urban accommodation. Without the madam's permission or knowledge, he slept with Linda in the skylight location. Linda was an ardent Christian, and the couple began eventually to argue about her commitment to her religion. "[H]e didn't want I must go to the church. He made me cross." Linda put a swift and efficient end to his nagging. "I kicked him out."[49]

For men who believed that the old rules still applied—that, "[w]hen I get to my house . . . I must feel I am being welcomed and everything is done to make me feel back home—a husband feels he should be appreciated when he gets home"—life in a back room could prove a rude awakening.[50] Sally M.'s husband experienced such a shock. Originally from Soweto, but having lost title to the family house, he thought their housing problems were solved when Sally secured a domestic position. He moved in with her. Given her familiarity with her employers' hours and habits, she felt it necessary to set the rules of the household herself. Fearful of detection by the white family living just a few yards away, she had to remind him, repeatedly, "Don't light a candle," "Use less water," "Speak more softly," "Come in the dark." He eventually left her, she said, because he could not accept her placing restrictions on him.[51]

There were frequent cases of domestic abuse in the servants quarters; women did not have absolute power there. But even this violence may have been less a sign of men's continuing control over their women than a symptom of its disintegration. In the rooms that they controlled, and by virtue of the fact that they controlled them, African women took giant steps in their efforts to acquire a new sense of their own dignity.[52]

Conclusion

By housing their men, workers opened the doors of the city to "illegal" African immigration from the countryside, thus undermining one of the basic assumptions of apartheid, that of white control over urban space. By the mid-1980s, even before the dismantling of apartheid, the National Party government abolished influx control. Its proven impracticability was an important factor in its eventual elimination. Ironically, much of the movement of Africans that so undermined the intent of apartheid's planners took place literally under the noses of domestic workers' white employers. Equally ironically, it was just because this activity took place on private property that it could happen at all.

Most English-speaking whites, even if they disagreed with the government's position on African influx control, did not like the idea of boarding African families in their backyards. But what many disliked even more was the rough intrusions of police—most of whom were working-class Afrikaners—onto their properties. Many argued vehemently, and somewhat disdainfully, with officers literally from the other side of the tracks who tried to get past their private gates to search for undocumented Africans. On principle, they refused to cede their rights to control entry onto their lots. The police had to turn away unsatisfied when an angry madam threatened to turn the dog on anyone who tried to step past her, or when a master swore that he would take the officers to court if they ever disturbed his dinner again.

For other homeowners, a different principle was at stake. A small minority felt so strongly opposed to the government's influx control policies that they practiced civil disobedience in protest, choosing to fight apartheid as it appeared literally at their doorsteps. Precious M.'s madam not only allowed her children to visit during school holidays, she put them up in her own guest room in the main house.[53] Susanna M.'s employer went to jail for fifteen days in protest of apartheid policy rather than pay a fine for illegally harboring an unregistered worker.[54]

White suburbia, the ostensible nurturing grounds for the white nuclear families that formed the core of the apartheid state, served simultaneously as a vast underground railroad station for Africans (fig. 5.9). And the least remarkable structure in these places, the simple domestic worker's back room,

Fig. 5.9. Suburban neighborhood, Parkview, Johannesburg. Few whites suspected all that went on behind the walls and hedges.

was the key to the whole operation. By exploiting their control of these structures and their social and physical environments, servants were able to make space in the city for their loved ones. In the process, they also forged important new places for themselves.

Notes

Many thanks to the South African Domestic Workers Union, its leadership, and members for their warm and supportive cooperation with my research. Thanks, too, to my research assistant, Peggy Twala, for her invaluable help. My research was funded by the University of California's African Studies Center, the Ford Foundation, the Graduate Division of the University of California, and my father. Thanks, as always, to my adviser, Dell Upton, for his encouragement and example.

1. On early, male-dominated domestic service in Johannesburg and the reasons for its collapse, see Charles van Onselen, "The Witches of Suburbia," in *New Nineveh, Studies in the Social and Economic History of the Witwatersrand*, 1886–1914 (Johannesburg: Ravan, 1982).
2. Mabel T., interview by author, tape recording, Johannesburg, June 29, 1996. I have changed the names of all my informants in order to protect their privacy.
3. Unnamed source, cited in Joanne Yawitch. "The Relation between African Female Employment and Influx Control in South Africa, 1950–1983" (master's thesis, Univ. of the Witwatersrand, 1984), 299.
4. Yawitch, "The Relation between African Female Employment and Influx Control," 211–12.
5. Eleanor Mary Preston-Whyte, "Between Two Worlds: A Study of the Working Life, Social Ties, and Interpersonal Relationships of African Women Migrants in Domestic Service in Durban" (Ph.D. diss., Univ. of Natal, Durban, 1969), 62.
6. Cherryl Walker, "Gender and the Development of the Migrant Labour System, c. 1850–1930," in *Women and Gender in Southern Africa to 1945*, 191–94; Virginia Naomi Charlotte Van der Vleit, "Black Marriage: Expectations and Aspirations in an Urban Environment" (master's thesis, Univ. of the Witwatersrand, 1982), 66–67.
7. Walker, *Women and Gender in Southern Africa to 1945*, 187–96; I. Schapera, *Migrant Labour and Tribal Life. A Study of Conditions in the Bechuanaland Protectorate* (London: Oxford Univ. Press, 1947), 67.
8. Unnamed source, cited in Van der Vleit, "Black Marriage," 133.
9. Walker, *Women and Gender in Southern Africa to 1945*, 187–96; Schapera, Migrant Labour and Tribal Life, 67.
10. See, for example, Philip Bonner, "African Urbanisation on the Rand between the 1930s and 1960s: Its Social Character and Political Consequences," *Journal of Southern African Studies* 21, no. 1 (1995): 123.
11. Allen Drury, *"A Very Strange Society": A Journey to the Heart of South Africa* (London: Verso, 1968), 6.
12. Nikolaus Pevsner, "Johannesburg: The Development of a Contemporary Vernacular in the Transvaal," *Architectural Review* 113, no. 679 (June 1953): 361–82.
13. Populations varied during the period under consideration in my paper, from about 1960 until about 1976, but these figures, based on the Reports of the Director of Non-European Affairs Department, City of Johannesburg, for the years in question (Johannesburg Municipal Archives) provide a sufficient sense of size and proportion.
14. On apartheid-era service in South Africa, see

Jacklyn Cock, *Maids and Madams: Domestic Workers under Apartheid* (Johannesburg: Ravan 1980); Eleanor Preston-Whyte, "Race Attitudes and Behaviour: The Case of Domestic Employment in White South African Homes," *African Studies* 35 (1976); Deborah Gaitskell et al., "Class, Race and Gender: Domestic Workers in South Africa," *Review of African Political Economy* 27/28; Michael Whisson and W. Weil, *Domestic Servants: A Microcosm of "The Race Problem"* (Johannesburg: SAIRR, 1971).

15. Precious M., interview by author, tape recording, Johannesburg, July 19, 1995.
16. Alberta S., interview by author, tape recording, Johannesburg, July 17, 1995.
17. Martha T., interview by author, tape recording, Johannesburg, June 29, 1996.
18. Candace N., interview by author, tape recording, Johannesburg, Feb. 14, 1998.
19. Alberta S., interview.
20. Linda S., interview by author, tape recording, Johannesburg, July 17, 1995.
21. Jacqueline M., interview by author, tape recording, Johannesburg, June 29, 1996.
22. Domestic workers did not form relationships with African men only. Although it is beyond the scope of this paper, because it raises a host of additional issues, they also entered liaisons with white, Coloured, and Indian men. However, these cases were a minority. Also beyond the scope of this paper, though a topic that deserves attention and seems to have received none, is lesbian relationships among African workers. When I tried to broach this subject, I was told by informants that it was unthinkable. The taboo nature of the subject has doubtless made it a difficult one for researchers to pursue.
23. Most domestic workers also entered the city illegally, but many had their status regularized by their employers. Those that did not suffered the same insecurities as men who did not have their papers in order.
24. Unnamed source, cited in John McNamara, "Social Life, Ethnicity and Conflict in a Gold Mine Hostel" (master's thesis, Univ. of the Witwatersrand, 1978), 106.
25. McNamara, "Social Life, Ethnicity and Conflict."
26. Dr. Harry Seftel, cited in L. Menge, "'Bachelor' Life Is Breeding Disease," *Star,* Aug. 26, 1972, Univ. of the Witwatersrand Archives, newspaper collection.
27. John McNamara, "Social Life, Ethnicity and Conflict in a Gold Mine Hostel," 106.
28. See, for example, Aubrey Sussens, "If Elias goes, then I must go . . . and so it goes on," *Star,* Sept. 20, 1956, Univ. of the Witwatersrand Archives, newspaper collection.
29. Van der Vleit, "Black Marriage," 198–99.
30. Sally V, interview by author., tape recording, Johannesburg, July 21, 1995.
31. One reason many women sought to keep their boyfriends or lovers at close hand was that they feared the fathers of their children, if not closely supervised, might fail to contribute to the maintenance of those youngsters, being raised by kin back in the rural areas.
32. Ebony D., interview by author, tape recording, Johannesburg, July 2, 1995.
33. Roberta M., interview by author, tape recording, Johannesburg, July 15, 1995.
34. Jacqueline M., interview by author, tape recording, Johannesburg, June 29, 1996.
35. Sally V., interview.
36. Sophia B., interview by author, tape recording, Johannesburg, Feb. 14, 1998. Though this sounds a little preposterous, other informants confirmed the existence of this practice, apparently not an uncommon one.
37. Molly T., interview by author, tape recording, Johannesburg, June 29, 1996.
38. Linda M.

39. Emily M., interview by author, tape recording, Johannesburg, July 19, 1995.
40. Lydia M., interview by author, tape recording, Johannesburg, July 6, 1996.
41. Flora M. interview by author, tape recording, Johannesburg, July 22, 1995.
42. Candy M., interview by author, tape recording, Johannesburg, July 15, 1995.
43. Anita S., interview by author, tape recording, Johannesburg, July 17, 1995.
44. Amy K., interview by author, tape recording, July 22, 1995.
45. Elizabeth M., interview by author, Johannesburg, July 18, 1995.
46. Mrs. Mthinkulu, cited in Deborah Posel, "Marriage at the Drop of a Hat: Housing and the Politics of Gender in Urban African Communities in South Africa, 1930s–1960s" (paper presented at the conference on Africa's Urban Past, SOAS, London, June 19–21, 1996), 23.
47. Van der Vleit, "Black Marriage," esp. 73, 259–67
48. See also Dolly Mapumulo, "Back-room Love Affairs Are Full of Drama, Intrigue," *Star,* Dec. 10, 1963, Univ. of the Witwatersrand archives, newspaper collection.
49. Interview, Linda M.
50. Unnamed source, cited in Van der Vleit, "Black Marriage," 193.
51. Sally M., interview by author, tape recording, Johannesburg, July 27, 1995.
52. Van der Vleit, "Black Marriage," 243.
53. Precious M., interview.
54. "Motherless—By Order," *Star,* Feb. 12, 1973. Univ. of the Witwatersrand Archives, newspaper collection.

CHAPTER 6

Zeynep Kezer

Familiar Things in Strange Places: Ankara's Ethnography Museum and the Legacy of Islam in Republican Turkey

The Ethnography Museum opened its doors to the public in 1930 as one of Ankara's most prominent landmarks. The building's highly visible location atop the Namazgah Hill was punctuated by a cast-bronze Atatürk monument standing in front of its marble portal, on axis with its central dome. From here, hovering over the din and drone of life, the nation's leader silently commanded the city, which, since becoming the new national capital, had been transformed into a giant construction site. Kemal Atatürk was the founder of modern Turkey. He had unified the nationalist movement and masterminded the Independence Struggle against foreign occupation following the defeat and eventual collapse of the Ottoman Empire at the end of World War I. In 1923, upon victory, rather than restoring the empire, he founded the Turkish Republic and chose to relocate the capital from Istanbul to Ankara with the support of a close cadre of nationalist supporters. This was a turning point in Turkish history that marked the country's passage to nation-statehood. In the subsequent years, the nationalists continued to work under his guidance to transform this small, long-forgotten, charmless, and poverty-stricken Anatolian town into what popular propaganda publications defined as "an absolutely new city" that would "symbolize the breakaway from the Ottoman Empire and its heritage" (fig 6.1).[1]

Despite the passionate determination of Atatürk and his followers, the transition from an empire to a nation-state and the relocation of the capital to Ankara were risky moves. The longevity of the neophyte Turkish state depended upon the acknowledgment of its legitimacy externally by its peers and internally by the nation itself. External recognition was achieved at the end of the Independence Struggle with the Lausanne Peace Treaty, in which Turkey's political integrity as a nation-state within a system of modern states was internationally recognized. Nevertheless, internal recognition continued to be a challenge, because in Turkey the people had not yet defined themselves as a nation to the exclusion of other competing, especially religious, identities with strong local and historical roots. To complicate matters more, the general population had little in common with the ruling republican elite, who came from socially and culturally privileged backgrounds and had limited knowledge about the diversity of Anatolian social life and customs.[2]

To facilitate national consolidation, Turkey's leaders broadened the state's jurisdiction to regulate more aspects of people's lives than ever before. While this modernized state apparatus, with its centralized institutional and administrative network performing standardized tasks uniformly throughout the national territory, undoubtedly provided a useful scaffolding for the nascent state by providing procedural unity in bureaucratic pro-

Fig. 6.1. A view of the Ankara Ethnography Museum and the Atatürk Monument in the front. The building in the foreground is the headquarters of the People's Houses, the popular community centers which were used for cultural, recreational, and educational activities. From Fotografla Türkiye Ankara: Matbuat Umum Müdürlüg, 1936.

cesses, it was not sufficient for achieving a stable degree of social cohesion. Building a nation-state also required cultural integration, but the people of Turkey continued to have significant local and regional differences and did not necessarily identify themselves with the goals set for them by their rulers. To remedy this situation, the nationalist leaders also introduced a series of reforms intended expressly to homogenize the polity and consolidate its communal allegiances around the idea of nationhood. At the same time, they tried to eliminate or suppress particularisms that could potentially threaten the sovereignty and the integrity of the neophyte nation-state. One of the top strategies used by the nationalists was to instill in the minds of the people a sense of continuity from the past into the future as a nation with a shared history and a common destiny. Using all the resources available to them, Turkey's leaders single-handedly attempted to define what constituted the nation's history, its destiny, and the path of continuity between the two. Historiography, at the hands of state officials, became a prime tool for forging national unity, used simultaneously to fabricate venerable pasts that never were, and to erase collective remembrances that challenged official ideology.

In this chapter, through the example of the Ethnography Museum, I examine the use of official historiography as a tool for national unification in Turkey. The implications and internal discrepancies of this state-propelled strategy may best be understood through an analysis of spatial practices and material artifacts because it relied heavily on the manipulation of space and its uses. In Turkey, constructing a nationalist historical narrative was a twofold process which simultaneously entailed creative and destructive interventions. During the early years of the Republic, the nationalists introduced new kinds of sociospatial practices designed for the public reaffirmation of nationalist ideals. Hence, official history was not disseminated exclusively through books; it was also spatially constructed and enacted in a variety of ways, ranging from ritual pageants, which incorporated prominent public places into their stylized narratives, to the nomenclature of streets, which made explicit references to selected meaningful events from the past. Didactic spaces by definition, museums and exhibitions, which made use of tangible props to convey their messages more convincingly, were seen as particularly useful tools of indoctrination and were, therefore, frequently used for this purpose. At the same time, the nation's leaders were determined to erect impregnable barriers between the present and the immediate past. They were particularly concerned about the persistence of certain sociospatial practices that reaffirmed premodern communal allegiances. Nationalists believed the sheer existence of these practices in the present was a threat to the national unification process and to the official history, and they felt compelled to alter or sometime completely purge such practices from the public sphere.

The Ethnography Museum provides a particularly significant site for inquiry because it simultaneously embodied the creative and destructive impulses triggered by the nationalist ideology. On the one hand, as a novel institution in Ankara's cultural landscape, the museum was a crucial didactic space for the material representation of the official history of the nation. On the other, the context from which it drew the materials for its collections was the battleground of cultural politics. While within the museum the nationalists tried to define local religious allegiances as obsolete, outside the museum these ties were very much alive. The boundaries the museum intended to establish between the past and the present remained under relentless contestation. Inextricably implicated in both processes, the story of the Ethnography Museum is, therefore, a useful parable for understanding the coexistence of widely divergent kinds of experience, imagination, and remembrance within the same physical space despite their glaring contradictions.

The Ethnography Museum as a Tool for Official Historiography

The leaders of the neophyte Turkish state regarded the making of a new capital as an opportunity to inscribe the structural transformation of the state into the physical landscape, and they allotted a significant portion of the state's resources to various construction projects in Ankara. Theirs was an ambitious venture that required substantial human and material assets, but in the aftermath of long and devastating wars, Turkey's funds were limited and skilled labor was scarce. Consequently, despite intense efforts, the completion of major government buildings stretched for over two decades as several offices continued to be housed in makeshift structures and competition for construction funding remained stiff. Under these circumstances, the nationalists' decision to grant priority to the Ethnography Museum suggests that they expected it to perform an indispensable function within the cultural life of the new capital.

Embracing the new Ankara in the front, but built on the brim of the old town, with the citadel at its back, the museum stood like a threshold between the two parts of the town (fig. 6.2). Interestingly, the sense of physical in-betweenness exuded by the building's location seemed to echo its intended function as a jarring separator between the past and the present. The museum was surrounded by a cluster of new buildings, all of which housed the novel cultural institutions generated by the republic.[3] Together, these buildings clearly faced forward, bridging the present into the future. But the museum did so through a curious use of the past. On the one hand, the past served as a frame for the building, highlighting its newness and its future-bound outlook. Seen from the boulevard, tall and white, it sat on the Namazgah Hill in stark contrast against the fabric of the old town at its back. On the other hand, the museum itself was intended to be the frame through which the past was to be viewed, since its collection was advertised as consisting mainly of historic artifacts. By juxtaposing the past and the future as frames for one another, the museum also became a metaphorical threshold between them, a vantage point whence it was possible to look both ways simultaneously.

The museum's stately entrance was accentuated by two wide flights of white marble stairs leading to a colonnaded portico. Inside the building, past the handsome brass doors, was a space unlike anything the people of Ankara were likely to have seen before. Upon walking in, the visitors found themselves in the main hall, where myriad colorful artifacts such as exotic costumes, ornaments, and antique guns lured them back in time. This central hall featured a mixture of exhibits consisting of various artifacts from different parts of Turkey as well as objects from such faraway lands as North America, Australia, and the Pacific Islands.[4] Moving to the right, the visitors could walk through a sequence of interconnected smaller rooms surrounding the entrance hall (fig. 6.3). In these side spaces, the focus of the collection shifted closer to home and the objects on display looked decidedly more familiar. The exhibits in these rooms included tools, furnishings, and other accouterments pertinent to village life and agricultural production in the Turkish countryside; specimens of various regional traditional handicrafts; and religious artifacts.

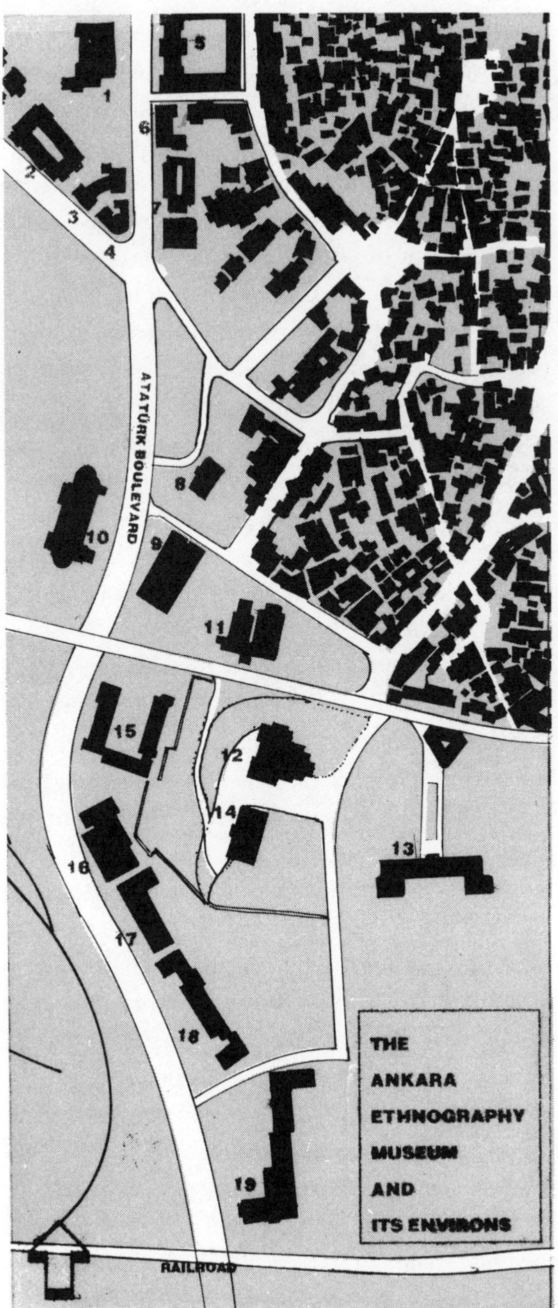

Fig. 6.2. Site plan of the Ethnography Museum with other important buildings constructed during the first fifteen years of the Republic (drawing by the author): (1) Headquarters of the State Agricultural Bank; (2) Belvü Palas, Apartotel building, rented mainly by high government officials and members of parliament; (3) the general directorate of Pious Endowments; (4) Ottoman Bank; (5) Tasmektep, late-nineteenth-century school building used during the independence struggle and in the early years of the republic as the headquarters of the Joint Chiefs of Staff; (6) State Customs and Monopolies Administration Headquarters; (7) Housing Credit and Orphans Bank; (8) first building of the Ankara Law School; (9) ministry of Foreign Affairs; (10) State Exhibition Hall; (11) New School of Commerce; (12) headquarters of People's Houses; (13) Ankara Model Hospital; (14) Ankara Ethnography Museum; (15) Turkish Aviation Society; (16) Municipalities Bank; (17) Ankara Radio Offices; (18) Ismet Pasha Institute for Girls; (19) Faculty of Language History and Geography.

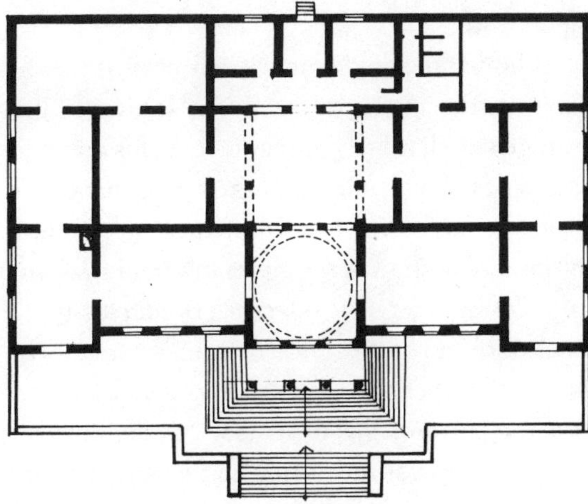

Fig. 6.3. Plan of the Ethnography Museum. Drawing by the author, based on sketches from the archives of the Ethnography Museum.

These were randomly interspersed with occasional archaeological finds brought from Roman and Hittite excavation sites around Ankara.[5]

Uprooted from their familiar surroundings, these artifacts had been tossed together with objects from faraway lands and remote times, and had little in common with each other beyond the dislocation they all had undergone. The indiscriminate mixture of religious, utilitarian, exotic, and archaeological items glossed over their historical and geographical differences. The rather eclectic and anachronistic arrangements of the displays further highlighted the complete disentanglement of these artifacts from the collective practices that bestowed them with meaning. Since the exhibition provided little contextual information about their uses, similarities, origin, or the criteria for their selection, the exhibits stood in a peculiar arrangement that highlighted their formal properties over their cultural significance.

Although the apparent arbitrariness of the displays in the museum made the logic of their arrangement hard to grasp at first, a closer examination of these artifacts and their provenances revealed a purposeful pattern in their selection. A substantial portion of the museum's holdings came from *tekkes* (dervish lodges) and *zaviyes* (guild lodges), places of religious communion and learning used by the members of Sufi orders known as *tarikats* (Sufi orders).[6] Tarikats were religious sects that practiced various vernacular versions of heterodox Islam and used tekkes and zaviyes as their congregational spaces. In addition to furniture and various accessories used in rituals, tekke and zaviye complexes were also rich repositories for ancient literary texts and arts and crafts such as calligraphy, illumination, and marquetry. Tekkes and zaviyes, of which there were thousands scattered throughout the country, provided ample source material for the museum. Once in the museum, the functional and spatial relations that connected these artifacts at their places of origin were overridden by their curators' classificatory principles and practical concerns. Hence, rather than reconstructing the contextual relationships between the objects by placing the object brought from the same tekke together, the displays provided typological series where artifacts of the same kind were exhibited together regardless of their provenance. As a result, rosaries from different parts of the country and different tarikats were placed in the same glass case and headdresses were placed in another. Irregularly shaped larger articles were placed according to the availability of space in their new settings. Hence, the door of a tekke from Sivas found a place at the side of a casket of a Sufi dervish from Ankara and next to the glass cases containing the headdresses and rosaries (fig. 6.4). In short, the displays deliberately refrained from reconstituting the interior of an actual tekke or suggesting how these objects were used or placed in it. Instead, the dates and short descriptions labeling each item depicted it as a unique piece frozen at a particular moment in the flow of history. Moreover, the glass cases surrounding the exhibits rendered them physically inaccessible to the viewers and symbolically demarcated them from the present. The effect of this conceptual compartmentalization between the past and the present was particularly disconcerting to an audience who, for the most part, had never visited a museum.

Museums and exhibitions have their roots in the Enlightenment, but proliferated with the emergence of the modern state. By the end of the nineteenth century in Europe, museums and exhibitions were commonly regarded as instructional settings with a looser format and a broader audience than formal educational institutions, and several Euro-

Fig. 6.4. A hand-carved wood pulpit on exhibit. From *La Turquie Kamaliste* (1943).

pean states used them as major instruments in shaping the orientation of the moral values of their respective populations.[7] Museums and exhibitions were designed to facilitate learning through the actual performance of circulation in space, and they relied on the persuasive power of the material artifact held as the physical evidence of an argument conveyed spatially. In Turkey, museums as public buildings with a didactic purpose were relatively new, and they certainly were unprecedented in Ankara. The only precedent available to the nationalists was the Istanbul Archaeology Museum, which was inaugurated in 1891 as the first of its kind in the Ottoman Empire.[8] Curated by the French-trained scholar Osman Hamdi Bey, the Archaeology Museum showcased findings from various excavations of Greek and Roman sites within the empire.[9] Beyond a lesson in classical archaeology, the museum was meant to convey a political statement claiming the unity of the Ottoman Empire through a collective display of its historical commonwealth in its capital at a time when emergent nationalisms and colonial capitalism was gnawing at its borders on all sides.[10] The existence of a local example in Istanbul, and the nationalists' own exposure to various European prototypes through either their education or their travels, provided them with crucial ideas and strategies for deploying space for political purposes in Ankara. Although, by comparison, the Ethnography Museum was smaller in size and its contents were not as numerous, it had clearly been based upon these models. Similarly, even though it fell short of the standards set by its European counterparts due to a chronic lack of funds and the kind of expertise necessary to run a comparably large enterprise, it certainly shared similar goals of instilling the ideological agenda of the state in the minds of its people.[11]

What set the Ethnography Museum apart from its predecessors, making it decidedly a product of the early republican period in Turkey, was the focus of its collection. In those years—and until recently—the display of artifacts pertinent to "exotic" foreign cultures in order to highlight the sophistication of the collectors' culture was a common practice. But in the Ethnography Museum, the exhibits consisted of familiar things still part of everyday use, which were labeled as historical and placed on display for the viewing of the locals. These objects were presented as props of a premodern way of life that had already been left behind in the nation's quest for modernity. By taking the familiar out of its context and thereby estranging it from its common users, the Ethnography Museum deliberately attempted to seal off from the present the practices and objects that defined a way of life that, according to the official ideology, was to remain in the past. This was official history at work, negotiating the boundaries of the past and the present in the physical space of the museum. Such an arrangement conveyed a teleological notion of civilization and suggested that in this process of linear development, equipped with a grasp of objective knowledge and harnessed to technological improvements, the people of Turkey, too, would evolve into a modern civilized nation. In other words, the nation's history was a long single-minded journey toward modernity, the milestones of which were preserved in museums as relics of the past to be remembered but carefully kept at a safe distance. Accordingly, history and destiny were envisioned as the two ends of a single, unified, and unifying path that extended into eternity.

While the nationalists regarded official history as an indispensable tool for constituting the Turkish nation out of people who lived in Turkey, they were neither accurate nor consistent in the way they used it. Hence, for instance, while the Ethnography Museum was expressly designed to exclude aspects of the immediate present by situating them in the past, Archaeology Museum, located just a few hundred yards away, was used to "revive" historical lineages that did not exist in the first place. In the latter museum, the growing collection of artifacts from various archaeological excavation sites were held as the evidence of Asia Minor's rich history, reinforcing its position as "the cradle of civilization." In their attempt to stretch the origins of Turkish presence in the land further back in time, the nationalists took license to include preclassical cultures such as the Hittites and Phrygians in the master narrative of the nation's history.[12] Official historiography, as represented in these museums, silenced rival narratives and alternative paths and prohibited criticism. In defining the nation's "manifest" path toward modernity, the nationalists monopolized the places and means by which the collective memory was to be stored.

Religious Landscapes as the Battleground of Cultural Politics

Museums and heritage sites, Dean MacCannell suggests, "establish in consciousness the definition and boundary of modernity by rendering concrete and immediate that which modernity is not."[13] Further, he maintains that "the best indication of the final victory of modernity over other sociocultural arrangements is not the disappearance of the non-modern world but its artificial preservation and conservation in modern society."[14] Yet what makes the story of the Ethnography Museum interesting is the incompleteness of its conquest of the premodern ways of life and its failure to frame them exclusively as history. Despite their widespread use for precisely that purpose during the early years of the republic, it would be naive to assume that museums and exhibitions could single-handedly achieve the kind of indoctrination prescribed by the state. In the case of the Ethnography Museum, the exhibits were not merely withdrawn from their former realms of circulation, and thus severed from their functional contexts, but were placed in another realm with a different and narrower audience. The museum was the domain of the educated republican urban elites who conceived it in the first place. A strange place by definition, it remained outside the experience of most of the common people, for whom it was intended to serve as a didactic tool and whose lives were already disrupted when objects essential to their daily lives were extracted to be made an exhibit.

In contrast to the solemn silence inside, outside the confines of the museum the landscape was a battleground, because every novelty introduced displaced something old and deeply ingrained. The modernizing mission of the state took the form of constant attacks on precisely those premodern ways of organizing life that had been placed under preservation in the museum. But while the museum pretended to portray them as obsolete, they survived, albeit shaken and transformed. In turn, their persistence challenged and at times shook the grounds of the museum and the ideology it stood for. If, as Adorno suggests, we can envision the gap between reality and ideology as irony's medium, we may look at the museum as a threshold in yet another sense, as an ironic threshold between competing realities, the existence each of which calls the other into question.[15] Thresholds and boundaries are not mere separators but also advantageous positions that afford critical juxtapositions of the realms they are meant to demarcate. Hence, while the nationalist leaders intended to use it as a barrier between the modern and the premodern, the museum, standing between reality and ideology, was also a threshold that offered a rare glimpse into the discrepancies of the process of rapid cultural transformation propelled by the state.

Having traced the lineage of the museum, we now need to turn in the other direction and trace the exhibits back to their sources and examine how the extraction of familiar things from their habitual surroundings was linked to larger forces at work. Consequently, it is more productive to assess the museum not exclusively in terms of the novel sociospatial experience it offered, but also as part of a broader process of dismantling an entire cultural landscape for the making of another. At an abstract level, this process entailed legislative maneuvers but became most painfully visible when it cut into the fabric of everyday life through the elimination or the radical modification of some social and spatial relations. State presence became evident when interventions small in scale but broad in scope began to affect the cycle of life in the most immediate environment.

As a key element in the constitution and sustenance of social life that could—and did—rival nationalism, religion was the prime target of such interventions. In a speech delivered in Kastamonu, Atatürk announced that the "mentalities that [were] incapable of accepting the revolutionary drive to modernize and civilize the nation [would] be irrevocably purged" because it was not possible "to bring the light of truth into the minds of such people."[16] Commanding the heads of tarikats to close their tekkes immediately, he declared, "May it be well-known to all, that the Turkish Republic is no place for *sheikhs* (tarikat leaders), their disciples, and sympathizers."[17] According to him, if the ultimate purpose of a tarikat was the procurement of worldly and spiritual happiness for its followers, from then on the truest tarikat (path) had to be that modern civilization. In this age of science and rational thinking, it was unacceptable to be so naive as to seek those in the so-called wisdom of a sheikh.[18] Atatürk saw the activities of tarikats not merely as roadblocks on "the nation's manifest path toward modern civilization" but as a divisive threat to the integrity of the nation and the sovereignty of the state as well.[19] According to the government, these had become breeding grounds for subversive political activities under the guise of religious practices. What is more, sheikhs, dervishes, and other men of the cloth with ulterior motives were luring the masses and manipulating public opinion against the policies of the state.

Consequently in an attempt to preempt religion's stronghold over collective allegiances and to repattern them around secular nationalist ideas, the nationalist leaders actively engaged in eradicating the physical presence of religion in the landscape. This process became especially noticeable in the landscape because it took the form of spatial obliteration. Beginning in 1925, all sacred sites were closed, such as mausoleums, shrines, lodges, and other congregational spaces that belonged to tarikats and in which locally based heterodox forms of Islam were practiced, and related offices were outlawed by a series of executive decisions.[20] The closures were conducted under the supervision of local commissions consisting of administrative officers and representatives from the State Directorate of Pious Endowments (Vakifs) and they were highly conspicuous acts of severance. The members of these commissions went to every single known site, inspected the interiors, itemized their contents, and produced several copies of the inventories for archival purposes. Moreover, they assessed the value of every object, picked out those of artistic or historical value, and discarded the rest. Upon departure, they sealed the doors with a bright red sign, forbidding trespass—let alone use—under any circumstances. The pieces chosen by the commissions, including entire sets of interior furnishings, carpets, kilims and prayer rugs, hand-carved mihrabs, and bookstands, clothing and accessories, musical instruments, and even the caskets of mystics and sect leaders from various parts of the country, were then packed and sent to the museum in Ankara. Once at the Ethnography Museum, a further selection was made and the pieces with higher artistic merit or intricate craftsmanship were picked for exhibition, while hundreds of others were placed in storage.

The demise of the tarikats did not exclusively entail the closure of their congregational spaces or sites of pilgrimage. Rituals and prayers were not the only functions that engaged communal allegiances. The practice of vernacular religion transcended the purely spiritual and extended into the landscape in a variety of ways as an ever-growing network of commercial, pious, civic connections that bound people together, reinforcing the sense of social cohesion. Commercial and agricultural properties and their revenues that had originally been granted as pious endowments to support the tarikats were also appropriated by the state and funneled into new projects. It was as though a layer was forcefully being peeled off of the landscape. As a result, what had once been busy street corners or tucked away congregational spaces, shrines, and other sacred sites—in short, nodes of social life large and small—were sealed away from the patterns of everyday use. The charities they sustained also died with them: street fountains that quenched the thirst of passersby dried; endowed stores, orchards, and fields changed hands; lodges and retreats were razed; schools and student dormitories were taken over.

Moreover, while the collections of the museum served as a safe repository for the clothes and accessories worn by the followers of these orders, the wearing of these items in public was banned by law with very serious penalties for violations.[21] Previously, in the Ottoman town, what one wore and how he carried himself in public were primarily an expression of the self as part of his devotion to a particular tarikat and the community of its followers. Religious garb was about distinction. It was not simply worn but attained after the

Fig. 6.5. Mevlevi Dervishes wearing accessories that indicate their position within the order in a mid-nineteenth-century photograph. From *The Dervish Lodge: Architecture, Art, and Sufism in Ottoman, Turkey*, ed. Raymond Lifchez (Berkeley: Univ. of California Press, 1992). Courtesy of the University of California Press.

completion of a series of rites, and it proudly displayed one's specific persuasion and rank within the order. Far beyond mere appearances, clothing and accessories were part of a system of meanings, a medium of communication where at least a rudimentary recognition of the coding was essential for one's orientation within the urban landscape (figs. 6.5, 6.6).

Even death did not do away with such distinctions and merit. When the saints and mystics, notables, and elders who lived among the people and commanded their respect died, they were usually buried in neighborhood cemeteries, frequently adjacent to the lodge itself where they remained close and present. Their gravestones, sculpted out of marble, identified who was buried at that site, because the stones were carved to resemble the distinctive headdresses of the individual devotees, and a few verses of poetry paid tribute to their pious deeds in this world.[22] These burial grounds en-

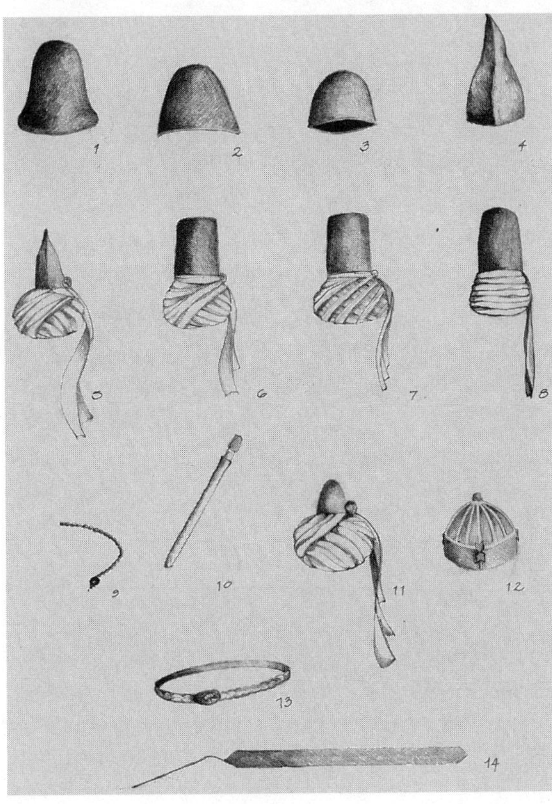

Fig. 6.6. Miscellaneous ritual headdresses and accessories used by the members of the Mevlevi order (1) dal sikke; (2) seyfi külah yandan; (3) arakiyye yandan; (4) seyfi külah (front view); (5) cüneyd-i destar; (6) seker avize destar (wrapped destar); (7) seker aviz kafes-i destar (destar wrapped in lattice pattern); (8) dolama destar (simple wrapped destar); (9) habbe (accessory made of a semiprecious stone attached to a silver or nickel chain, worn usually on the shoulder or the chest); (10) hizmet ("service"), an accessory symbolizing the dervish's formal training in the two kitchens of the Mevlevi order, where the production and consumption of food was an important part of the ritual practices; (11) örfi destar (sikke wrapped in melon form); (12) sikke-i duvazdeh-küngüre (cap of Shams, a close friend of Mevlana Celaleddin Rumi and one of the founding fathers of the order); (13) kemer (belt with ornamental buckle and semiprecious stones); (14) Elif-i nemed (cummerbund). Drawings by the author, based on sketches by Abdülbaki Gölpinarli in *Mevlana'dan sonra Mevlevilik* (Istanbul, 1953).

sconced in cul-de-sacs or nestled in small yards were common and frequent components of the Ottoman townscape. They were open, visible, and accessible. Yet small cemeteries sprinkled in neighborhoods and several larger ones in more prominent locations of town were also expropriated. While valuable and aesthetically pleasing samples of gravestones were transported to the backyard of the Ethnography Museum, others were often discarded (fig. 6.7).

Religion received an even more shattering blow when in 1928 the government moved to prepare a master list of mosques in the country. Accordingly, all the mosques in Turkey were inventoried and classified according to size of staff and congregation, the number of services offered, and historical and aesthetic values. The result was a catalogue containing information about their numbers, locations, contents, land holdings, and liquid assets that supported them. Based on this data, neighborhood mosques deemed too small to be sustainable were to be shut down. The numbers were to be curtailed so that no two mosques would be closer to each other than five hundred meters.[23] Hence, one by one in Ankara, as elsewhere, small mosques that had defined neighborhoods by sound, with the range of human voice summoning the people to prayer five times a day, were sealed and closed. As a result, the sights and sounds that gave definition to a particular spatial organization were gradually changing (fig. 6.8).

Despite active state intervention in placing restrictions on the public performance of religious rites, forbidden sites were open to constant sur-

Fig. 6.7. Dervish gravestones from the Mevlevi order in an Istanbul cemetery. The stones are carved to resemble the headdresses provided in fig 6.6. From *The Dervish Lodge: Architecture, Art, and Sufism in Ottoman, Turkey,* ed. Raymond Lifchez (Berkeley: Univ. of California Press, 1992). Courtesy of the University of California Press.

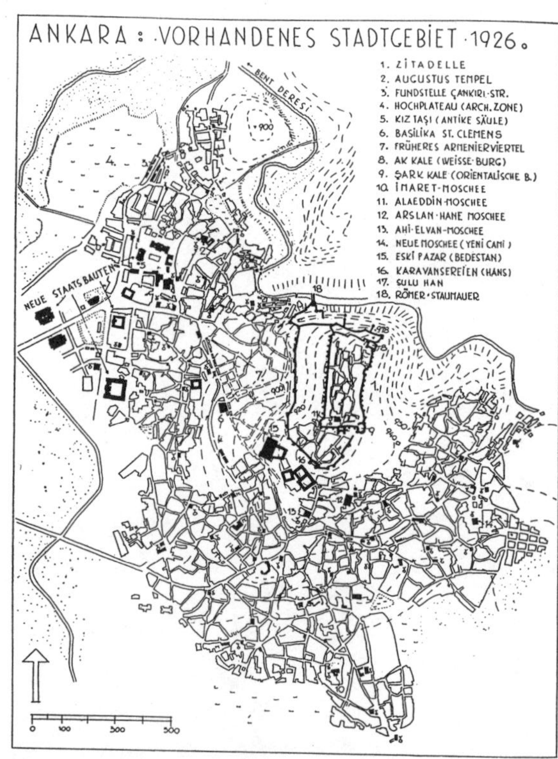

Fig. 6.8. The plan of Ankara in 1926 before the expansion of the new capital. In addition to the larger and more remarkable mosques named in the key of the plan, the small darkened squares with the sign indicate mosques. From Alfred Cuda, *Stadtaufbau in der Türkei* (Burg b. M.: Druck von A. Hopfer, 1939).

reptitious forays. Neither religious activities nor allegiances could be obliterated by the closure and confiscation of sacred sites. These practices were pushed toward the margins of visibility and at times severely penalized, but they continued to exist clandestinely.[24] At the heart of the old town, for instance, the Friday rituals performed by the followers of the Bayrami order at the mausoleum of Haci Bayram Veli had been outlawed in 1925. While a lock and a red seal conspicuously declared the site off limits to the general public, when night fell, skittish flocks of believers gathered at the mausoleum and lit candles by its doors and prayed in quiet. Ironically, the silent mumbling of prayers often included the voices of the members of the nationalist elite as well. According to the neighborhood residents who watched and partook in the nightly pilgrimages, women, "elegantly dressed in fur coats and high heels, with rouge on their lips," sometimes even accompanied by their spouses, dressed in suits, joined the "superstitious" natives in making wishes and lighting candles.[25] Policing local sites of pilgrimage such as Haci Bayram did not help either. As if to defy the administration, for every crackdown more people found ways of sneaking in and leaving cryptic carvings to evidence their visits in the dark. The street signs that changed the name of the district frequently disappeared, the seals were broken and locks were cut, but prosecution was rendered impossible by the deliberate silence of the people who chose to claim them to be the mystical vengeance of Muslim saints who had been sacrilegiously dislocated by the government's harsh actions.[26]

Religion had historically played a constitutive role in Turkish society, shaping moral and cultural values and permeating popular imagination in every conceivable way. It mediated spiritual matters between God and the individual and social matters between individuals within their communities. No one, not even the leaders of the republic as demonstrated by their own ambivalences at the gates of the Haci Bayram Mausoleum, was immune to its pervasive presence. Therefore to take religion on in a direct head-on collision would be a dangerous step for the state. Yet the nation's leaders clearly felt the need to regulate religion and confine its domain of influence because it threatened the constitution of the nation-state at two levels: First, the practice of orthodox Islam, which promoted the unity of all Islamic peoples, conflicted with the premises of a nation-state because it transcended national boundaries, expanding into far-flung lands. Second, the practice of heterodox Islam also conflicted with nationalism because the presence of local enclaves of power that came to life in tangible and immediate communal practices threatened to fragment the national territory.

The former was an allegiance that at the time did not pose any actual political danger, and in terms of its formulation and practical mechanisms was as "imagined" a community as the modern nation was. The leaders of the republic were quick to seize upon the similarity and deployed orthodox Islam for the purposes of the state, using it as a means of homogenization across the country. The administration of religious services was brought under the auspices of the Directorate of Religious Affairs, which was in charge of keeping strict checks on the qualifications of the religious personnel, the views divulged by them, and the overall homogenization of religious activities. Moreover, in 1930 the language of prayer calls was switched from Arabic to Turkish, and Friday sermons were standardized throughout the country, becoming channels for the dissemination of nationalist themes from the pulpit to the masses.

In contrast, vernacular heterodox Islam was a

very real threat, and state policies were intently geared toward the eradication of its subversive presence. Hence, a closer reading of the laws with the structure of the land tenure in mind reveals that it was the mosques and the lodges of the heterodox vernacular Islam that were more likely to be closed down. Their lands and assets were more prone to appropriation. Urban real estate and agricultural lands, the ownership of which became obsolete with the banning of tarikats and/or closure of mosques, were swiftly handed over by the government to new owners for new and more "acceptable" uses, or the properties simply fell into disrepair as if to bespeak their extinction.

Expropriations and other property transactions resulting from the government's attempts at undermining the constitutive role of Islam within the fabric of everyday life and relegating it to the past were particularly visible in Ankara because the republican leaders intended the new capital as a model for the rest of the country. A surprising number of Ankara's most outstanding buildings were built on endowed properties or were funded by revenues appropriated from the pious foundations that owned them. It was on such an expropriated property, which had historically been used for mass prayers, that on one early morning in April 1925 the foundations of the Ethnography Museum were laid.[27] The Namazgah Hill, which meant "the place of prayer," on the brim of the old town, was where for generations the natives of Ankara had gone to pray for rain and bounty of crops as well as to lay their dead on the hillside overlooking the plains extending westward. And not so long ago, during the independence struggle, they stood in prostration to pray for victory together with the would-be republican elites. With the construction of the museum and the neighboring modern institutions, the cemetery on the hill was displaced and a handful of small mausoleums, which had been sites of pilgrimage for people coming to make wishes and pay respects to the fallen saints of their faith, were dislodged forever. Yet in a most portentous twist of fate, when in 1938, Kemal Atatürk himself died at the age of 57, the domed entrance hall of the museum was designated as a temporary resting place for his body for fifteen years, until a permanent mausoleum was built for him. Once more, the Namazgah Hill, with the museum at its top, became an official pilgrimage site, ironically bringing this story to a full circle. In the end, as new layers of Ankara's spatial palimpsest were placed on the Namazgah Hill, the museum became not only a strange place for familiar things, but also a strange thing in a familiar place.

Notes

1. Anonymous, "Ankara-Istanbul," *La turquie kamaliste* (Apr. 1944): 44.
2. Atatürk and most of his acolytes had a military-bureaucratic background. While few were sons of wealthy and powerful Ottoman families, many came from an urban middle-class background and had a good education, especially by the standards of the time. Their professional training, fashioned after Western models, had exposed them to European history and philosophy during their formative years. Long before becoming actively involved in the founding of the Turkish Republic, Atatürk and his cohorts were members of clandestine groups that criticized the Ottoman imperial administration and sought alternatives for reform and modernization. Their connections with Turkish intellectuals who lived and studied in France and their own language skills gave France a particularly prominent position as a source of ideas and strategies in formulating their own solutions to what they saw to be the problems of the Ottoman Empire. They shared a common

interest in the French Revolution, and, not surprisingly, they tapped into the ideas and strategies they had observed in the modernization of France when formulating their own break from the Ottoman heritage. A comparison of the strategies used by the French revolutionists and later government administrators to break with the past and to homogenize national culture bear a striking resemblance to those used by the Turkish nationalists. For a detailed account of these strategies in France, see Lynn Hunt's *Politics, Culture and Class in the French Revolution* (Berkeley: Univ. of California Press, 1984), Eugene Weber's *Peasants into Frenchmen* (Stanford: Stanford Univ. Press, 1977), and Eilean Hooper-Greenhill's *Museums and the Shaping of Knowledge* (London: Routledge, 1992). For the case of Turkey, see Bernard Lewis's *The Making of Modern Turkey* (Oxford: Oxford Univ. Press, 1962). For the connections between Turkish nationalism and French thought, see Serif Mardin, *The Genesis of Young Ottoman Thought* (Princeton: Princeton Univ. Press, 1962).

3. The buildings around the Ethnography Museum included the new school of commerce, the Ankara Model Hospital, the headquarters of the People's Houses (national community centers), the Turkish Aviation Society Headquarters, and the Faculty of Language History and Geography, to name a few.
4. Ernest Mamboury, *La guie touristique de Ankara* (Ankara, 1934), 229–30.
5. Ibid., 230.
6. The following short definitions are based on those provided in the Raymond Lifchez, ed., *The Dervish Lodge* (Berkeley: Univ. of California Press, 1992):

   Dervish: The term literally means "seeker of doors," more commonly it is used to refer to the follower of a tarikat.

   Tarikat: The Sufi path as a whole; the inward dimension of a religion; a Sufi order associated with the name of its founder.

   Tekke: Dervish lodge, a congregational space for the members of the tarikat.

   Zaviye: A congregational space for the members of guilds. Anatolian guilds *(ahilik)* were professional fraternities with a strong religious aspect; membership practices often included devotional practices similar to those of a tarikat.

7. T. Bennet, *The Birth of the Museum* (London: Routledge, 1995), 89–90, 100; Susan Pearce, *Museums, Objects and Collections* (Washington, D.C.: Smithsonian Institution, 1993), 3–4.
8. Although the military gear and weaponry collections of the Ottoman Army were put on display as early as the mid-1800s, the accessibility and audience of that exhibition was extremely limited.
9. Arik Remzi Oguz, Türk müzeciligine bir bakis (Istanbul: Milli Egitim Basimevi, 1953), 3–4.
10. I am indebted to Ayfer Bartu for pointing this out in a discussion.
11. Pearce, Museums, *Objects and Collections*, 3.
12. Even a brief scanning of high school history textbooks, scholarly and nonscholarly journals of the time, and a stream of government-sponsored propaganda publications reveals the recurring theme in Turkish historiographical discourse of Asia Minor as the cradle of ancient civilizations.
13. Dean MacCannell, *The Tourist* (New York: Schocken Books, 1976), 84.
14. Ibid., 84.
15. Theodor Adorno, *Minima Moralia* (London: Verso, 1985), 218.
16. Bernard. Lewis, *The Emergence of Modern Turkey* (Oxford: Oxford Univ. Press, 1968), 410.
17. Mustafa Imece, *Ataturk'un sapka devriminde*

kastamonu ve inebolu seyahatleri (Ankara: Is Bankasi Yayinlari, 1975), 63.

18. Ibid., 64.
19. Ibid.
20. *Vakiflar kanunu*, Zabit Ceridesi, 1928 art. 677, Vakiflar mecmuasi (Ankara: Vakiflar Umum Müdürlügü, 1942), 9–13. More information about the closures of orders and the confiscation of their property is available in the surveys by Nazif Öztürk in his book *Türk yenilesme tarihi cercevesinde vakif müessesesi* (Ankara: Diyanet Vakfi Yayinlari, 1995) and Hikmet Tanyu in *Ankara ve cevresinde adak yerleri* (Ankara: Ankara Üniversitesi, 1968).
21. *Kiyafet kanunu*, Zabit Ceridesi, 1926.
22. Hand Peter Laqueur, "Dervish Gravestones," in *Dervish Lodge*, ed. Raymond Lifchez (Berkeley: Univ. of California Press, 1992), 284–94.
23. *Vakiflar mecmuasi*, 16.
24. Tanyu, *Ankara ve cevresinde adak yerleri*, 82–84.
25. Ibid., 76–77, 81. See also Nezihe Araz, *Anadolu evliyalari* (Istanbul: Atlas Kitabevi, 1975), 79.
26. Tanyu, *Ankara ve cevresinde adak yerleri*, 68, Araz, Anadolu evliyalari, 147–48.
27. Osman Aksoy, *Etnografya müzesi rehberi* (Istanbul: TTOK Yayinlari, 1980), 3.

CHAPTER 7

Elaine Jackson-Retondo

Manufacturing Moral Reform: Images and Realities of a Nineteenth-Century American Prison

On an early summer afternoon in 1831 James Whittier, a young banker's apprentice in Boston, set forth with two companions in search of entertainment. They ventured first to the commons, found nothing to their liking, then proceeded to the navy yard in Charlestown to tour the man-of-war *Columbia*. Still in want of further distractions, the three young men walked down the road to the state prison with the intention of taking a tour. Upon arrival, they unexpectedly encountered an entrance fee of twenty-five cents per visitor. Unwilling to pay, they left with their curiosities unfulfilled, walked across Prison Point Bridge to Lechmere Point, and concluded their day at the Glass House (fig. 7.1).[1] The path traveled by Whittier and his friends during this one afternoon united four otherwise unrelated places into a common landscape of casual didactic entertainment. The interest of the trio was not unusual; had they been prepared to remit the fee they would have added to the thousands of visitors who toured the state prison annually.[2] A variety of people, including local citizens and foreign dignitaries like Gustave Beaumont and Alexis de Tocqueville, visited the institution. Like James Whittier, many also toured other local attractions.

Guidebooks to the city of Boston provided the potential prison tourist with detailed descriptions and high points of prison tours.[3] R. L. Midgley's 1856 *Guide to Boston and Suburbs* not only told potential visitors what they might see at the Massachusetts State Prison, but also suggested how to interpret what they would experience: "A visit to the workrooms, comprising the shoemaking, whip

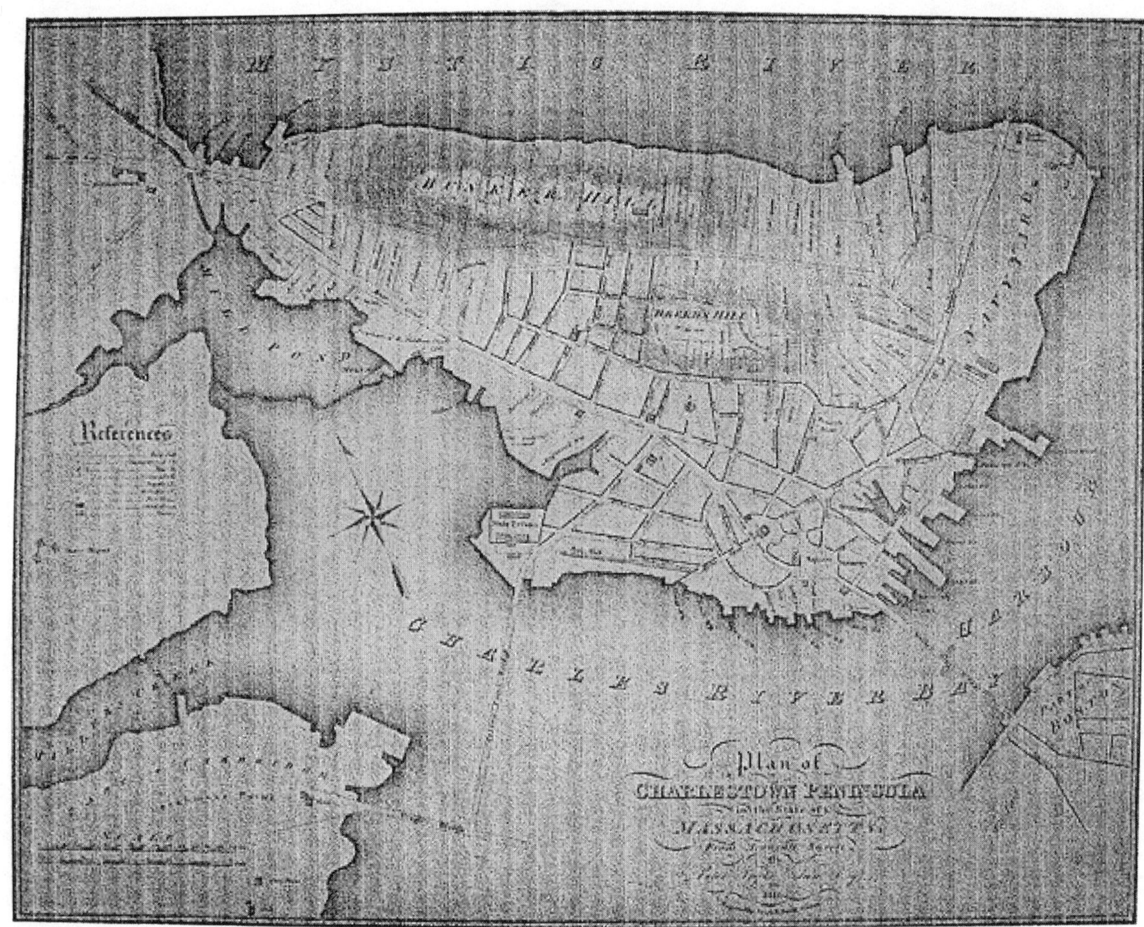

Fig. 7.1. Charlestown Peninsula, 1818. Courtesy of American Antiquarian Society.

making, cabinet making, stone cutting, blacksmithing, upholstering and other departments, generally pleases the visitor, and calls forth encomiums for the stillness, order and cleanliness observed."[4]

But not all visitors, nor those directly involved in the institutional routine, interpreted their prison experiences through the lens of guidebook boosterism or reform rhetoric.

British author John Ross Dix, for example, offered a different interpretation of the manufacturing scene in his book *Local Loiterings and Visits in the Vicinity of Boston*, which he published in 1845 under the pseudonym of "a looker-on."[5] After a visit to the Massachusetts State Prison, Dix wrote: "Here were heaps of furniture in different stages of manufacture; and if the men about had not worn the prison dress, I should have imagined myself to have been in a cabinet maker's wholesale establishment. All around were workshops of different trades."[6] Unlayered with symbolic interpretation, the scene is presented for what it was: a commercial enterprise operating within the confines of a penal institution.

The workshops were arguably the most dynamic spaces within the prison. Here reformers' beliefs, the public view of ordinary citizens, and the interests of officials, legislators, convicts, and independent contractors dovetailed to determine the daily interactions and practices of both the workshops and the institution at large. Yet scholarship regarding nineteenth-century prisons often limits itself to the idealized forms and the theoretical relationship of the inmate to prison authority presented in reform literature. Beyond these there were underrepresented spaces like the workshops and unprescribed experiences and interactions that played an important role in the constitution of the prison landscape. This chapter analyzes the disparity between an image of the prison based in reform theory and the realities of prison experience, space, and form. Prison workshops and the ways various actors interacted with and experienced the prison are at the forefront of the discussion.

The most well-known accounts of reformed prisons were seminal interpretations written during the 1970s (David Rothman, 1971; Michel Foucault, 1975; Michael Ignatieff, 1978).[7] In these works, the longstanding interpretive model that had explained nineteenth-century prisons and prison reform in terms of humanitarian intentions "compounded by unintended consequences" was abandoned for an approach geared toward analysis of the relationship nineteenth-century prison reforms had to political, economic, and social structures.[8] Building upon the social theories of Emile Durkheim, Karl Marx, Max Weber, as well as other theorists, Rothman, Ignatieff, and Foucault connected punishment practices to larger social patterns of interaction, domination, and power. While the methodologies of these works continue to influence academic discourse, the evidence for the three interpretations is derived primarily from extraordinary circumstances and the idealized forms and theories presented in reform literature. Daily practice, actual built environment, and everyday experience of prisons fall through the analytical frameworks.

The Massachusetts State Prison at Charlestown was a physical product of interests founded in prison reform ideals, democratic principles, cultural ethics, public sensibilities, previous efforts, and a capitalist economy.[9] Within that icon of social order these intertwined interests collided and at times conflicted with one another, creating a complex reality. This prison and others like it were at once emblems of a progressive humane society and places of manufacture based upon a regressive system of penal slavery.[10] For the convicts, the prison was home, workplace, house of worship, and both barrier from and conduit to liberty. Prison officers, too, experienced the institution as workplace and as home in many cases. To the average citizen, the prison was a cloistered environment, experienced from afar, although for some, such as James Whittier, a paid fee opened the curiosity for public view.

The observations of John Dix and James Whittier's diary entry reveal ways in which prisons existed in the nineteenth-century United States. Dix's description presents evidence that structures of everyday life permeated the theoretically isolated specialized landscape of the prison. Whittier's summary of the events of a summer afternoon frames the prison in a nonpenal realm of existence. And both represent the real life experience ordinary people had with the institution. Others experienced the prison through indirect means: news accounts, which often focused upon the spectacular events of escape, inmate violence, and insurrection; novels and didactic children's stories; social commentaries such as Charles Dickens's *American Notes;*[11] and magazines, including *Niles Register and Gleason and Ballou's Drawing Room Companion.* These sources generally presented one-dimensional opaque depictions of the institution. Although the simplistic representations offered a different interaction between viewer and subject than an actual visit provided, they did constitute the sole means of prison experience for many. A variety of people encountered the prison through different means for a variety of purposes. Their multiple perceptions varied in relation to each person's identity and physical proximity to the prison. The diverse experiences, interactions, interpretations, and interests transformed the prison from buildings and space to complex cultural landscape.

The 1797 plans for the Massachusetts State Prison at Charlestown commenced during the early stages of European and American penal reform. Theoretical underpinnings and initiative for nineteenth-century prison reform are usually identified with Milanese jurist Cesare Beccaria and his brief yet influential work, "An Essay on Crimes and Punishment (1764)," and John Howard's *State of the Prisons in England and Wales* (1777).[12] Beccaria's treatise offered theoretical basis, means, and goals for reform, while Howard's concerns identified material goals that would distinguish prisons of the past from those of the nineteenth century. The influence of the two works could be seen in the reform rhetoric, prison discipline, and siting of the Massachusetts State Prison at Charlestown as well as other nineteenth-century penal institutions. However, Beccaria's treatise and Howard's recommendations would have fallen upon deaf American ears if the catalysts for change had not already been present in the culture.

More than a decade prior to the creation of the Charlestown prison, Massachusetts faced serious economic difficulties and a seemingly uncontrollable increase in antisocial and amoral behavior. In 1784 state legislators found that it had become "necessary to the safety of the industrious inhabitants of the Commonwealth, to provide some place other than common gaols, for the reception and confinement to hard labor of persons convicted of larcenies, and other infamous crimes." The military outpost known as Castle Island, located a few miles off the South Boston shore, was designated as the place of confinement for this new class of convicts and would become Massachusetts's first state prison (figs. 7.2, 7.3).[13]

The use of an active garrison to detain civilian prisoners was not far removed from the long-standing use of common jails for prisoners of war. The function of the prison was, however, new.[14] Colo-

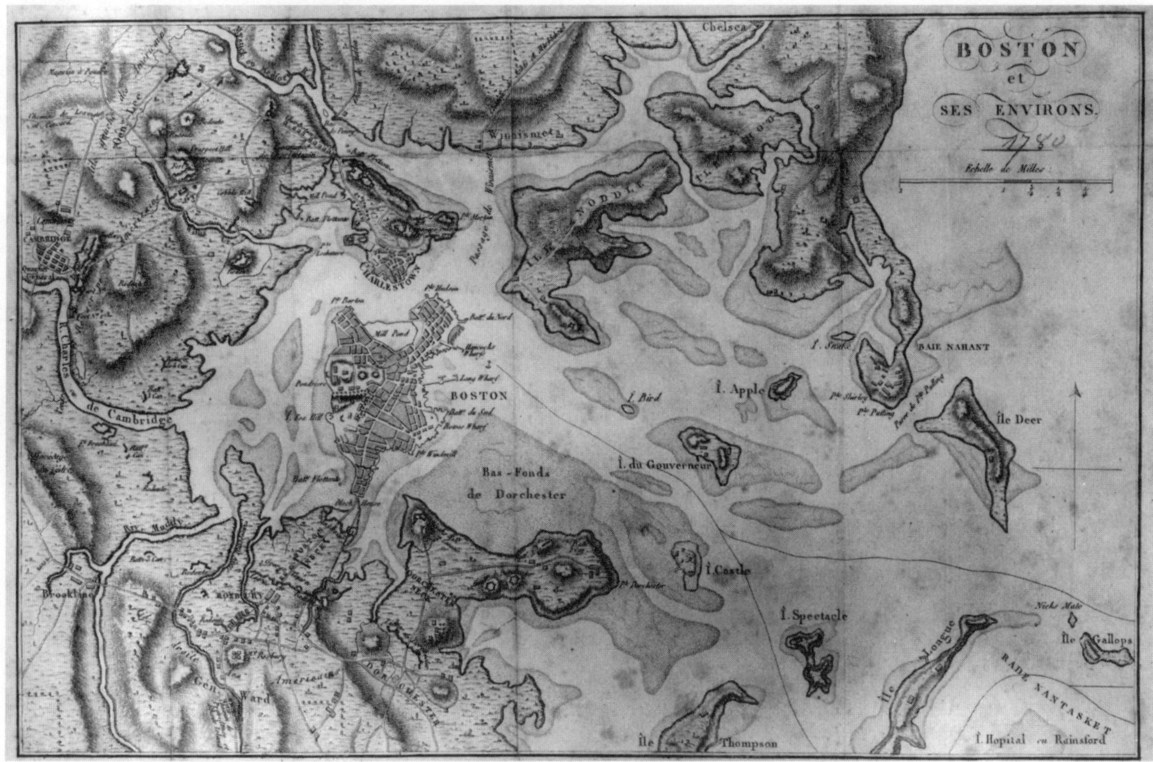

Fig. 7.2. "Boston et ses Environs, 1780." Courtesy of American Antiquarian Society.

nial jails had primarily been used for the detainment of those awaiting trial or sentencing, those unable to pay their fees for detainment, and debtors. A place, owned and operated by the state, for the reception of convicted criminals had never existed in Massachusetts until Castle Island.[15]

Fig. 7.3. View Castle Island, 1789. Courtesy of American Antiquarian Society.

Massachusetts's first state prison would eventually prove a short-lived experiment in early-nineteenth-century prison reform. Little time passed before the inadequacies of the ad hoc accommodations were realized. In 1785 a legislative committee visited the island prison and declared the "bomb-proof,"[16] which served as the prisoners' barracks, unhealthful and resolved that an appropriate building sufficiently strong and with proper ventilation and light be built, "together with out houses and workshops as may be necessary for accommodation and employment to the greatest advantage of said convicts."[17] Twelve years after the first prisoners were sentenced to the garrison, Castle Island was ceded to the federal government and the state's prisoners, who previously had been identified as too dangerous and their crimes too infamous for local jail detainment, were sent back to these places of confinement.

Less than three years after the closure, a legislative committee was appointed to "select and procure a piece of land in Charlestown to erect a State Prison thereon."[18] As successor to the island experiment, the new prison became an opportunity to not only reestablish a state prison in the commonwealth but also a chance to incorporate new ideas about criminal control and possibly redeem Massachusetts's efforts in prison reform.[19] In November 1800 the state legislature approved payment of two thousand dollars for a large lot at Lynde's Point, and Charles Bulfinch was appointed "agent for building the state prison" on this marshy piece of land that would eventually become known as Prison Point.[20]

The general specifications for the prison's design, issued by the state legislature, requested an enclosure large enough to include the "principal building or prison in its finished state, with the different workshops, & other necessary buildings" and the construction of "partition walls of such materials, & the Rooms of such dimensions, and in such situations, as will in their judgment, be best adapted to the purposes of safe confinement & penitentiary reformation." The outside walls of the "principal building or prison" were to be constructed out of stone and built sufficiently large to house one hundred convicts and designed in such a manner to allow for easy enlargement.[21]

Within these parameters, Bulfinch proposed a design that incorporated leading penitentiary reform theory as well as his own stylistic preferences, which were rooted in English neoclassicism. Massachusetts State was designed to accommodate a system of group labor during the day and solitary confinement at night by providing a free-standing workshop (for which there is little information) and laying out the "principal building" with solitary cells. In this respect the proposal clearly forged ahead of existing practices. Twenty years later this penological theory would be "codified as the 'Auburn system.'"[22]

While elements of Bulfinch's proposal would have been regarded as progressive, the overall layout and massing of the principal building were older institutional forms. Bulfinch had proposed two three-story single-loaded wings of solitary cells arranged colinearly about a central administrative pavilion.[23] The design was accepted with revisions. The width of the structure was doubled in a manner that created double-loaded corridors of cells. Another floor was added, and the more progressive solitary cells, which became prominent in the 1820s, were constructed only on the first two floors with group night rooms, a spatial division reminiscent of older institutions, constructed on the subsequent levels. Unfortunately, the windows on the lower two floors were also eliminated and "small apertures" were instead provided, significantly reducing the chance of escape but also minimizing the admittance of light and ventilation (fig. 7.4 and 7.5).[24]

The underlying intentions of Bulfinch's design were compromised by the changes. He had planned the prison with the intent that it would make possible the moral reformation of the state inmates. This goal, the efforts toward achieving it, and the requisite changes culminated in a prison representative of both continuity and change in its form, spatial divisions, and daily practices. Bulfinch captured this characteristic, perhaps unintentionally, with the inscription he had hoped to have inscribed

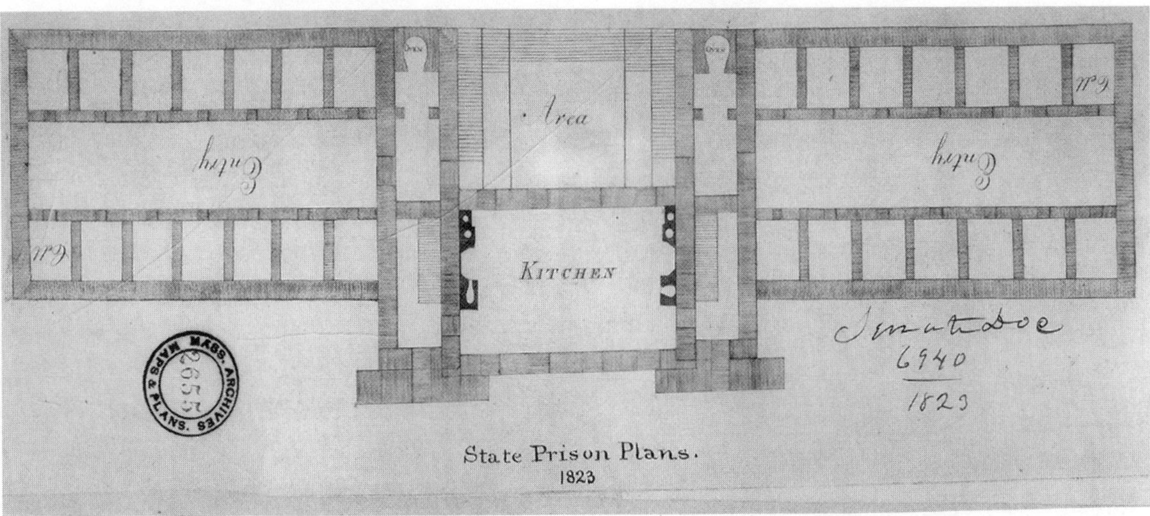

Fig. 7.4. Plan of principal building at Massachusetts State Prison, Charlestown. Courtesy of Massachusetts State Archives.

Fig. 7.5. Elevation of principal building at Massachusetts State Prison Charlestown, by Samuel Etheridge, 1806. Courtesy of Boston Athenaeum.

above the main entry: "Correction. Reformation." Correction was a goal that belonged to the past, while reformation and the belief that architecture could aid the process reflected new theories and intentions toward crime and punishment.

The following description of the Massachusetts prison, which appeared in various state documents, provides a sense of the institution's situation at the mouth of the Charles River and the principal building's original form.

> The Massachusetts State-Prison, or Penitentiary, stands on the westernmost point of the peninsula of Charlestown, at Lynde's Point, a pleasant and healthful spot, commanding a rich variegated and extensive prospect. The wall which encloses it, is washed on the west and north sides by the tide waters. This building [the principal building], erected in 1804–05, is two hundred feet long by forty four wide. The two wings are each four stories, the centre five stories . . . The outer walls are four, and the partition walls two feet thick. Each cell has two openings for the admission of air and light; each two feet in height and four inches wide.[25]

Additional details about the impressive size, weight and quantity of stonework and iron were offered as assurance that the new state prison was both impervious and healthy. Officials felt compelled to reassure the public that concentrating prisoners whose crimes previously would have been considered capital offenses in one place would not pose an increased danger to the free population. These concerns are worth quoting at length:

> To what extent this indulgence [abolishing capital punishment for Robbery, Burglary and Arson] may prevail, consistently with the safety of this populous and wealthy community, will be discovered upon satisfactory evidence, in the progress of the experiment now commencing within this State . . . What has been known, of the numerous collections of desperate criminals, of their dangerous outrages and insurrections, and of other distressing circumstances, which have occurred in the places of confinement in other States, where the punishment of death has been suddenly and almost indiscriminately abolished suggests many inducements to a more deliberate procedure on the present occasion.[26]

Spatial separation of prisoners became the overriding formal support to criminal reformation and secure detainment throughout the United States. This new class of prisoner, their almost instant large numbers, and reformers' focus on physical isolation and "moral architecture" shaped new prisons that were distinctive physical entities.[27] Stacked rows of purpose-built therapeutic cells surrounded by "frowning walls" stood as both a "silent yet

Fig. 7.6. View of Massachusetts State Prison, Charlestown. Illustration from the *American Magazine*, Oct.–Dec., 1837. Courtesy of Boston Athenaeum.

impressive monitor, reminding the evil doer that *the way of transgression is hard*" and as a symbol of a well-ordered social landscape where all were treated with humanity.[28] The prison's geographical location and cell size, placement within the building shell, and juxtaposition to the guard room were the physical elements that gained the most attention from reformers and architects in their efforts to create therapeutic environments.

These carefully planned features did not, however, exclusively define the prison. A large portion of the prison's physical environment consisted of ordinary and residual space that accommodated convict labor and other daily activities. A legislative mandate requiring prisoners to labor from sunrise to sunset meant that most Massachusetts state prisoners spent the majority of their waking hours in this realm and not under the influence of the carefully planned cells. This was common practice and prisoner experience in most congregate prisons.

The 1802 legislation that established the parameters for the prison's buildings was specific about the, size, materials, and spatial divisions for the principal building containing the cells, but it left the specifics of the shops for others to decide: "And the said Agents are further directed to erect within the area aforesaid, a number of workshops of stone or brick sufficient for the use and employment of the different kinds of trades."[29]

The structures needed for blacksmithing, brushmaking, cabinetmaking, cordwainery, coopering, stonecutting, weaving, and whipmaking were established as utilitarian backdrops without special rehabilitative construction, space, or form. The shops were initially housed under one roof with interior partitions separating the trades. Some of the more space-consuming activities took place in the surrounding yard. The original workshop structure at Massachusetts State was 122 feet long by 25 feet wide and two stories high, excluding the basement.[30] Within ten years after the institution opened, the length of the workshops had expanded to 227 feet in length, nearly doubling the original square footage (fig 7.7). It is worth noting that inmate housing received no increase during the same time frame.

Reformers prescribed workshops as places where prisoners could learn a marketable skill and steady habits of industry, the cure for their propensity to

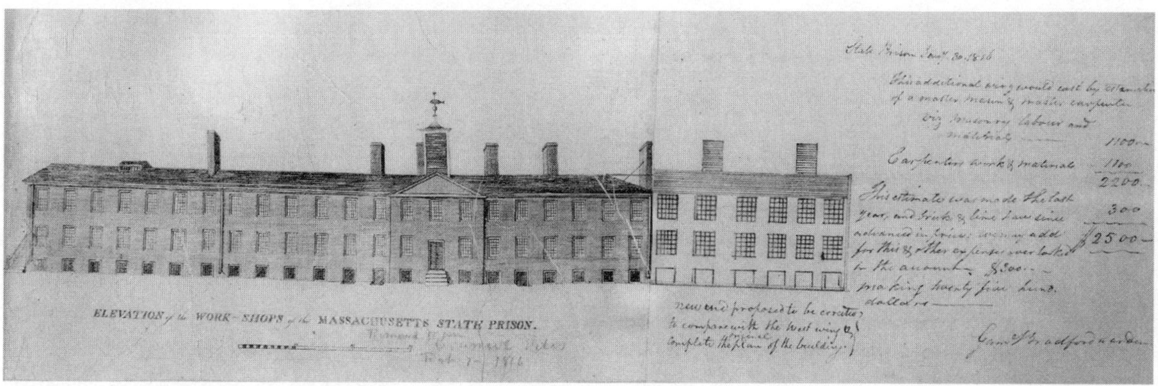

Fig. 7.7. Elevation of workshops at Massachusetts State Prison, Charlestown. Courtesy of Massachusetts State Archives.

idleness, which was the first step down the slippery slope toward intemperance and finally crime. In practice, however, opportunities for profit replaced reform theories. Convicts were rarely given the time or instruction to master a skill and instead learned patterns of shiftlessness as they were moved between trades depending on profit margins and the contracts the warden was able to obtain. Administrators were open about the motivating economic factors in their decisions. In 1807 the warden reported that the making of screws and augers was not profitable.[31] He therefore recommended that they no longer engage in this activity. If the market for a product dried up, such as nail-making after the War of 1812, then the operation was shut down and the inmates assigned to another task.

Prisoners who were diligent efficient workers could, at different points in the history of the institution, earn a small share of the profits from their labor. Motivating prisoners to meet their daily quotas was at times difficult, and some prisoners rushed through their work with the hope of idling away the remainder of the time set aside to labor. Responding with a typical sanction of solitary confinement was not conducive to production. An incentive was, therefore, offered to constructively address these issues. The prison established accounts for each convict who produced more goods than were necessary to cover his costs. Each prisoner was supposed to receive the money from this account upon release from the institution, provided he never required discipline during confinement. The number of prisoners who actually received all that they earned is not clear. In 1807, the Board of Visitors voted to provide one prisoner with $8.80 of the $48.80 he had earned. The Board kept the rest as profit for the commonwealth.[32] This particular case seems to be a typical one during the early years of the prison.

Prison manufacturing was a landscape of opportunity defined by each participant's personal interest and position within the prison apparatus. Prisons became places of opportunity for contractors to make money through the use of cheap labor. Outside contractors were allowed to set up shop inside the prison. They were provided with convict laborers for a below-market daily rate if this was the most profitable arrangement for the prison, such was the case for brushmaking and whitesmithing. If an outside contractor's operation proved especially lucrative, then the state took over the trade, bought the raw materials, and oversaw production. Stonecutting, which was the prison's biggest profit-making activity during the nineteenth century, followed this pattern.

Evidence soon showed that manufacturing activities and the compartmentalized shop arrangements allowed prisoners to define their own opportunities. Convicts were routinely found with weapons, false keys, and counterfeiting plates handmade in the shops and with crowbars and other tools of escape stolen from the shops.[33] The congregate arrangement necessary for efficient manufacturing also provided opportunities for communication, organization, and insurrection. Charles Dickens described this type of manufacturing environment in the following terms: "The noise of the loom, the forge, the carpenter's hammer, or the stonemason's saw, greatly favor those opportunities of intercourse—hurried and brief no doubt, but opportunities still—which these several kinds of work , by rendering it necessary for men to be employed very near to each other and often side by side without any barrier or partition between them, in their very nature present."[34]

Officers at the Massachusetts State Prison experienced the results of such "collaboration" more than once during the prison's history. One of the more serious incidents resulted in the destruction of an entire workshop through an act of arson. This near insurrection occurred in 1822, the same year that Boston mayoral candidate Josiah Quincy accused the prison administration of obfuscating rehabilitation goals with an "undue regard for profit."[35] Two years later a near insurrection occurred with prisoners rushing "from the workshops arming themselves with clubs, knives, hammers, chisels and every variety of weapon within their reach."[36] The warden quickly judged the uprising beyond his ability to resolve and called in the marines and their commander, Major Wainwright, who were stationed at the navy yard. The rebellion was quelled without bloodshed. However, this incident precipitated plans to lessen the opportunities for recurrence of such an incident.

In 1827 plans to eliminate the unintended opportunities that convicts gained by laboring in the shops were introduced. The focus was on the built environment. Instead of partitioning laboring prisoners from one another, as suggested by Dickens, the warden and Board of Inspectors chose to create a workshop without partitions or any other physical barrier that could obscure visual surveillance. An 88-by-144-foot, single-story open floor plan was selected in 1827 as the physical remedy against the "evils" of the manufacturing environment.[37] In their second annual report the Prison Discipline Society of Boston made further suggestions toward regulating the shops through spatial articulation. The general heading for the strategy, "A place for every man and every man in his place," projects the general tone of their approach.[38] Specific recommendations for the shops included assigning convicts to the same place in the shop every day and not allowing the convicts to face one another during their work.[39] While these methods may have helped to prevent communication, they were not conducive to profitable production for many of the trades and were therefore not implemented in the workshops. However, the open floor plan identified by the Discipline Society as superior for surveillance did not compromise manufacturing efficiency. The new work sheds, which closely resembled other contemporary workshops in overall form, were built exclusively for the prison's stonecutting operation. The decision to use an open floor plan for the new work shed resulted from the amount of space needed to handle the ashlar masonry. These utilitarian needs dovetailed nicely with the desire for visual surveillance in determining the stone shed layout (fig 7.8). Additional existing workshops for other trades remained in use upon completion of the new stone sheds, resulting in a hybrid of old and new manufacturing space totaling four times the square footage of the original workshop.

In 1827 an additional spatial armature against prisoner collaboration was planned. The individual cells on the first level of the original principal building were used for solitary confinement of new and refractory prisoners. The remaining sixty-two cells were shared by the other convicts, who likely numbered more than 250. These conditions were thought unacceptable for many reasons, not the least of which was an inability to closely monitor prisoner interaction. If each prisoner were physically isolated from one another, insurrections would be more difficult to plan. A new granite cell block, broadly referred to as the new prison, was constructed with prison labor and ready for their occupation in 1829.

The legislative action necessary for the construction of the new cells occurred at a time when two prisons had risen as paragons of American prison reform, the New York State Penitentiary at Auburn and Eastern State Penitentiary in Philadelphia, still under construction. The proponents of both the Auburn and Eastern systems believed that communication among convicts was dangerous, and

Fig. 7.8. Interior view of the stone shed at Massachusetts State Prison, Charlestown. From *Ballou's Pictorial Drawing Room Companion*. Courtesy of American Antiquarian Society.

they advocated physical separation, labor, and moral instruction as essential elements in the rehabilitation process. Each principle was assigned a different level of importance in the two models. Eastern State's separate system aimed to keep prisoners in physical isolation during the entire length of their imprisonment. Labor, meals, and worship were conducted in isolation. Double-loaded corridors of cells radiated from a central control node, creating a hub-and-spoke configuration. Individual exercise yards were placed adjacent to each of the ground-level cells. Auburn's congregate system, as it was referred to by reformers such as Samuel Gridley Howe, was structured to house the inmates in individual cells at night with group worship and labor during the day. Meals were taken in the isolation of the cell. During congregate activities strict silence was the disciplinary code enforced through corporal punishment. The U-shape of Auburn's main building, which resembled the eighteenth-century Walnut Street Jail in Philadelphia, was not as unique as Eastern State's.[40] However, the interior layout at Auburn—a row of multitiered back-to-back solitary cells fronting upon multistory galleries—was considered innovative and was characterized as a prison within a prison. Through essays, pamphlet literature, and new prison construction, proponents of Auburn and Eastern State Penitentiaries engaged in an extensive debate about each system's relative merits.[41]

Pressed by the need to provide more housing for its convicts and the desire to improve the prison's reputation as a reform institution, the Massachusetts State Legislature made a decisive attempt to emulate the Auburn model by constructing three hundred solitary night cells, three and one-half feet wide, seven feet long, and seven feet high. The decision to implement the Auburn system was a relatively easy one. Bulfinch's original unaltered design for the prison foreshadowed a congregate system of operation at the prison, and the existing system of prison discipline at Massachusetts State most closely resembled that at Auburn. The congruencies between Auburn and the state prison at Charlestown were reinforced by a dependency on a certain level of profits, not unattainable in an Eastern State separate system. The warden, Gamaliel Bradford, as well as the Boston Discipline Society, advocated for the Auburn model in both philosophical and practical terms: "a man, if ever again destined for society, should not, by any punishment, be disqualified for enjoyment and usefulness in it. But a long confinement in total solitude might destroy his social feelings, and produce a sort of stupid apathy, which would render him very unfit for an useful or happy member of society. There is one other objection to keeping a convict entirely alone . . . and that is, as it regards labor; and this objection will apply both to its moral effect, and to the pecuniary interest of the institution where he may be confined."[42]

With the completion of the stone sheds and new cell block, in 1829 the original Bulfinch buildings became dwarfed secondary structures. Many of the daily operations, originally housed in the principal building, had been parceled out into separate buildings (fig. 7.9). The warden now lived in a detached house adjacent to a small fenced yard located to the south of the original main building. The chapel, kitchen, and a schoolroom shared a building located to the northeast of the original main building. This building was constructed at the same time as the new cell block and lay immediately adjacent to it.

In the interim the internal arrangement of Bulfinch's "principal building" had also undergone numerous renovations and served different functions. The east wing was gutted and refitted with the Auburn cellular arrangement. The central pavilion of the Bulfinch building still served administrative purposes and housed officers. The existing cells on the first two levels of the west wing were still used for those sentenced to solitary confinement. The upper two west-wing levels were used for the hospital and for the female prisoners, whose daily routine and spatial experience differed greatly from their male counterparts.

Like many other general discourses of the early nineteenth century, the subjects of prison discipline theories were inherently male. American female convicts were an afterthought in the process, often dealt with on an ad hoc basis and commonly housed in residual spaces, such as attics and older portions of the institution no longer utilized for men. At Massachusetts State, women, depending on the year, represented from less than 1 percent to 7 percent of the prison's population. Massachusetts's state female convicts, in essence, lived an eighteenth-century carceral existence within an institution that embraced and incorporated nineteenth-century reform principles for its male prisoners. Female prisoners at the Massachusetts State Prison in Charlestown were not addressed in 1829 renovations. Women also figured in the prison landscape as matrons, visitors, and the wives of officers.

The renovations of the late 1820s were the first in a series of projects aimed toward improving conditions within the prison. During the next two

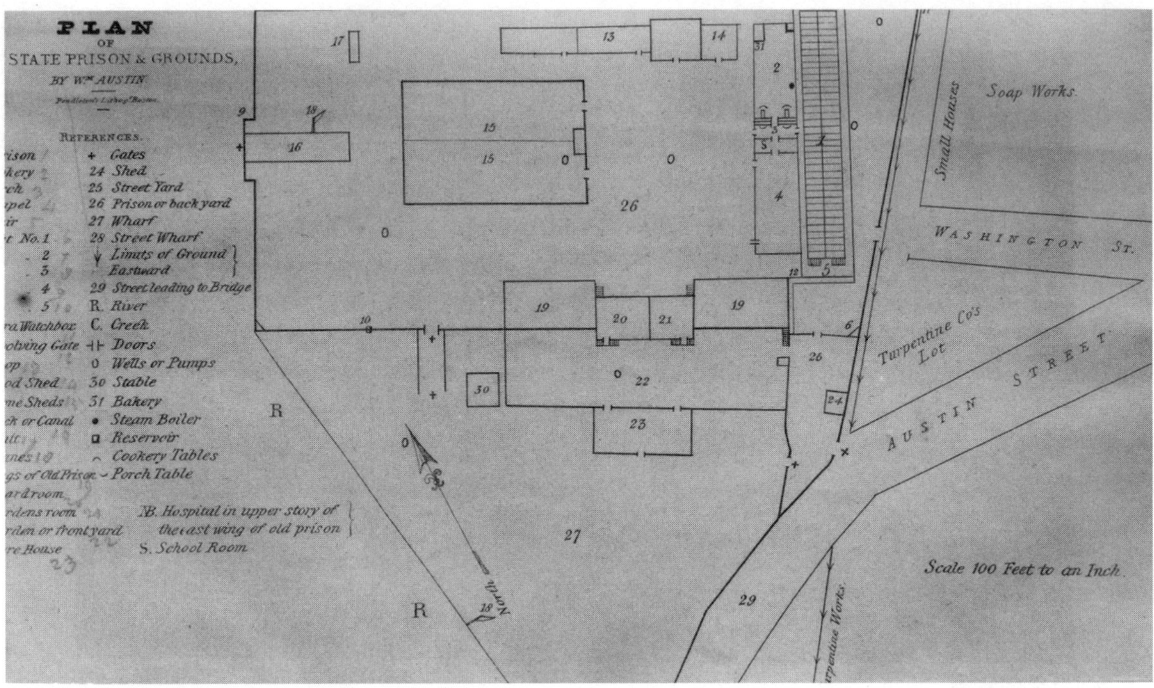

Fig. 7.9. 1829 Site Plan of Massachusetts State Prison, Charlestown. From *Laws of the Commonwealth for the Government of the Massachusetts State Prison, with the Rules and Regulations of the Board of Inspectors* (Charlestown: State of Massachusetts, 1830). Courtesy of Boston Athenaeum.

decades the original workshop was further engulfed by more additions and a new one was constructed in the southwest corner of the compound. Another significant building campaign was initiated in 1850. During this effort the 1829 cell block was connected to the original Bulfinch building via an octagonal central hub (fig 7.10). This configuration was viewed as the most efficient form for visual surveillance. The new central pavilion housed a kitchen, guard room, chapel, and hospital.

A new five-story wing of minutely larger cells, laid out in accordance with the Auburn plan, was attached to the south end of the hub during the 1850 expansion project. The designers of the new building components, Louis Dwight and Gridley Bryant, incorporated the thickness of the cell walls in the prevention of "evil communication" between prisoners. The extraordinarily thick interior walls aimed at preventing communication and were also intended to block the prisoners' ability to see an approaching sentinel by aligning the cell doors to the inside edge of the wall.[43] A portion of the new wing was identified as a good place for a workshop and "particularly adapted to shoemakers and tailors, who may be arranged on seats in two rows, with their faces towards the south and their backs towards the guard room, so that the master mechanic . . . may oversee them without being overseen by them."[44] The 1850 renovations resulted in a building that Dwight and Bryant characterized as "favorable to order."[45]

This midcentury expansion had been chosen over another course of action proposed at the same time as the Bryant and Dwight plan. Annual reports show that total profits from prison manufacturing, especially stonecutting, could prove

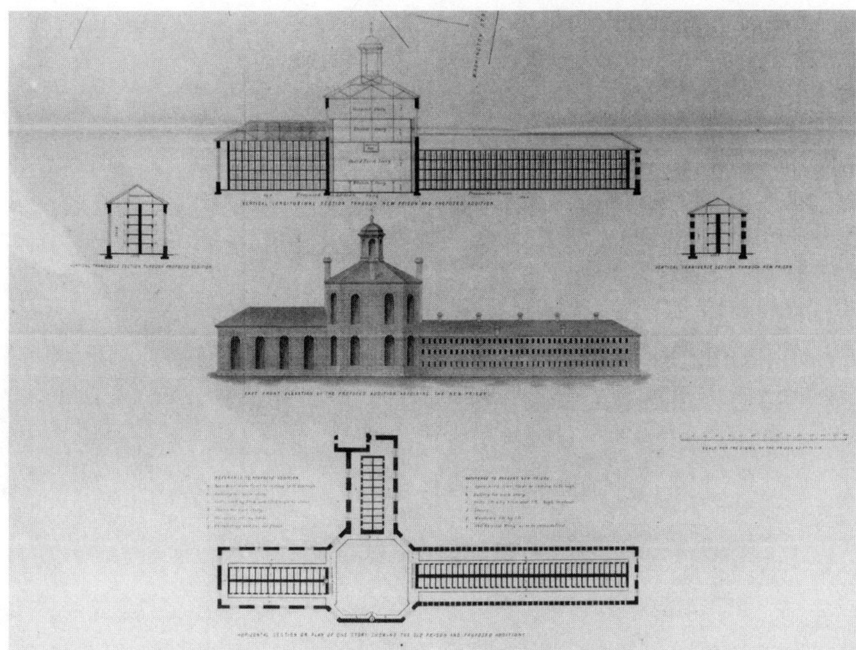

Fig. 7.10. Plans, sections, and elevations of 1850 additions to Massachusetts State Prison by Louis Dwight and Gridley Bryant. From Massachusetts State House Doc. No. 140. Courtesy of American Antiquarian Society.

significant.[46] This fact was the driving force behind the other proposal. In 1850, members of the Standing Committee on Prisons, intent on exploiting the prisoners' earning potential, recommended relocating the prison to Quincy or Fitchburg for the express purpose of gaining greater profits from the stonecutting operation. "At this time about one-quarter of the number of convicts are engaged at the stone cutting business . . . If the stone department were connected with a quarry, at least three quarters of the convicts it is believed, could be employed at hammering and quarrying, by which a large revenue would ensure to the State, if the institution were well conducted. . . It would be a good investment, giving good dividends, without exhausting capital."[47] Perhaps in an effort to attract broader support for relocating the institution the committee emphasized that the Charlestown site had lost its original advantages and was actually detrimental to the convicts' rehabilitation. What was once an isolated corner of the peninsula now was encroached upon by urban fabric. In the committee members' view, the close proximity to the "very heart of a dense city population" defeated the purposes of the institution. "Irreclaimable rogues" visited the prison for "improper purposes," and a location away from an urban center would make visits from "this class of persons" less frequent.[48] Unconvinced by the proposal, the state legislature resolved to maintain the Charlestown site as the location for the state prison and go forward with the Dwight and Bryant expansion.

By the end of the nineteenth century the confines of the prison had been expanded making room for a perpendicular addition to the workshop in the north part of the complex. Another shop was built in the new southwest corner; a new school room to the south of the original main building and a new administrative wing and wardens house were added to the east side of the octagonal pavilion. Throughout the piecemeal construction that transformed the prison's interior landscape, its "frowning walls" remained a stolid omnipresent symbol of social order and progress.

Symbolic imagery came to represent the nineteenth-century American prison. Simplified depictions of prisons portrayed pure forms or ideal orderly landscapes, uncomplicated by the colliding realms of experience and operation that existed inside the carceral compound. The bucolic renderings belied the reality of the daily operations and physical conditions within the prison by placing the walled compound as a backdrop to a republican view of virtuous order. The compositions resemble paintings of medieval landscapes where castles are the background to obedient peasants placed in the foreground. The images considered in tandem represent idealized versions of cultural landscapes and capture a reversal in social spatial ordering.

The idealized prison image, a potent emblem of progressive republicanism, also became a bourgeois iconic commodity appearing on ephemera such as dessert plates. Later in the century, photographic views of the prison were brought into the realm of parlor entertainment through novelties like the stereoscope. Using the device, one could get a three-dimensional view of the prison, its inmates, and overseers from the comfort of one's home. The backs of the viewing cards often served

Fig. 7.11. View of Massachusetts State Prison, Charlestown, from inside the walled complex. The building in the left background is the cell block built in 1829. In the left foreground are the chapel and meal hall. The original Bulfinch building is located in the center background. From *Laws of the Commonwealth for the Government of the Massachusetts State Prison, with the Rules and Regulations of the Board of Inspectors* (Charlestown: State of Massachusetts, 1830). Courtesy of Boston Athenaeum.

as order forms for other images or were used as advertisement space, thus merging the prison, casual entertainment, and nineteenth-century commercialism into one cultural artifact.

The images that have come to represent the Massachusetts State Prison at Charlestown were established early in the institution's history. The first rules and regulations pamphlet for the prison was printed in 1806. Two engravings of the prison were included in the document. One is a plan and the other an elevation of the principal building. No other elements within the prison compound are depicted. These engravings ignore the workshops and naturally exclude the multiple renovations that subsequently transformed the physical environment of the prison. Yet they have been used in historical accounts to represent the prison resulting in a static and incomplete presentation of the prison environment.[49] A later more complete depiction of the prison was included in the 1829 version of the rules and regulations. A plan that shows the entire prison compound and an interior view of the prison that portrays the inmates in formation marching out of the workshops are included in the 1829 document (figs. 7.9, 7.11). Although the latter image reinforces the imagery present in the bucolic renderings by depicting a pristine physical environment inhabited by orderly industrious convicts, it also captures a dark ominous quality of the prison environment. This 1829 plan and view, perhaps less appealing and ideal than the earlier and simpler image, fell to the wayside, and the 1806 engravings became the preferred representative image of the prison.

Similarly, representations of America's model prisons, Auburn and Eastern, were visually reduced to geometrically rigid ideal plans. Eastern State's hub-and-spoke configuration was, and often still is, reduced to a pristine uniform structure. When Eastern opened in 1829 only two wings were complete. By the conclusion of the nineteenth century, expanded two-story versions of the remaining original seven wings had been completed as well as four additional wings that were wedged in between the original long blocks of cells. Nonetheless, the original symmetrical seven-winged design by the architect John Haviland and an idealized pastoral engraving created by a prisoner have dominated Eastern State's historical image.[50] Auburn's multistoried U-shaped form received a far more drastic simplification. A singular three-story rectilinear structure with the characteristic spine of cells down the middle became the representative architectural form for the Auburn system.

These icons became the emblems of principles for which nineteenth-century American prison reform wished to be recognized. New American prisons, such as Massachusetts State, adopted sentences of detainment with hard labor in lieu of many longstanding sanguinary and corporal punishments. They were intended by their designers, both architectural and theoretical, to be viewed primarily as places of reform and not profit-making manufactories. Many prison officials were, nonetheless, preoccupied with the manufacturing principles of product marketability and profit. This fact produced a physical impact upon the prison environment.

Two constants are present when the landscape of Massachusetts State is viewed in its entirety and over time: the institution never fit into any one ideal form and it was an amalgam of competing, at times overlapping, interests. In the early history of the prison, both old and new spatial patterns defined the principal building. The overall form was that of an older institutional building that contained a combination of progressive solitary cells and eighteenth-century group night rooms. And, the workshops were ordinary buildings similar to structures found outside the prison compound. By midcentury the housing unit displayed a hybrid of the two competing models of American prison reform. The overall form of the housing unit resembled the hub-and-spoke configuration of Eastern State Penitentiary, while the interior layout was that of an Auburn system. And, the numerous workshops which now encircled the housing unit on two sides competed with the cells for physical dominance of the prison environment. These incremental changes and transformations are an historical record of the built form experienced by the nineteenth-century people who visited, worked, and lived at the Massachusetts State Prison at Charlestown.

Rarely are the workshop realm and daily practices presented in historical accounts, although they were clearly major determinants in the development of the prison complex and its cultural identity. The ad hoc spaces as well as those consciously built, daily practices as well as the intentions, and the entire built form as well as the desired image contribute to the significance of the prison in nineteenth-century American culture. The manufacturing realm is one of the overlooked constituent elements in the complex environment of intertwined landscapes that helped define the spatial and experiential reality of this nineteenth-century icon of social reform. An understanding of elements connected with a manufacturing presence within the prison landscape and an understanding of the way people interacted with the institution allows a historical understanding based not only in the imagery but also in the reality of daily practice and experience of the prison.

Notes

1. James Whittier, Diary, 1830–1831, American Antiquarian Society, Worcester, Mass., 151–52. "Glass House" referred to the large glass factories that were the mainstay of the East Cambridge economy.
2. This number comes from the amount of money collected as visitors' fees listed in the prison's 1825 and 1826 "Expense and Income Reports," reprinted in the *Second Annual Report of the Board of Managers of the Prison Discipline Society, Boston* (Boston, 1828), 60.

   In June of 1807, the Board of Visitors logged the following comments regarding visitors in the meeting minutes: "Whereas the greatest inconvenience and interruption has arisen to the Visitors from the almost incessant applications for permits to visit the Prison. Ordered that except in such cases as are expedient no permits shall be granted but on Tuesdays and Saturdays, from two to six o'clock in the afternoon. And that the Super be authorized at those times either by personal attendance or permits to persons whose characters he is satisfied, to admit the citizens of this Commonwealth, or others to view the Prison, in company with the Keeper, Underkeeper or an Assistant"; State Prison Records, Massachusetts State Prison, Charlestown, Board of Visitors Minutes, Massachusetts State Archives, Dorchester, Mass., 1807, 45.

   Gamaliel Bradford, a warden at the prison, stated that visitors were "daily frequent (I am apt to think too frequent)" in *State of the Prisons and the Penitentiary System Vindicated* (Charlestown, 1821), 46.
3. For further discussion of the prison as part of tourism, see John Sears, *Sacred Places: American Tourist Attractions in the Nineteenth Century* (New York: Oxford Univ. Press, 1989), 87–100.
4. R. L. Midgley, *Guide to Boston and Suburbs* (Boston, 1856), 163.
5. John Ross Dix, *Local Loiterings and Visits in the Vicinity of Boston* (Boston, 1845). Dix, whose real name was George Spencer Phillips, was drawn to many of the same types of

provocative scenes that attracted his fellow countryman Charles Dickens. Observations at the Lowell factories, the public institutions in South Boston, and other curiosities fill the pages, yet he was true to the claim with which he opens his book—that his interest was with "plain matters, with common facts," and what he presented were "records of every-day subjects, and chronicles of common things" (9). He published at least one other book on life in America, *Transatlantic Tracings; or Sketches of Persons and Scenes in America* (London, 1853).

6. Dix, *Local Loiterings*, 88.
7. David Rothman, *Discovery of the Asylum* (Boston: Little Brown and Co., 1971); Michel Foucault, *Discipline and Punish: The Birth of the Prison*, 2d ed., trans. Alan Sheridan (New York: Vintage, 1979); Michael Ignatieff, *A Just Measure of Pain: The Penitentiary in the Industrial Revolution, 1750–1850* (New York: Pantheon, 1978).
8. Ignatieff, *A Just Measure of Pain*, 209.
9. The idea of multiple interests underlying the development of nineteenth-century penal practices has been previously discussed by other authors. Michel Foucault identifies the agency of multiple interests at the level of an overarching cultural phenomenon. Foucault locates early-nineteenth-century penal reforms within a "new distribution of the power to punish." He asserts that "many different interests came together to instigate" this shift in general punishment power relations and identifies prison institutions as supporting tools within this more pervasive physical exercise of punishment. Foucault also addresses multiple interest, or the "pluralization of causes," in "Questions of Method," an interview in *The Foucault Effect*, ed. Graham Burchell, and Gordon Miller (Chicago: Univ. of Chicago Press, 1991), 73–86.

   Adam Hirsch in *Rise of the Penitentiary* places the agency of the multiple interests at the level of penal ideology and identifies the three ideological strains that came together to allow prison labor ideology to become a part of reform theories. Hirsch states that "the beauty of hard labor was its capacity to serve simultaneously as threat and therapy . . . and fountain of support," which worked for both utilitarian and philanthropic reformers.
10. For an extensive discussion of penal slavery starting with the ancient Greeks, see Thorsten Sellin, *Slavery and the Penal System* (New York: Elsevier, 1976). In *Rise of the Penitentiary: Prisons and Punishment in Early America* (New Haven: Yale Univ. Press, 1992), 79, Adam Hirsch reminds us that this type of slavery later became a protected practice under the Thirteenth Amendment, which reads: "Neither slavery nor involuntary servitude, except as punishment for crime whereof the party shall have been duly convicted, shall exist within the United States, or any place subject to their jurisdiction."
11. Charles Dickens, *American Notes for General Circulation* [1842] (Middlesex, England: Penguin, 1972).
12. Cesare Beccaria, *Essay on Crime and Punishment,* trans. Mons. de Voltaire, trans. from French (London, 1767).
13. State of Massachusetts, *Acts and Resolves, 1784–1785* (Boston, 1886), 163.
14. Hirsch, *Rise of the Penitentiary,* New Haven, 7.
15. State of Massachusetts, *Acts and Resolves, 1784–85,* 163.
16. "Bomb proof" was the noun used in the eighteenth-century literature to refer to the subterranean shelter. Ironically, its location proved advantageous for potential escapees.
17. State of Massachusetts, *Acts and Resolves 1784–85,* 928. The record is unclear as to whether the structures were ever built.

18. State of Massachusetts, *Acts and Laws of Massachusetts, 1799, 558.*
19. According to economic historians H. Faulkner, H. Schieber, and H. Vatter, a "spirit of rivalry lay behind many of the state projects that took the form of public enterprise—undertakings, financed, planned and managed by the states themselves." They also state that the principal enterprises in this category were under way from the 1820s through the 1840s. However, state rivalry in the area of prison reform was clearly evident much earlier, although the expenditure for the projects was much less. See H. Faulkner, H. Schieber, and H. Vatter, *American Economic History*, 9th ed. (New York: Harper and Row, 1976), 102.
20. State of Massachusetts, *Acts and Laws, 1802–03*, 861
21. State of Massachusetts, *Acts and Laws of the Commonwealth of Massachusetts* (Boston, 1802), 381.
22. Harold Kirker, *The Architecture of Charles Bulfinch* (Cambridge, Mass.: Harvard Univ. Press, 1969), 211–15.
23. In 1829 Bulfinch apparently stated the prison was planned with nine-by-seven-feet cells. However, the dimensions on the Bulfinch plans read twelve feet by sixteen feet.
24. State of Massachusetts, *Acts and Laws, 1802*, 381.
25. Massachusetts State Prison Board of Directors, Rules and Regulations for the Government of the Massachusetts State Prison (Boston, 1806), iii. It is worth noting that John Ross Dix described the prison's location as "dismal, damp and sloppy"; Dix, *Local Loiterings*, 83.
26. Samuel Sewall, *Communication from the Hon. Samuel Sewall, Esq. and the Hon. Nathan Dane, Esq. Accompanied with Several Bills for the Regulation of the State Prison, and an Alteration of the Criminal Codes of the Commonwealth* (Boston, 1806), no pagination.
27. This term has been commonly used in reference to nineteenth-century reformers' focus on architectural solutions for the reformation of convicts. Cellular separation was viewed by reformers as the remedy for various moral contagion, including the corruption of novice offenders by hardened criminals, sodomy, and conspiracies to escape. See Rothman, *Discovery of the Asylum*, 84.
28. Gideon Haynes, *Pictures from Prison Life, an Historical Sketch of the Massachusetts State Prison with Narratives and Incidents, and Suggestions of Discipline* (Boston, 1869), preface. For a more extensive discussion of the prison as a model of social order, see Rothman, *Discovery of the Asylum*, and Sears, *Sacred Landscapes.*
29. State of Massachusetts, *Acts and Laws, 1802,* 381.
30. *An Account of the Massachusetts State Prison by the Board of Visitors* (Cambridge, Mass., 1806), no pagination.
31. Visitors Records 1807: State Prison Records, Massachusetts State Prison, Charlestown, Board of Visitor Minutes, Massachusetts State Archives, Boston, Mass., 48.
32. Ibid., Dorchester, Mass., 1807, 39.
33. Journal, Massachusetts State Prison Daily Reports, 1805–1863, Massachusetts State Archives, Dorchester, Mass., 1805; Journal of Transactions in the State Prison, Massachusetts State Prison Daily Reports, 1805–63, Massachusetts State Archives, Dorchester, Mass., 1807; Prison Discipline Society, *First Annual Report of the Board of Managers, of the Boston Discipline Society, Boston, June 2, 1826*, 5th ed. (Boston, 1827), 15–16; Prison Discipline Society, *Second Annual Report of the Board of Managers, of the Boston Discipline Society, Boston, June 1, 1827* (Boston, 1828), 62.
34. Dickens, *American Notes for General Circulation*, 100.

35. Josiah Quincy, *Remarks on Some of the Provisions of the Laws of Massachusetts, Affecting Poverty Vice and Crime* (Cambridge, Mass., 1822), 21.
36. Haynes, *Pictures from Prison Life,* 132–37.
37. Boston Discipline Society, *Second Annual Report,* 57.
38. Ibid., 36.
39. Ibid.
40. The Walnut Street Jail did not employ the Auburn system of prison discipline. A portion of the prison was adapted for solitary confinement in 1791 and was the precursor for Eastern State Penitentiary.
41. For examples from the debate, see William Roscoe, Esq., *Observations on Penal Jurisprudence, and the Reformation of Criminals (London, 1825); Letters on the Comparative Merits of the Pennsylvania and New York System of Penitentiary Discipline, by a Massachusetts Man* (Boston, 1836); Samuel Gridley Howe, *An Essay on Separate and Congregate Systems of Prison Discipline* (Boston, 1846); Francis Lieber, *A Vindication of the Separate System of Prison Discipline from the Misrepresentations of the North America Review, July, 1839* (Philadelphia, 1839); Francis Lieber, *A Popular Essay on Subjects of Penal Law, on Uninterrupted Solitary Confinement at Labor Contradistinguished to Solitary Confinement at Night and Joint Labor by Day . . .* (Philadelphia, 1838).
42. Bradford, *State of the Prisons and the Penitentiary System Vindicated,* 19. The Boston Discipline Society supported hard labor on the basis that it was healthy, productive, provided a means of support upon release, was reformatory, and "consonant with republican principles," *Second Annual Report,* 34.
43. Louis Dwight was a well-known reformer and secretary of the Boston Discipline Society. Gridley Bryant was a prison architect responsible for the design of many institutions in Massachusetts, including the Charles Street Jail, which was completed prior to the construction at the state prison. The cruciform is found in both the jail and prison as well as others designed by Bryant.
44. State of Massachusetts, Standing Committee on Prisons, *House Doc. No. 140,* 1850 (Boston, 1886), 17.
45. State of Massachusetts, *House Doc. No 140,* 18.
46. In 1825 the profits from prison manufacturing at Massachusetts State totaled $58,574 with $51,957 coming from the stone sales. In 1826 labor profits totaled $57,351 with $49,717 from stone sales. It is also worth noting that the total profit from visitor fees exceeded $500 for both 1825 and 1826. This sum represented two thousand visitors for the year, or an average of thirty-eight visitors daily.
47. State of Massachusetts, *House Doc. No. 140,* 23–24, 27.
48. State of Massachusetts, *House Doc. No. 140,* 28.
49. Rothman, *Discovery of the Asylum,* 91.
50. One exception to this trend is Norman Johnston, *Eastern State Penitentiary: Crucible of Good Intentions* (Philadelphia: Philadelphia Museum of Art, 1994).

CHAPTER 8

Anna Vemer Andrzejewski

The Gazes of Hierarchy at Religious Camp Meetings, 1850–1925

In September of 1920, the first camp meeting at God's Holiness Grove was held on the northwest bank of the Susquehanna River in central Pennsylvania (fig. 8.1).[1] For ten days, the devout set aside everyday concerns to commune with fellow Christians, traveling ministers and exhorters, and their God in this eight-acre wood lot in rural Snyder County. During the first year, they camped in canvas tents and worshipped in a canvas tabernacle; clearing the dense brush in early summer left little time or money to erect substantial buildings. However, the next year they constructed a frame dining hall, as well as a forty-by-sixty-foot frame tabernacle, partially enclosed, but with removable walls. In 1924, they built a caretaker's house near the main road and replaced some tents with frame, weatherboarded cabins, each averaging thirteen feet by twenty feet in size. One by one, these cabins, nearly identical in construction and level of finish, supplanted the original canvas tents. By 1947, the camp meeting had attained its current layout, having ninety-nine cabins laid out in parallel rows around the tabernacle in a U-shaped configuration (fig. 8.2).[2]

The founding of God's Holiness Grove Camp Meeting represented only one chapter in a long camp meeting history extending back to the late eighteenth and early nineteenth centuries, when the first camps appeared on the American landscape. Presbyterians, Baptists, and Methodists all held camp meetings and revivals during the Federal period, perhaps as early as the 1780s and certainly by 1800 and 1801, when large meetings took place on the Kentucky and Tennessee frontier.[3] Presbyterians and Baptists gradually abandoned

Fig. 8.1. View of first camp meeting held at God's Holiness Grove Camp Meeting, Village of Hummels Wharf, Snyder County, Pennsylvania, in 1920. Courtesy of God's Holiness Camp Meeting Association and the Sunbury Daily Item.

Fig. 8.2. Aerial photograph of God's Holiness Grove Camp Meeting, Village of Hummels Wharf, Snyder County, Pennsylvania, c. 1950. Courtesy of God's Holiness Camp Meeting Association.

the practice of attending annual camp meetings during the first quarter of the nineteenth century, but Methodists continued to establish and hold camp meetings well into the Victorian era and beyond. Methodists, more than any other religious denomination, exploited camp meetings to gain members, founding hundreds if not thousands of camps throughout the eastern and middle United States prior to the Civil War.[4] The late-nineteenth-century holiness movement breathed new life into what had become a predominantly Methodist camp meeting institution. Originating as a faction largely within Methodism but rapidly evolving into an interdenominational movement, the holiness effort promoted the Wesleyan idea that, following conversion, Christians could seek sanctification, a kind of "second blessing" that brought them even closer to God. In addition to holding holiness services at traditional Methodist camp meetings, holiness leaders founded camps devoted especially to sanctification, of which God's Holiness was an early-twentieth-century example.[5]

At Methodist camp meetings established during the middle decades of the nineteenth century, and holiness ones founded after the Civil War, lines of vision played an essential part in religious activities.[6] The highly ordered layout of the grounds worked to direct gazes between and among buildings and their users. The physical and symbolic focus of these camps, the tabernacles, occupied strategic central locations. At God's Holiness Grove Camp Meeting, the tabernacle stood at the center of the rows of cabins that surrounded it (fig. 8.3). From here, especially from the raised preaching stand inside, the entire camp, including benches for worshippers inside the tabernacle and the cabins encircling it, was visible, especially when the tabernacle's walls were removed. Likewise, the benches and cabins faced inward, offering worshippers views of the pulpit inside the tabernacle and the events that took place there. The careful design of God's Holiness and other Methodist and holiness camps around these lines of vision raises questions about the function and significance of

Fig. 8.3. View from edge of "circle" of cabins looking toward the tabernacle at God's Holiness Grove Camp Meeting, Village of Hummels Wharf, Snyder County, Pennsylvania. Photograph by the author, 1997.

"gazing" at camp meetings erected throughout the United States during the nineteenth and early twentieth centuries.[7]

This chapter investigates the complex nature and multiple meanings of "gazes" at Methodist and holiness camp meetings built and used between 1850 and 1925. I use the term *gaze* to describe a mode of vision characterized by a sustained and purposeful "look," which has as its intent processes of transformation and the goal of influencing behavior through the very act of looking. Rather than casually survey, this kind of gaze actively shapes the object of its focus. The gazes discussed here are not synonymous with the masculine "gaze" as discussed in postmodern and feminist theory. Writers in this tradition have examined dominant modes of vision in modern society which place the man-as-viewing-subject in sharp contrast to the woman-as-viewed-object, thereby setting up an active-passive relationship between the (male) seer and the (female) seen.[8] As I will show, gazes at religious camp meetings resist easy co-option into such discussions about the gendered nature of visual practices in modern (Western) society. At camp meetings, men and women both assumed active and passive positions through the gazes they exercised there. Further, visual exchanges at camp meetings were usually reciprocal, such that either party could become both subject and object of the gaze simultaneously.[9] With the blurring of the lines between active/passive, male/female, and subject/object in this reciprocal gaze, notions of control, authority, and domination that logically follow from discourses about the masculine all-powerful gaze also break down—authority comes to rest in the gaze itself as a mediator between the viewing parties intent upon negotiating their places at the camp meeting.

At Methodist and holiness camp meetings, I argue that gazes worked in multiple directions between and among participants as a means to create, negotiate, and reinforce boundaries between people and groups. From his elevated pulpit, the minister or exhorter gazed upon the congregation, delivering the gospel to the audience in attempt to save a soul or two. But equally significant, the worshippers looked at the speaker in hopes of reaching a higher level of religion, potentially looking beyond the minister/exhorter toward a "higher power." Gazes also worked to define camp meeting attendees' places relative to one another; pursuing and finding one's place in the camp's religious hierarchy involved looking at others. The design of camps participated in these processes by fostering these multiple and often reciprocal visual exchanges and by collapsing boundaries between public and private space. Exploring what I call the "gazes of hierarchy" at Methodist and holiness camp meetings considers how gazes between camp meeting goers served as a means of negotiating their position in relation to other worshippers, ministers and exhorters, and God.

Earlier discussions of architecture and vision focus on sites of confinement, largely within the context of authority and punishment. Michel Foucault and his followers, among others, have examined prisons and other types of institutional buildings in terms of theories and practices of "surveillance."[10] In this paradigm, gazes work in one direction and from a privileged vantage point, an oft-cited example being the all-powerful gaze of the sentinel in the watchtower. The prisoners' status as condemned persons places them in subservient positions to the guards who look upon them. Within the punitive context of surveillance, Methodist and holiness camp meetings are unlikely spaces where such disciplinary, authoritative gazes would be found. But thinking of gazes at camp meetings solely in terms of discourses of surveillance is interpretively limiting; it fails to account for the important role of gazing in the camps' religious services and avoids recognizing how gazes there worked outside the Foucauldian model of surveillance in several important ways.

In contrast to the surveying gazes found in prisons and other institutions, gazes operating at religious camp meetings were often reciprocal. Although *gaze* by definition implies a single viewer, the kinds of gazes at camp meetings often involved two parties who simultaneously looked at one another, each with purposeful intent. By using the term *reciprocal* to describe this kind of gaze, I refer to the two-way visual interchange between camp meeting goers, including gazes between worshippers, between worshippers and preachers, and between both and God. These reciprocal gazes held the potential to transform both the seers and those seen; through their mutual visual exchange, the gaze-as-action also shaped and transformed itself. Even when gazes were not returned in this kind of reciprocal arrangement, gazes worked in multiple directions at camp meetings between these different participants, in sharp contrast to the monocentric and autocratic mode of vision discussed by Foucault.

These gazes also functioned within a hierarchical context rather than a punitive one, serving as a way through which campers negotiated their places relative to one another. Retreating into the woods to camp meetings, genteel manners that placed restrictions upon unabashed stares and self-display relaxed, as gazing between and among all participants was allowed and even encouraged. For example, women often assumed leadership roles at camp meetings as exhorters, a very visible "public" role that Victorian society at large would have condemned.[11] As "rules" such as this waned, so did everyday economic and social hierarchies. At camp meetings, these hierarchies were temporarily suspended in favor of those based on religion, as an 1849 defender of camp meetings explained: "the pride and pomp of the city, with the multiplied cares and distinctions of society, are laid aside, and all meet as members of one family, entitled to equal attention, and destined to the same immortality."[12]

Despite this defender's claims, however, members of camp meeting "families" were not all the same. Positions within these communities varied, especially according to the degree to which one possessed religion. This created hierarchical relationships between camp meeting goers, all of which were highly visible on the grounds. In using the terms *hierarchy* and *hierarchical* in this essay, I refer to the often unarticulated but nonetheless prominent classification and organization of different camp meeting goers into categories or groups based on their religious status (sinner, saved, or sanctified). These hierarchical relationships between camp meeting goers were constantly in flux, since one's level of religion constantly underwent negotiation and renegotiation during religious services and other camp activities.[13] Since they held their first camp meetings on the frontier, Methodists went there to pray to God for forgiveness from their sins. Through rituals occurring at the altar, worshippers received God's blessing during their conversion, resulting in the creation of hierarchies between the "sinners" and the "saved." Although Methodist camp meetings continued to serve as sites for conversion through the early twentieth century, the post–Civil War holiness movement influenced rituals there dramatically. Where holiness was a concern, religious hierarchies became even more complicated; in addition to distinctions between the "saved" and "sinner," new hierarchical relationships took shape between the "merely saved" and those who had been "sanctified," thought to be the highest level of Christianity attainable.

Even if these categories changed through time, gazes between campers played an important part in the negotiation of religious hierarchies at Methodist and holiness camp meetings during the late nineteenth and early twentieth centuries. The hierarchies forged through gazes could be divisive, serving to mark divisions between people and groups, as in relationships between "saved" and "unsaved," as well as affirmative, in terms of strengthening ties between them, as in the idea of "family," which united those who attended camp meetings.[14] Examining Methodist and holiness camp meetings offers a way to destabilize earlier discussions of architecture and vision and unpack an expanded interpretation of the gaze by recognizing its reciprocal nature and its workings within a context of hierarchy.

Comparing the physical layouts of camp meetings erected between 1850 and 1925 offers a means to investigate the complex nature of the gazes operating at them. Camp meetings, whether Methodist, holiness, or otherwise, usually adhered to one of several plan types, all of which had become established by the mid-nineteenth century, as Charles Johnson and others have discussed.[15] God's Holiness Grove Camp Meeting exemplified a popular layout, which Johnson called the "open horseshoe." At God's Holiness, ninety-nine cabins formed a rectilinear U-shape around the tabernacle (fig. 8.4). Two parallel rows of cabins extended along the north and south sides of the tabernacle, while a single row of cabins marked the west row behind it. As Johnson noted, the open-horseshoe plan originated during the early nineteenth century, subsequently being used at Methodist and holiness camps of all sizes. Another holiness camp meeting, Elm Grove Camp, founded in the 1920s near the village of Center Valley in Lehigh County, Pennsylvania, displayed a U-shaped layout on a much smaller scale, containing only fourteen double cabins.[16]

Other arrangements employed at Methodist and holiness camps included the rectangular, circular, and radial layouts. Cleona Camp, founded by the

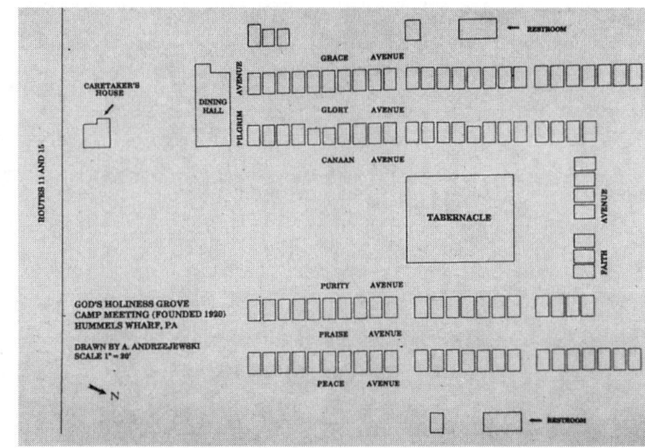

Fig. 8.4. Site plan of God's Holiness Grove Camp Meeting, Village of Hummels Wharf, Snyder County, Pennsylvania.

United Christian Church in 1896 and located near Cleona in Lebanon County, Pennsylvania, displayed a rectangular plan (fig. 8.5). The cabins at Cleona were laid out in a single row around a central tabernacle; but at other rectangular-plan camps, such as Balls Creek Camp Meeting Ground, a Methodist camp established in 1853 in Catawba County, North Carolina, several rows of cabins surrounded the tabernacle.[17] Another popular option was the circular plan, or a semicircular variant of it, such as the plan of the grounds of Mountain Grove Camp founded in 1872 in Luzerne County, Pennsylvania.[18] Like the square or U-shaped plans, the tabernacle stood at the center while the cabins encircled it. The circular and semicircular plans had limits in terms of expansion, since cabins could not be added in the circle as the camp grew. Instead, as with the rectangular layout, new cabins usually formed extra rows immediately behind the first.[19] The radial plan developed around this anticipated need of expansion. An original plan of Highland Park Camp Meeting, a Methodist camp founded in 1893 near Sellersville in Bucks County, Pennsylvania, showed that the original cabins were to be built around the tabernacle in a square, but that later cabins would be erected along avenues extending from the corners and sides (fig. 8.6). According to Merv Werst, a former president of the camp, these later avenues followed this radial pattern so that campers would have unobstructed views of the tabernacle from their cabin porches.[20]

Despite their differences, these camp meeting layouts possess similarities that establish a camp meeting typology for Methodist and holiness camps built between 1850 and 1925. The worship space formed the heart of these camp meetings, always standing at the center of the grounds.[21] At most late-nineteenth- or early-twentieth-century camps, a tabernacle occupied this space. Often the first tabernacle was temporary, being replaced several years later by a more permanent structure, as was the case at God's Holiness. The preaching stand, where itinerant ministers delivered sermons, was located at one end of the tabernacle. In front of this stand stood the altar, and benches or seats stood behind it, most of which lay under the roof of the

Fig. 8.5. View of "circle" of cabins at Cleona Camp, near Annville, Lebanon County, Pennsylvania. Photograph by the author, 1997.

Fig. 8.6. View looking at one of the radiating avenues extending off the main rectangular "circle" of cabins at Highland Park Camp Meeting, near Sellersville, Bucks County, Pennsylvania. Photograph by the author, 1997.

tabernacle. Lodgings for worshippers, referred to collectively as the "circle," flanked the tabernacle.[22] At most camps, the first accommodations were impermanent structures, which were gradually replaced by more sturdy cabins of frame construction. Boardinghouses, the domain of curious visitors to camp meetings, and stores were rare, usually found only at large late-nineteenth-century camps, in which cases they stood on the edges of the grounds. Man-made or natural boundaries, such as fences, tree lines, or creeks, surrounded camp meetings, separating them physically and symbolically from the outside world and marking them off as sacred spaces.

Lines of vision held an important place within this typology. Besides providing a physical separation, the boundaries on the edges of camp meeting grounds directed visual attention inward toward the camp and away from the outside world and the concerns of everyday life. With the exception of the radial plan, cabins faced the tabernacle, making an architectural gesture toward the physical and symbolic nucleus of the camp meeting.[23] The central and elevated preaching stand afforded speakers views over the benches, themselves arranged so that every seat in turn yielded a view of the stand. Even if the ministers could not literally see into all of the cabins, especially at night, when the podium would have been brightly illuminated, the position of the stand at the center of and above the worshippers implied a prospect that spanned the entire camp. Regardless of their type, date of construction, or layout, Methodist and holiness camps shared this emphasis on centralized planning, which facilitated gazing among and between camp meeting participants.

The architectural design of these camp meetings encouraged gazes between worshippers, who had many opportunities to view each other throughout the grounds. The proximity of cabins to each other and the lack of yards, fences, and dense clusters of trees on the grounds made privacy all but impossible. Ellen Weiss recognized this in her study of Wesleyan Grove, a Methodist camp meeting founded during the mid-nineteenth century at Martha's Vineyard, Massachusetts. Weiss observed how doors and windows dominated the facades of the cottages there, facilitating the very act of looking.[24] Even if not to the same degree, cabins at other camp meetings, Methodist and holiness alike, displayed multiple doors and large windows. Benches and large porches stood outside many of the front doors, encouraging campers to spend time in view of others. Camp rules also stressed the importance of visibility. Rule 13 of the 1889 Manual of Crystal Spring Camp Meeting, a Methodist camp established in Fulton County, Pennsylvania, in 1885, stated that lights must be on in cabins during night services and front doors must stay open, exposing the private space of the camp meeting "home" to the watchful eyes of other worshippers.[25]

Visibility between campers is a dominant theme of an 1874 novel by Mary Harriott Norris entitled *Camp Tabor,* based on a Methodist camp meeting founded in 1868 in Morris County, New Jersey. Relating the camp meeting experience through the eyes of four children, Norris repeatedly raised the idea of negotiating space through the viewing act. The following focuses on the close contact between campers, highlighting the role that gazing played in negotiating relationships at camp meetings:

> Charlie thrust his curly head through his tent-curtains at the identical moment that Bentie looked out from hers. The black eyes, intent on seeing the new comers, looked straight into the gray ones, determined to take in all of their surroundings.

> The two children were so surprised at their relative positions that for a moment they gazed unabashed. Then each head disappeared, to come out a moment after for a second view.[26]

On another morning, Trot, the youngest child, walked through camp: "with no other object than to have a peep into the cottages." On her jaunt, she noticed a small tent set away from the others. Curious, Trot thought nothing of peeking in to observe a woman saying her prayers.[27] Norris used these vignettes in part to show the children's naïveté, but they also reveal how dependent the organization and operation of the camp meeting is on the condition of viewing and being viewed.

Another gaze at religious camp meetings involved the visual exchange between worshippers and the preachers who took turns leading religious services. This kind of gaze related to the religious end of camp meetings: to encourage camp meeting goers toward higher spirituality. At Methodist camps founded before the Civil War, ministers and exhorters aimed chiefly to convert sinners; but at camp meetings held later in the nineteenth and early twentieth centuries, speakers also attempted to help the already-converted attain sanctification. Whatever the circumstances, reciprocal gazes between speakers and worshippers were important means of assuring the latter's participation in services, thought to be absolutely critical to the success of camp meetings. Drawings from the popular press, nineteenth-century camp meeting manuals, and minister biographies illustrate the visual intercourse between worshippers and preachers. A sketch of Deal's Island Camp Meeting from an 1861 biography depicts a famous Methodist exhorter, Joshua Thomas, speaking to worshippers who in turn gaze upon him (fig. 8.7). Although some campers on the fringes of the circle engage in conversation while a few others bow their heads in prayer, the eyes of most dutifully focus upon the speaker. The preaching stand, in this drawing in the open air rather than a tabernacle, facilitated these gazes, occupying a central and elevated position on the grounds. Further, the benches on which the worshippers sit radiate outward from the stand, affording many good views. Behind them, all of the cabins in the circle face the central preaching space.[28]

In his 1859 autobiography, William Henry Milburn, a Methodist preacher, addressed the reciprocal nature of this minister-worshipper gaze. Milburn articulated his desire for eye contact with his congregation, asserting that it was through this visual exchange that his power, and hence the power of God, appeared. He expressed anxiety about his rhetorical prowess, because he was blind: "Who has not felt the matchless power of the human eye? . . . Men not only see with their eyes, but hear; for the beaming eye and expressive face speak a language that articulate sounds can never ex-

Fig. 8.7. Deal's Island (Maryland) Camp Meeting, anonymous illustration from Adam Wallace, *The Parson of the Islands; A Biography of the Rev. Joshua Thomas* (Philadelphia: Adam Wallace, 1861). Courtesy of the University of Delaware Library, Newark, Delaware.

press—a language more moving, soft, and irresistible than ever entered the soul through the galleries of the ear. Through the eye, the speaker enters into sympathy with his audience, by it he perceives their capacity, reads their wants, appreciates their condition; by it they are persuaded of his simplicity, earnestness and faith . . . so true is it, here at least, 'that seeing is believing.'"[29] Milburn deemed "vision" essential to all of his ministerial pursuits. Although he discussed his fears in the context of his duties as chaplain for the U.S. Congress, his anxiety extended to his duties as a camp meeting exhorter as well. Milburn felt that it was in and through a reciprocal gaze that conversion of sinners occurred. In his case, vision extended beyond the biological act of seeing to encompass other senses, signaling the need to consider gazing at camp meetings in multisensate and even metaphorical terms. Even if he could not "see," Milburn looked at his worshippers through his words and physical and symbolic position as minister while also functioning as the focus of their watchful and dependent gaze.

These multiple, reciprocal gazes operated at Methodist and holiness camp meetings within a context of hierarchy. Through them, one's physical, social, and religious position at the camp was created, negotiated, and reinforced. Religious hierarchies are even written into the tenets of the Christian faith. For example, in chapter 8 of the book of Numbers in the Old Testament, the narrator explained how God chose the Levites from among the sons of Israel to serve him at the tent of meeting after their conversion and baptism, creating a hierarchical relationship between them and other followers.[30] Practiced by the evangelical denominations, baptism and conversion have hierarchy at their essence, since as a result of these events, a higher level of Christian is believed to emerge. Further, the evangelical tradition stresses the responsibility of converted Christians to lead by example, as the Methodist Rev. A. P. Mead explained in 1859: "When our souls are thus baptized, and purified, and filled with love, we are prepared to lead sinners to Christ. This love will lead us to seek lost sinners."[31] Camp meetings were an important forum for negotiating religious status, since religious awakenings of various types remained a major goal of the annual retreats, from the conversion-oriented Methodist camps in the nineteenth century to holiness ones founded mainly after the Civil War that accommodated sanctifications in addition to conversions.

Hierarchical negotiations played out at these camp meetings at multiple levels and between the participants in many different ways, with vision serving an important role. Since the earliest camp meetings were held on the frontier, gazes exchanged between campers involved distinguishing religious from nonreligious attendees. In his 1823 biography, Rev. Jesse Lee articulated a distinction that became commonplace in later descriptions of Methodist camp meetings: "disorder originates from the disorderly spectators, and not from the orderly worshippers who assemble for the sole purpose of spiritual benefit."[32] In Lee's and other Methodists' writings, "worshippers," who engaged in the religious activities of camp meetings, were sharply differentiated from "spectators," who came for social reasons or entertainment. In 1859 Reverend Mead adopted this distinction when asking a friend why he did not like camp meetings: "Did you attend as a *spectator,* or as a *worshipper?* Perhaps you stood aloof and looked on, and thus you saw some incidental things that you could not approve . . . did you take any part in the religious exercises, and thus identify yourself with the good work?"[33] In using the term *spectator* to refer to those who did not actively participate in camp meeting activities, Lee and Mead raise the possibility of interpreting camp meetings within the context of spectacle.[34] In this context, a spectator merely looked upon the events with a passive eye, intent on merely watching the striking show of events but refraining from a participatory role. This type of vision contrasted sharply with the active gazes of worshippers within the camp meeting circle, which aimed to transform the behavior of both seer and seen.

Whether one experienced camp meeting as spectator or worshipper directly related to the physical position that these different types of campers occupied on the grounds. At services, spectators took seats at the back of the worship space or stood outside it. Usually, they stayed on the grounds only for the day or, at most, two. If they stayed overnight, they resided in cabins, tents, or boardinghouses at the margins of the grounds. Worshippers, on the other hand, took good seats on benches in the tabernacle and lived in cabins on the circle.[35] Given the visibility of the nineteenth-century camp meeting environment, distinctions between devout worshippers and idle spectators would have been very apparent. The differences between them can be seen in the frontispiece from Methodist preacher B. W. Gorham's 1854 *Camp Meeting Manual* and in an undated engraving of a camp meeting in Clinton County, Pennsylvania (figs. 8.8, 8.9). In each illustration, worshippers are depicted sitting in front of the preaching stand looking intently at the speaker, in sharp contrast to spectators who are shown paying little attention to the religious activities. In the drawing from Gorham's book, a pair of rather disinterested dandies linger by the tree at the rear of the meeting, similar to the way the finely dressed male and female spectators dawdle about on the edges of the Clinton County camp. As in everyday Victorian society, camp meeting goers would have read appearances as a means of knowing others; but at camp meetings, appearances were somewhat less deceiving than in society at large. In this context, any show of fashion

Fig. 8.8. Frontispiece from Barlow Weed Gorham's *Camp Meeting Manual: A Practical Book for the Camp Ground* (Boston: H. V. Degen, 1854). Courtesy of the University of Delaware Library, Newark, Delaware.

Fig. 8.9. Interior view of West Branch camp meeting, Clinton County, Pennsylvania, n.d. Reproduced courtesy of the Department of Prints and Photographs, Library of Congress, Washington, D.C.

was perceived as a sign of spiritual malaise, and automatically marked those who wore such dress as spectators.[36]

An anonymous 1849 essay suggests some ways in which Methodist camp meeting goers in the mid-nineteenth century negotiated their position on the sliding scale of the worshipper-spectator hierarchy. The author stressed that the influence of good Christians upon less fervent ones pushed the latter toward spiritual growth. For spectators, camp meetings provided a forum for them to mend their ways. The author argued that here they encountered good Christian worshippers to emulate:

> They need to *see* and *hear* a higher order of Christians, and feel their regenerating influence . . . Camp-meetings bring together the best spirits within a large circumference. Those who possess most of the divine influence, and are best informed in the science of salvation, are much inclined to such meetings. They love to retire from the world, to commune with God and his people. They delight to talk of his word and works—of the blessedness of religion; to sing his praise and tell of his goodness. How appropriate then is the place for the stupid and the impenitent![37]

The author asserted that worshippers held a role almost as important as that of the preachers. It was their responsibility to "take the difficulties out of the sinner's way . . . and bring him under the most powerful stimulants to duty possible," by which the author meant their own pietistic behavior.[38] If worshippers did not behave like model Christians, he knew spectators would see: "great care should be exercised in regard to our *general deportment*. . . . The rules of the ground are to be strictly observed. If we [good Christians] violate them, how can we enforce them upon others?"[39] This writer's anxiety about visual influences highlights how relationships between Methodists at mid-nineteenth-century camp meetings were bound to the viewing act.

At Methodist camp meetings held through the early 1860s, gazes between worshippers and spectators furthered the latter's move toward Christian conversion. At these camps, religious hierarchies revolved around whether one was "saved" or not, and one's position there, both physical and religious, turned on this distinction. At camp meetings where holiness was a concern, most of which were held after the Civil War, hierarchical distinctions between campers became more complicated. To the categories of "sinners" and "saved" were added "seekers of holiness" and "sanctified." Although the worshipper-spectator distinction remained in use, in this context spectator could refer to the believer who came to camp with no intention of seeking sanctification as much as to the nonbeliever. Rev. R. V. Lawrence, a holiness preacher, explained: "[T]he mere fact of being on the camp-ground in the midst of all these holy persons and influences will not make you more holy . . . The most heavenly scenes of the camp-ground, witnessed as a spectator, but not engaged in as a participant, will harden and disgust. The mere spectator had better hurry off the ground before the devil of ridicule and dislike creeps into his soul."[40] Knowing who had received the second blessing, who sought it, and who was there as a spectator was important at camp meetings where holiness was practiced. Through contact with the "holy," the sanctified confirmed their beliefs while seekers moved closer to attaining holiness.

The sanctified and seekers of holiness had responsibilities besides confirming and advancing their religious beliefs.[41] At the 1873 National Camp Meeting for the Promotion of Holiness in

Landisville, Pennsylvania, a holiness preacher stressed to seekers of the second blessing and to those who possessed holiness that they had a mandate from "above" to lead others in their spiritual pursuits. He urged them to "win a soul for Jesus" by focusing on campers who needed to be converted or sanctified and bring them along in their quest.[42] Another minister at this camp, Rev. L. C. Matlock, explained how the sanctified had the important responsibility of converting others by their visual example: "These souls become magnetic centers of attraction, filled with God's gracious power, their light shines and is seen of men. They radiate pious influence over a vast circumference. Instrumentally they fulfill the Savior's words, 'I, when lifted up, will draw all men unto me.' "[43] At camp meetings where holiness was practiced, the creation of another religious category, the "sanctified," produced an even more complicated worshipper-spectator hierarchy—but one that was equally dependent upon gazing as a means of forging relationships between campers, who watched one another to secure their relative place in the camp meeting's religious hierarchy.

Hierarchies were also negotiated through the reciprocal gazes exchanged between worshippers and the preachers and exhorters. In evangelical churches, the devout usually relied upon one minister to lead religious services; but Methodist and holiness camps attracted multiple itinerant preachers and exhorters who took turns leading the exercises. At camp meetings, the figure of the preacher or exhorter served as a guiding force, regardless of who occupied the pulpit at a particular time. During services, the presiding speaker and other ministers stood on a centrally located and elevated stand that emphasized their prominence, as this 1859 account of a camp meeting illustrates: "[On the campground] . . . Hundreds of worshippers, occupying the rude benches are listening . . . Nearly a score of ministers occupy a seat directly back of the speaker, and in full view of the congregation . . . lights burn brightly behind the altar, surrounded by darkness . . . nothing here to divert attention."[44] The physical position of the speakers at the center of and above the worshippers dovetailed with their duties as leaders of camp meetings. In his 1854 manual, Reverend Gorham emphasized the need to keep in place the distinctions between ministers and worshippers: "On the campground, as in the army, and for similar reasons, there must be a general Head."[45] The leadership of the itinerant ministers was thought to assure that worshippers focused on religious goals, such as worship, conversion, and sanctification. Further, preachers served as exemplars for camp meeting goers to emulate, even more so than the "model" worshippers discussed above.

Descriptions of nineteenth-century Methodist camp meetings show the key role that ministers and exhorters played, converting souls through their example. These accounts emphasize how conversions involved the facility with which worshippers saw the preacher, how successfully their gaze was returned, and how religious status was negotiated through it. An example is found in an 1861 account of a camp meeting on Deal's Island, Maryland. The writer described how the Rev. Joshua Thomas attracted the attention of his congregation during his exhortation:

> The eyes of the congregation kindled, as they followed him [Thomas] in his movement towards the "stand." . . . "At first I thought the man was a fool, and the preachers were to blame for asking him up. I was about leaving my seat in disgust and indignation and retiring from the ground; for, though I was not a professor of religion, I respected its order too much to see it cari-

> catured in that manner. I finally concluded to stand it out, rather than attract attention by my departure. I took a steady look at him, and in that instant one of the strangest sensations I ever had experienced, came over me . . . for the first time in all my life, I trembled from head to foot, under a new and over-powering conviction that I was a lost sinner."[46]

In this vignette, the narrator's conversion took place through the very act of fixing his eyes upon the minister. Similar accounts abound in descriptions of Methodist and even some holiness camp meetings of the late nineteenth and early twentieth centuries, which recount how conversions at camp meetings was closely tied with the reciprocal gaze between preacher and worshipper.[47]

At holiness camp meetings, gazes between ministers and worshippers were believed to impel those seeking sanctification toward their goals. Although some sanctifications actually occurred at camp meeting services, in many cases the recipient did not secure the second blessing until several days later. However, attending to the preacher or exhorter was believed to push seekers toward sanctification, even if they did not achieve it during the sermon. An 1873 description of the exhortations of holiness pastor R. V. Lawrence illustrates his persuasive power, through which he propelled his congregation toward holiness: "Brother Lawrence *employed largely the power of description, and illustration* . . . he understood that a successful pulpit must arrest attention, hold it, and concentrate the thoughts of the hearer upon the great truths of salvation." Through gazing upon "this man of God," many in Lawrence's crowd had joy awoken in their hearts, even if for many, the "joy" of sanctification itself followed later.[48] Further, at holiness services it was not just the gaze from worshippers to ministers, but the reciprocal gaze between them, that furthered religious experiences. Beverly Carradine, a holiness evangelist, explained how during a camp meeting in 1911, he felt he saw into the souls of people gazing back at him, which in turn spurred him to more emphatically preach his holiness message to them.[49]

The role of the ministers and exhorters as focal points of the worshippers' gazes transcended their own physical being. Although they were the acknowledged leaders at camp meetings, they also served as vehicles for and to a "higher power." A Methodist preacher explained his purpose as an agent of God in a sermon directed at sinners invoking biblical verse, when he demanded: "'Look unto me and be ye saved, al ye ends of the earth; for I am God, and there is none else.'"[50] Through the figure of the minister, holiness worshippers also hoped to look toward and upon their God, and in the process find sanctification. Through gazing upon the holiness preacher J. L. Brasher, seekers explained how his powers of illustration helped them "see" God, as J. Lawrence Brasher wrote in a recent biography of the famous minister: "Letters from Brasher's listeners testify to 'eyes opened only in spiritual vision' during his preaching. After hearing him in 1907 at White Cross Camp Meeting near Oneonta, Alabama, Eloway Hurst wrote, 'The sermon you preached Sunday was the richest I had heard for awhile. It seemed to me sometimes my poor little narrow contracted soul would burst out of its fetters . . . and soar into the heavenlies.' A listener in Conneaut, Ohio, told Brasher that his eloquence brought her 'face to face with God Himself.'"[51] Thus gazes at both Methodist and holiness camp meetings extended beyond reciprocal gazes between the ministers and their congregation to involve a third, if not actually physical, player: the spirit that reigned above them in the religious hierarchy, but who spoke through the ministers and exhorters to whom the worshippers looked for guidance.

At God's Holiness, as at many Methodist and holiness camp meetings before it, the annual meeting closed with a circular procession around the campground. "Marching around Jerusalem," as this event was sometimes called, appears to have been intended to strengthen the commitment of camp meeting goers as members of the Christian faith before they returned to their everyday lives. In 1859, Reverend Mead described an emotional closing ceremony at a Methodist camp: "The procession starts from the right of the stand, and passes on within the inner circle of tents . . . We are marching to the music of Zion! We are in the grove! The winds are still . . . How touching is the scene! Here is manhood with its strength and hope; but who can resist the current of sympathy that flows from heart to heart?"[52] Regardless of their religious position within the camp, Mead explained that at the closing ceremony all campers perceived themselves as part of a Christian family. Rev. Edgar Levy preached a similar kind of unity in a sermon at the close of the Sixteenth National Camp Meeting for the Promotion of Holiness at Landisville, Pennsylvania, in 1873, stressing how holiness meetings brought together a Christian brotherhood: "As it is the nature of sin to separate, disintegrate, and repel, it is the nature of holiness to unite, adjust, and harmonize."[53] These rituals reminded campers of their shared mission to bring God's word into the world, while simultaneously impressing upon them that their own devotion to God should not wane after leaving the campground. Gazing held an important place in these ceremonies, since the gazes of camp meeting goers across the circle would have reinforced the sense of community and commitment at the heart of the closing ritual.

By emphasizing the unity that bound camp meeting goers together, Mead's and Levy's accounts of these closing ceremonies might appear to contradict the very notion of the existence of hierarchies advanced earlier in this chapter. Just as the cabins encircling the tabernacles tend to present a uniform appearance, worshippers promenading in the circles may seem to have no distinguishing position relative to one another. But gazes of hierarchy operated here as well, if in a different and more complicated manner. Even if new divisive hierarchies emerged at Methodist and holiness camp meetings as this essay as shown, the very act of going to camp and participating in its events simultaneously assured camp meeting goers' positions as devout Christians relative to those who did not attend camp meetings. Further, the ritual offered campers the chance to affirm their positions within their hierarchical groups as worshippers or spectators or, at holiness camps, as saved or sanctified. Viewing their fellow worshippers across the circle, their gazes assumed a unifying, reinforcing function quite different from the gazes that divided them into groups but which were still hierarchical in nature.[54] Rather than forge divisions, the closing ceremony attests to the affirmative role of gazes at Methodist and holiness camp meetings. Both the divisive and affirmative gazes point to the complex nature of vision at work in these spaces and, perhaps more significantly, the complex ways in which the practice of gazing in a larger sense pervaded the everyday lives of persons during the nineteenth and early twentieth centuries.

Notes

1. I would like to thank those who supported me during the research and writing of this essay. A Henry Luce Foundation American Art Dissertation Research Award administered through the

art history department at the University of Delaware made travel connected with this project possible. I thank the Department of Art History, the Graduate School of Arts and Sciences, and the Office of Women's Affairs, University of Delaware, and Cultural Heritage Research Services (CHRS) of North Wales, Pennsylvania, for funding my travel to the 1997 VAF Annual Meeting. Gabrielle Lanier, Nadine Miller Peterson, and Wanda C. Parrish gave generously of their time to help me visit and document camp meetings throughout Pennsylvania. I also appreciate the feedback of those who read the manuscript at various stages: Bernie Herman, Gabrielle Lanier, Patricia Keller, Monique Borque, Cynthia Falk, Tom Ryan, Ann Kirschner, Louis P. Nelson, Mark Parker Miller, Dell Upton, Bill Littmann, Rebecca Siders, Sally McMurry, Annmarie Adams, Kenneth O. Brown, three anonymous readers, and especially my VAF session chair, Ellen Weiss. Matt Andrzejewski patiently dealt with my never-ending anxiety, always willing to lend an ear even when he was fretting about his own research. I also appreciate the assistance (and patience) of librarians, volunteers, and archivists at the Free Library of Philadelphia; the Library of Congress; the University of Delaware (especially the Special Collections Department and Interlibrary Loan Office); the Columbia County, Pennsylvania, Historical Society; the Union County, Pennsylvania, Historical Society; and the Archives at Drew University. Above all, thanks to the camp meeting goers who allowed me access to their camps and records, especially James Leininger, Scott Schambach, and Charles Robinson of God's Holiness Grove Camp Meeting, who were willing to share much of their time enlightening me about the history of this very special wooded grove.

2. Most information about the camp's history comes from two locally published histories. See Lodge W. Chappell, Harry J. Daniels, and John P. Campbell, *Camp Meeting Memories: A Short History of Holiness Camp Meetings in Central Penna* (Sunbury, Pa.: Sunbury Daily Item, 1951) and Rev. Howard J. Frey, Rev. R. Marlin Hain, and Harold F. Koppenhaver, *Fifty Years of Spiritual Ministry* (pamphlet, 1970). Also helpful were conversations with persons associated with the camp, including Al and Sue Carroll, Scott Schambach, and Rev. James Leininger. Most of the original buildings survive, although some have been renovated, including the tabernacle, which now measures approximately 105 by 80 feet in size.
3. The oft-cited example of the first camp meeting is the one held at Cane Ridge, Kentucky, in 1801. Kenneth O. Brown has taken issue with the prevalent chronology in camp meeting studies that meetings emerged spontaneously in the wake of the success of Cane Ridge. Despite Brown's well-reasoned and convincing argument that details the gradual popularization of camp meetings and revivals in the late eighteenth century, Cane Ridge was one of the earliest examples and likely contributed at some level to the flourishing of a broader camp meeting "movement" during the nineteenth century. See Brown, *Holy Ground: A Study of the American Camp Meeting* (New York: Garland, 1992). Useful sources on the history of the camp meetings include Brown, *Holy Ground;* Ellen Weiss, *City in the Woods: The Life and Design of an American Camp Meeting on Martha's Vineyard* (New York and Oxford: Oxford Univ. Press, 1987); Dickson D. Bruce, *And They All Sang Hallelujah: Plain-Folk Camp-Meeting Religion, 1800–1845* (Knoxville: Univ. of Tennessee Press, 1974); Charles Albert

Johnson, *The Frontier Camp Meeting: Religion's Harvest Time* (Dallas: Southern Methodist Univ. Press, 1955); and Ray McKinzie Goodrow, "From Sacred Space to Suburban Retreat: The Evolution of the American Camp Meeting Ground" (master's thesis, University of Virginia, 1994). The numerous studies of individual camp meetings and meetings of denominations other than Methodism, many of them scholarly, are far too numerous to list here.

4. Johnson emphasized the importance of camp meetings to Methodism, discussing how they became a "weapon" through which the denomination gained adherents during the early nineteenth century. See Johnson, *The Frontier Camp Meeting,* esp. 84–85.
5. On camp meetings and the holiness revival, see Melvin Easterday Dieter, *The Holiness Revival of the Nineteenth Century* (Metuchen, N.J., and London: Scarecrow Press, 1980), esp. 96–155; Charles Edwin Jones, *Perfectionist Persuasion: The Holiness Movement and American Methodism, 1867–1936* (Metuchen, N.J., and London: Scarecrow Press, 1974); and J. Lawrence Brasher, *The Sanctified South: John Lakin Brasher and the Holiness Movement* (Urbana and Chicago: Univ. of Illinois Press, 1994).
6. This essay focuses on the religious aspects of camp meetings. As Weiss, Goodrow, and others have shown, many camp meetings evolved into summer resort communities in the late nineteenth century, bringing together those who wished to recreate in a Christian environment. However, many camps remained focused on religious activities, or included religious activities as part of them.
7. Although gazing likely held an important place at camp meetings of other denominations, this essay is based on research in the specific contexts of Methodist and holiness camps.
8. The literature on the "male gaze" and power is extensive and cross-disciplinary. Notable studies may be found in the areas of literary criticism, psychoanalysis, philosophy, and art history. Some of the most notable, influential, and useful studies come from film theory and photography criticism; see Laura Mulvey, "Visual Pleasure and Narrative Cinema," *Screen* 16 (autumn 1975): 6–18; Jacqueline Rose, *Sexuality in the Field of Vision* (London: Verso, 1986); and Kate Linker, "Representation and Sexuality," *Parachute* 32 (fall 1983): 12–23. Many of these texts make use of the writings of Jacques Lacan and his rewriting of Freud's theories regarding the "structures of sexuality" in terms of active and passive relations. One of the more accessible examples of Lacan's work that discusses this is "Guiding Remarks for a Congress on Feminine Sexuality" (1958), reproduced in *Feminine Sexuality: Jacques Lacan and the École Freudienne*, ed. Juliet Mitchell and Jacqueline Rose (New York: W. W. Norton, 1982); see also Lacan's writings in *Écrits: A Selection,* ed. Alan Sheridan (London: Tavistock; New York: Norton, 1975). On the male gaze in art history, see John Berger, *Ways of Seeing* (London: British Broadcasting Company and Penguin, 1973) and Rozsika Parker and Griselda Pollock, *Old Mistresses: Women, Art, and Ideology* (New York: Pantheon Books, 1981).
9. In the language of feminist criticism, I recognize that this would mean that men and women both take on the "male" gaze, meaning they both have active control over the ability to look. See Mulvey, *Visual Pleasure and Narrative Cinema.*
10. Michel Foucault, *Discipline and Punish: The Birth of the Prison,* trans. Alan Sheridan (New

York: Vintage Books, 1977) and Power/ Knowledge: Selected *Interviews and Other Writings, 1972–1977,* ed. Colin Gordon, trans. Colin Gordon, Leo Marshall, John Mepham, and Kate Soper (New York: Pantheon Books, 1980). See also Robin Evans, *The Fabrication of Virtue: English Prison Architecture, 1750–1840* (Cambridge & New York: Cambridge Univ. Press, 1982) and Michael Ignatieff, *A Just Measure of Pain: The Penitentiary in the Industrial Revolution, 1750–1850* (New York: Pantheon Books, 1978).

11. On the anxiety about the gaze in the nineteenth century, see Karen Halttunen, *Confidence Men and Painted Women: A Study of Middle-Class Culture in America, 1830–1870* (New Haven and London: Yale Univ. Press, 1982) and John F. Kasson, *Rudeness and Civility: Manners in Nineteenth-Century Urban America* (New York: Hill and Wang, 1990). The different roles women assumed at Methodist and holiness camp meetings far exceeds the scope of this study; good discussions of women's place at camp meetings include Bruce, *And They All Sang Hallelujah,* esp. 73–132, and Joe L. Kincheloe Jr., "Transcending Role Restrictions: Women at Camp Meetings and Political Rallies," *Tennessee Historical Quarterly* 40 (summer 1981).
12. Anonymous (James Porter?), An Essay on Camp-Meetings, by the Author of "The True Evangelist" (New York: Lane and Scott, 1849), 20–21.
13. Bruce discussed the negotiation of hierarchies at camp meetings between 1800 and 1845 in *And They All Sang Hallelujah,* 73–132. However, he did not examine how these hierarchies were negotiated through vision or examine Methodist or other camp meetings after 1850.
14. My thoughts on affirmative and divisive hierarchies at camp meetings derive from Dell Upton's discussion of style and mode in architecture and its functioning within a social context (itself derived from linguist Basil Bernstein's concept of restricted and elaborated codes). See Upton's "Toward a Performance Theory of Vernacular Architecture: Early Tidewater Virginia as a Case Study," *Folklore Forum* (1979): 173–96 and *Holy Things and Profane: Anglican Parish Churches in Colonial Virginia* (New York: Architectural History Foundation; Cambridge and London: MIT Press), 99–162.
15. This typology is based on my study of over thirty Methodist and holiness camp meetings throughout central and eastern Pennsylvania and secondary sources, including Johnson, *The Frontier Camp Meeting,* 41–44; William M. Clements, "The Physical Layout of the Methodist Camp Meeting," *Pioneer America* 5 (January 1973): 9–15; Goodrow, "From Sacred Space to Suburban Retreat," 16–28; and Weiss, *City in the Woods.* Johnson identified three main plan types: the open horseshoe, the oblong square, and the circular; my findings differ slightly from his. Although my focus here is on Methodist and holiness camps, these other sources address camp meetings of a variety of denominations, at which many of these same layouts are used.
16. An example of a Methodist camp meeting that employs the U-shaped layout is Perkasie Park Camp Meeting, located in Perkasie, Bucks County, Pennsylvania (1882).
17. Information on Balls Creek Camp Meeting comes from Goodrow, "From Sacred Space to Suburban Retreat," 29.
18. Information on Mountain Grove Camp Meeting comes from Craig A. Newton, "Of Piety's Pleasure: The Mountain Grove Camp Meeting," *Pennsylvania Heritage* 11 (Spring 1985): 12–17. Another excellent example of the circular plan is Indian Fields Methodist Campground (c. 1848), in Dorchester County, South Carolina. On this camp meeting, see

Records of the Historic American Buildings Survey (HABS), No. SC-595, held in the Library of Congress, Department of Prints and Photographs, Washington, D.C.

19. This occurred at Northeast Nazarene Camp founded in the early 1900s in Northeast, Maryland. In January 1997 one of the caretakers of the camp, Muriel Wetzel, explained that initially all of the original cabins flanked the tabernacle in an oval shape. Later, an additional row of cabins was added behind the first, and, subsequently, additional cabins were built outside the original plan.
20. Conversation with Merv Werst, January 1997. The original plan is located in private papers located in the camp's office. Another example of the radial-planned camp meeting is found in Goodrow, "From Sacred Space to Suburban Retreat," 25, at Pitman Grove Camp Meeting Ground (1872), in Pitman Grove, New Jersey.
21. Johnson, *The Frontier Camp Meeting,* 42.
22. In many cases, ministers and exhorters also lived in cabins on the circle, although other times they resided in buildings located behind the preaching stands.
23. On the edges of larger camps, where facing the tabernacle was not possible, the cabins faced one another, perhaps the next best alternative to gazing upon the minister. This arrangement is seen at Northeast Nazarene Camp, in Northeast, Maryland. With radial plans, the layout itself was symbolic of "inward looking." The cabins actually did not face the tabernacle, but toward roads that led toward it. While the actual view of events occurring in the tabernacle would not have been as comprehensive as views from cabins in the "circle," in most cases cabins in radially planned camps were positioned such that from their front porches they could see some of the activities occurring at the center.
24. Weiss, *City in the Woods,* 30–38, 70–75.
25. *By-laws, Rules and Regulations of Crystal Spring Camp Meeting Association of Brush Creek, Fulton County, PA, Chartered 6 December a.d. 1886* (Everett, Pa.: John C. Chamberlain, 1889), 12. Rules such as these were thought to prevent certain indiscretions, such as drinking and illicit sexual encounters, from occurring on the sacred grounds. On indiscretions and methods to prevent them, see Johnson, *The Frontier Camp Meeting*, 54, 89–92; and Weiss, *City in the Woods*, 73.
26. Mary Harriott Norris, *Camp Tabor: A Story of Child Life in the Woods* (New York: Phillips and Hunt; Cincinnati: Cranston and Sloan, 1874), 25.
27. Ibid., 32.
28. This sketch appears in Adam Wallace's book *The Parson of the Islands: A Biography of the Late Rev. Joshua Thomas* (Philadelphia, 1861). See also the frontispiece from Barlow Weed Gorham's *Camp Meeting Manual: A Practical Book for the Camp Ground* (Boston: H. V. Degen, 1854).
29. William Henry Milburn, *Ten Years of Preacher-Life: Chapters from an Autobiography* (New York: Derby & Jackson, 1859), 116–17. The equation of "seeing" with knowledge of God has a long history as a metaphor in Christianity; a good discussion of this tradition may be found in Martin Jay, *Downcast Eyes: The Denigration of Vision in Twentieth-Century French Thought* (Berkeley, Los Angeles, and London: Univ. of California Press, 1993), esp. chapter 1.
30. Num. 8:5–15.
31. Rev. A. P. Mead, *Manna in the Wilderness*; *or, the Grove and Its Altar, Offerings, and Thrilling Incidents* (Philadelphia: Perkinpine and Higgins, 1859), 89. See also Anonymous, *An Essay on Camp Meetings,* esp. pages 27–35.
32. Jesse Lee, *Memoir of the Rev. Jesse Lee, with Extracts from His Journals* (New York: N. Bangs and T. Mason, 1823), 289.

33. Mead, *Manna in the Wilderness,* 29–30. The Rev. Barlow Weed Gorham makes a similar distinction, noting the different classes of those that attend camp meetings, even if he does not use the terms spectators and worshippers: "He that goes to church merely to see or be seen accomplishes that object and returns home. He that goes to be entertained with the intellectual qualities of a discourse, listens to it in a corresponding temple of mind, and is acted upon accordingly; but he that goes to church hungering and thirsting after righteousness shall be filled." Gorham, *Camp Meeting Manual,* 45.
34. This context is discussed in much greater detail in chapter 4 of my forthcoming Ph.D. dissertation, "Architecture and the Ideology of Surveillance in Modern America, 1870–1940" (Newark, Del.: Univ. of Delaware, 1999).
35. Bruce, *And They All Sang Hallelujah,* 79. Brasher raises this issue of one's religious status determining the space he or she occupied in the southern Methodist church in *Sanctified South*, 23, although he does not apply this to camp meetings.
36. Halttunen, *Confidence Men and Painted Women, and Kasson, Rudeness and Civility.*
37. Anonymous, *An Essay on Camp Meetings,* 25.
38. Ibid., 30.
39. Ibid., 78–79.
40. Rev. E. H. Stokes, Rev. George Hughes, and Rev. Adam Wallace, *The Earnest Minister: A Record of the Life, Labors and Literary Remains of Rev. Ruliff V. Lawrence, for Sixteen Years an Itinerant in the New Jersey and Philadelphia Conferences* (Philadelphia: Adam Wallace, Methodist Home Journal Office, 1873), 330–31.
41. Rev. R. V. Lawrence articulated this well: "Be active in helping others. What! were you so selfish as to come all the way to this Camp Meeting for your own sole benefit. How unlike Jesus! . . . Be active. There is a blessing here for you; find it." See Stokes et al., *The Earnest Minister,* 330–31.
42. Adam Wallace, ed., *A Modern Pentecost: Embracing a Record of the 16th National Camp Meeting for the Promotion of Holiness, Held at Landisville, Pennsylvania, July 23rd to August 1st, 1873* [1873] (Salem, Ohio: Convention Book Store, 1970), 16.
43. Ibid., 126. Stories like these appear repeatedly throughout the holiness camp meeting literature. See also Stokes et al., *The Earnest Minister*, 63, 164; Revs. A. McLean and J. W. Eaton, eds., *Penuel; or, Face to Face with God* [1869] (New York and London: Garland, 1984), 14; and Brasher, *The Sanctified South.*
44. Mead, *Manna in the Wilderness,* 136.
45. Gorham, *Camp Meeting Manual,* 151.
46. Wallace, *The Parson of the Islands,* 222–23.
47. Further evidence of the importance of "seeing" in the conversion process relates to Joshua Thomas's own conversion. After many attempts to be converted in private (out of fear of having to lose his composure at the altar in front of the watchful eyes of other worshippers), Thomas finds that his conversion could only occur as he stood at the altar at the feet of the presiding speaker and God. Looking on at the services for him was essential. See Wallace, *The Parson of the Islands*, 88–90. Meanwhile, Mead discussed the more complex case of William Wyatt, who, while not a good-looking man, had the spirit in him. Thus, he still attracted the congregation's attention and converted many. See Mead, *Manna in the Wilderness,* 286–93.
48. Stokes et al., *The Earnest Minister,* 120–21, 129.
49. Brasher, *The Sanctified South,* 103; Beverly Carradine, *Graphic Scenes* (Cincinnati: God's Revivalist Office, 1911), 254.
50. Mead, *Manna in the Wilderness,* 239. See also

Wallace, *The Parson of the Islands,* 222–23, and John Franklin Grimes, *The Romance of the American Camp Meeting* (Cincinnati: Caxton Press, 1922), 84.

51. Brasher, *The Sanctified South,* 103–4.

52. Mead, *Manna in the Wilderness,* 410.

53. Levy is quoted in Wallace, *A Modern Pentecost,* 114.

54. On divisive and affirmative hierarchies, see Upton, *Holy Things and Profane,* 99–162.

PART III

THE INTERPENETRATION OF PRIVATE AND PUBLIC

CHAPTER 9

Michael Ann Williams and Larry Morrisey

Constructions of Tradition: Vernacular Architecture, Country Music, and Auto-Ethnography

Vernacular architecture scholars have increasingly studied the products of automobile tourism, although often with a wink of the eye or with tongue planted in cheek. We are still quick to separate the "authentic" material representations of traditional culture from the stereotypical portrayals produced by our consumer culture. Perhaps we have been too quick in our judgments. As some scholars have argued, our contemporary culture is "auto-ethnographic"; it creates its own ethnographic depictions of itself. If this is true, then the role of the scholar engaged in ethnography (including the student of vernacular architecture) needs to change. Shouldn't we study and understand how a culture chooses to document and represent itself?

Tourism is one agency of the transformation of culture into a consumable commodity, and the earliest auto-ethnographic landscapes predate our advanced consumer culture. As Dean MacCannell argued over twenty years ago in *The Tourist: A New Theory of the Leisure Class,* tourists are modern people in search of an authenticity they do not find in their own lives. Mobility is a basic requirement for tourism. While tourism in some form has perhaps existed since ancient times, the invention and mass production of the automobile made the widespread development of tourism possible. Beginning in the 1920s, Americans increasingly took to the road to see how others live. Those on the receiving end of this activity not only needed to provide goods and services for the tourist, they needed to provide "authentic" experiences for the tourist to consume, including easily digestible depictions of the local culture. Clearly, then, the development of auto(self)-ethnography is linked to auto(mobile) tourism.[1]

Another industry that has engaged in the indigenous self-documentation of auto-ethnography is the country music business. Since its commercial beginnings in the 1920s, country music has been strongly self-referential, constantly making notes of its own authenticity. This referencing also takes place on the individual level; it is not enough to perform, write, or produce country music, one must authenticate one's own life experiences. Autobiography in a variety of forms is pervasive in country music. Despite the artifice of the genre and its show business roots in vaudeville and the traveling medicine show, "real" cowboys, cons, and coal miners' daughters abound.[2]

Although scholarly notice has been scarce, auto tourism sites connected to the country music industry are not uncommon. While they range from "Little Oprys" to large theme parks, most employ some form of auto-ethnography and many use representations of vernacular architecture as part of their self-authentication. In this chapter we will examine two auto tourism sites which span a half a century of country music's history. Sources of information include field examination of the sites themselves, published literature, oral history, and writings (and music) of the sites' creators. Renfro Valley, country music's first auto tourist site, and Dollywood, created in the 1980s, contain compelling testimonies to the changes in the lives of individuals in the upper South during the early to mid-twentieth century and provide alternative perspectives from those found in the "authentic" and official material representations of life during that period.

One of the central themes explored by country musicians over the years has been the loss of home and separation from a rural environment. As rural southerners migrated in huge numbers to the northern industrial cities during the first half of this century, romanticized images of rural vernacular architecture became popular subjects in country music lyrics. The types of architecture most often referenced are rural structures, such as in the songs "Dreaming of a Little Cabin" and "The Old Country Church." During the late 1920s and early 1930s, radio programs that featured country music were often called "barn dances," linking them with traditional rural music events that frequently had been held in barns. Although these shows often employed musicians and other entertainers with rural backgrounds, all of them originated from studios or theaters in urban areas.[3]

The first person to create a physical link between country music and the rural structures referred to in its songs was John Lair, the creator of the Renfro Valley entertainment complex. It was located approximately 130 miles south of Cincinnati in Rockcastle County, Kentucky. Begun in 1939, Renfro Valley was arguably the first country music auto tourism site. It featured live country music shows that were performed in a barnlike structure and broadcast over network radio. During the 1940s and 1950s, Renfro Valley was immensely popular, attracting a large radio audience and drawing huge crowds at the complex itself. In order to accommodate the visitors, the complex included a restaurant, tourist cabins, post office, and gift shops in addition to the barn where performances were held. All of these structures were built in a style reminiscent of the vernacular architecture found in the area during the previous century. These structures might be viewed by architecture scholars and preservationists as specious representations of rural southern architecture. However, when they are viewed in relation to Lair's efforts to document the past, specifically his own past, the Renfro Valley complex can be revealed as his attempt at self-documentation or auto-ethnography. While Lair presented Renfro Valley as his way of preserving the "early American way of living,"[4] the buildings at the complex more accurately reflect the central incongruity of Lair as a man with strong rural roots who became successful through the manipulation of modern consumer culture.

John Lee Lair was born in July 1894 in Livingston, Kentucky, and grew up on a farm in Rockcastle County, a short distance from where he would eventually establish the Renfro Valley complex. After attempts at a number of different careers, Lair wound up in Chicago in the late 1920s working for an insurance company. He became interested in the new medium of radio through the performances of early country singer Bradley Kincaid (also a Kentucky native) on the station WLS, home of the National Barn Dance. He began working for this station in the early 1930s on a part-time basis, bringing in performers from his home area and finding them spots on different shows at WLS. Eventually he became a full-time station employee, working as a music librarian as well as recruiting talent and producing shows.

During this time Lair began to formulate his unique vision for presenting country music. He utilized his rural background in writing the scripts for his programs, portraying his performers as members of a small mountain community who got together to entertain each other. They sang songs and reenacted activities from social occasions that Lair remembered from his childhood. The performers' image as mountaineers was further reinforced by the stage clothes Lair had them wear; the women wore long dresses and high-topped shoes and the men plaid shirts with work boots. Although the creation of the Renfro Valley complex was only an idea in the back of Lair's mind at this time, he was already constructing and shaping the identities of his performers.

The success of the shows Lair developed for WLS enabled him to turn his dream of the Renfro Valley complex into reality. He moved his show to the station WLW in Cincinnati in 1937 to build up funds for the business. While the Renfro shows played to nationwide audiences on WLW (which was then operating at 500,000 watts)[5] and to large crowds on personal appearances in Ohio and the surrounding states, Lair supervised the construction of the complex in Kentucky. Upon the completion of the Old Barn and other primary structures, the show began broadcasting from the Valley in November 1939.

When discussing the reasons for building Renfro Valley, Lair frequently explained it as his attempt to preserve the past. He wanted to "move backward across time" and present Renfro Valley as "a page in the history" of this country.[6] However, it is important to note that the main historical texts that Lair employed in this work were his own experiences. The authenticity of the complex, its shows, and architecture were all tied to Lair's own history. Writing in 1947, Lair explained, "The Renfro Valley set-up is not new . . . It is as old as John Lair's earliest recollections . . . of his home neighborhood."[7] Rather than a documentation of Appalachian culture as a whole, Renfro Valley can be "read" more accurately as Lair's attempt to document his own life.[8]

Lair built the complex on land nearby his childhood home, which provided him endless opportunities to intertwine the presentation of the history of the area with his own past. However, the history of the region and his ties to it were not the only reasons he chose the site. The Renfro Valley property was built alongside U.S. Highway 25, one of the roads that made up the Dixie Highway, a collection of state roads connecting upper Michigan with southern Florida. These roads were built during the early 1920s and allowed the first access for long-distance auto travel through the American South into Florida. By the time Lair began building Renfro Valley in the late 1930s, the Kentucky segment of the Dixie Highway had been an active road for over a decade and many businesses had already been built alongside the road that catered to the auto traveler, proving the economic viability of the area to Lair.

Through writings and interviews, Lair acknowledged the influence of increased auto travel as one of the main factors in his decision to start Renfro Valley. He told one interviewer, "I thought, well now, the townspeople like to get out in the country. And they're more able to do it, they've got more money and better automobiles. Why don't I build a show outside of town and let the townspeople come to it?"[9]

In addition to putting on a music show for the urban auto travelers, Lair also provided them with meals, lodging, and souvenirs. The Renfro complex was not only a place for Lair to present his interpretation of the past, it was also a full-service tourist destination. Lair's attempts to mediate between his interest in his personal history and the demands of the entertainment and tourism industry was a central theme found throughout his work, including the architecture of Renfro Valley.

Fig. 9.1. The old barn. Renfro Valley Keepsake 1947.

The building at the complex most important to the story of Renfro Valley was the Old Barn (fig. 9.1). It served as the main auditorium and the central icon in the promotion of the complex. When experienced firsthand by a visitor, the structure appeared to meet all the necessary requirements of an authentic barn. It had a simple frame construction, proper interior features like bales of hay and horse bridles on the stage, and lack of ventilation and heating, making it as uncomfortable in the summer and winter as a real barn.[10] But the building's true authenticity was supplied by Lair's recollections of attending social events in his neighbors' barns as a young man. His frequently used narrative of the "lantern-lit loft of the Staverson barn where the bright-eyed boys and rosy-cheeked girls of the neighborhood came together,"[11] helped authenticate the building for the live audience and radio listeners.

In addition to functioning as a physical prop in Lair's narratives, the barn was also the primary icon in promotions of the Valley. Lair always mentioned on his radio programs and in print advertisements that his show was "the only barn dance in America broadcast from a real barn."[12] The barn was also useful in drawing in passing motorists. The message emblazoned on its roof, "Home of the Renfro Valley Barn Dance," distinctly marked the building as part of the roadside architecture appealing for patronage by auto tourists.

The integration of aspects of the local vernacular style with the elements of modern business and technology required for the success of the complex was also noticeable in the Museum Building at Renfro Valley (fig. 9.2). The exterior of this structure evoked a dogtrot plan with its partial log construction and open front-to-rear central passage. The usage of the building, however, negotiated Lair's interest in history with the complex's need for technology. The Pioneer Museum was located on the upper floor of the building. It offered Lair the opportunity to showcase his numerous collections of historical items, including muzzle-loading rifles, sheet music, and tools. Lair's personal collection was enhanced by items donated by Renfro Valley fans. Listeners were encouraged to donate or lend "souvenirs, pioneer relics, and family treasures"[13] to the museum for exhibition. Also, this aspect of Renfro was not without the presence of the John Lair story. Within the museum's collection were several relics saved from Lair's boyhood.

In contrast to the historical ambience upstairs, the first floor of the Museum Building was devoted to the business concerns of Renfro Valley. One-half of the floor was taken up by the administrative offices, home to the clerks, auditors, and booking agents who kept the complex running. The other half of the floor was taken up by a studio, where recording and production work for Renfro Valley's radio programs was done. In the late 1950s the studio also became home to WRVK, a small radio station which Lair began. This station was primarily for the local audience and it featured a show that played current rock-and-roll records in addition to Renfro's standard country fare.[14]

The tourist cabins at Renfro Valley were another successful melding of Lair's needs for buildings that both referenced the past and adequately served the modern traveler (fig. 9.3).[15] Since these were the buildings at the complex with which the visitor would have the most intimate and prolonged contact, Lair went to great lengths to ensure that the cabins were both "authentic" and comfortable. In the illustrated "keepsake books" he sold to his visitors, Lair explained in considerable detail the old-time building techniques used by local men (referred to as "the neighbors")[16] in constructing the cabins. Nevertheless, he also made sure to note that the tourist's expectations for modern lodging would also be met. "It was all very well for the exterior of the cabin to look like the boyhood home of a Senator or a President," Lair noted, "but the interior had to make some concession to modern living."[17] Therefore, each cabin was outfitted with heating and plumbing, allowing the visitors both "the quaint charm of early pioneer days with all the conveniences of the modern age."[18]

The structure at Renfro Valley that perhaps best displayed Lair's negotiation of his rural background with his success in modern business was his family's

Fig. 9.2. Museum building. Renfro Valley Keepsake 1947.

Fig. 9.3. Tourist cabins at Renfro Valley.

Fig. 9.4. Lair family home.

home, which was built on land adjacent to the complex (fig. 9.4). Lair wrote that the house was "copied after the prevailing style of the neighborhood a hundred years ago."[19] The home was of partial log construction, but its large size and distinctive features (including a two-car garage, a sunken living room, and a second-story external deck) put it more in line with the modern upper-middle-class homes of the time period. The exterior of the home presented a mixture of architectural features. Horizontal log and stone walls were combined with board and batten siding cut to resemble Victorian fish-scale siding and second-story dormer windows. These features placed the home outside of the local vernacular style and any other general architectural categorization.[20]

However, like the tourist cabins at Renfro Valley, Lair claimed vernacular status for his home by noting the raw materials and building methods used in the construction of the house rather than pointing out its structural similarities to other homes in the area. Lair observed that the flooring was secured with wooden pegs, much of the hardware for the doors was made in local blacksmith shops, and the interior paneling was prepared "using old carpenter tools more than eighty years old."[21] In addition, the stones used in the construction of the house were quarried from the Lair ancestral homeplace, allotting the structure its necessary connection to Lair's past.

The Lair Family home serves as an excellent example of how its owner attempted to create a balance between traditional life and the consumer culture. The seemingly free interchange of local vernacular and modern architectural features found in the Lair home can be viewed as a physical manifestation of Lair's ambiguity over his need to stay linked to his past while still being able to enjoy his newfound prosperity.

The Lair home also demonstrated the ambiguous line that demarcated Lair's private life from his public one. Although the home was the private property of the Lair family, it was presented as an element of the tourist landscape of Renfro Valley. Its log and stone construction matched many of the commercial Renfro buildings, and it was frequently featured in literature produced for the visitors to Renfro Valley. This attention resulted in frequent visits to the house by tourists eager to meet the owner of Renfro Valley. Lair's daughter Barbara remembered her father's reaction to these visitations: "He always, much to my mother's chagrin, stopped what he was doing and would go out the door. And you could hear somebody say, 'I came all the way from so-and-so a place just to shake your hand' . . . and he always sat and talked to them."[22] This reflects how Lair's conception of Renfro Valley as a community on display extended beyond the parameters of his programs and enveloped his entire existence, including the time he spent with his family.

In addition to the buildings previously investigated, there were numerous other structures that were part of the Renfro Valley complex. Several of them were built, moved, modified, and ultimately removed from the complex. These included a grandstand for outdoor events, a series of shops built to resemble an old-time Main Street, and a replica of a water mill connected to the lodge building. Lair was an enthusiastic presenter of history and tradition, but he was also an entrepreneur who was constantly developing new ventures that he could tie into his business. Although he promoted the complex as "The Valley Where Time Stands Still," Lair made frequent changes to the built landscape at Renfro Valley in order to better serve his patrons and increase the profitability of the business.

Renfro Valley continues to operate today but is without the leadership of Lair, who died in 1985. The business still offers live country music shows for auto tourists, but the story that the complex now tells about itself is different from the one that Lair employed. Unlike the Renfro Valley of the 1940s and 1950s, which found its historical "truth" in the childhood experiences of Lair, the current organization relies on the story of the successful earlier era at the complex for its historical validity. Constant referrals to the golden age of Renfro Valley are found in the newer buildings at the complex. The "New Barn," a large auditorium that was constructed in 1990, is a thoroughly modern facility with little structural similarity to the original barn, yet it has the same board and batten exterior as the 1930s-era Old Barn. Images of the Renfro Valley performers from the 1940s and 1950s are placed throughout the complex. Their photos line the walls of the New Barn's lobby and their likenesses are used on signage on other new buildings. The new owners of Renfro Valley have continued Lair's practice of self-ethnography, but they have shifted their focus to include a portrayal of the complex's role in the history of the development of the country music industry.

Roadside country music shows are now a common form of entertainment offered to auto tourists, but Renfro Valley was the first instance of these two American traditions being successfully joined. John Lair presented his complex as a historically re-created mountain community, but the site actually reflected his negotiation of the past and the rapidly emerging consumer culture's need for entertainment. Lair was never able to return to the Renfro Valley that he had known as a boy, but he was able to present a selective version of his past to the thousands of people who listened to his radio programs and visited his complex.

While John Lair was beginning to dream of a nationally broadcast radio show emanating from his home county in eastern Kentucky, the federal government was busy creating a national park in the Great Smoky Mountains. Unlike the largely uninhabited western lands that had earlier become parkland, the three eastern national parks authorized in the 1920s and created during the 1930s (Mammoth Cave, Shenandoah, and the Great Smoky Mountains) were inhabited. In the Smokies over a thousand families lost their homes, the largest park removal in U.S. history.[23] Those who lost their land to eminent domain in the creation of the eastern parks became part of a larger population of dislocated southerners. In the Smokies the dispossessed also included individuals who sold their farms during the boom and bust of the local timber industry, families who were displaced by the construction projects of the Tennessee Valley Authority, and those who could simply no longer support their families by farming during the years of the Great Depression.[24] While some families displaced by the park relocated to nearby communities outside the park boundaries, others joined the great southern migration to industrial cities of the North, the milltowns of piedmont Carolina, the coalfields of central Appalachia, or the timber camps of the Northwest.

In creating the Great Smoky Mountains National Park, the first impulse of the government was to destroy all signs of human habitation, granting families salvage rights and burning other houses to prevent squatters from moving in. Park superintendent J. Ross Eakin believed that "houses should be razed as soon as their occupants move out," although he noted that the destruction of former homes aroused "considerable ire among residents."[25] By the mid-1930s, however, the park service moved to make preservation of traditional culture part of the park's mission in the Great Smoky Mountains.[26] Over seventeen hundred structures were documented during the 1930s, due mostly to the tireless efforts of a single individual employed by the Civilian Conservation Corps, Charles Grossman. While Grossman dreamed of a "comprehensive program to preserve the architecture of the region in natural settings," the park's preservation efforts were ultimately selective, preserving a number of nineteenth-century log homes but neglecting to preserve the most common type of dwelling built in the mountains during the early twentieth century, the Appalachian boxed house. Grossman's documentation, now in the park archives, demonstrates the ubiquitousness of these single-wall vertical-plank structures, but not a single one survives within the park's boundaries.

The Smoky Mountains region is notable for the conservative retention of log building techniques. Dwellings of log were constructed and lived in as late as the early twentieth century. However, in the more prosperous communities, such as Cataloochee and Cades Cove, frame houses were not uncommon. A few were left standing within the park, although generally they were destroyed in preference for the more rustic log houses. By the beginning of the twentieth century, however, the most common construction method for housing was probably the vertical-plank "boxed" house. Although the construction technique was known in the southern mountains during the nineteenth century, boxed framing became popular in the Smokies with the advent of wide-scale timbering. Boxed houses were used not only in timber camps but also on family farms. Many of these homes were still built cooperatively by community members, but neighbors, now pulled increasingly into "public work" (paid employment away from the farm) simply had less time to spare. The boxed house required a greater cash outlay than a log house but could be built much faster. Most rural residents of the mountains saw them as "nice and new" and at least equivalent, if not better, than log homes, as indicators of social and economic status. However, outsiders who tended to romanticize the log cabin, dismissed boxed houses as poor housing for poor people.[27]

Despite Grossman's recommendation that at least one representative boxed house be preserved, all were removed. It was not just that the architectural or historical significance of boxed houses was unrecognized; these homes did not tell the story that Park Service wished to convey about the Smokies. As legal suits over condemnation dragged on, it was the supposed uniqueness of the culture of the Smokies that was stressed. As one 1937 park memorandum stated: "there has survived a manner of living, an entire cultural complex, which almost everywhere else within the boundaries of the United State has disappeared entirely. The Smokies might be conceived as a cultral [sic] island, to a great extent, isolated from the outside world, where we are able to see the survival in our contemporaries of language, social customs, unique processes, that go back to the 19th century and beyond."[28] In order to reinforce this fairy tale, not only must the boxed houses vanish from the landscape, but also evidence of industrialization, most public and commercial buildings, as well as the great majority of the larger frame homes. The attempts to obscure the reality of the early twentieth century in the Smokies through selective preservation and interpretation has largely been successful. As one former resident of Cades Cove put it: "All those [frame] houses were torn down. They left the cabins, you know, more pioneerish . . .[Visitors] can't believe that people used to be here and you had schools and stores and churches and stuff like that . . . Lots of people think that we never did go out to town, you know, and people here just lived and died and never went to the city. But, cars were in here in 1915, the first car came in. My mother was fourteen years old."[29] By leaving the impression that a unique way of life, as well as wilderness, was preserved in the Great Smoky Mountains National Park, the park service avoided telling the story of the human toll of the park removals.[30]

In 1946, approximately a decade and a half after the park removals, a child was born in Sevier County, Tennessee, not too many miles outside the park's boundary, who was destined to become one of the region's best-known success stories. Some counties put up statues to the war dead in front of their courthouses. Sevierville has a statue of its hometown heroine, country music singer Dolly Parton (fig. 9.5). Raised poor in a boxed house, Parton did not stay in the mountains long. Immediately after graduating from high school she packed her bags and left to seek her fortune in Nashville.[31]

While Dolly Parton was proving her talents as a singer and songwriter, as well as one of the shrewder business minds in country music, her home county was being transformed. From the outset, the public justification for the creation of the Great Smoky Mountains National Park was the preservation and restoration of natural wilderness. However, local support came mainly from business interests, the chambers of commerce, and supporters of the "good roads" movement. While the federal government depended on this local support, the National Park Service fought against commercial development at the park gates. It appropriated land to create a buffer zone, denied leases of land to local people who wished to build

Fig. 9.5. Statue of Dolly Parton in front of Sevier County courthouse.

tourist accommodations, and generally tried to prevent "the hotdog stand, the soft drink stand, the gaudy filling station, the stand selling celluloid dolls and the billboards from marring the natural beauty of our gates." They lost this battle in a rather spectacular way as the sleepy towns of Cherokee, North Carolina, and Gatlinburg, Tennessee, became major destinations for the auto tourist.[32]

By the 1980s touristic development of Gatlinburg, wedged up against the park boundaries, had reached critical mass, and commercial growth spilled over into adjoining Pigeon Forge. In 1985 Dolly Parton teamed up with Herschend Enterprises of Missouri to transform an existing four-hundred-acre theme park, Silver Dollar City, into Dollywood. Dollywood, like Dolly, is glitzy, even tacky, and commercially successful. The transformation of Silver Dollar City into Dollywood proves that, in terms of visual imagery, the Wild West, Victoriana, and Appalachiana are largely interchangeable in the tourist world of the theme park. Parton herself likens Dollywood to the "big, flashy attractions" of the county fairs and carnivals of her youth.[33]

Dolly Parton's public persona would seem to have little to do with her mountain roots; but, it might be argued that it has everything to do with country music's roots in vaudeville and the medicine show. In her interviews, her autobiographical writings, and in some of her songs, Parton also markets the "real" Dolly, the poor mountain girl who learned to sing in her grandfather's Church of God congregation. Dollywood encompasses both sides of Parton's persona. A re-created rural church within the theme park sponsors one of the annual local shape-note singings, and the park's museum offers up the Parton legend, including "the coat of many colors" that inspired one of her hit songs about her childhood.[34] Still, Parton argues, the theme park is "much more about the culture of the people who live there than it is about Dolly Parton." She just happens to be "the most famous hillbilly from those particular hills."[35]

At the heart of the material representation of the authentic Dolly is Parton's reconstruction of her homeplace, a simple boxed house (fig. 9.6). Keyed to another of Parton's popular songs, "My Tennessee Mountain Home," this site is a popular destination within the complex. Although the authenticity of the reconstruction is questionable—the real house, which still stands, has only vertical boards, not boards and battens, and is not air-conditioned for the comfort of the visitor—what is notable is the interior reconstruction based on the memories of Parton's family members. According to the sign outside the house, the reconstruction was built by Dolly's brother, Bobby, and the interior was reproduced by her mother, Avie Lee (fig. 9.7). Many of the items on display are original.

The self-documentation of Parton's Tennessee Mountain Home achieves something the National Park Service typically fails to do: it gives the tourist a feel for how the house was lived in. It's not an

Fig. 9.6. Reconstructed home place, Dollywood.

empty shell. The park service, even when it does attempt to furnish its historic structures within the Smokies, always fails to present the complex, multilayered, traditional use that was typical of the small homes that sheltered large families in the region. Parton's reconstructed homeplace does achieve the sense of visual clutter and intensive usage that was well known to residents of southern Appalachia. Visitors most often wonder how a large family could survive in such a small house. However, the reconstructed home manages to convey pride, not grinding poverty.

Dollywood's Tennessee Mountain Home also gives visitors a peek into an era that the Great Smoky Mountains National Park is reluctant to interpret. Within the park, interpretation generally focuses on nineteenth-century pioneer life and deliberately leaves the impression that the residents of the Smoky Mountains were forever fossilized in this past. The park removals themselves are largely an untold story. While Parton was born after the removals, they were a recent memory during the period of her childhood. The replication of the Parton home is a more accurate depiction of the way many lived in the Smokies when the park was created than any of the structures interpreted within the park's boundaries.

Fig. 9.7. Sign in front of Dolly's reconstructed home.

Tourist sites are sometimes viewed in the scholarship as "authorless texts," and their self-documentation is seen as the product of institutions and power structures.[36] However, it is not always trivial to identify the "authors" of these sites. The autoethnographic aspects of Renfro Valley and Dollywood cannot be fully understood without reference to their creators, and, while they are partially products of institutions, they are also both highly personal presentations of culture.

As vernacular architecture scholars well know, the architecture we study may not be just *of* a tradition, it may be *about* a tradition. Of particular interest are those representations of traditional architecture which are, in themselves, vernacular in nature. In this chapter we have explored the relationship between vernacular representations of southern folk architecture and a vernacular music form which, as often as not, alludes to tradition rather than simply being traditional. As we have seen, these representations of vernacular culture can take both a musical and a material form. Along with this cross-genre look at self-representation, the examination of these two country music–linked tourist attractions furthers our understanding of the relationship between the development of tourist sites and auto-ethnographic expression.

Tourism has also been viewed by critics (and not without justification) as economically and culturally exploitative. It "appropriates" culture, offering stereotypical representations.[37] However, tourism also provides an opportunity for those with certain means to present their own culture, intermixed with biography or autobiography. Other vernacular tourist sites linked to the history of country music include the Carter Family Fold developed at A. P. Carter's old general store in Scott County, Virginia, by Janette Carter; Loretta Lynn's homeplace (also a boxed house) maintained by Lynn's brother, Herman Webb (fig. 9.8); Bill Monroe's relocation of his Uncle Pen's cabin to Bean Blossom; and the relocated Merle Travis homeplace in Muhlenberg County, Kentucky. All of these sites allow families and local communities to make money from tourists, but they also provide the opportunity for local people to document and depict their own culture and history. If we see

Fig. 9.8. Loretta Lynn home place, Butcher Hollow, Kentucky.

tourism as a form of ethnography, then these vernacular representations of vernacular culture are particularly compelling. They offer us a viewpoint not found in the scholarly literature or purveyed by official institutions of cultural representation such as the National Park Service.

Notes

Thanks to Brian Gregory for his assistance in additional research and to Dr. Erika Brady for her comments on the manuscript. Parts of the information on the Great Smoky Mountains National Park and Dollywood appeared in another form in Michael Ann Williams, *Great Smoky Mountains Folklife* (Jackson: Univ. Press of Mississippi, 1995).

1. For the relationship of tourism and auto-ethnography, see especially Dean MacCannell, *The Tourist: A New Theory of the Leisure Class* (New York: Schocken Books, 1989) and John D. Dorst, *The Written Suburb: An American Site, An Ethnographic Dilemma* (Philadelphia: Univ. of Pennsylvania Press, 1989). While MacCannell addresses "modernity," Dorst examines the condition of "postmodernity." The question raised by Dorst is whether the massively auto-ethnographic nature of the culture of advanced consumer capitalism precludes traditional ethnographic methods. While this question is beyond the scope of the chapter, we do question the merits of presuming auto-ethnographic "texts" to be either spontaneous or authorless.
2. Thanks to Erika Brady, associate professor, folk studies, Western Kentucky University, for her thoughts on autobiography and country music. The standard history of country music is Bill C. Malone, *Country Music U.S.A.* (Austin: Univ. of Texas Press, 1985). For a recent consideration of country music and authenticity, see Richard A. Peterson, *Creating Country Music: Fabricating Authenticity* (Chicago and London: Univ. of Chicago Press, 1997).
3. Among the earliest radio barn dances was the National Barn Dance, created in the mid-1920s at WLS in Chicago. The master of ceremonies, George Hay ("The Solemn Old Judge") moved to WSM in Nashville in 1926, where he created the Grand Old Opry.
4. Taped segment of Lair speaking recorded during an interview with Ann Lair Henderson by David Baxter, May 16, 1995.
5. For more information on WLW's broadcasting at 500,000 watts, see Lawrence Wilson Lichty, "'The Nation's Station': A History of Radio Station WLW" (Ph.D. diss., Ohio State University, 1964).
6. Henderson interview, May 16, 1995.
7. John Lair, *Renfro Valley Keepsake* (Renfro Valley, Ky.: Renfro Valley Enterprises, 1947), 6.
8. A comprehensive survey of the vernacular landscape of Rockcastle County, Kentucky, has not been conducted. Generally the folk architecture of the region is typical of patterns found in the upper South. For an overview of the folk architecture of Kentucky, see Lynwood Montell and Michael Morse, *Kentucky Folk Architecture* (Lexington: Univ. Press of Kentucky, 1976). For descriptions of some of the commercial structures in Rockcastle County, see Lynn David, Kentucky Historic Resources Group Survey Form (KHC 91-2) for the Mt. Vernon Business District (Group No. RK 02), Kentucky Heritage Council, 1996; and, Lynn David, Kentucky Historic Resources Group Survey Form (KHC 91-2) for the McKenzie Motor Court (Group No. RK 02). For Renfro Valley itself, see Mary Breeding, "An Historic Survey and Analysis of Renfro Valley Entertainment, Inc. Properties and Surrounding Properties," report prepared for Renfro Valley Entertainment and Cumberland Valley Area Development District, 1989.

9. Tape-recorded interview with John Lair by Reuben Powell, Oct. 26, 1967, Berea College, Special Collections.
10. The Old Barn was probably loosely based on a transverse-crib plan, which would have been typical of the larger barns found in Rockcastle County during Lair's youth.
11. Lair, *Renfro Valley Keepsake* (1947), 6.
12. "Howdy Folks! Welcome to Renfro Valley" (advertisement), *Louisville Courier-Journal,* Jan. 1, 1942, 12.
13. "Cornerstone Laid to New Museum," *Renfro Valley Bugle,* Nov. 15, 1945, 1.
14. For more information on programming and shows on WRVK, consult tape-recorded interviews by Larry Morrisey with Jonelle Simunik (Jan. 17, 1997) and Virginia Sutton-Bray (May 22, 1997).
15. For comparative purposes, see Lynn David's survey for the McKenzie Motor Court, a motel that provided a temporary home to many Renfro Valley performers. See also, John A. Jakle, Keith A. Sculle, and Jefferson S. Rogers, *The Motel in America* (Baltimore: Johns Hopkins Univ. Press, 1996) and Chester H. Liebs, *Main Street to Miracle Mile: American Roadside Architecture* (Boston: Little, Brown and Co., 1985), 174–81.
16. Lair, *Renfro Valley Keepsake* (1941).
17. Ibid.
18. Ibid. (1947), 26.
19. Ibid.
20. Lair's home and stable, though not the other historic structures at Renfro Valley, are on the National Register. See David Baxter, National Register of Historic Places Form for John Lair House and Stables, Rockcastle County, Kentucky, 1996.
21. Lair, *Renfro Valley Keepsake* (1947), 26.
22. Tape-recorded interview with Barbara Lair Smith by David Baxter, Mar. 3, 1995.
23. For histories of the park removals in the Smokies, see Margaret Brown, "Power, Privilege, and Tourism: A Revision of the Great Smoky Mountains National Park Story" (master's thesis, Univ. of Kentucky, 1990); W. O. Whittle, "Movement of Population from the Great Smoky Mountain Area," *University of Tennessee Agricultural Experiment Station Bulletin,* 1934; Michael Ann Williams, *Great Smoky Mountains Folklife* (Jackson: Univ. Press of Mississippi, 1995), 9–11; and Carlos Campbell, *Birth of a National Park in the Great Smoky Mountains* (Knoxville: Univ. of Tennessee Press, 1970).
24. During the 1940s land was added to the Great Smoky Mountains National Park following the Tennessee Valley Authority's construction of Fontana Dam. Several hundred families who lived adjacent to the park boundaries lost their land when the new lake inundated communities and flooded the only access road to communities along the north shore.
25. Superintendent's reports, Great Smoky Mountains National Park Archives, Sugarlands Visitors Center.
26. Park records do not make clear the reasons for this change of heart on the part of Superintendent Eakin and the National Park Service. While it is tempting to attribute it to the implementation of New Deal policies, such a change in policy did not occur in the two sister parks, Mammoth Cave and Shenandoah, which were created at the same time and also involved removal of local residents. The cultural preservation efforts in the Smokies seemed to be the result of the efforts of three individuals, H. C. Wilburn and Charles Grossman, both on the Civilian Conservation Corps payroll, and park naturalist Arthur Stupka.
27. For attitudes toward boxed housing in the region, see Michael Ann Williams, "Pride and Prejudice: The Appalachian Boxed House in

Southwestern North Carolina," *Winterthur Portfolio* 25, no. 4 (winter 1990): 217–30. Other descriptions of traditional building in the Smoky Mountains area include Michael Ann Williams, *Homeplace: The Social Use and Meaning of the Folk Dwelling in Southwestern North Carolina* (Athens and London: Univ. of Georgia Press, 1991); Williams, *Great Smoky Mountains Folklife,* 65–78; John Morgan, *The Log House in East Tennessee* (Knoxville: Univ. of Tennessee Press, 1990); and Robbie D. Jones, *The Historic Architecture of Sevier County, Tennessee* (Sevierville, Tenn.: Smoky Mountain Historical Society, 1997).

28. Park archives, Sugarlands Visitors Center.
29. Tape-recorded interview with Bonnie Meyers by Michael Ann Williams, July 29, 1993.
30. For an account of the park service's interpretation of local culture, see Williams, *Great Smoky Mountains Folklife,* 127–32.
31. For Parton's own account of her life, see Dolly Parton, *Dolly: My Life and Other Unfinished Business* (New York: HarperCollins, 1994).
32. For an examination of the National Park Service's effort to control tourism at its gates, see Jane Stewart Becker, "Selling Tradition: The Domestication of Southern Appalachian Culture in 1930s America" (Ph.D. diss., Boston University, 1993), 428–31.
33. Parton, *Dolly,* 279–82.
34. See Pat Arnow, "Dollywood: Changing the Profile of Pigeon Forge," *Now and Then 8,* no. 1 (spring 1991): 8–10; and Williams, *Great Smoky Mountain Folklife,* 183–85.
35. Parton, *Dolly,* 278.
36. Dorst, *The Written Suburb,* 4, 208–9.
37. For critical examinations of tourism in Sevier County, Tennessee, see Michael Smith, *Behind the Glitter: The Impact of Tourism on Rural Women in the Southeast* (Lexington, Ky.: Southeast Women's Employment Coalition), and the special issue on tourism in *Now and Then 8,* no. 1 (spring 1991).

CHAPTER 10

Travis C. McDonald Jr.

Constructing Optimism: Thomas Jefferson's Poplar Forest

In 1806 Thomas Jefferson finally turned to a project of great personal consequence. In that year he began construction of his long-awaited villa retreat, which he named Poplar Forest, after its setting in a majestic old-growth forest on the eastern edge of the Blue Ridge Mountains on the Virginia frontier (fig. 10.1). With two more years to go as president and with the rebuilding of Monticello accomplished, Jefferson anxiously launched another building project. While all his architectural projects can be called personal, this one was intimate. Its creation was one of private pleasure, both in the autobiographical nature of its architecture and in the anticipated peace and quiet the retreat would afford him in retirement. Poplar Forest provided the privacy Jefferson had always craved.

After Jefferson's time the site was lost for more than 150 years—lost to Jefferson histories and lost in original form. While the primary corpus of Jefferson documents and his well-known architectural works have been repeatedly analyzed for over a century, Poplar Forest offers new insights into Thomas Jefferson. In contrast to the more traditional analyses of Jefferson's buildings, which focus on design and style, this particular study focuses on the construction tradition of Jefferson as practiced at his private retreat. What distinguishes Poplar Forest regarding its workforce, its location, and its materials? Ultimately, what does its construction story tell us about the intellectual role of its designer/supervisor, about construction's psychological purpose for Thomas Jefferson, or about the reality of construction as dictated by tradition and circumstance?

Fig. 10.1. North (front) elevation of Poplar Forest. Drawing by Mesick Cohen Wilson Baker Architects.

Reading the actual building allows us to make more sense of the conventional documents such as drawings, journals, and letters, enlightening our perspective on Jefferson as a builder, as a materials supplier, as a recruiter of skilled labor, and as a construction manager.[1] Through this understanding of Poplar Forest as an artifact of Jeffersonian construction, we can compare the intended design with the actual execution. For Jefferson the builder, the logistical difficulties of building in the early republic compromised the realization of his ambitious architectural design, yet he never relinquished his patient optimism. Jefferson's optimism for executing his building projects might very well be the key to understanding his never-ending process of construction—that the act of construction, of "putting up and pulling down," might have been a contributing source for his optimism—of effecting change for some superior result.[2]

Thomas Jefferson's established role as owner/architect/builder played a major part in this story, but the location of Poplar Forest played an even greater role in its construction. More specifically, location related to supervision, workforce, and market. Poplar Forest was located a three-days' journey from Jefferson's home base at Monticello, and much farther from Washington (fig. 10.2). This distance posed obvious challenges for a man with a legendary obsession for detail and control. Distance between the site and its labor force formed the second obstacle; Jefferson used the same group of hired and slave workers for two simultaneous,

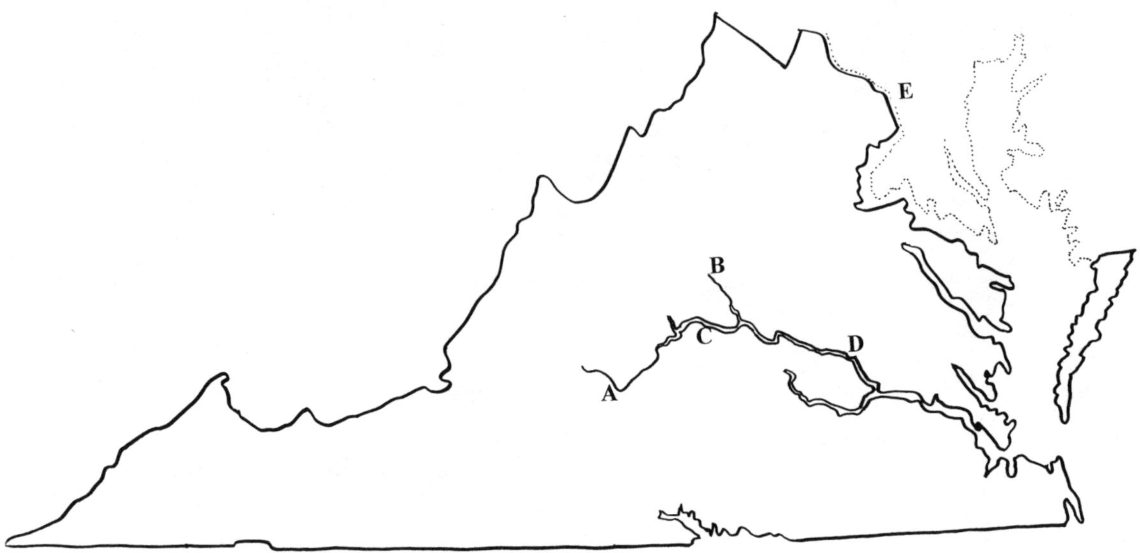

Fig. 10.2. Map of Virginia showing the location of Poplar Forest (A), Monticello (B), the James River (C), Richmond (D), and Washington, D.C. (E).

yet distant, construction projects. The third challenging factor involved the market location for certain construction materials. Jefferson not only specified uncommon materials that were hard to obtain, he also relied on his remote Monticello shops to produce finished parts for Poplar Forest, with inconvenient consequences regarding transportation. These three things—construction supervision, workers, and materials—run like an autobiographical thread through Thomas Jefferson's life and form a tradition in which to understand his construction practices.

History of the Site

The remoteness of Poplar Forest was, in fact, its raison dêtre. Situated on the eastern slope of the Blue Ridge Mountains in the county of Bedford, ninety miles south and west from Jefferson's principal house, Monticello, Poplar Forest suited Jefferson's need for a private retreat away from the bustle of visitors. The property consisted of two working plantations on nearly five thousand acres when it passed to Jefferson's wife upon her father's death in 1773. A workforce of slaves, supervised by overseers, lived on the property adjacent to the cultivated fields.[3] Jefferson relied heavily on its income from tobacco and later wheat. President Jefferson finally set into motion in 1805 plans for his long-awaited villa retreat. Like many things in his life, the execution of a retreat represented a fervent desire long delayed, and in a very real sense, an optimism fulfilled. Brick making began in the fall of 1805. Construction followed in the summer of 1806. By his retirement in 1809, Poplar Forest offered a somewhat habitable site which was finished over the next sixteen years. The ultimate in Jefferson's lifetime of octagonal designs, Poplar Forest equaled a brick repository for his collected and refined architectural concepts, mixing Roman ideas from the ancient world, Palladian interpretations from the Renaissance world, and

French conveniences from the modern world (fig. 10.3).[4] Its landscape design blended architecture and nature in an ongoing horticultural experiment.[5]

Change first occurred in 1814 when Jefferson altered his idiosyncratic retreat house into one for more conventional arrangements with an eastern wing of four service rooms called "offices." This asymmetrical addition to the house perhaps anticipated grandson Francis Eppes and his wife living there and inheriting the property. Eppes took up residence in 1823 and sold the property in 1828, two years after Jefferson died. Fire struck in 1845, destroying all but the brickwork. Quickly rebuilt in the then-fashionable Greek Revival style in 1846, the house lost Jeffersonian spaces, forms, and details except for the general octagonal shape. Modernization further altered the house in the 1940s.

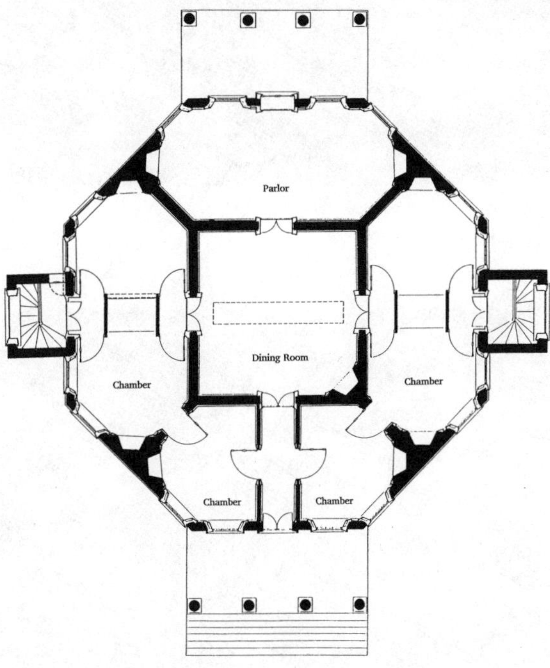

Fig. 10.3. Principal (upper) floor plan of Poplar Forest. Drawing by Mesick Cohen Wilson Baker Architects.

Rescued in 1983, the house has undergone intensive historical, architectural, and archaeological analysis. Through this architectural analysis a great deal has been learned about Jefferson's intention for the design, his alterations during construction, the techniques and skills of his workmen, and the subsequent alterations to the building (figs. 10.4, 10.5).[6]

Long-Distance Coordination and Control

The "when" of Poplar Forest's construction bears a great relationship to its "why" and "how." Losing patience with public life, Jefferson chose to begin his project in 1806 while still occupied as president in Washington. The impatience signified by this awkward timing must be seen in the context of Jefferson's lifelong attempts to build a private retreat.[7] Repeated pressures of public life pushed Jefferson's delayed dream into reality sooner than later. Jefferson must have felt his retreat was almost too late in coming. Nevertheless, his intense desire for privacy put into action another major building project before he had finished paying for the last. Because of his impatience to get started, Jefferson created the challenge of long-distance control and supervision.

Thomas Jefferson's remote supervision of his construction projects had become routine by 1806. During the initial period of construction of Monticello, 1770–84, Jefferson occupied positions in Williamsburg, Philadelphia, and Richmond,[8] and the post-Paris rebuilding of Monticello took place from 1794 to 1809, years when Jefferson served in Philadelphia as vice president (1797–1800) and then in Washington as president (1801–9).[9]

At Poplar Forest, Jefferson put even greater faith

Fig. 10.4. Restored north elevation of Poplar Forest. Photograph by the author.

in the unsupervised workforce and, consequently, on correspondence.[10] He did not enjoy the trusted family supervision there that he had established at Monticello. Besides the field hands, only overseers occupied the plantation. Duties kept him away for as long as two years during the beginning work. He simply sent working drawings and written instructions directly to the workers and occasionally to the overseer. His letters might include the

Fig. 10.5. Restored south elevation of Poplar Forest. Photograph by Robert Ziegler.

phrases "you will find in your instructions," "I now send you a sketch in ink," or "I enclose a drawing." In a letter to the bricklayer after visiting the site for the first construction visit, Jefferson wrote: "Everything is drawn so plainly that no further explanation is necessary. Take care of the drawings as they will be necessary for Mr. Perry, and I do not reserve another copy for him."[11] As important as the working drawings and sketches were, the written instructions were more crucial for their explicit descriptions.[12] Most importantly, Jefferson relied on return letters to inform him of the completed work.

Any letter in this correspondence usually indicated one or more episodes, out of many, in a complicated coordination of details. A typical letter will illustrate this. On June, 7, 1808, Jefferson wrote from Washington to his Monticello overseer Edmund Bacon: "As soon as the sashes are ready for Bedford, furnish Mr. Randolph 3 of your best hands, instead of his waterman, who are to carry the sashes, tables, and other things up to Lynchburg, and to give notice of their arrival to Mr. Chisolm, who will then be in Bedford, and will have Jerry's wagon there, which he must send for the things to Lynchburg. In the meantime, they must be lodged at Mr. Brown's at Lynchburg. Jerry is to go to Bedford with his wagon as soon as Mr. Chisolm goes."[13]

This letter indicates many things characteristic of the Poplar Forest process. Foremost is Jefferson's long-distance supervision from the president's house in Washington. Frequently, however, the directives pass through his core of workers and workshops at Monticello, where rebuilding work was still taking place in the first decade of the nineteenth century.[14] The letter principally discusses the Poplar Forest window units, which were made and finished at Monticello rather than at the actual building site. Due to the fragile nature of the glazed sashes, Jefferson instructed that they be sent by boat "up" to Lynchburg. He also directed the slave Jerry and "his wagon" to Poplar Forest, where Hugh Chisolm the bricklayer would also be headed from Monticello. Finally, Jefferson explained that the three slaves were to stay with the goods in Lynchburg until the sashes could be transported by wagon ten miles to the building site. This letter is typical of hundreds that describe the process at Poplar Forest. Other letters between Jefferson and his various workers fill in the details of this constant ebb and flow of directions, materials, and workers at the two sites and of the reality imposed by long-distance supervision.

These letters document the close relationship and trust between Jefferson and his hired workers, as well as the difficulties typically encountered, such as the saga of the window sashes. Jefferson's favorite master house joiner at Monticello, James Dinsmore, made the Poplar Forest sashes at the same time he made new sashes for Monticello. Although the letter refers to "sashes," it is the entire window-frame unit with double-hung and triple-hung sash that was made at Monticello. No documentation ever places Dinsmore at the remote house site, only at the principal carpenter shops at Monticello. In December 1806 Jefferson instructed Dinsmore at the start of the prolonged window project that "The window frames at Poplar Forest may be of poplar dug out of the solid, with locust sills, tho I do not know why the sides and top might not also be of locust dug out of the solid."[15] Typically, this letter reveals Jefferson "thinking out loud" about materials or techniques in corresponding with his most trusted workers whose opinions he valued and with whose decisions he could usually live. Circumstances occasionally determined the matter, as when Dinsmore wrote ten months later: "You expressed a wish to have the sashes for Poplar Forest made of walnut. If you still desire it you will please to let me know that we may have the walnut got to kiln dry along with the plank. I would beg leave however to observe that I am afraid there is none to be had about here but what is so much given to warp that it will render it very unfit for that purpose."[16] In response, Jefferson allowed Dinsmore the choice based on his best judgment: "I should certainly prefer walnut for the Bedford sashes, because well rubbed on the inside and unpainted it has a richer look than a painted sash, and I believe no wood is more durable but if you cannot get it good, then certainly good pine will be preferable to bad walnut. It must therefore depend on your being able to get good walnut and without delaying the work. The sashes for the lower rooms may be pine."[17] Jefferson not only trusted Dinsmore's opinion, but also frequently took the time to explain his rationale in a mentoring manner. Jefferson's correspondence to other workers reflected the same thoughtful explanation. A letter to carpenter John Perry in 1808 explained the rationale for materials as related to their specifications for production: "The floor at Poplar Forest being intended for an under floor must be laid with oak. Poplar would not hold the nails, and pine is too distant & dear. All the floors of Europe are of oak, so are the decks of ships. Good nailing will secure it against warping. Perhaps it may be easier done in herring bone, as the hall floor at Monticello was. In that case your sleepers should be but 14 I. from center to center, in order that the plank may be cut into two feet lengths."[18]

Jefferson sometimes delayed the Poplar Forest work to take advantage of the best craftsmen at one site instead of two.[19] Such was the case with master painter Richard Barry from Washington, who arrived at Monticello to glaze and varnish window sashes and to faux-grain all the interior and exterior doors to imitate mahogany.[20] Jefferson instructed Barry to glaze the Poplar Forest sashes, still at Monticello, and finish them in a manner similar to the Monticello sashes with a varnished interior side and a painted exterior side. Having delayed the sashes, Jefferson responded to bricklayer Hugh Chisolm's request for the window and door frames in June of 1807 by saying: "if the window frames are ready it is better to put them up & work the wall to them, but if not ready, they are not to be waited for. They can be put in afterwards, tho' with more trouble."[21] Chisolm could not wait and consequently installed the window frames later with considerably more trouble for himself and the carpenters, but not before further delivery delays resulting from Jefferson's choice of materials (fig. 10.6).[22]

The quality of light in a room mattered greatly to Jefferson. This quality depended upon a larger-than-usual size of window glass. Jefferson wrote from Washington to James Donath in Philadelphia in October 1807 to order oversized glass of twelve by eighteen inches "to be very exactly cut to their measures, because in the country those who could trim them are few & awkward & occasion great loss. To be of the same quality you formerly furnished me, that is to say Hamburg or Bohemian glass of the middle thickness."[23] Subsequent letters in October and December 1807, and then January 1808, lament the absence of the glass. The next month Jefferson relayed to Dinsmore that the glass couldn't leave Philadelphia until the Delaware River thawed. The glass eventually made its way to Washington in March, was forwarded to a ship in Alexandria, sailed to Hampton Roads and then upriver to the inland port Richmond, and by late April it had, at last, arrived at Monticello. Two months later Jefferson wrote the letter to Bacon, quoted earlier, instructing that the windows be sent by boat to Poplar Forest.

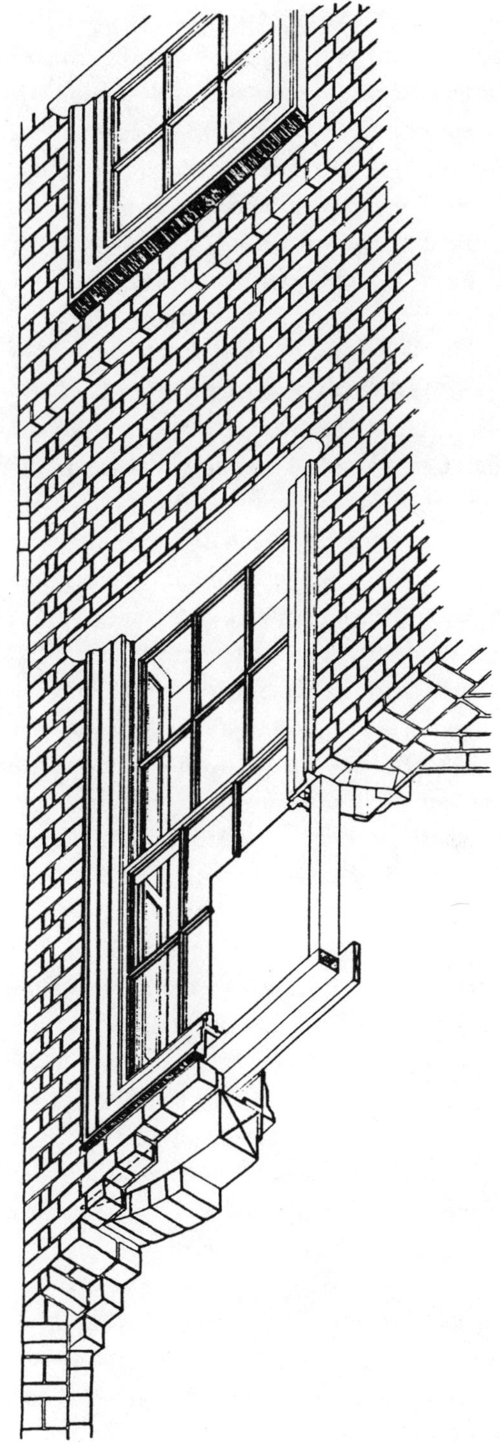

Fig. 10.6. Isometric of wall construction showing relationship of rough frame and finished window frame. Drawing by Mesick Cohen Wilson Baker Architects.

Dinsmore finally responded to Jefferson in June that he sent fifty-seven metal sash weights for the windows and sheet lead for gutters, among other items on the wagon, but "the sashes will not be ready before harvest."[24] Jefferson received a letter from Bacon, his overseer, at the end of June confirming this: "The window sashes are not done glaseing [sic]."[25] The next letter from Dinsmore clarified the situation in early July when he reported that he did not have enough sash cord, there were no window pulleys left, and "The waggon was obliged to leave the sash weights behind being so overloaded so that we must send them and the cord along with the sashes, which will be ready in a fortnight."[26] Thus ended the lengthy ordeal of getting the finished windows to the site to be installed by carpenter John Perry. Jefferson's use of the shops and craftsmen at Monticello to produce finished parts for Poplar Forest, together with his insistence on hard-to-obtain materials and on the problems of long-distance transportation, exacerbated the difficulties of building in a remote location.

Numerous other materials and parts of the house were at various stages in the same protracted and frustrating sequence of difficult procurement, transportation, and construction. In addition to the window units, solid exterior and interior doors and interior sash doors were made at Monticello and sent to Poplar Forest. Letters between Jefferson and his workmen often mention numerous construction subjects complicated by simultaneous projects at both Poplar Forest and Monticello. They provide a wonderful, yet dense and dizzying, paper trail of construction details squeezed into the busy life of a president with myriad interests. Jefferson even found time on December 28, 1806, to write James Dinsmore to discuss the type of wood with which to construct the window frames for Poplar Forest. In addition to the usual presidential duties, distractions that day included Meriwether Lewis, who had miraculously arrived back at the president's house from his long, incredible trip![27]

The Workplace, the Workforce, and the Work

Jefferson's experience with absentee coordination of building projects did not quite prepare him for the challenges presented by the remote Poplar Forest site. One of the very first letters of communication regarding the beginning brickwork at Poplar Forest should have been an indication of difficulties ahead. In June 1806 Jefferson wrote from the president's house in Washington to his daughter: "I find by a letter from Chisolm that I shall have to proceed to Bedford almost without stopping in Albemarle. I shall probably be kept there a week or 10 days laying the foundation of the house, which he is not equal to himself." The 2.5-degree shift in the foundations found during investigation might be related to this letter, presumably reflecting Jefferson's correction by some precise measurement. Jefferson's ability, or inclination, to drop presidential duties and take control at the building site says a great deal about his insistence on proper details. However much he might have been tempted to repeat this dedicated commitment, it was only to be repeated once more while he was in office.

Remarkably, a letter written from Poplar Forest could reach Washington in just four days, and yet Chisolm's early correspondence was infrequent and seemingly timed for needed cash rather than for conscientious reporting. One of only two known Chisolm letters of 1807 in the second season of building starts with "I thought proper to inform you of my progress" and closes "You will please to send me thirty dollars as soon as it is convenient."[28] Workers' letters helped convey a sense of optimism on Jefferson's part since they frequently contained only the opinion of the worker. In the case of Hugh Chisolm, that opinion reflected either exaggeration or deceit regarding the quality of what he had done. In later years, perhaps stung by his experience with Chisolm, Jefferson sent his accomplished slave John Hemings to the Poplar Forest to execute classical details with the instructions: "Send me a letter every Wednesday. In these letters state to me exactly what work is done, and what you will still have to do."[29]

Jefferson usually repeated the same basic materials, details, and structural techniques in his construction, establishing a tradition known to his workers. The tradition varies, however, in the execution of those materials and details. Brick construction provides one comparative aspect of a Jeffersonian building tradition. Close, and even cursory, analysis of the brickwork at Poplar Forest reveals poorly executed details when compared to Monticello, the University of Virginia, or even to other contemporary buildings of the region. Jefferson sent his Monticello bricklayer Hugh Chisolm to Poplar Forest as a known quantity. What went wrong, even in the absence of supervision, remains a mystery.

Chisolm traveled to Poplar Forest in the fall of 1805 to prepare for brick making.[30] He made bricks at the site in 1806, 1807, and 1808. They are typical sand-mold bricks, ranging in color from orange to plum. Special shapes included the corner squint bricks, the beveled fireplace back bricks, the semicircular column bricks, and the molded Tuscan order bricks for column bases and capitals (fig. 10.7). The exterior bond is Flemish above grade, and the interior is two- and three-course common bond.[31] By the second season, Chisolm had finished the walls, columns, the stair pavilions, and the two detached octagonal privies.[32] Despite the surviving physical evidence that Chisolm did use string lines inside and out, he must not have used a level because the courses are not straight. In several prominent places crude corrections were made for off-level coursing by turning bricks on their stretcher faces to acquire more height. Despite a specific caution from Jefferson to leave enough room for the window openings adjacent to the pavilions, Chisolm got it wrong and had to shift a window opening by cutting one jamb and adding to the other. Chisolm did not bond the pavilions into the main wall; he did not fully align the Flemish bond; and he chose to fully bond stretchers on the inner common bond rather than on the stronger, outer Flemish bond, resulting in a fractured wall when the foundationless pavilions settled. This created structural and conservation problems from the beginning which have only recently been corrected.[33] The idiosyncratic pattern of makeup bricks in Chisolm's Flemish bond is wildly varied, with little consistency of double headers, double stretchers, bats, or closers. Worse still was the interior brickwork, whose quality, they must have reasoned, would eventually be hidden by plaster. Some inner wythes of brick suggest the shortcut of grouting wall cavities with a liquid mortar rather than using the stronger mortar. Other areas indicate a bricklayer's hurried work of throwing down trowels of mortar on an inner wythe without fully spreading the mortar. Perhaps nervously, Chisolm wrote Jefferson on several occasions remarking on the high quality of his work and stated that the Tuscan columns would be "elegant" when finished. After two seasons of construction, Jefferson made a trip to the site in the fall of 1807. Having seen some of the sloppy brickwork on the lower walls at that time, Jefferson later wrote to Chisolm saying that he must come to Monticello, "where I wish some work done under my own eye."[34]

Fig. 10.7. North portico Tuscan order columns made of brick and rendered with stucco. Photograph by the author.

Some of the poor brickwork quality can undoubtedly be attributed to Chisolm's crew, and probably to his own failings at supervision. Jefferson recorded in his account book that he paid Hugh Chisolm twenty dollars a month, "4 inferior hands" ten dollars a month, and at another time he paid Chisolm and his brother John and "two boys." Jefferson left no opinion of the sloppy brickbond, of the poorly molded capital bricks, or of the incorrect diameter of the Tuscan order columns. For a man obsessed with these details, he must have been sorely disappointed, if not mortified. Characteristically, Jefferson's loyalty, and surely his optimism, ran deep when his workers were concerned. He went on to recommended Chisolm to his friends. While Hugh Chisolm's brother John was left behind to plaster two rooms in the lower level, Hugh left Poplar Forest in 1808 to work for James Madison at Montpelier. Jefferson later called Chisolm back to Poplar Forest in 1812 to complete the plastering in the main house and again in 1814 to do more plasterwork as well as the brickwork and stonework for the attached wing of offices. He worked for Jefferson at Monticello as late as 1820.

How did the carpenters fare as compared to the bricklayers? The physical work of hired carpenters John and Reuben Perry cannot be completely judged at Poplar Forest, having been consumed by the fire of 1845. Jefferson employed Charlottesville carpenter/house joiner John Perry at Monticello as early as 1806 and hired him to work on the University of Virginia buildings in the 1810s and 1820s. Perry went back and forth between Monticello and Poplar Forest from 1807 to 1809. During that time at Poplar Forest he installed the wood framing for floor and roof systems, the windows and doors, and the exterior trim. The timber frame roof structure was somewhat typical for the time, except for the octagonal roof shape with the twenty-foot cube room projecting at its center and top. The four-by-ten ceiling joists were connected by four-by-four posts to tapered four-by-six roof rafters (the posts being tenoned to the joist and toenailed to the rafter). The ends of the joists and rafters met in an unusual bird's-mouth joint

Fig. 10.8. North-south section drawing looking east. Drawing by Mesick Cohen Wilson Baker Architects.

rather than a butted or false plate juncture (fig. 10.8).[35] After 1809 Reuben Perry, a house joiner in Lynchburg, took over from his brother and installed plaster grounds, among other things, at Poplar Forest. Nailing nogs and ghosts of plaster grounds suggest that the quality of Perry's work was not superior. Jefferson wrote Reuben Perry in 1812, saying: "I find that for wanting of plumbing the grounds in the parlour, several of them will have to be taken down when we go to putting up the architraves and cornices. I pray you to have strict attention paid to this in the rooms still to be done."[36] In turn, Perry probably cursed the bricklayer for the inconsistent and nonplumb walls.

Beginning in 1816, and continuing for ten years, Jefferson's highly trained slave joiner John Hemings executed all the finest finish work on the interior of Poplar Forest. Hemings had apprenticed under the best Monticello craftsmen, held an elevated status among the Jefferson slaves, received an annual salary, and gained his freedom upon Jefferson's death. Hemings executed Poplar Forest entablatures, sash doors (made in the Monticello shop), and door, window, and wall trim. Hemings also constructed the classical balustrade, the Chippendale-style Chinese rail, and the louvered exterior window blinds. Corresponding with his master regularly about his work, Hemings not only communicated in a fairly literate manner, but as one conversant in classical detail. Jefferson put great trust in Hemings's work, frequently sending him unaccompanied to Poplar Forest to work with his two carpenter aids at a time when he could have supervised the work himself. Hemings wrote from Poplar Forest to Jefferson in 1821: "I am at work in the morning by the time I can see and the very same at night." When Jefferson replaced the "rafter roof" over the central twenty-foot cube room with his new favorite "terras" or "zigzag" roof in 1819, he proudly wrote about Hemings's work: "a more compleat and satisfactory job I have never seen done."[37] Hemings continued to work on the house after 1823, even when Jefferson had stopped visiting the property. By that time Jefferson's grandson Francis Eppes and his wife were living there.

A roof fire in 1825 prompted Jefferson to anxiously write Eppes, saying, "I will spare J. Hem. to you & his two aids and he can repair everything of wood as well or perhaps better than any body there."[38] Eppes responded that his own man repaired the damaged roof, "but the balustrade and railing are I am afraid beyond his art."[39] Jefferson quickly replied that Hemings, when he finished covering Monticello's roof with tin shingles, would go to Poplar Forest and replace the fire-damaged Chestnut shingle roof with tin shingles.[40] Anticipating this, Jefferson ordered his Richmond merchant to "send to Lynchburg 15 boxes of tin addressed to F. Eppes by the first boats."[41] By July 23 Hemings reported to Jefferson: "we begin to tin the west side of the house and we have used 52 boxis. We shal in a few days finish that side except the Potcos."[42] The following month Hemings reported that he was putting the final pieces back on the roof, preparing the "chines railing & putting up the ornaments of the hall."[43] He referred to the Chinese rail on the top of the roof and to the Doric entablature of the central cube dining room (figs. 10.9, 10.10). Hemings most likely referred to the dining room as a "hall" since it was centrally located and probably served as an old-fashioned, all-purpose hall. On this same trip Hemings also repaired the east wing terras roof and deck and prepared the entablature parts for installation in the parlor on the next trip. One of the last letters Jefferson received before his death was Eppes's letter of June 23, 1826, sadly informing his grandfather that the newly installed roof was leaking, "not in one but a hundred places."[44] Eppes blamed this

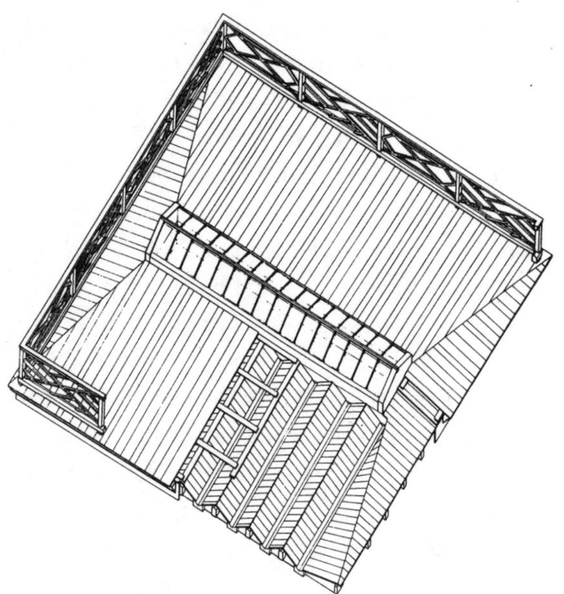

Fig. 10.9. Axonometric of terras roof over central room. Drawing by Mesick Cohen Wilson Baker Architects.

Fig. 10.10. Restored roof showing terras deck with Chinese railing and skylight, tined shingles, and balustrade. Photograph by the author.

problem on Hemings, and without the long-term relationship or loyalty of his grandfather's with the carpenter, he was unforgiving. In a letter to his cousin Jeff Randolph after Jefferson's death, Francis commented: "I have just had a workman here examining the roof of the house. There appears to be a radical fault in the putting on of the tin which can be remedied only, by removing and recutting it . . . I have engaged him thereupon to recover the house. so much for J.H. god dam him!"[45] Hemings had made a rare mistake with one of his last known projects at Poplar Forest. This news about his beloved house, and his trusted slave, likely hastened Jefferson's end.

Transportation

Along with supervision and workers, the crucial factor of location most affected the transportation of materials.[46] Acquiring and transporting materials to the remote building site posed problems for all concerned. Over a twenty-year period special materials had to be ordered: sheet iron, lead, glass, paint, hardware, entablature ornaments, marble, and tin. While some of these items were domestic, they still had to come from New York, Philadelphia, and Washington via Richmond—Richmond being the closest port. Monticello was frequently designated the first point of delivery for commonly used goods, with needed portions then going on to Poplar Forest. Other items, such as the window frames and sash, came from the Monticello shops. The problem is readily apparent on a map: Monticello and Poplar Forest are both upriver beyond the fall line from Richmond and thus not navigable. Frequent descriptions of "up" in the correspondence no doubt refer to "upriver" because once goods were floated down the Rivana River from Monticello, they had to be poled up the James River to Lynchburg.[47] Jefferson preferred that delicate goods come by boat and not by wagon. Jefferson directed in the same letter for his Richmond merchant to "send 8 boxes of tin by the first *wagon*" and to "send me by the first *boat*" 100 panes of glass. Jefferson wrote to carpenter Reuben Perry in 1811: "My boat will start to Lynchburg as soon as it has got all my flour down from hence . . . She will carry the 4. pair of glass doors with their jambs & soffites [*sic*] & the semicircular windows, all ready glazed for hanging."[48] When corresponding with William Coffee, the New York sculptor who made the significant interior entablature frieze elements for Poplar Forest, Jefferson instructed that the clay ornaments be "forwarded by water" through Richmond to Lynchburg.[49] Jefferson's taste demanded things not produced locally or even in the region. These choices had consequences effecting availability, transportation, and the construction schedule.

Regarding materials produced locally, the most frequent frustration over a fifteen-year building period involved Captain Martin and his sawmill.[50] Getting mill-sawn lumber depended on a consistent water source in the area. Without one, the house became a mixture of pit-sawn and mill-sawn lumber, although Jefferson preferred the expensive option of milling the lumber.[51] Jefferson wrote of one failure: "I shall feel Capt. Martin's disappointment very heavily as we shall be obliged to get our stocks sawed by hand & to work them green & for outside work too."[52] On another occasion, Jefferson wrote to his overseer: "I hope Capt. Martin will consider what a loss and disappointment it will be to me if these people [John Hemings and his carpenter assistants] have to return for want of the stuff desired."[53] In that particular case, the overseer replied that "Capt. Martin has completed the first bill of timber, but will not be able for want of water to do any thing with the other this season."[54] John Hemings replied once to Jefferson that he had to go as far as twenty-five miles to find a working mill, although he mentioned the reason most mill owners refused to cut timber in July was for "feare of the worms."[55]

Occasionally Jefferson tried to purchase in Lynchburg items normally made at Monticello.[56] When trying to purchase 6,000 wrought nails from his merchant in Lynchburg in 1815, Jefferson was told that only "cut nails" were available.[57] In March 1809 Jefferson referred to 700 pounds of nails sent from Monticello to Poplar Forest "by Jerry" in 1807.[58] Wrought L-head finishing nails were used to fasten the exterior entablature trim in 1808, but by 1812 machine-cut L-head finishing nails fastened the interior work as well as the balustrade erected in 1815.[59] In this regard Poplar Forest spanned a technological transition, with the rebuilt Monticello of the 1790s constructed entirely with wrought nails and the University of Virginia from 1817 onward constructed with cut nails.[60]

For twenty years, Jefferson's workmen relied on a single wagon and a cart, split between Monticello and Poplar Forest. "Jerry's waggon" proved indispensable for transporting materials as well as the seasonal expedition of workers and their tools. It was mentioned during all times of the year—sometimes as a custom, as in "when the waggon goes in the spring" or "when the wagon goes at Christmas time." Jefferson frequently instructed that the wagon or cart "must stay but one day" or not go one day prior to the workers being ready to come home. In a letter of June 1807, Jefferson wrote: "P.S. We are in great distress for Jerry's waggon at Monticello. I pray you therefore to press the finishing what is for him to do at Poplar Forest."[61] Once there, the wagon or cart did many things such as hauling wheat into Lynchburg and picking up sand for plaster on the return trip, hauling lime, and hauling a "waggon load of plank."[62] The wagon most often transported finished goods from the Monticello workshops in the early years: chairs, tables, books, or musical instruments. In the later years, when the house was being finished through seasonal expeditions, the wagon generally helped Johnny Hemings and "his gang" or "his people." In 1819 Jefferson wrote from Poplar Forest to request a carpenter and his three helpers from Monticello, explaining: "It is so inconvenient for the house to spare the little mule and cart, and so few tools will be wanting here that they may bring them on their shoulders. They will need 2 hand saws, 2 jack planes, 2 pair chisels broad and narrow, some augers for common framing, a foot adze, and one of the narrow adzes which were made here to dig gutters in the joists. These things divided among three will weigh little. Let them bring their own provision for the road."[63] Clearly, the wagon did its duty for materials and goods and the workers generally walked, except in rare occasions or when the wagon was free, as evidenced in this letter from Jefferson to Hemings: "The carpenters will go up in the spring . . . Lilburne has a hurt on his leg which will disable him from walking back. Eston must drive the cart therefore and Lilburne stay and come in the waggon."[64]

Optimistic Traditions

So far this study has examined the construction context of Poplar Forest—the materials, the workers, the effort, and the constructed work. It has also attempted to tie those threads to its owner/builder's intention and to the site's function. We can move beyond this to glimpse an insight into the character of Thomas Jefferson. Jefferson's difficulties of long-distance supervision during his most demanding public office, the remoteness of Poplar Forest from the central workforce and workshops at Monticello, and the extensive effort to obtain certain manufactured goods places the construction of Poplar Forest squarely in a history and tradition of Jefferson's construction choices and their consequences, both in terms of process and product.

Beyond the mere observation that unsupervised work can be inferior when compared to supervised, can we read more into the details at Poplar Forest? I'd like to suggest we can. There existed a relationship between Jefferson, his architecture, and his workers which in some ways seems a metaphor for understanding him as a person.[65] When seen in the broadest perspective, Thomas Jefferson exhibited a personal and professional optimism fueled by a clarity of purpose most conveniently wrapped up in the title of Enlightenment. Jefferson's fundamental goal was to create order and reason in the world, both at large and his own.[66] Much has been written about Jefferson's specific political optimism and his intellectual dedication to those ends. Might we not say that Jefferson's intellectual capacity and need for architecture, and all that the construction efforts returned to him, benefited from this optimistic drive? Jefferson never stopped his own process of architectural evolution, whether in structure, convenience, or beauty. Adding the indoor toilets, skylights, and alcove beds together with the favorite forms of Palladian orders and regional construction details became the interesting personal process that we call both autobiographical and idiosyncratic. At the same time, the lifelong growth and maturity of Jefferson the designer, supervisor, and builder belies the fact that the reality of construction sometimes got harder, as in the case of Poplar Forest, rather than easier. The extreme difficulties of getting the Poplar Forest window units built, shipped, and installed underlies both an intention and desire for a certain detail and a practiced patience (optimism) for achieving those goals. Observing the quality of brickwork at Poplar Forest after his long absence,

Jefferson should have dismissed Hugh Chisolm without further adieu, much less without further work. The opposite actually happened.[67]

Against all odds of time and money, Jefferson pursued his architectural ideas and ideals with an amazing commitment driven by his optimism. At times this optimism can only be summarized as either naive or irrational. Financially, Jefferson's well-known debt at the end of his life should have precluded any other major personal building projects. Jefferson scholars who have most closely studied his habitual record keeping state that "the daily ritual of recording pecuniary events gave Jefferson an artificial sense of order in his financial world."[68] Coming on the heels of an overextended personal budget that had paid for an extravagant, yet federally underfunded, presidential lifestyle, Jefferson might have been expected to complete the restyled and reconstructed Monticello. However, to also incur the expense of a completely new villa retreat indicated a fundamental need, a necessity, for a private man long trapped in a public life.[69] Had the need for a retreat been less of a psychological necessity, Jefferson could have deferred construction of Poplar Forest until better financial times, or for just three years until he left the presidency and could supervise the work himself, as he occasionally did for fourteen years with the subsequent finishing of the interior. He couldn't wait; the retreat represented a dream unrealized for too long. The function of Poplar Forest suited the irrational means to its end perfectly. One characterized definition of the classic villa, especially as conceived by Jefferson from its Roman prototypes, was its power and ability to be "impervious to reality."[70] To Jefferson, a large part of his reality seemed rooted in an optimistic vision of future possibilities, not the least of which was his own villa retreat, where he could block out worries and still contemplate hopes and dreams.[71] With the physical and mental limits of the once nearby frontier now pushed to the western sea, Jefferson could look out the expansive lights of the triple-sash parlor/library windows at Poplar Forest and still think of the future. His most frequent Poplar Forest companions were his granddaughters Ellen and Cornelia, representing the next generation and learning at his side.

The incredibly minute details Jefferson carefully noted in letters to his workers became juxtaposed with the reality of the workers' skill and the unsupervised results, whether good or bad. Ironically, the quality of work produced by Jefferson's most highly paid workers fell beneath that of his slave. While the record is embarrassingly silent on Jefferson's opinion of Chisolm's brickwork, the bricklayer's incorrectly proportioned Tuscan columns on the front and back porticos of Poplar Forest become the defining character of the place: the most consistent intellectual tradition of Jefferson's architectural efforts, and yet the most noticeably wrong feature of his intimate and cherished retreat. Perhaps like the poplar tree logs serving as temporary columns on the west facade of Monticello, which for so long waited correct classical replacements, or the east facade stone columns at Monticello, so damaged in their rebuilding that they required a painted faux stone finish, the improper Poplar Forest columns probably stood noted on an optimist's "to redo" list never realized. Similarly, the wing of four service rooms added to the east side of the house in 1814 clearly called attention in its asymmetrical form to a balancing future wing unrealized on the west. Out of lifelong habit, Jefferson's mind could not stop the physical and metaphysical pairing of architectural improvement with a future state of perfection and his own sense of completeness. With his life quickly drawing to a close, several years after he had stopped traveling to Poplar Forest, Jefferson ordered John Hemings to finally install the entablature ornaments for the parlor at Poplar Forest, which for five years had been sitting in their boxes. This final directive completed, at long last, the retreat Jefferson never seemed too anxious to complete once he had occupied it.[72]

Jefferson's highly controlled and personal desire for specific details, even details long delayed, had become inextricably tied to his experience and outlook on life: one of difficulty and optimism. Yet, as we see in some of the details of Poplar Forest, those ideals were compromised in their physical manifestation, a contradiction among many in Jefferson's life which he justified or accepted in his own way. Jefferson's need to control details represented perhaps some anchor of stability in a life of incredible change wrought by political as well as personal circumstances. Distance and absence from the building site, especially when the site moved to the frontier and when the owner/builder happened to be president, increased the need for control through correspondence, both in a psychological as well as a practical sense. In other ways, the close attention to detail on paper sometimes obscured the reality rather than confirming it, like in his detailed financial record keeping. Jefferson's architectural details represented his own contribution to the spread of civility and refinement, in both public and private venues, and they extended his lifelong commitment to Enlightenment beliefs as well as providing some order and reason in his own world, even if that world at Poplar Forest became detached from reality.[73] Moreover, Jefferson's characteristic optimism extended to his workers, resulting in a trust well secured by habit, if not always borne out by results. He trusted his workers to help him achieve his lifelong goal of constructing a physical place where his optimism could renew itself.[74] Thomas Jefferson created his villa retreat within an intellectual harmony of his own mind and for his own mind. That he accomplished what he did regardless of the inherent difficulties provides us with a humanistic, sympathetic, and understandable perspective of this place and its creator.[75]

Notes

ABBREVIATIONS

TJ	Thomas Jefferson
CSmH	Henry Huntington Library, San Marino, Calif.
DLC	Library of Congress, Washington
MHi	Massachusetts Historical Society, Boston
PPAMP	American Philosophical Society, Philadelphia
Vi	Virginia State Library and Archives, Richmond
ViW	Swem Library, William and Mary University, Williamsburg
ViU	University of Virginia, Charlottesville

1. The only definitive history of Poplar Forest is S. Allen Chambers, *Poplar Forest and Thomas Jefferson* (Forest, Va.: Corporation for Jefferson's Poplar Forest, 1993, 1998). This history did not include the investigation details of the house itself, except for the preliminary restoration drawings.
2. Jefferson's often-quoted line, "Architecture is my delight and putting up and pulling down one of my favorite amusements," is credited to Margaret Bayard Smith, *A Winter in Washington* (New York, 1824), 2:261 as quoted in Dumas Malone, *Jefferson and the Ordeal of Liberty,* vol. 3, *Jefferson and His Time,* 222 n. 4. The two best overall treatments of Jefferson as a builder are Richard C. Cote, "The

Architectural Workmen of Thomas Jefferson in Virginia," (Ph.D. diss., Boston Univ., 1986); and Jack McLaughlin, *Jefferson and Monticello: The Biography of a Builder* (New York: Henry Holt and Co., 1988).

3. Archaeologists have been exploring two slave quarter sites that appear to predate the villa house. An overseer's house was used by Jefferson on the few trips he made to the property before constructing the house in 1806.
4. For a discussion of the autobiographical nature of *Poplar Forest*, see Travis C. McDonald Jr., "Ghost Stories: The Architectural Investigation of Poplar Forest," in *Notes on the State of Poplar Forest, Volume 1*; and Travis C. McDonald Jr., "Poplar Forest: Synthesis of a Lifetime," in *Notes on the State of Poplar Forest, Volume 2* (Forest, Va.: Corporation for Jefferson's Poplar Forest, 1991, 1994).
5. Jefferson sited the house against an ancient forest of tulip poplars so that the forest provided a dense natural layer at the front; in the back, Jefferson created a man-made landscape. The best treatment of the landscape is found in C. Allan Brown, "Poplar Forest: The Mathematics of an Ideal Villa," *Journal of Garden History* 10 (1990): 117–39.
6. For information on the process of architectural and archaeological investigation, see *Notes on the State of Poplar Forest,* vols. 1 and 2; Travis C. McDonald Jr., "Poplar Forest: A Masterpiece Rediscovered," *Virginia Cavalcade* (winter 1993), 112–21; Jane Brown Gillette, "Mr. Jefferson's Retreat," *Historic Preservation* (July/Aug. 1992), 42–49; Vernon Mays, "A Villa through Time," *Inform* 2 (1997): 22–25; and Dale Mackenzie Brown, "Jefferson's Other House," *House Beautiful* (Dec. 1997): 48–50, 139.
7. For a history of Jefferson's attempts at retreats see McDonald, *Notes II*; Mark Wenger has discovered a relationship between Jefferson's designs for the governor's palace in Williamsburg and a Poplar Forest plat, providing a possible date of 1781 for the plat; "Jefferson's Designs for Remodeling the Governor's Palace," *Winterthur Portfolio* 32, no. 4 (winter 1997). The significance of this date is that Jefferson drew a small house plan on the plat, indicating an early desire for the tract as a retreat; Jefferson later added a second plan to the plat showing his evolution to the full octagon form he eventually constructed.
8. Jefferson's first important public work, the Virginia State Capitol, was also constructed without his supervision. He wrote virtually nothing about it, being disappointed after having seen it upon his return from Paris. This certainly provided a good early warning about unsupervised construction projects.
9. At Monticello, Jefferson relied on family and overseers to supervise the work when he was away. Occasionally he wrote that the workers "must suspend their work during my absence" because he could not "trust them with its execution in my absence" (TJ to Count Constantin Francois de Volney, Apr. 3, 1797, DLC, quoted in McLaughlin, *Jefferson and Monticello,* 262). For the most part, however, work at Monticello proceeded without its owner's presence. Jefferson was aware of the potential social problems of unsupervised workers when left without a coordinating and mediating owner. Most often he chose to ignore or accept the inherent and inevitable traits. In one such episode, at Poplar Forest, plasterer John Richardson complained to Jefferson about an overseer in a letter of resignation: "I have quited for several reasons which I will inform you, there is too much party work going on here" (John Richardson

to TJ, Jan. 16, 1810, Mhi-7). Following a dispute at Monticello between an overseer and a worker, Jefferson explained: "It is my rule never to take a side in any part in the quarrels of others, not to inquire into them" (TJ to James Oldham, Nov. 30, 1804, DLC). Jefferson's optimism for things in general, and especially for people, extended to his "family" of workers, in whom he put a strong faith.

10. From his remote location in Washington, Jefferson directed and coordinated all manner of construction: detailed instructions to hired and slave workers, work and travel schedules, wagons, and the flow of materials between many locations. Jefferson also needed to coordinate the supervision of field hands and crop production at Poplar Forest. Cash crops, especially at Poplar Forest, formed the basis for either cash or speculation credit, paying for the purchase, movement, and use of materials and construction labor. To keep track of this effort, Jefferson used a polygraph machine to make copies of his own letters to workers and overseers. The flow of letters back and forth gives us an explicit view of his process. The obvious exception was when he could supervise the construction work at Poplar Forest directly during his occasional visits after 1809. In those cases the written record ceases except when Jefferson needed something from the Monticello workshops.
11. TJ to Hugh Chisolm, Sept. 7, 1806, MHi-5.
12. Unfortunately none of the working drawings referred to in the letters are known to survive.
13. TJ to Edmund Bacon, June 7, 1808, cited in James A. Bear Jr., ed., *Jefferson at Monticello* (Charlottesville: Univ. of Virginia Press, 1976), 67–68.
14. Jefferson first constructed Monticello between 1770 and 1784. When he left for France in 1784 the house was not quite finished, lacking interior trim. The rebuilding of Monticello began in 1794 and continued until about 1809, when all but the porticos were completed.
15. TJ to James Dinsmore, Dec. 28, 1806, Vi, TJ Personal Papers, 24807.
16. James Dinsmore to TJ, Oct. 16, 1807, MHi-5.
17. TJ to James Dinsmore, Oct. 25, 1807, MHi-5.
18. TJ to John Perry, Mar. 29, 1808, CSmH-6. Another letter to Jefferson's overseer at Poplar Forest in 1815 went into more detail about having a stock of scantling produced (TJ to Joel Yancey, July 25, 1815, MHi-8.):

    > [G]ive the inclosed bill to Mr. Atkinson & get him to saw it immediately so as to have it ready on the arrival of the carpenters. There are, I imagine, belted poplars in the cleared grounds sufficient to furnish the stocks, for I do not suppose they will take more than 3 or 4 trees. He will need help in pitting, but the shorter he makes the stocks the less help he will need.

    A Note for Mr. Atkinson.
    I shall have occasion for 600 feet, running measure of scantling 5 1/4 inches square, clear of the saw, all of heart poplar, without a speck of sap. When we use it will be cut into lengths of 2 ft. 8 I. for balusters. The stocks therefore must be of such lengths as to cut into these smaller lengths of 2 ft. 8 I. without waste.
    For example a stock of 8 feet will give 3 lengths
    10 f. 8 I.———4 lengths
    13 f. 4 I.———5 lengths
    16 f.————6 lengths
    to be done immediately so as to be ready on our arrival.
19. James Dinsmore to TJ, Oct. 24, 1807, MHi-5.

20. The first-period doors of Monticello (1770s) have raised panels. The second-period doors (1790s) have flat panels. Barry's graining technique was to run a double stripe as imitation inlay around the edge of the raised panels or in the position of the raised edge on the flat panels, both with a burl pattern in the area of the sloping panel. The question of whether the stripe was put on the raised panels just to match the imitative one on the flat panel has not been completely answered. Other examples such as Prestwould Plantation would indicate that raised panels can have a stripe on their edge. Paint analyst Frank Welsh believes this was common practice. The question of whether the exterior face of a faux-grained door would have imitation inlay or burl is also at question. Again, Preswould Plantation in Mecklenburg County, Va., has a stripe on the exterior face of a grained door. Paint analysis by Frank Welsh on the south parlor door at Monticello revealed graining but no details about the inlay or burl.
21. TJ to Hugh Chisolm, June 5, 1807, MHi-5.
22. Given the usual practice of spanning masonry openings with brick arches, putting in a window unit at a later time would not have been a major challenge. Jefferson's designs were not usual, however. He preferred that the segmental brick window arches be hidden on the exterior. This posed a problem for the bricklayer. What would hold up the outer four-inch veneer of brickwork in front of the arch and its arched white oak lintel beneath? Investigation revealed that Chisolm constructed a rough frame against the straight portions of the splayed window jambs with a vertical one-inch board, above which spanned the opening and evidently held a temporary board to support the brickwork.
23. TJ to James Donath, Oct. 9, 1807, MHi-5.
24. James Dinsmore to TJ, June 24, 1808, MHi-6.
25. Edmund Bacon to TJ, June 30, 1808, ViU-6.
26. James Dinsmore to TJ, July 1, 1808, MHi-6.
27. Chambers, *Poplar Forest and Thomas Jefferson,* 37.
28. Hugh Chisolm to TJ, June 1, 1807, MHi-5.
29. TJ to John Hemings, Nov. 27, 1819, MHi-10.
30. For a detailed account of Jefferson and brickwork, especially at Poplar Forest, see Travis C. McDonald Jr., "The Brickwork at Poplar Forest: Mr. Jefferson Builds His Dream House," *APT Bulletin* 27, no. 1–2 (1996): 36–46.
31. Lynchburg builders continued to employ Flemish bond through the 1840s.
32. The two stair pavilions he added after the main walls were done, telling Jefferson, "I had rather put them up after than to build them with the out walls of the house as the angles where they join interfear so much with the line that I work by"; Hugh Chisolm to TJ, June 1, 1807, MHi-5. Chisolm referred to a string line held by wrought-iron pins pushed into wet mortar for setting level brick courses.
33. The stair pavilions are an interesting feature of the Poplar Forest plan. Based on a letter Jefferson sent to Chisolm after the initial visit when construction began, and also on a preliminary floor plan, the stair pavilions were not part of the initial scheme, nor were the porticos, leaving just a pure octagonal form. Like many ideal things compromised for their practicality, Jefferson then realized that the pavilions were absolutely necessary as the only means of communicating with the lower floor; even with their addition the food had to come through the east chamber to reach the central dining room. This is why the east chamber was altered in 1816, probably with the sealing of the central alcove bed in order to provide a more public "pantry" on the south side of the room for food coming up the east stairs from the newly constructed wing. McLaughlin proposes that the staircase in Jefferson's work

stood as a symbol of democratic life when compared to European prototypes (*Biography of a Builder,* 6–7). He goes on to suggest that the Monticello staircases, in addition to their comparative plain and democratic form, also reflected a psychological symbol of Jefferson's personality in their "dark, cramped" way, symbolic of "its owner's difficulties with free access and disclosure." If we engage this psychological explanation, we might then comment on the Poplar Forest stair pavilions: they were wider, less steep and more comfortable, filled with plenty of light from a huge lunette window, and yet privately dedicated, one pavilion for each large chamber, and providing private access to the lower floor or to the outdoors—an open, free, and unguarded state of mind, perhaps. Multiple means of access, even in such a private house, echoed Jefferson's infatuation with French plans, even when made to work in symmetrical Palladian forms. Each stair would also provide access to the exterior octagonal necessaries beyond the respective mounds on the east and west. However, in keeping with personal privacy and convenience, Jefferson's west stair pavilion became even more private when he retroactively squeezed an indoor toilet (not a water closet) underneath the stairs, similar to the need for one added to his chamber suite at Monticello.

34. TJ to Hugh Chisolm, June 5, 1807, MHi-5.
35. This assumes the same roof framing details as at Monticello, which had just been completed by the same workers.
36. TJ to Reuben Perry, Dec. 10, 1812, ViW.
37. TJ to Brockenborough, Sept. 1, 1819, DLC-51.
38. TJ to Francis Eppes, Feb. 17, 1825, ViU-10.
39. Francis Eppes to TJ, Feb. 25, 1825, MHi-14.
40. Jefferson used the tin shingles at the University of Virginia as well. Monticello has restored their tin shingle roof and the university has restored four out of ten pavilion roofs. Poplar Forest now features a restored tin shingle roof. Jefferson reported to a friend about the tin covering: "Altho the operation is so simple that any person of common sense may learn it in 3 hours as well as 3 years it would take sheets of writing to give all its details. . . . The tin costs us 13. D. a box, which does a square and a half (150 sq. ft.) and a man puts it on in 2 days. The machine we use to make the tuck is not worth a dollar." TJ to Pryor, Oct. 16, 1824, MHi-12.
41. TJ to Peyton, May 6, 1825, MHi-12.
42. John Hemings to TJ, July 23, 1825, MHi-12.
43. Ibid., Aug. 7, 1825, MHi-12.
44. Francis Eppes to TJ, June 23, 1826, MHi-14.
45. Francis Eppes to Thomas Jefferson Randolph, Sept. 21, 1826, ViU-1397-5, Edgehill Randolph Papers. It seems, in fact, that Hemings must have installed the tin shingles in their whole sizes of ten by thirteen inches instead of half sizes. Jefferson once cautioned a friend: "Some workmen with us put the tin on in whole sheets. The half sheet is what 100 years experience elsewhere has approved. In larger pieces it may contact and dilate too sensibly, and there is no reason to justify the innovation" (TJ to Paxton, Sept. 10, 1824, MHi-12). To another friend Jefferson speculated: "If your tin covering has failed, it must have been from unskilfulness. Perhaps it was been put on in whole sheets, or plain like shingles, which will not do" (TJ to Pryor, Oct. 16, 1824, MHi-12).
46. The subject of manufactured goods and their movement and marketing is a larger subject under current research by the author. Research regarding the state of consumer goods in Richmond relative to the War of 1812 shows that a transition occurred from foreign to domestically produced goods and that the war, trade restrictions, and blockades only had a

minor effect on availability. Current research is being conducted into Lynchburg goods regarding their availability upriver from Richmond.

47. Flat-bottomed bateaus, having carried tobacco or wheat downriver from Monticello or Lynchburg to Richmond, could bring goods back up—although with much more difficulty above the fall line, where ships could not travel. Shipping from around the world to upriver ports at the fall line, such as Richmond, posed little problem. An unusual example is that of the Wickham House in Richmond. John Wickham commissioned Alexander Parris of New England to design and build his fashionable new house in 1812. Parris, coming south due to the recession around Boston, not only provided a New England feel to the design of the house (later critiqued by Benjamin Latrobe), but he also used his crew of New England workers who had also come with him and even constructed a good deal of the interior using New England white pine! It is a powerful example of economic determinism regarding labor and materials relative to transportation and distance, not to mention the conservative choices of a Tory owner.

48. TJ to Reuben Perry, May 10, 1811, ViW. In error, Jefferson's Richmond merchant thought the shipping address wrong and sent the Poplar Forest ornaments to Monticello instead of going by boat to Lynchburg. Jefferson wrote to Coffee of the mistake, saying: "Col. Peyton's mistake now made it necessary for me to send them in a waggon by land 90 miles . . . The consequence which falls to my lot by that of Col. P. I hope I may remedy by bedding my boxes in a good quantity of straw in the waggon." In addition, Coffee mistakenly confused the ornaments for the university with the ornaments for Poplar Forest, an error Jefferson caught at Monticello before the boxes were redirected.

49. TJ to William Coffee, Apr. 30, 1823, ViU-9. The middle room entablature at Poplar Forest is one Jefferson made up for that room from two different sources. When questioned about the inappropriate elements for the Baths of Diocletian, Jefferson responded that it was a "fancy which I can indulge in my own case, altho in a public work I feel bound to follow authority strictly" (TJ to William Coffee, July 10, 1822, MHi-11). Not surprisingly, the orders are hierarchical, beginning with a Tuscan order on the exterior and in the front passage, to a Doric order (albeit altered) in the middle room, and finally an Ionic order in the south parlor. The surrounding secondary chambers contained Tuscan orders as evidenced by the size of their grounds and ghost marks. All these orders follow Palladio's proportions with the exception of the diameter of the columns.

50. There is no mention of how the earliest framing members for the house were produced. The earliest mention of mill-sawn lumber is in 1810; most references after that time are to having stocks taken to the mill.

51. Ironically, the reconstruction of Poplar Forest after the fire in 1846 was entirely with hewn and pit-sawn lumber, mostly poplar. Houses in Lynchburg as late as the 1850s were still using pit-sawn lumber, although usually mixed with milled sash-sawn and circular-sawn lumber. The Hutter family barn from 1856 (date in mortar) at Poplar Forest was constructed of both new pit-sawn and circular-sawn lumber (dendrochronology dated to 1853) and reused pit-sawn lumber from a Jefferson barn constructed circa 1805 (dendrochronology date) and torn down in 1848 (*Hutter Farm Journal*). The two brick octagonal privies at Poplar Forest (1808) were constructed with pit-sawn joists and rafters.

52. TJ to Joel Yancey, Sept. 13, 1816. MHi-8.

53. Ibid., June 25, 1819, MHi-10.
54. Joel Yancey to TJ, July 1, 1819, MHi-10.
55. John Hemings to TJ, July 23, 1825, MHi-12.
56. In 1810 Thomas Jefferson wrote to Gideon Granger about Lynchburg: "Lynchburg is perhaps the most rising place in the U.S. It is at the head of the navigation of James River, and receives all the produce of the Southwestern quarter of Virginia . . . it ranks now next to Richmond in importance, it is already ahead of Petersburg with the advantage of being rapidly rising while Petersburg is declining." Quoted in S. Allen Chambers, *Lynchburg: An Architectural History* (Charlottesville: Univ. of Virginia Press, 1981), 38.
57. Jefferson to Archibald Robertson, Sept. 29, 1815, MHi-8. "Be pleased to send me by the bearer 3000 nails of the length of the longest sample sent & 3000 of the shortest. Wrought nails would be preferred, but cut ones will do." The response was: "Wrought nails of the description you wanted, could not be procured, I have therefore sent cuts." Even though Jefferson's nailery had been established at Monticello in 1794 and produced cut nails by 1796, it only produced a fourpenny cut nail. All other nails made by the slave boys were wrought. In a memorandum of 1807 to Monticello overseer Edmund Bacon, Jefferson states: "Get Mr. Perry and Mr. Dinsmore, an estimate of all the nails we shall want for the house in Bedford; and when you have no orders to execute for others, let the boys be making them, and keep them separate from all others; and when the wagon goes up at Christmas, send what then shall be ready" (TJ memorandum to Mr. Bacon, Dec. 1807, cited in Edwin Morris Betts, ed., *Thomas Jefferson's Garden Book* (Philadelphia: American Philosophical Society, 1944), 357–58)
58. Edmund Bacon to TJ, Mar. 19, 1808, MHi-13.
59. Based on surviving examples found during investigation.
60. Information from Robert Self regarding Monticello; inspection of Monticello and university buildings by the author. The university framing nails are hand-headed cut nails. Investigation of buildings in the Lynchburg area confirm an early use of small lath-size cut nails around 1800 followed shortly by the use of hand-headed cut nails (Woodborne: rural) and by mature cut nails by at least 1836 (Rosedale: rural setting) and 1840 (202 Norwood: urban setting). The 1846 rebuilding of Poplar Forest after the fire was done with mature cut nails and large wrought iron spikes used in the roof system; although some wrought nails were used in some attic framing, but might have been reused. Wrought rosehead and T-head nails of various sizes were found in the investigation of the house in a first-period Jefferson context, most of which was associated with the roof.
61. TJ to Hugh Chisolm, June 5, 1807, MHi-5.
62. TJ to Goodman, Oct. 18, 1812, CSmH.
63. TJ to Edmund Meeks, July 19, 1819, MHi-10.
64. TJ to John Hemings, Dec. 18, 1821, MHi-11. When the wagon and cart were unavailable, Hemings asked Jefferson to send the mules and their "tuge harness" from Monticello. Curiosity about the unreasonable reliance on one shared wagon and cart for twenty years was answered by the 1826 inventory at Jefferson's death. It listed just "1 road waggon at $100" and "1 ox cart at $25."
65. I am indebted to Mark R. Wenger, who challenged me to find the humanistic meaning in the construction story of Poplar Forest.
66. Dumas Malone, in his six-volume biography of Jefferson, refers repeatedly to his optimism as a lifelong character trait.
67. Jefferson recommended the bricklayer to his friends and used him again at Poplar Forest

and at Monticello. Of more significance, Jefferson chose Chisolm to undertake the brickwork at the first pavilion at the University of Virginia in 1817, a high honor in Jefferson's eyes. Despite the good comparative quality of Chisolm's work at Pavilion VII, especially with oil-stock brick, Jefferson's optimistic belief in his bricklayer faltered with a final recognition of his flaws. Chisolm did no further work at the university. Jefferson's displeasure with Chisolm's work on this most idealistic of projects resulted in some of the tightest masonry specifications of the time for the remaining university construction, written, optimism aside, for the yet-untried and unknown personalities who would finish the work (*Lynchburg Press and Public Advertiser*, Mar. 19, 1819). For more information on the initial construction story of the University of Virginia, see William B. O'Neal, *Jefferson's Buildings at the University of Virginia: The Rotunda* (Charlottesville: Univ. of Virginia Press, 1960); Cote, "Architectural Workmen"; Richard G. Wilson, ed., *Thomas Jefferson's Academical Village* (Charlottesville: Univ. of Virginia Press, 1993); Travis McDonald "The Brickwork at Poplar Forest: Mr. Jefferson Builds His Dream House," APT 27, no. 1–2 (1996): 36–46; and Mendel Mesick Cohen Waite Hall, series of historic structure reports on several pavilions published for the University of Virginia in the 1980s and 1990s.

The public newspaper ad on March 19, 1819, called out Jefferson's expectations for quality materials and workmanship at the University of Virginia:

> It is proposed to lay about a million of bricks this season in buildings so far distinct that the undertakings may be in one or more portions of about an hundred thousand bricks each, the undertakers finding materials as well as work, the front walls are to be faced with oil stock bricks, the others with sand stocks, the interior mass to be of plane bricks, all to be laid with good bond to be clinkers, and not a single sammell brick to be used in any part of the work under a penalty of 5 cents for every such brick, nor more than 2 bats to 9 whole bricks, the inner mortar to be one third lime and two thirds clean and gritty sand without any mixture of earth, the outer 1/2 lime and 1/2 such sand and the whole to be grouted with a mortar of the inner quality.

68. James A. Bear Jr. and Lucia C. Stanton, eds., *Jefferson's Memorandum Books, Accounts, with Legal Records and Miscellany 1767–1826* (Princeton, N.J.: Princeton Univ. Press) as quoted in McLaughlin, Jefferson and Monticello, 378.
69. At the time of his leaving the presidency in 1809, the year in which he started living at Poplar Forest, Jefferson discovered, despite his record keeping, that he was $10,000 more in debt than he realized (McLaughlin, *Jefferson and Monticello,* 378).
70. James S. Ackerman, *The Villa: Form and Ideology of Country Houses* (Princeton: Princeton Univ. Press, 1990).
71. See Gordon S. Wood, "The Trials and Tribulations of Thomas Jefferson," and Merrill D. Peterson, "Afterword," both in Peter S. Onuf, ed., *Jeffersonian Legacies* (Charlottesville: Univ. of Virginia Press, 1993), for further discussions of Jefferson's optimism. At Poplar Forest, Jefferson resumed his correspondence with John Adams, sometimes wondering if the battle for the Enlightenment had been lost. Adams responded to Jefferson with the same worries: "Is the Nineteenth Century to be a

Contrast to the Eighteenth? Is it to extinguish all the Lights of its Predecessor?" Forces had been aligning against the Enlightenment: Jacksonian Democracy, romantic emotions, and popular religious revivals. It is no wonder that Jefferson stopped reading newspapers and returned to the classical authors of his educational and optimistic foundation to resecure this failing optimism at his retreat.

72. Jefferson's greatest public project, the University of Virginia, was considerably completed when he died in 1826.
73. Gordon S. Wood, "The Trials and Tribulations of Thomas Jefferson," in Peter S. Onuf, ed., *Jeffersonian Legacies* (Charlottesville: Univ. of Virginia Press, 1993); Mark R. Wenger, in "Thomas Jefferson, Tenant," *Winterthur Portfolio* 26, no. 4 (winter 1991), demonstrates that even in rented accommodations in New York and Philadelphia, Jefferson undertook physical change to personalize his private space.
74. The peace and quiet of Poplar Forest allowed Jefferson to design his ultimate Enlightenment monument and, we might say, his most fervent optimistic hope for the future: the University of Virginia.
75. The process of researching, investigating, conserving, reconstructing, and restoring Poplar Forest for the past nine years has been a transcending experience. The commitment of philosophy and time from the board to "do it right," the commitment from donors to fund the project, and the commitment from the architectural team to tackle each and every detail in the spirit of a greater good has meant all the difference. Most of all, by trying to follow the details and techniques of the original work has meant reliving the frustrations of Jefferson regarding supervision, workforce, materials, and details. We can get no closer to his process. My own natural optimism in people and in projects mirrors Jefferson's in perfect, ghostly precision. This story of construction is humbly dedicated to the committed craftsmen whose work stands as testament against the current theories asserting that the traditional connection between head and hand has been lost; for those reasons, this work is dedicated to all the restoration craftsmen who have given it their best, and especially to master restoration craftsman Douglas Rideout.

CHAPTER 11

Ann Smart Martin

Commercial Space as Consumption Arena: Retail Stores in Early Virginia

Becca, an enslaved woman, was found guilty of theft in Petersburg, Virginia, in 1807. Her story sets the scene for a new understanding of stores in early Virginia. Becca had entered a well-appointed store and asked to look at some lace in a show case on the counter. The storekeeper, William Ingles, unlocked the case and showed her several pieces. None suited her fancy, so he closed the case but did not lock it. She then asked to examine some bonnets high on a shelf behind him, which he turned to procure and handed down. None pleased her, and he left the room. As he returned into the store, he saw a piece of lace fall from "her Bosom or Some Where about her" onto the floor. Quickly recovering from her error, she picked it up and asked if the merchant "could sell her such a Bargain of Lace as that." Ingles, seeing his mark on the lace, claimed she had stolen it. Becca denied his charge, saying she had gotten it from another woman. To her poor fortune, her friend denied her story and the theft was charged.[1]

An enslaved woman shopping for lace was not unusual. By the end of the eighteenth century, retail stores were semipublic arenas where a broad cross section of society—men and women, rich and poor, black and white—participated in a common act of consumption performance. What is remarkable in a society defined by formal stratification of class, race, ethnicity, and gender is that no group seemed to be systematically excluded from participating in the new world of goods by shopping at stores. Despite occasional rhetorical dismay and attempted legal boundaries, even blacks, the most fettered of all Virginians, crossed the store's thresholds to buy and sell with regularity.[2]

This triangulation of merchant, customer, and artifact was continually redefined based on the performers, the setting of the stage, and its location in town or country. The richest matron and the poorest slave both faced a merchant across the counter in the store. Yet only one might be invited to the office to have tea. To be consumers, wives might be freed from husbands, slaves from masters, and girls from mothers. They then entered a distinct relationship—to the merchant, the market, and the world of goods. Even men stepped out of their more comfortable business identity to negotiate the vagaries of fashion and consumer choice. It is in this sense that stores were places where larger cultural paradigms are acted out and recast in new economic and social scenarios.

The store building's form and finishing both shaped and responded to these paradoxes of social action in commercial life. This chapter demonstrates how stores evolved in response to increasing consumer demands for new amenities and fashions by a broader cross section of the population. The needs of the merchant to display goods to entreat purchase and control them to prevent loss form one axis of his ability to succeed in business. The merchant's need to control access for some and to cultivate business for others is another. His larger purpose was to make money, and how he achieved that goal tells us much about the larger world of Virginia society.

By the end of the eighteenth century, retail stores were perhaps the most common nondomestic buildings on the Virginia landscape—in towns, at crossroads, or on plantations. With our rising scholarly interest in commerce and culture—consumerism as a cultural form and the economic shifts to capitalism—these buildings are gaining fresh interest as one of the most important institutions and places of everyday life. Historians have shown a rising tide of household consumption in the late seventeenth and eighteenth centuries; most of these new things were manufactured goods brought to the Chesapeake in exchange for the staple crop of tobacco.[3]

The provision of imported manufactured goods to seventeenth-century Virginians was problematic. There were few specialized places where goods were sold. More common may have been entrepreneurs who opened a pack of goods and hence carried on the trade. Wealthy planters also imported and sold a limited range of goods on their property. There were thus options for consumption, but probably few purpose-built structures with extensive choices. Several important factors changed the business climate after 1730. The Tobacco Inspection Act that year removed the onus of judgment from the merchant to the inspector. Greater population density enabled the regular stocking of goods on a year-round basis and changing business organization put full-time storekeepers or merchant partners on the ground to buy tobacco and sell goods. An important result of these changing business conditions was the building of retail stores as permanent structures at specified locations.

Thus, by the middle of the eighteenth century, the single most important source for new consumer goods for most of the population was the local retail store. Like the village shops of England, these stores supplied the colonists with the common necessities and amenities of life. Such objects were usually purchased on credit, with payment made in crops, cash, or services. Because the wealthiest planters were most likely to use the consignment system of marketing—selling their own crops and obtaining goods on account in England—the patrons of local retail stores were usually lesser farmers who turned to the local storekeeper, often an agent of an English or Scottish firm. One Virginia merchant wrote in 1767 that "the best customers a store can have" were "those people who have one or two h[ogsheads] to dispose of" and who wanted goods instead of cash.[4] The demand of these customers was for local access to consumer goods in the latest styles at reasonable prices, and twice yearly it was customary for merchants to complete an extensive order of the goods necessary for the following season's trade.

While the organizational details of these retail businesses differed, a common problem faced all merchants. By the third quarter of the eighteenth century, too many merchants had made competition fierce and the selection of goods for sale became even more important. One merchant wrote with exasperation to his supplier that his success depended on the completion of his orders for goods "with dispatch, exactness and judgement in the choice of the goods." They were to be particularly attentive to the "quality, collours, patterns and fashions."[5]

As consumers became more particular about the kinds of things for sale, merchants also competed by providing better shopping experiences. Simply put, at the beginning of the eighteenth century having goods appropriate to the market was a basic predictor of a merchant's success. A century later a merchant needed to store, display, and actively present a wide array of fashionable amenities and luxuries to assure patronage. Providing the appropriate consumption arena meant a fixed place of a recognizable form that controlled access and movement of customers but simultaneously allowed the powerful desires of consumption to unfold. A new stereotypical figure thus emerged: the man behind the counter, willing to please. By the end of the nineteenth century the department store could arise as consumption palace.

But many questions remain. We know little about the physical environs of shopping. Did men and women jostle at a counter? Were objects for sale draped seductively about or enveloped tightly in wrappers? How did Virginia stores compare to the highly ornamented and sophisticated world of London shopping? How did Virginia structures evolve? What did it mean for a store to be "completely fitted up"?[6]

Vending consumer goods in Virginia responded to pragmatic difficulties of climate and slow stock turnover. While London trade cards and prints often show elegant displays, particularly of fabric bolts draped to display them at best advantage, Virginia stores may have kept much of their general goods covered to avoid devastating losses from insect, rodent, and moisture damage. For example, the inventory of goods in John Bates's store in 1720 included fabrics and clothing items that had been eaten by rats or moths, and some drugget that had suffered from both. Some handkerchiefs were "spoiled and rotten." It is in this context that we can further understand the reluctance of merchants to have too much stock left at the end of the season.[7]

Another problem was how to organize and keep sorted the myriad goods that filled these buildings. James Robinson advised John Turner always to keep his goods in "proper order," adding that it will help them sell. He urged Turner to take them down often and retie them, presumably in papers.[8] Norfolk merchant Henry Fleming also complained about an assortment of poorly made gloves that he and his assistants are "frequently called upon to shew them & hitherto have had as often the trouble of putting them up again."[9] Taking down items from shelves, returning them, and putting them back in order was the heart of a hypothetical scene between a shopping lady and mercer where she tested his patience by having him "tumble" several thousand pounds of goods from shelves for her viewing.[10]

Nonetheless, the solution of the polarities of security/access and storage/active display evolved over the course of the eighteenth century. Three extant inventories of store goods, two with accompanying plan or room size, are rare evidence of the detail of goods, their organization, and location. In combination, they can help assess change over time and differences in rural and urban stores. Increasing consumer desires were demonstrated as the axis tilted toward organized goods and display, a process that was accelerated in urban situations.

The first clue can be found in a Virginia probate inventory of 1728. The appraisers of Richard Walker's store in rural Middlesex County in 1728 carefully listed the goods for sale and defined seven spaces by name: "Store loft, below stairs, under the shelves on the floor, lower floor, middle floor, new house, and dwelling house." The goods were mainly stored *in something;* containers for small items shipped in quantity (a cask of nails, for instance) or a jumble of goods in a chest, crate, or barrel. In the loft were two trunks, three chests, two barrels, and seven boxes of assorted goods. One shelf was listed separately holding hose, hats, and eight pieces of fabric. "Under the shelves on the floor" were numerous books, shoes, ironmongery (tools and small metal goods), and small items like beads and spectacles. In a box on the floor was a jumble of stoneware, glass, marking irons, combs, needles, pewter, sugar, and books. In the "New House" was an assortment of tools and other metal wares, such as chaffing dishes and engineer rules, and a hogshead of ship bread. Along with the heavy iron objects were two boxes of pipes, earthen chamber pots, punch bowls, and other ceramics not contained or packed in any box. In the dwelling house were scattered dozens of pairs of hose and gloves, pins and primers. The overall picture is one of chaotic combinations of objects and spaces.[11]

This early-eighteenth-century rural store can be compared with John Hook's in rural Franklin County seventy-five years later. A detailed 1801 inventory taken by court commissioners combined with a standing structure gives some of our best evidence of how goods were organized and displayed in rural Virginia stores at the end of the eighteenth century.[12] No shelving remains in the extant fifteen-by-twenty-foot storeroom, but a shelving plan is extant from the same merchant a decade earlier (fig. 11.1). Ten pigeonholes were well filled with different sized buttons, and there were 124 papers of different kinds. Two holes contained razors; others were filled with an extraordinary array of small consumer goods, from knives and forks to ribbons, nearly all wrapped in paper. Elsewhere around the store were barrels of ginger, brimstone, shot, and pepper, casks of brandy and whiskey, even an anvil. Breakable items were nearly all in trunks, such as the forty-one different sizes of looking glasses or the glass goblets, decanters, and vials. Creamware was packed in three crates, window glass in two boxes. But the textiles were all listed separately, as were individual books and household goods, such as pewter, tin, and iron. This suggests, albeit tentatively, that those items may not have been boxed but stacked on shelves or hung in relative proximity to each other. On the counter may have been the two pair of small brass scales and weights next to a few pounds of tea and indigo. Nearby may have been the barrels of brimstone, pepper, and shot that would have been measured. Boxes of chocolate, bags of ginger, and bladders of putty may have been on shelves near barrels of copperas or brown sugar, seed cotton in bags, bushels of salt, chests of tea, and tin candle boxes full of candles.

The snapshot of the contents of this store is remarkably different from the jumble seen at Rich-

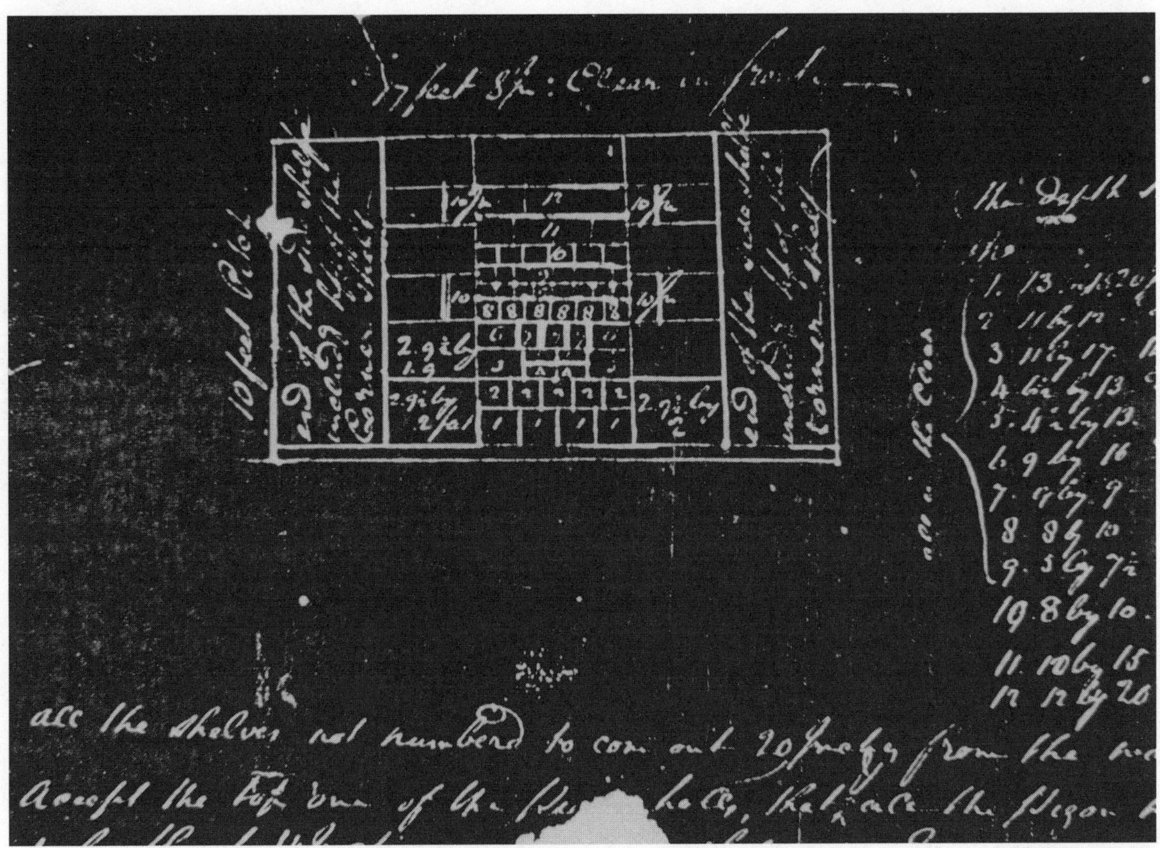

Fig. 11.1. Shelving plan from John Hook's 1771 store. Original Hook store drawings, New London, Bedford County, Virginia. John Hook Papers, undated. Rare Books, Manuscripts, and Special Collections Library, Duke University.

ard Walker's store in 1728. While barrels and boxes still probably lined the walls, the picture here is one of relative order. Small consumer goods were stored in pigeon holes, and breakable items were packed together. It is not clear how the immense array of fabrics were stored or displayed, but they were also listed in a distinct and organized way.

Urban store goods at the end of the eighteenth century were even more carefully organized and displayed. William Parrott's Richmond estate inventory in 1798 also remarkably listed the goods on the shelves and can be combined with a Mutual Assurance Society plat recorded less than a year earlier.[13] At thirty by twenty feet, the storeroom was larger than John Hook's. Shelves completely lined two walls and at least a part of another. The inventory takers moved through the space, first recording large quantities of alcohol in casks. Shelves on the east wall were filled with carefully grouped grocery items, followed by textiles and clothing. The far end of those shelves and the south and west wall shelves were stacked with less expensive and breakable ceramics and glassware. On the floor on the west side were bushels and barrels of foodstuffs, like corn, salt, potatoes, and preserved fish. Shelving continued in the front two windows, and one was stacked with glass plates. An ancillary lumber house contained large quantities of alcohol, another sacks of salt and barrels of corn.

These three inventories show the evolution of spaces with specialized architectural fittings, like shelves and pigeonholes. They also demonstrate the increasing wish to display goods in an orderly way in rural stores. If some objects remained in shipping crates in late-eighteenth-century rural stores, gone is the sense of jumble and chaos. In urban stores the need to display, not just store, was perhaps even stronger. Ceramics and other breakables were still in boxes in Hook's rural establishment, but they were stacked in view in William Parrot's store. Shelving, too, continued in the front windows to entice the customer from the street. Shopping was still hardly self-service, as the merchant worked hard to protect (from eager rodents or sticky fingers), show, and sell. Nonetheless, the duality of display and protection had begun to shift.

The buildings themselves give further evidence of the importance of wooing yet controlling customers. Before the second quarter of the nineteenth century most Virginia stores employed the same vocabulary as domestic dwellings. Some standing stores moved from dwellings to stores and vice versa, and eighteenth-century property sellers sometimes hinted that stores could be transformed to dwellings at small expense. Like houses, their size varied greatly, depending on wealth, location, and the wish of merchants to impress. Interior space on the first floor ranged from 300 to more than 1,000 square feet. Within those walls, a store and a counting room or office were the norm with occasional additional spaces and ancillary buildings for other uses.[14]

While these two basic units were most common, the placement of the rooms on the lot, alignment to street, addition of other rooms, and location of doors and windows differed. One simple organizing plan predominated. In one version, seen here in the Prentis store in Williamsburg, the gable end faced a street: a large room served as the store, with the counting room or office behind it (fig. 11.2). The most salient feature is the fenestration: the placement of windows and doors easily identified purpose-built store structures. A door and flanking windows pierced the gable end. If there was storage upstairs, a hoist and door might enable easy loading. Windows clustered toward the back of the side wall, lighting the back of the store and the office. A broad uninterrupted wall space allowed for continuous shelving, even if it left an asymmetrical facade. In a second example illustrated by the John Hook store, the building's long side faced a street and the two rooms stood side by side, often with two doors on the street. This allowed access to carry out business in the office, even if the storeroom remained locked. The need for long uninterrupted continuous shelving still affected the placement of doors and windows (fig. 11.3).

The heart of the building was the main storeroom. It was often square or nearly square and ranged in size from about 200 square feet (16 by 14 feet, for example) to almost 500 square feet. Typical are the drawings for John Hook's store in New London from 1772 (fig. 11.4).

The long side of his 42-by-20-foot building faced onto the street on his two-acre lot. On the ground floor were a store, counting room, and a storage room that Hook may have referred to as the "lumber room." The storeroom was 20 by 20 feet with a 2-foot-10-inch-wide counter nearly bisecting the room on its east-west axis. On the street side (to the south) was a door and two windows; the facing wall—behind the counter—was lined

Fig. 11.2. Prentis and Company Store, Williamsburg, Virginia, 1739. Photograph by author.

with thirteen shelves and forty-nine small pigeon holes, ranging from 4.5 by 13 inches to 13 by 20 inches (fig. 11.1). A door on the east wall to the storage room was on the public (south) side of the counter; the door on the west wall to the counting room was behind the counter, thus controlling public access. Under the counter were three tiers of cross-divided drawers, including a cash drawer. This structure no longer exists, but its appearance was probably similar to that of the Farish Print Shop on King Street in Port Royal, Caroline County, which has a quite similar plan and size (fig. 11.5).[15]

Fig. 11.3. John Hook Store, Franklin County, Virginia, c. 1784. Photograph by author.

Several discrete zones split the storeroom; one for customers, the other for the merchant. The counter and shelves framed the merchant's world. Although a table or desk could serve a similar func-

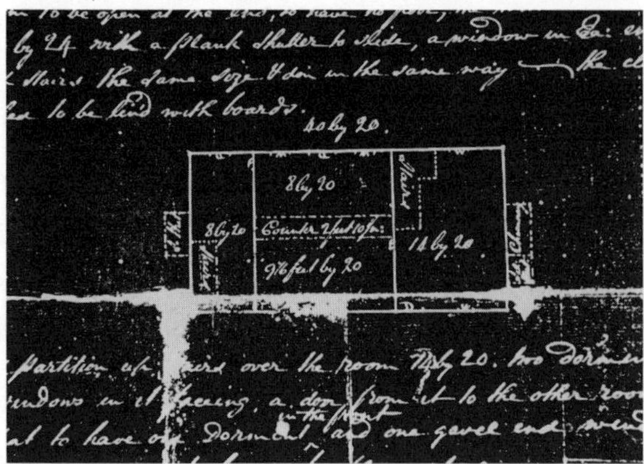

Fig. 11.4. Plan of building. Original Hook store drawings, New London, Bedford County, Virginia. John Hook Papers, undated, probably 1771. Rare Books, Manuscripts, and Special Collections Library, Duke University.

Fig. 11.5. Farish Print Shop, Port Royal, Caroline County, Virginia. Photograph by author.

tion, the counter emerged as the standard surface for writing, measuring, and displaying goods. On the counter, bundles were unwrapped, goods shown and handled, and money weighed. The propensity for small items to disappear from open counter displays can be seen by the small glass cases increasingly for sale. The most specialized stores included glass casing, such as the "three mahogany counters, with glass fronts, fit for a jeweller's shop" advertised in Charleston, South Carolina, in 1803.[16] Drawers underneath counters also allowed control of goods and money. Finally, the counter served as a barrier over which a thief must reach to acquire his or her prize. The counter thus not only demarcated a physical space but a symbolic zone as well. The poem "The Village Merchant" published in 1792 contains the long travails of a young farmer's plan to become a merchant, although he speaks with pride of a counter "behind whose breast-work none but he might stand." Only a "brother merchant from some other place" could broach his place of honor.[17] "Life behind the counter" became a catch phrase for a shopkeeper's career (fig. 11.6).

Few standing stores contain their original shelving and trim. The White Store in Isle of Wight County probably dates to the middle of the eighteenth century, and an elaborate system of pigeonholes and shelves covered the entire back wall. The store at Marmion Plantation in King William County is another early surviving example, and its construction date probably closely followed mid-eighteenth-century house construction (figs. 11.7, 11.8). The storeroom was sheathed with unpainted vertical boards (as was common) and the walls capped with crown molding. A waist-high shelf on brackets still lines the side wall. Ghost lines there also indicate the presence of shelves, and the missing shelf and brackets lie in a pile of lumber in the corner. Nails and hooks above the shelf indicate that other items were probably hung for easy viewing (fig. 11.9). Another set of hooks of unfinished (bark-covered) wood clustered in the southeast corner of the store at six feet high and approximately two-foot intervals. Next to each hook was

Fig. 11.6. "Captain Andrew Johnson, Merchant," Lewis Miller (1796–1882) Sketchbook. Courtesy, The Historical Society of York County, Pennsylvania.

a large wrought-iron nail. A second set of wrought spikes was probably placed in the eastern wall later in the century. While it is unclear what hung from these large spikes, nails, and hooks, we might imagine a zone of larger agricultural tools, implements, hanging ropes, and saddlery items. The Marmion store also allows us to see other probable zones of storage; the northeast corner, for example, had no shelves or hooks but may have had a place for larger containers and hogsheads. Indeed, in that corner can still be found a packing crate of southern pine with wrought-iron hardware of probable eighteenth-century origin. The counter was likely removed along with the original floor, making its placement conjectural; but it undoubtedly fronted the shelves, dividing the space on its north-south access. Defining features of rural storerooms are sheathed walls, exposed joist ceilings, shelving and a counter, and a lack of any form of heating.

While no original interiors for urban stores have been located, urban plans were often more refined. The Langley Store in Washington at the end of the century was on a street corner and included a large window flanked with colonnades or pilasters over cellar caps on each street providing two directions of lighting into the storeroom. The semicircular shelves below the windows could be used to display objects to passers-by. Inside, a long counter sided on one window with shelving on the two opposite walls.

Stores (like other commercial structures such as taverns) were paradoxical spaces, privately owned but open to the public. Nonetheless, like churches and courthouses in colonial Virginia, architectural fittings defined zones of exclusion. A patron only advanced to the middle of the room to be stopped by the counter; only his or her gaze could travel ahead and sometimes around. This more exclusionary zone in courthouses and churches is often marked by railings and contains the symbolic elements of the power of church and state. In commercial enterprises like stores, the demarcated power is the world of goods.

The other major room in store buildings was the office or counting room, where the merchant tended books and entertained customers. The higher level of architectural finishing suggests a different kind of space than the storeroom. These counting rooms were most often finished like a domestic interior; walls were most likely lathed and plastered, with chair boards and washboards. Some were papered. They were also heated and may have been quite well furnished. The presence of chairs,

Fig. 11.7. Store at Marmion Plantation, King George County, Virginia. Photograph by author.

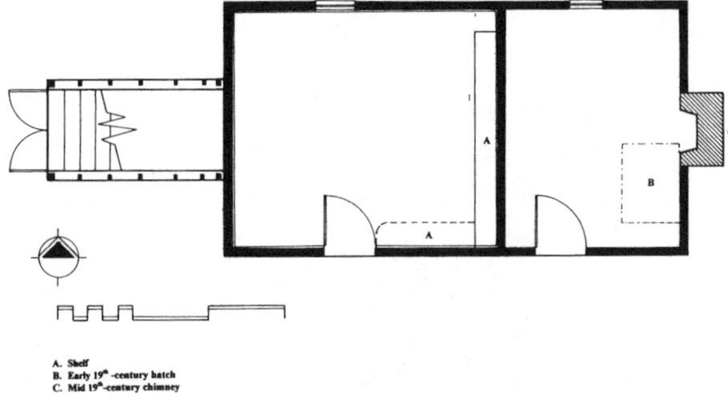

Fig. 11.8. Plan of store at Marmion Plantation. Measured by Carl Lounsbury and author. Drawing by Carl Lounsbury.

drinking vessels, and tea equipment demonstrate the entertainment necessary in the wooing of customers. Indeed, James Robinson urged a new storekeeper to give "all good usage and drink in abundance."[18] Access to this room was carefully arranged. There was often a separate public entrance from the street so that the storeroom could remain locked if the merchant withdrew. In other cases, the counting room could only be entered through a door behind the counter in the storeroom. A set of stairs could lead upward for storage or living space for assistants.

The counting house of the Alexandria firm of Hooe and Harrison contained desks, tables, chairs, scales, money chests, and a bed. All the equipment for writing was there: quires of paper, ink bottles,

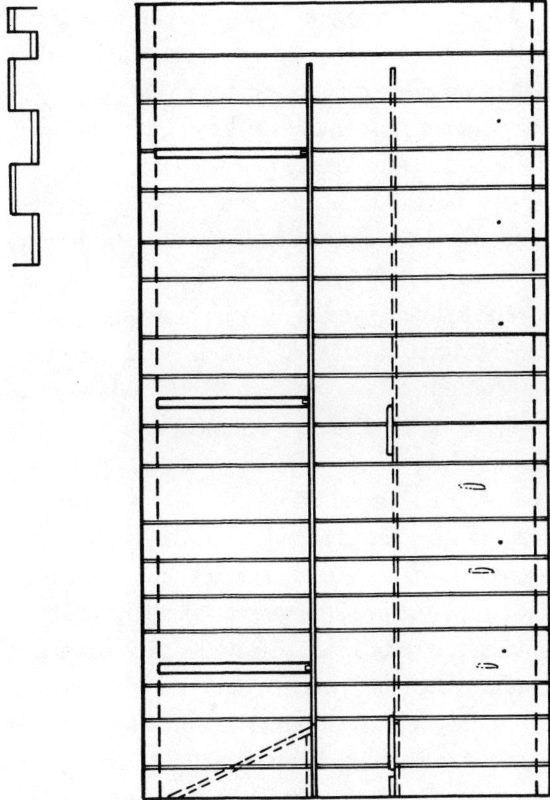

Fig. 11.9. Interior elevation of east wall shelving, Store at Marmion Plantation. Measured by Carl Lounsbury and author. Drawing by Carl Lounsbury.

lead pencils, Dutch quills, paper cutters, seals, and, of course, the set of books for the firm. The merchant could consult several published treatises on trade and law, reading late at night with the aid of the "compting House Candlesticks" (valued at an extraordinary seventy-five pounds) or by the light of the fire. When tired, he could stretch out on his bed, put his head on his pillow, pull up his sheets and blankets, and enjoy a good night's rest.[19]

Other ancillary structures and spaces completed the store's setting. Some merchants had a need for (and could afford) extra storage and sleeping for shopkeepers, apprentices, or slaves, hence the added extra rooms on the first or second floor. Clerks often slept on the premises for security, usually upstairs or in the office. The Syme store in Newcastle included a "bedroom" as well as a counting room. Back shedding was not uncommon. Others added stables, warehouses, granaries, and log houses for storage of goods and the reception of slaves for sale. On more elaborate sites, two stores were built, one to accommodate dry goods, the other for liquors and bulky wholesale items. Underlying the use of space in all these commercial establishments was a basic need to store, unpack, and/or display goods (both wet and dry), keep books, conduct business, entertain important clients, and receive slaves or other servants on errands.

Urban plans also often combined domestic space for the merchant and his family with store space for goods. For instance, the Dudley Digges store in Yorktown was advertised in 1754 as a "commodious Brick store-house which has necessary Apartments for private family."[20] But how the commercial and private spaces were combined is less clear. One option for providing domestic space was to include a side passage or alley to allow access to a back or side entry to an upstairs living space. Another was to provide a second block with side entrance leading to a stair passage. The plan of the Langley Store shows how stores were combined with dwelling houses and multiple outbuildings on urban lots. The door opened out on the corner of South Capitol Street and South N Street, allowing access from two directions. The counting room was heated with access from the storeroom. A commodious parlor lay behind with a separate entrance onto a stair passage; the other living spaces lay overhead. A kitchen behind faced a fenced courtyard with a large warehouse with gable entrance (fig. 11.10).[21] William Parrot's two-story structure also combined domestic and commercial space. A one-story structure on the site by 1796 was occupied as a grocery; by 1798 it had been expanded to a two-story building with a one-story back counting room. Entrance to the upper floor was probably through a side entrance into a back passage with staircase. Upstairs were a back chamber and a well-finished front parlor. The garret contained more sleeping space.

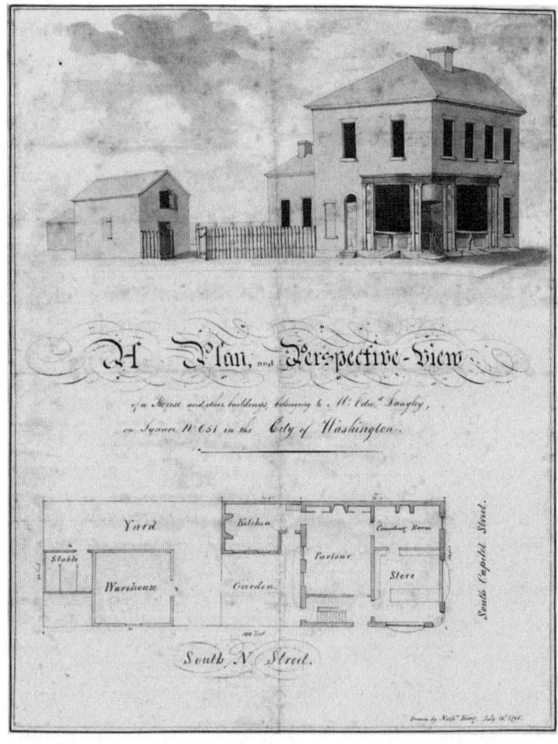

Fig. 11.10. "A Plan and Perspective-View of a House, and other Buildings, belonging to Mr. Edward Langley, on Square No. 651 in the City of Washington" by Nicholas King, July 14, 1798. Courtesy of Winterthur Library, Joseph Downs Collection of Manuscripts and Printed Ephemera.

While the Parrott store was rebuilt to add domestic space, other stores were renovated as their ownership evolved from commercial to domestic.[22] The Spooner store in Fredericksburg was built as a house and a store for the lot owner's daughter and her new husband, the merchant and shipping agent George Spooner (fig. 11.11). Two years later the family relocated, and Spooner listed the structure for sale the following year as a "well finished two story House with a passage, two rooms, and a store on the first floor; and a passage and three rooms on the second floor, a cellar under the whole house." The lot included "every necessary outbuilding, with a well-enclosed garden." The store was home to different tenants and changed hands repeatedly in the next forty years. A second merchant purchased it and ran a store in 1803; after his death in 1811 the building was reconverted to a dwelling for his widow, and later their married daughter. It would not return to its commercial function until 1835, when it was used as a grocery, but probably for only the next two years. From 1796 to 1835 it can be precisely documented as a store for eight years, run by three different merchants. Its owners also had other commercial interests, from auctions to taverns, some of which may have been carried on in that building.[23]

This cycle—from store to dwelling and dwelling to store—makes analysis of its current plan even more difficult (fig. 11.12). Renovations have obliterated some of the important original fabric necessary to discern precise changes in plan. Of special interest, however, are the ghost lines of shelves on boxed and beaded ceiling joists, with traces of original blue paint on the north wall of the front room. It is likely that the front room was unheated and the current fireplace added in the early nineteenth century, when the store was converted to a dwelling. A partition may then have been added and later removed. The door to Caroline Street prob-

Fig. 11.11. Spooner Store, 1794, Fredericksburg, Virginia. Photograph by author.

ably entered at the center of the room. The advertisement for two rooms and a store on the first floor in 1799 is perplexing but suggest that the back room may have been divided into two spaces, one for business (counting room) and one for family use (parlor). Upstairs was a second commodious room that may have served as another formal living space, as it was more highly finished than the other chambers.

Urban stores continued to evolve plans to accommodate family residence with commercial use. Again, issues of security and access arise. On the one hand, living space on the first floor meant that merchants could join family at meals while keeping the store open and available.[24] On the other hand, arrangement of landscape and domestic space to enable access only to appropriate parties was a continuing concern of Virginia's hierarchical society.[25] William Parrot may have solved this by moving family space upstairs while providing downstairs sleeping space for a hired clerk, as expressed by the bed and gun in the back counting room. Thus, amongst all the shifts in plan to accommodate family residence, office space for the merchant, and outbuildings and cellars for storage, the storeroom remained the central core from which decisions flowed.

The combined architectural and documentary evidence helps provide a detailed analysis of the environment of shopping. The ordinary consumer confronted a building to the scale of a large dwelling; the storeroom itself may have matched the size of many Virginia dwellings.[26] It was constructed in a conventional plan of several rooms designed to con-

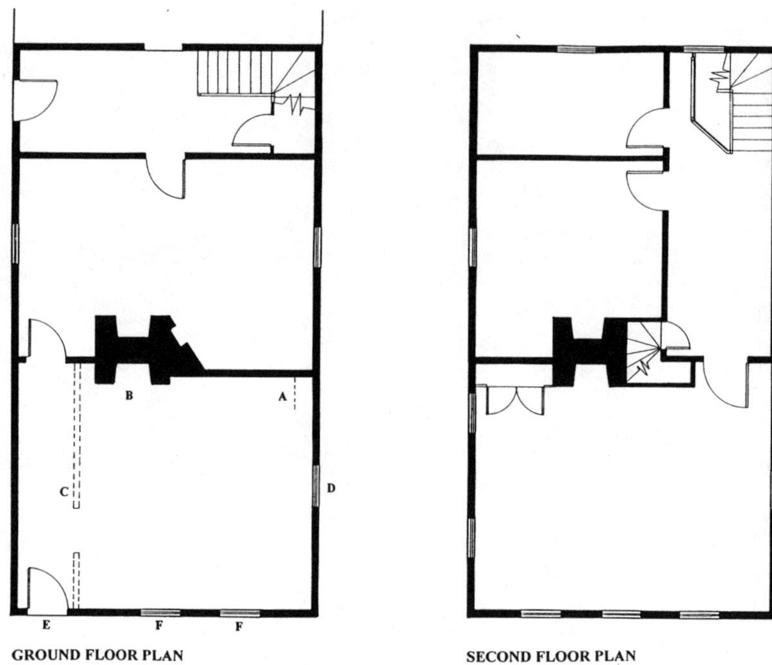

Fig. 11.12. Plan of Spooner Store, 1794, Fredericksburg, Virginia. Measured by Gary Stanton, Carl Lounsbury, and author. Drawing by Carl Lounsbury.

trol their access to goods through the use of doors and counters. Light came nearly all from one wall; thus the store may have been relatively dark, and we might imagine the merchant pulling items from the shelves behind the counter and carrying them to the better-lit side of the room on cloudy days. The storeroom was not heated; a customer could have been invited into the warm counting room, which was architecturally finished to the standard of a good dwelling. Merchant and consumer could have sat, socialized, or haggled. At the same time, even if a customer did not have complete access, goods were stacked enticingly around the store. While many remained wrapped in paper or stored in large hogsheads, boxes, or other containers, a large number of items may have been on shelves in plain view.

Combining this evidence suggests that Virginia stores, like Virginia dwellings, represented a broad range of options. Some, especially rural stores, may have been little more than shelters for the valuable stock of goods inside. Increasingly, however, the structure itself came to be a large investment for a merchant; the store and its related buildings ranged in value from £300 to £1,000. The size and interior finishing of these stores reflect permanency and year-round use, but also a need to store and display a vast range of consumer goods to suggest both order and fashion. Important business clients had to be entertained with drinking and treating, and in most cases storekeepers, clerks, or slaves needed housing. A number of supporting ancillary structures may have given the store a look of a little plantation.

Moreover, the most important point might be that by the third quarter of the eighteenth century these stores were often only that: a single-function building where goods were stored, displayed, sold, and traded in a standardized setting. That specialization of place means that the act of consumption was something distinctive, defined by action and reinforced by space. The store building for many Virginians was as defining a place on the landscape as house, church, tavern, and courthouse. Behind those doors a whole world was inside—a world of color and fashion, hard-nosed bargaining, and impulse decisions.

Between 1750 and 1830 market economics and consumer demand shifted massively throughout the Western world. Retail stores stocked more and different goods to please more and different people. The ability of consumers to see and touch and handle new things further released new desires. Nonetheless, *how* Virginia stores evolved as specific shopping environments tells about the particular economy that produced them and the society that frequented them. Virginia merchants relied mainly on imported manufactured goods in exchange for agricultural products, and as the economy diverged from a reliance on tobacco to a more diverse market economy more petty entrepreneurs arose. Merchants could no longer, at face value, judge a customer's ability to pay. As more people of differing classes, races, and genders wanted ribbons and teapots, stores changed to serve them. The need to display goods to entreat purchase and control them to prevent loss, to allow access for people on the economy's margins, and to court patronage for the well heeled continued to guide merchants' actions in how they allowed the consumption performance to unfold. That slaves bought ribbons did not release them from bondage; that women bought teapots did not make the legal or household structure less paternal. These actions, nonetheless, created new social performances in an economic setting. Thus the dialectic of stage and performance continued to evolve. Changes in form and fitting were incremental, but together they began to create an environment that encouraged shopping as leisure. As the nineteenth century progressed, purveyors of the world of goods continued to peel back the skin of the building, insert multiple large windows filled with commodities to lure the customer, and add heating and lighting. A Virginia girl's diary in 1836 describes repeated visits to local stores to see the new goods and ogle the neighborhood young men. One day a large group dallied for several hours in a store, then one more hour in another. On another visit, a merchant treated them with almonds and candy.[27] This was shopping as entertainment, the new triangulation between merchant, customer, and consumer goods at the new local store.

Notes

1. Examination of Becca, a slave the property of Robert Nicholson, July 23, 1807, Petersburg City Hustings Court Minute Book 4, 1800–1807, n.p. My thanks to Mick Nichols, who generously shared records of this and other store thefts.
2. For analysis of slave purchases at Virginia stores, see Ann Smart Martin, "Complex Commodities: The Enslaved as Producers and Consumers in Eighteenth-Century Virginia" (paper presented at the Omohundro Institute of Early American History and Culture Annual Conference, Winston-Salem, June 1997), and John T. Schlotterbeck, "Internal Economy of Slavery in Rural Piedmont Virginia," in *The Slaves' Economy: Independent Production by Slaves in the Americas* (Portland, Oreg.: Frank Cass and Co., 1991), 176.

3. The literature on consumerism in the eighteenth century is growing rapidly and cannot adequately be summarized here. A good place to start is Cary Carson, Ron Hoffman, and Peter J. Albert, eds., *Of Consuming Desires: The Style of Life in the Eighteenth Century* (Charlottesville: Univ. Press of Virginia, 1996). Neil McKendrick, John Brewer, and J. H. Plumb, *The Birth of Consumer Society: The Commercialization of Eighteenth-Century England* (Bloomington: Indiana Univ. Press, 1982). T. H. Breen, "An Empire of Goods: The Anglicanization of Colonial America, 1690–1776," *Journal of British Studies* 25 (October 1986). Richard L. Bushman, *The Refinement of America: Persons, Houses, Cities* (New York: Alfred A. Knopf, 1992). For a summary of the literature on consumerism from the view of the consumer goods, see Ann Smart Martin, "Makers, Buyers, and Users: Consumerism as a Material Culture Framework," *Winterthur Portfolio* 28, no. 2–3 (summer/autumn 1993): 141–57.
4. James Robinson to Bennett Price, Oct. 7, 1767, in *A Scottish Firm in Virginia, 1767–77*, ed. T. M. Devine (London: Clark Constable, 1982), 2.
5. John Hook to Walter Chambre, Dec. 28, 1773, Letter Book 1763–84, 1796, 1797, n.d. Virginia State Library, Richmond.
6. Property sale advertisement of Theodorick Bland in Prince George County; *Virginia Gazette* (Rind), July 23, 1767.
7. Inventory of the Estate of John Bates, Merchant. Goods in Poplar Spring Storehouse, June 10, 1720. York County Order and Will Book 15, 1716–20. Johnathan Newell's store inventory from 1672 included coarse men's castor hats "eaten with the Ratts around the Brims"; a dozen women's castors, some "damnified"; and "4 dozen and 4 Ratt eaten Cabbidge Nets"; Feb. 29, 1671–72, York County Deeds, Orders, and Wills 6, 1677–84.
8. James Robinson to John Turner, Apr. 22, 1769, in T. M. Devine, ed., *A Scottish Firm in Virginia, 1767–77* (Edinburgh: Clark Constable, 1982), 12.
9. Henry Fleming to Fischer and Bragg, July 29, 1774, Fleming Letterbook, 1772–75, Cumbria County Council Archives Department, Microfilm, CWF.
10. Daniel Defoe, *The Compleat English Tradesman* [1727] (New York: Augustus M. Kelley, 1969), 68.
11. Inventory of Richard Walker, Mar. 7, 1728, Middlesex County Will Book B: 1714–34, 335–43. Walker's total estate (including personal goods) was valued at over £1,300.
12. "Inventory of John Hook's property relieved by the Supersedens issued from the High Court of Chancery, sworn 16 January 1802, Ross. vs. Hook, Chancery Court of Virginia." Microfilm, Special Collections, Perkins Library, Duke University.
13. Inventory of William Parrott, Jan. 8, 1798, Richmond City Hustings Court Deed Book 2, 1792–96, 391–95. Mutual Assurance Society, vol. 13, no. 297, reel 2. Both documents found at the Library of Virginia.
14. An earlier version of this analysis can be found in Ann Smart Martin, "Buying into the World of Goods: Consumerism and the Retail Trade from London to the Virginia Backcountry" (Ph.D. diss., College of William and Mary, 1993). The database for this expanded study comes from multiple sources with help from many: Architectural plans of rural stores from the Agricultural Buildings Project, Colonial Williamsburg, early 1980s, partially summarized in Edward A. Chappell, "Architectural Recording and the Open-Air Museum: A View from the Field," *Perspectives in Vernacular Architecture* (Columbia: Univ. of Missouri

Press, 1986), 35–36. Williamsburg's four important standing stores are detailed in Donna Hole, "Williamsburg's Four Original Stores: An Architectural Analysis," Colonial Williamsburg Research Report Series 188, 1980. The author has examined eight additional stores in Fredericksburg, Petersburg, Falmouth, and the counties of Franklin, Prince George, and King George. Camille Wells culled nearly two hundred store advertisements in her study of the *Virginia Gazette,* and I thank her for sharing that information. From that database and with additional evidence from newspapers, court cases, insurance records, and merchant records, the size of more than twenty additional stores were documented. Willie Graham, Gary Stanton, and especially Carl Lounsbury have been wonderful partners in fieldwork and all have shared information with enthusiasm and have taught me new ways to look and think. Mick Nichols generously shared his urban court documents, including the Petersburg thefts and William Parrot's store inventory. The combination of documentary and field evidence recorded details of Virginia stores spanning from about 1740 to 1830.

15. For a brief description of the Farish Print Shop, see Ralph Emmett Fall, *Hidden Village: Port Royal Virginia, 1744–1981* (Verona, Va.: McClure Printing, 1982). The Farish shop has one less dormer window for lighting the upstairs storage area, and the office and storage area are of slightly different dimensions. The chimney is also placed differently. Overall, however, the forty-by-twenty-foot size, organization of space, and the fenestration of the first floor are remarkably similar; Hook even mistakenly wrote the dimensions forty by twenty on his plan, although the room dimensions added up to forty-two by twenty. The structure may have been used as a tavern in the late eighteenth century. Port Royal, like New London, was also a small mercantile town, home to five or six Scottish merchants and about twenty or thirty houses in 1775, although it lay on navigable water. Robert Honeyman, *Colonial Panorama 1775: Dr. Robert Honeyman's Journal for March and April,* ed. Phillip Padelford (Freeport, N.Y.: Books for Libraries Press, 1971), 1.

16. *Charleston Courier,* Jan. 14, 1803. The ultimate solution to the merchant's dilemma—the competing pressures for control and display—was thus found in a relatively small material culture innovation. The small glass case on the counter from which Becca the enslaved woman could pilfer some lace might only be expanded to counter size at large expense, justified by the value of the jewelry for sale within. With changing technology, glass could be made in larger sheets and at a smaller price. The same process that enabled larger shop windows was used to address the continual problem of theft, dirt, and order. By the later nineteenth century, glass counters were advertised as a means to promote viewing (and consumer desire) and prevent shoplifting (seemingly rampant when goods were left unguarded on counters).

These glass cases were promoted at the end of the nineteenth century as allowing the customer to see (hence saving the merchant's time in handing down goods that did not suit) and keeping goods clean (from dust and too much handling). The most important theme throughout advertisements for these store fittings was that "goods can be displayed without risk from the nimble fingers of the shoplifter" (78). These three themes were the heart of the eighteenth-century merchant's dilemma, although later nineteenth-century thievery seemed to have turned from the more marginal part of society to middle-class women. Elaine Abelson ultimately argues it is the consumption palace that released consumer desire, sometimes in ways that could not be controlled by the individual; *"When Ladies Go A-Thieving" Middle-Class Shopkeepers in the Victorian Department Store* (New York: Oxford University Press, 1989).

17. Judith R. Hiltner, *The Newspaper Verse of Philip Freneau: An Edition and Bibliographical Survey* (Troy, N.Y.: Whitson, 1986), 487. Thanks to Vanessa Patrick for this reference.
18. James Robinson to John Turner, Oct. 4, 1768, in Devine, Scottish Firm, 11.
19. "Inventory of Household and Other Furniture on hand belonging to the Concern of Hooe and Harrison at Alexandria, December 31, 1779," Hooe, Stone, and Company Invoice Book, 1770–84, New York Public Library (microfilm, Colonial Williamsburg Foundation). For sleeping in the store, see *Virginia Gazette* (Hunter), Sept. 16, 1737. Mr. Lidderdale's storekeeper and another man were sleeping in the store in Prince George County when three "rogues" came to the store while Lidderdale was away. The intruders demanded entry on the pretense of leaving a letter, "rush'd in, bound the Two Men, and stole about 70 pounds in Cash, a Watch, A pair of Pistols, several Shirts, etc."
20. *Virginia Gazette* (Hunter), Sept. 20, 1754.
21. The 1798 "Plan and Perspective-View of a House, and other Buildings, belonging to Mr. Eward Langley, on Square No. 651 in the City of Washington" by Nicholas King, July 14, 1798, Collection of the Henry Francis du Pont Winterthur Museum, Joseph Downs Manuscript Collection.
22. Mutual Assurance Society Records, vol. 12, no. 12; vol. 13, no. 238, Richmond: Library of Virginia. The rear addition was removed and the store returned to a dwelling by Parrot's heirs in 1804.
23. Patricia Kent, "1300 Caroline Street: A Brief History of the Structure and Early Owners," in "Historic Fredericksburg Foundation, Inc. Research Committee Historic Marker Program," 1991, unpublished report, Archives, Historic Fredericksburg Foundation, Inc. My thanks to Gary Stanton for this information and help in measuring and discussing the building and to Carl Lounsbury for this close scrutiny and completing the drawing.
24. For example, see the examination of Vina Nash, a free mulatto woman on suspicion of theft from the store of James William Latouche, Aug. 5, 1805, Petersburg City Hustings Court Minute Book 4, 1800–1807, n.p.
25. This theme pervades the study of Chesapeake domestic architecture. See, for example, Dell Upton, "Vernacular Domestic Architecture in Eighteenth-Century Virginia," *Winterthur Portfolio* 17, no. 2–3 (summer/autumn 1982): 95–119.
26. Estimates of square footage of Virginia dwellings comes from newspapers and tax lists. For advertised properties, see Camille Wells, "The Planter's Prospect: Houses, Outbuildings, and Rural Landscapes in Eighteenth-Century Virginia," *Winterthur Portfolio* 28, no. 1 (spring 1993): 6. Rare tax information on house size from Virginia is described in Pamela L. Higgins, "'Lands, Houses, and Slaves': The 1798 Federal Direct Tax in Spotsylvania County, Virginia," *Journal of Fredericksburg History* 1 (1996): 59, 65.
27. Eliza Barksdale diary, Charlotte Courthouse, May–August 1836, Virginia Historical Society, Richmond.

CHAPTER 12

Jeanne Catherine Lawrence

Chicago's Eleanor Clubs: Housing Working Women in the Early Twentieth Century

Philanthropist Ina Robertson established a series of boardinghouses for young working women in Chicago in 1898.[1] These boardinghouses, called Eleanor Clubs, reached the height of their popularity in the 1910s and 1920s, when six residential clubs housed a total of six hundred young women. By having residents pay a fair price for their room and board, the Eleanor Clubs were intended to be self-supporting; thus, they were distinct from the paternalism of "charity" associated with similar homes for working women (such as the YWCA). In accordance with these principles, the Eleanor Clubs began on a small, affordable scale: the first clubs were in rented premises that had originally been built as large single-family homes or small-scale hotels and apartment buildings. Gradually, each of the clubs moved to larger buildings. Whether they had been built as houses, apartment buildings, hotels, or institutions of some kind, these buildings were adapted, as well as possible, to their new use. Experimentation with various types of existing buildings helped Robertson determine, over time, the features and characteristics of an ideal group home for working women, one in which they would be given the opportunity to develop "the best that was in them" by being brought into "intimate association" and learning "to live and work together in hearty cooperation." Such a club would, she felt, create an atmosphere conducive to the development of another goal: the Christian ideal of "love expressing itself in service" to the community.[2] Concern for young women's "physical and social well-being" was also critical.[3] These ideals and goals provided the philosophical foundation for every Eleanor Club, but they were finally realized in built form in the design of two purpose-built clubs constructed in 1914 and 1916.

The evolution of the Eleanor Clubs to ever-larger buildings and, eventually, to commissioned purpose-built structures provides insight into the complexities of housing the single female wage earner in early twentieth-century urban America. It also sheds light on the adaptive reuse of the built environment and, specifically, on the problems encountered when attempting to transform or adapt existing structures to suit the needs of, or cultural expectations for, women. In the case of the Eleanor Clubs, a combination of social and economic factors contributed to the conception of an "ideal" organized home for young, single working women —a home that allowed them to exercise their independence but taught them to live harmoniously together, and provided them with protection and security. Thus, the Eleanor Clubs also provide a case study of the evolution of a building type. As Anthony King has noted, architecture as an instrument of social control is not simply a question of society's ideas and beliefs being incorporated into built form. One must ask, "on the basis of *whose* beliefs, *whose* values or *whose* view of the world are decisions based?"[4]

The eventual design of purpose-built Eleanor Clubs had everything to do with the specific experiences of Ina Robertson, the clubs' founder, and the cultural assumptions about appropriate avenues for middle-class women's participation in the public sphere (in this case, the field of philanthropy), as well as the broader cultural expectations of working women's behavior and needs. This essay examines Ina Robertson's own experiences and the choices she made on the path toward developing her concept of the ideal home for working women, considers the problems inherent in transforming buildings constructed for other purposes into Eleanor Clubs, and then analyzes the purpose-built clubs in order to determine what set them apart from other buildings (particularly college dormitories) designed to house single women in this period.

Ina Robertson was an Oregon native, the daughter of early settlers in the Pacific Northwest (fig. 12.1). Her father, at one time a farmer, had become a wheat merchant by the late 1860s. The members of her family were devoutly religious United Presbyterians. Robertson taught school for several years before graduating from Albany College (which is now Lewis and Clark College) in 1889. She then taught at, and served as principal of, the coeducational Waitsburg Academy, a United Presbyterian Home Mission school in Waitsburg, Washington. In 1895 the desire to continue her own education brought her eastward to attend graduate school at the newly established University of Chicago. Robertson initially enrolled in courses on English literature but soon transferred to the Divinity School, where she studied church history.[5] During this period of her life, Robertson lived in a rented room. And she ventured often into Chicago's downtown Loop district, where she met young women who were working in the city's big department stores. The ready availability of clerical and sales jobs in the city had lured many women to Chicago.[6] Many of these women had come to the city from small midwestern towns and were without friends or relatives in the city; the majority were young and intended to support themselves for only a few years before marriage.[7] Robertson's conversations with some of these "women adrift" led her to begin thinking about ways to make their transition from rural home life to urban business life safer and happier.[8]

Around this time, Robertson's life changed dra-

Fig. 12.1. Ina Robertson (1867–1916), founder and first president of the Eleanor Association. *Eleanor Record*, Dec. 1918, 2.

matically when James Law, a wealthy member of the United Presbyterian Church, designated her as trustee of his estate.[9] Along with her benefactor's elderly sister, whose name was Eleanor Law, Robertson was to oversee expenditures for philanthropic and religious causes. She promptly left graduate school and embarked upon the business of philanthropy.[10] In keeping with her new status and financial means, Robertson engaged the services of architect Howard Van Doren Shaw to build a home for herself and Eleanor Law in Hyde Park, near the university.[11] Not surprisingly, Shaw was the architect of choice for Chicago's conservative elites, especially those who lived in the Hyde Park area.[12]

Robertson's first philanthropic projects demonstrated her religious orientation and motivations. She and Law donated $12,000 to the United Presbyterian Church's Mission College in India and took over the operating expenses of the *Midland,* a Midwestern religious newspaper. By appealing for financial contributions through the *Midland,* the women secured funding to support an itinerant minister who served (via boat) the inhabitants of remote logging camps on the islands of Puget Sound. They also engaged the services of another minister for miners working in isolated districts around Spokane, Washington.[13] In Spokane, the two women established a low-cost boardinghouse for miners which stayed open for five or six years. Called Cliff House, this boardinghouse was a large wooden building containing eighty-one rooms; amenities for residents included a community room for smoking, meetings, and social affairs, and for religious services on Sunday afternoons. Cliff House operated on a self-sustaining basis in order to avoid "the shape or appearance of the so-called 'charitable' home."[14]

Based on the Cliff House experiment, Robertson began in 1898 to apply the concept of the low-cost boardinghouse to the problem of providing respectable and affordable housing for the "business girl" on the low wage in Chicago.[15] She located a suitable row house for rent on University Avenue, near the campus, and opened a low-cost boardinghouse to accommodate twenty-eight young women.[16] This first boardinghouse was called the Eleanor Hotel, both in honor of Eleanor Law and because "in its old Greek form [Eleanor] carried the meaning of 'light,'" which typified "the radiancy of the loving service and influence which a growing and united group of independent young women might render to the world about them."[17] Within a few years the name of the Eleanor Hotel was changed to the Eleanor Club, which Robertson felt evoked a social, communal atmosphere far better than the impersonal (and commercial) term hotel.[18] It was intended to be a safe haven from the dangers of urban life by providing "companionship and . . . homelike surroundings for the girl isolated in a great city."[19] Robertson had firsthand experience of this isolation—only a few years earlier she had been living alone in a rented room.

The provision of housing expressly for working women was not a new idea: as early as the 1850s, experimentation with approaches to the collective housing of working women was under way in New York.[20] Converted tenement buildings housed some five hundred women in a dormitory setting in the Working Women's Home of the 1850s, and department store magnate A. T. Stewart opened the doors of his luxurious Working Women's Hotel in 1878. Stewart's venture was especially audacious: his hotel provided individual rooms for single women, as well as rooms for two women to share, and a plethora of public spaces on the main floor, including parlors, reading rooms, a central dining room, and kitchen. Numerous rules and regulations, extra charges for services such as laundry, and prohibitively high rents doomed Stewart's Working Women's Hotel to failure (it soon reopened as the Park Avenue Hotel, a traditional hotel for well-to-do men and women), but Stewart's main problem was timing. As Elizabeth Cromley has noted, "in the 1870s and 1880s, younger respectable women did not have society's blessing to make independent homes of their own."[21]

The need to provide housing for women who had no alternative but to work was initially most successfully met by nonsecular reformers. A Ladies Christian Association in New York established a boardinghouse for working women as early as 1858, and the idea spread rapidly in the second half of the nineteenth century, becoming firmly associated with the Young Women's Christian Association (YWCA) by the late 1870s.[22] The YWCA became the most visible and numerous of the "organized boarding homes" that were launched throughout urban America in the last quarter of the nineteenth century. The term *boarding home* was consciously used by providers of this form of housing in order to evoke the more "homelike" atmosphere they strove to provide.[23] This distinguished them from mere buildings that provided room and board but did not promote or encourage the creation of a homelike atmosphere and the idea of the surrogate family.[24] Usually organized and run by a church group or denomination, organized boarding homes sought to counteract the loneliness and impersonality of the city by providing shared spaces and organized activities to bring residents together. In Chicago, there were thirty-one organized boarding homes for wage-earning women by 1914; the majority of these were associated with church groups.[25] These included the Chicago YWCA, which by 1902 occupied a large brick building seven stories high with seven bays evenly spaced across the street frontage at 288 Michigan Ave.[26] The Jane Club, associated with Jane Addams's Hull House, was another organized boarding home—it provided room and board for thirty young women.[27] Aspirations of creating "homes" for independent young women came into conflict with the perceived need for security at these residences, which usually included the careful review of applicants for residency, the monitoring of visitors, and the establishment of a curfew. As this form of housing became more popular and these homes became larger, there was also the problem of creating a homelike atmosphere and surroundings in a large building, where there would be less interaction between supervisors and residents and it would be more difficult to maintain the idea of the surrogate family.[28]

The notion of creating a "home" to protect those far from their own families' homes from the dangers, vices, and temptations of the city was shared by virtually all of these organized boarding homes. Indeed, it was a hallmark of Progressive housing reform. While Progressivism was by no means a unified movement, and reformers often held contradictory views, there was little question that on the subject of housing, the single-family house and the material trappings of the middle-class home were the ideal.[29] Both Joanne Meyerowitz and Lisa Fine have emphasized the ubiquity of this rhetoric among reformers providing low-cost housing for women in Chicago: they were simultaneously seeking to retain control of the domestic realm and to extend that realm to include territory well outside the traditional definition of "home."[30] Not surprisingly, in championing the cause of woman suffrage, Chicago settlement house founder Jane Addams argued that in order for women to maintain control over their own homes, they would need to expand their sense of duty and responsibility to include such public and civic arenas as education and industry—aspects of life once contained within the home but now carried on outside of it.[31] Like Addams and others, Frances Willard (president of the Woman's Christian Temperance Union) promoted this ideology of "municipal housekeeping," evident in her remark that "If I were asked the mission of the ideal woman, I would reply: *it is to make the whole world homelike.*"[32]

Ina Robertson's own efforts to make urban Chicago more homelike reached well beyond the sphere of housing. Tailoring her services for women working in offices and stores rather than factories, Robertson provided a facility downtown where a working woman could rest or read and enjoy "the privilege of making herself a cup of tea . . . after the rush and fret of the day."[33] If a woman planned to attend an event downtown in the evening, she no longer had to rush home after work, then rush back; likewise, she did not have to loiter aimlessly around the city waiting until the play or show began—she could go to the Central Eleanor Club. After opening in 1908, Central Eleanor moved twice to larger quarters. By 1920, it boasted a membership of 2,400 and shared almost an entire floor in the Stevens Building at 16 North Wabash Ave. downtown with the offices of the Eleanor Association, which governed the whole Eleanor operation. Central Eleanor hosted "evening classes, Sunday afternoon At Homes, dramatic entertainments, and community effort of every sort."[34] In 1916 alone, the Central Eleanor tea room served 58,000, while more than 2,000 young women attended classes in gymnastics, folk-dancing, dramatics, millinery, and English.[35] Robertson also established Eleanor banking facilities; a monthly magazine, *Eleanor Record,* written by and for club members; the Eleanor League for younger girls, aged twelve to sixteen; and a neighborhood social center for girls and women, located in Eleanor Club Six at the corner of Pierce Avenue and North Leavitt Street. In addition, hundreds of young women from Chicago enjoyed summer holidays at the Eleanor Camp at Lake Geneva, Wisconsin. The summer camp was not limited to Eleanor Club residents and Central Eleanor members, but was open to "any self-supporting young women of good character."[36]

Despite the elements of Progressivism that characterized Robertson's various enterprises, the Eleanor Clubs' single-sex, supervised housing was evocative of an earlier era. By the 1890s the boardinghouse was fast fading, as furnished rooms and rooming houses, often accommodating both men and women under the same roof, proliferated.[37] Whereas a boarding home landlady provided communal meals to all her boarders, the keeper of a rooming house had merely to supply residents with gas plates for cooking, allow them to use her kitchen, or let them otherwise cater for themselves. Rooming houses also gave roomers greater personal freedom to come and go as they pleased and to entertain in their rooms whomever they wished.[38] Areas just to the north, west, and south of the Loop became furnished room districts, where residents took their meals at cheap restaurants and cafeterias or cooked on gas plates in their own rooms.

This shift, from the "respectable" boarding home to the unsupervised rooming house, may in fact have encouraged Ina Robertson to found the Eleanor Clubs. Her clubs initially housed between fifty-five and eighty-two residents and provided simple furnishings and plain food to ensure that an affordable rent could be charged. The clubs attempted to counter the perceived deficiencies in available housing: First, they encouraged the creation of a "family" through communal meals and shared activities (such as monthly social events at each club and a lecture series each winter on a subject chosen by club residents).[39] These clubs were small enough for young women to meet others like themselves and form lasting friendships. In general, the clubs were an extension of the security and moral guidance of the home and therefore in direct opposition to the "moral lapse" many associated with hotels, rooming houses, and furnished room districts.[40] Second, the Eleanor Clubs strove to avoid the paternalism of charity, instead encouraging residents to be self-sufficient. As Meyerowitz notes, many young women disliked charity and the supervision it entailed and might instead become dependent upon men, in relationships "that fell somewhere between professional prostitution and marriage."[41] Robertson stressed, "We want the women to consider themselves as independent, and we give them the advantage of a good home, not out of charity, but because our careful management here enables us to meet expenses with a small income."[42] It was important to Robertson that the furnishings of each club be simple, homelike, and unostentatious—they should be the kind of furnishings the women would someday (or soon) be able to acquire for their own homes. By carefully managing funds, the clubs could charge a low weekly fee and still maintain their self-sufficiency: each club was expected to cover all of its expenditures with income from the residents' room and board fees. Third, while a live-in supervisor was in charge of each Eleanor Club, a House Council comprised of residents actually governed each club, and a General Council, also comprised of "Eleanor girls," oversaw the running of all the clubs.[43]

The first Eleanor Club appeared just when organized boarding homes, particularly the YWCA, were coming under attack by many residents for strict rules, unrealistic curfew hours, and a distinct class divide between residents and supervisors. Eleanor Club principles of self-governance and optional participation in religious services were in line with changes instituted at this time by the YWCA to increase the appeal of their boarding homes; for example, residents were allowed to participate more actively in the governance of the YWCA homes, and more reasonable curfew hours were established. The religious emphasis of the YWCA was diminished at this time, with attendance at "daily family worship" and Sunday services becoming voluntary rather than obligatory.[44] At the Eleanor Clubs, "the subject of religion [was] never broached" lest it alienate residents.[45]

Ina Robertson's first home for working women was located three miles from the central business district, but over a period of several months it gradually filled to capacity.[46] The Eleanor Hotel did not break even financially, however: Robertson kept careful expense accounts for three years and finally determined that the $2.50 rent per week paid by each resident was insufficient. Also, in addition to raising the rent, more residents were needed in order to cover overhead expenses.[47] Accordingly, in 1901, the boarding home moved to larger premises—an apartment building in the same neighborhood that could house eighty-two women (fig. 12.2).[48] At the same time, its name was changed to the Eleanor Club. The new name distanced the Eleanor boarding homes from connotations of the marketplace, as well as from some ideas currently gathering steam among middle-class moralists and reformers: for instance, that hotel living was lonely, that it allowed uncomfortably close contact with too wide a range of individuals, and that it led to the disintegration of manners, morals, and general human decency.[49] The term *club* also distanced the boardinghouses from Christian philanthropic organizations. The name Eleanor Club was collegial and businesslike and avoided an overtly Christian emphasis, which might have driven away prospective residents.

In 1905 the Eleanor Association became incorporated, with Ina Robertson as president. Interested individuals became stockholders.[50] Five directors, elected by the association's Board of Trustees,

Fig. 12.2. This former apartment building at 5656 Wabash Ave. housed eighty-two Eleanor girls when it served as Club One from 1901 to 1916. Courtesy of the Eleanor Women's Foundation.

tended to the business responsibilities of the organization. These directors elected an executive committee annually, which oversaw the management of the clubs and other Eleanor work.[51] When a new residential club was planned and a building leased, the association provided the money for the furnishings, but the club assumed all current expenses from the day the lease went into effect and paid back the loan of association funds at 5 percent interest.[52]

Following these guidelines, Robertson opened Eleanor Club Two in 1905 and four more clubs over the next nine years, quickly becoming one of Chicago's foremost independent providers of housing for young women. She constantly searched for new properties suitable for conversion into clubs and often moved established clubs into larger premises, always striving to locate them in respectable middle-class neighborhoods. These residential clubs provided each resident with her own single or shared bedroom and a host of communal spaces: parlors, reading rooms, sewing rooms, laundry facilities, and a dining room large enough to seat "the entire family" at once. Two meals a day (breakfast and dinner) brought all residents together.[53] Furnishings were "simple and serviceable," and while the food was "necessarily plain," every effort was made to keep it "well-balanced, well-cooked and bountiful."[54] This simplicity kept down the cost of Eleanor lodgings: after discovering that $2.50 per week was not enough, rates were raised—but not greatly. By 1918, Eleanor Club room and board rates ranged between $4.25 and $6.50 per week, at a time when women's average weekly wages were between $6 for a cash girl, and $12 for a bookkeeper.[55]

While the majority of women living in the Eleanor Clubs, especially in the early years, were office and store workers, any "self-supporting girl of good character" was eligible to join.[56] Students, too, were welcomed, especially those working their way through school. There was no age or wage limit, but the "young girl on the low wage" was always the first consideration, for, Robertson believed, that limited wage "exposed her in a peculiar manner to life's hardships and temptations."[57] Married and divorced women were not viewed as potential residents. The Eleanor Clubs were intended to be spaces of transition: the shift from girlhood to womanhood; the transition between a young woman's childhood home and the home she would eventually go on to establish herself; and the clubs made the broader transition of women "from home life into business easier and less dangerous."[58] When a young woman arrived in Chicago to work or to study, the Eleanor Clubs were there for her. One resident, whose experience was typical, recalled, "I came to Chicago in 1912, alone and a stranger; but fortunately, when I registered at the school I was to attend, I was given a booklet concerning the Eleanor Clubs; and before sundown I was safe in the protection of one of the residence clubs."[59]

From the beginning, Robertson strove to find the "proper relation between what a woman paid and what she received."[60] But she was reliant upon Chicago's rental housing, and she soon found that "only the cheaper class of buildings [were] available."[61] As a result, she had no choice but to place her residential clubs in buildings later described as being "badly suited" to her purpose.[62]

The first Eleanor Clubs were located in small, relatively intimate buildings, partly as a measure of economy (because the Eleanor Association could not afford to pay high rent, nor could it risk operating with empty rooms) and also because the venture was a new one—Robertson did not know how many boarders she would find. These buildings also lent themselves well to the creation of a homelike atmosphere. For instance, the building at 3216 Wabash Ave., which served as Club Two from 1905 to 1910 was constructed as a large single-family dwelling on what had been, at midcentury, one of Chicago's most fashionable streets (fig. 12.3).[63] By the turn of the century, urban expansion had pushed the wealthy farther and farther out, and this building became Eleanor Club Two, converted to accommodate fifty-five residents in single and shared rooms. Proximity to the South Side elevated railway (the El), constructed in the 1890s, increased the desirability of this location for Eleanor residents.[64]

Fig. 12.3. Eleanor Club Two (1905–10), shown here with club residents on porch and steps, c. 1905, was a single-family home adapted to house fifty-five women. Courtesy of the Eleanor Women's Foundation.

The process of turning single-family homes into boardinghouses has been carefully researched by Paul Groth, who explains that homes were usually adapted to the boardinghouse purpose by turning the parlors into rented rooms and adding closets and washbasins to each room. Groth finds that one of the problems with this form of housing was the fact that most homes had just one bathroom; even the largest of homes did not have enough bathrooms to accommodate large numbers of boarders. On the other hand, buildings constructed specifically as *rooming* houses could not easily be adapted to serve as Eleanor Clubs; since their ground floors could consist entirely of rented rooms, they did not have the requisite shared spaces, like parlors and dining rooms, and, most importantly, they lacked entrance lobbies that could be supervised to ensure that nonmembers (particularly, of course, men) could not gain access to the private bedrooms.[65] Such shared spaces and entrance lobbies were thought to be critical because the Eleanor Clubs housed women; no such proscriptions governed the design of buildings constructed (or adapted) to accommodate male residents.[66] Robertson believed it was particularly important that each club have a spacious ground-floor parlor where young women, "properly chaperoned," might receive their male friends.[67] Many of the nonsecular boarding homes did not allow men on the premises at all. Robertson felt this proscription pushed young women into unsupervised rooming houses, where they could entertain male callers in their rooms because they had no other place to entertain, a practice which was "frequently the first letting down of the bars of self-respect and reserve, the first step aside from the paths of rectitude."[68] The importance of the parlor, as well as of the domestic mission of the Eleanor Association, was underscored in a 1922 publicity pamphlet for the clubs, which described the parlors and reading rooms at Club Five as "especially large and homelike."[69]

Ina Robertson's diary, covering the years from 1905 to 1911, shows that she was constantly searching for buildings suitable for conversion into Eleanor Clubs.[70] But as she moved the Eleanor Clubs into ever-larger premises, she risked losing the homelike atmosphere she desired. And, as demand for Eleanor Club housing rose, she had trouble finding structures with the rooms and amenities she needed. Robertson's insistence that the clubs be situated in respectable and safe neighborhoods made her search even more difficult. Affordable buildings suitable for Eleanor Clubs were not always located in desirable neighborhoods. Robertson preferred to locate the clubs in her own Hyde Park neighborhood, in nearby Washington Park and Kenwood, and in a few other "good" neighborhoods on the South and West sides of the city.[71] Because Chicago was quickly expanding, the desirability of neighborhoods also changed rapidly as the class, racial, and ethnic constitution of an area changed. Less desirable areas offered more affordable rents, but there was a tradeoff in terms of safety and respectability. This was one reason the Eleanor Clubs moved to different locations so frequently. In 1909, Chicago resident Martha Freeman Esmond attended the opening of Eleanor Club Five at 3111 Indiana Ave., on Chicago's South Side. "This isn't such a good location as it used to be," Esmond wrote to a friend, "for many people are moving to the north side, but I have many friends who still remain there."[72] Esmond's letter highlights the fact that the Eleanor clubs were often located in transitional neighborhoods: areas that had once been quite fashionable or "good" but were no longer ideal. Real estate values had fallen, making property rents (like the hotel building adapted for use as Club Five) affordable, yet (because not everyone of means had abandoned the area) it was still a relatively safe location for Eleanor residents. In fact, directly across from Club Five was a theater (with capacity for 636 patrons) fronted by a row of shops; the club's other neighbors included a cigar factory, an upholstery business, a series of small shops, and seven small four-story apartment buildings, though farther down the block a number of single-family homes had not yet succumbed to the commercial development of the area.[73]

Club Five had originally been a small hotel; it would go on to serve as an Eleanor Club until 1913 (when it was relocated to a former "millionaire's home," which had more recently served as a dormitory for Presbyterian nurses at 430 S. Ashland).[74] Similarly, a small hotel building at the corner of Lake Park Avenue and Thirty-first Street served as Club Three from 1907 to 1911. Such hotels, built to accommodate fifty to sixty guests, had commercial spaces on the street level incompatible with Eleanor Club needs. Shops and small parlors were common, and a hotel's ground floor might also include such specifically male-oriented spaces as a tobacconist's shop, billiard room, smoking room, bar or saloon, and/or business offices. These small rooms at street level had to be converted into a large dining area and large parlor if the building was to serve as an Eleanor Club. Also, a hotel's multiple stairwells increased the chances of unwelcome guests and unsavory characters (or lecherous boyfriends) gaining access to a woman's private room.[75]

Further, hotels of the late nineteenth century traditionally provided both a main front entrance and a side entrance expressly for ladies (for purposes of privacy and discretion, and also so they could avoid going through the public reception area unescorted). By definition, a supervised home had to have just one public entrance, where everyone coming and going could be seen and accounted for.

Apartment buildings (such as that in fig. 12.2)

presented similar problems. They also lacked the ground floor spaces necessary for Eleanor Club life, such as dining rooms large enough for all residents, parlors, and large entrance lobbies. The ground-floor parlors in Club One (fig. 12.4) had been converted from a private apartment into public rooms; as indicated by the location of the fireplace so close to the doorway, this parlor was by no means large enough to accommodate the entire Club One "family" of eighty-two residents at once. Chicago's rental stock included many small apartment buildings like this one: in 1883 alone, 1,142 small three- to five-story apartment houses were constructed in Chicago, "mostly on the edge of the inner city, across major streets and railroad tracks from immigrant and slum neighborhoods."[76] A typical floor plan in such a modest hotel at the turn of the century was that of the housekeeping unit (today's efficiency apartment), which consisted of two rooms and a bath—one room was used for cooking and dining, while the other did double duty as parlor and bedroom (with the aid of a fold-up bed). This room configuration made conversion to an Eleanor Club difficult: it was awkward for each room to be occupied separately because of the connecting door. In such a situation, not every resident had a private entrance into her room from the public corridor.

The awkwardness inherent in Robertson's project of turning existing buildings into housing clubs for women is demonstrated in a few rare early photographs taken inside Eleanor Clubs, which show rooms not originally intended as bedrooms serving this new purpose. For example, one early photograph shows a room which might originally have been a parlor in a home, or one of the two rooms in an apartment or hotel suite. The beds are placed against the door, indicating that this room was being used for a purpose it was not originally intended to serve. Similarly, another photograph shows a room not designed to house two women; one bed stands against a door that must have opened into the room next door.[77] The bedrooms in the first Club One were, indeed, cramped. Fig-

Fig. 12.4. Apartment converted to public parlors at Club One, 5656 Wabash Ave., c. 1901. Courtesy of the Eleanor Women's Foundation.

Fig. 12.5. Single bedroom at Club One, 5656 Wabash Ave., c. 1901. Courtesy of the Eleanor Women's Foundation.

ure 12.5 shows a single bedroom at this club: an awkwardly shaped room (possibly the result of the conversion of a larger room into two or more smaller ones) crowded with bed, desk, dresser, window seat, and tables. Such furniture was provided in each Eleanor Club room; residents were encouraged to personalize their rooms with photographs, pictures, and personal possessions, as the occupant of this room has done.[78]

By 1911 the largest Eleanor Club housed 150 residents in a converted nursing home for elderly women at 3850 Indiana Ave. (fig. 12.6). This was Club Three, which had moved from a much smaller hotel building farther north on Lake Park Avenue. The brick, four-and-one-half-story corner building was connected to two four-story wings, one to the north and one to the west. This building no doubt contained many rooms not well suited to the Eleanor Clubs' needs (such as nurses' stations in each wing) and had multiple entrances. However, this building did contain the large public rooms for communal meals and social activities, which were relied upon to create the homelike atmosphere so important to Eleanor Club life. In 1926, former resident Thora Thorsmark looked back on "Old Club Three" and fondly remembered its "gracious, old-fashioned lobby" and its "fine old circular stair": "It was in the cozy corner under the stair

Fig. 12.6. Originally built as a nursing home for elderly women, this building at 3850 Indiana Ave. served as Eleanor Club Three from 1911 until the 1920s. *Eleanor Record*, Dec. 1918, 13.

that the girls read the Gumps, looked over the magazines, or 'just sat,' leaving the parlors for formality. It was on and about this stair that the girls gathered for Sunday morning service, those in morning dresses and slippers sitting at the top, around the curve, where they could hear without being seen."[79]

The location of this club was an improvement over its predecessor's. The previous Club Three had been located in a residential neighborhood but was right across the street from the tracks of the Michigan and Illinois Central Railroad and the Thirty-first Street railroad station. The noise and traffic must have been a consideration in the club's move to more sedate quarters. In its new location, though, Club Three was next door to a "5-cent Theatre," while the immediate neighborhood included two laundries, three saloons, three tailor's establishments, and a number of three-story houses converted to apartments with one flat per floor.[80]

Over the years, as they adapted buildings to suit Eleanor Club purposes, Robertson and her Eleanor Association colleagues began to develop an ideal Eleanor Club layout. The club building that probably came closest to this ideal had been a Baptist Missionary Training School, also on Indiana Avenue (fig. 12.7). This building served as Club Four from 1908 to 1918, housing seventy-six women. Before signing the lease on the building, Robertson visited it several times, remarking that she felt "favorable toward it for Club Four" in her diary.[81] Designed as a residential training school for young missionaries who would not reside there for long, it had appropriately sized bedrooms and a series of public rooms (including dining room and classrooms) easily adaptable to Eleanor Club uses. The surrounding neighborhood of two- and three-story single-family homes was also eminently suitable, though this neighborhood, too, was not devoid of commercial enterprise, including a steam laundry, a cabinet shop, and a large garage/auto-repair shop. Still, an Episcopal Church in the next block bolstered the area's respectability.[82]

Structures as suitable as the Baptist Missionary Training School were obviously hard to locate and secure, particularly in good neighborhoods. However, in 1914 the Eleanor Association was finally able to put the Eleanor ideals into "built form" when Mr. and Mrs. W. A. Wieboldt, founders of one of Chicago's most successful middle-income department stores, constructed Club Six specifically for rental by the Eleanor Association.[83] For the first

Fig. 12.7. Previously a Baptist Missionary Training School, Club Five at 2411 Indiana Ave. accommodated ninety "Eleanor business girls" from 1908 to 1918. *Eleanor Record*, Dec. 1918, 14.

time, the association could dictate, to some extent, what the building would look like, and so this building reveals the evolving ideology of the Eleanor Association (fig. 12.8). Indeed, it was heralded as "a new type" of building by Eleanor advocates.[84] As described in the souvenir booklet published for the grand opening of Club Six on April 18, 1914: "It will accommodate one hundred and fifty girls in residence and is the first building planned and erected to meet the requirements of an Eleanor Club. Its complete provision for the comfort and pleasure of its members will free the Association from the many handicaps found in buildings not adapted to the purpose, and should forecast a work of unusual achievement."[85] Located at 2155 Pierce Ave., Club Six was just two blocks from the El station at Robey Street and a twenty-minute El train ride to the Loop.

Club Six's brick-and-stone exterior and elements of the Georgian Revival style (keystones above windows, quoins at corners, pilasters inset above the ground floor at the center of both public-facing facades, balustrades at roofline over entrances) brought human scale to this imposing building, which bore great similarity to many contemporary apartment buildings. Since the World's Columbian

Fig. 12.8. Club Six at 2155 Pierce Ave., 1914. Built specifically for use as an Eleanor residence in 1914, this club housed a neighborhood Social Center, entered on the North Leavitt Street side (on the right in this photo), as well as rooms for 150 residents. Courtesy of the Eleanor Women's Foundation.

Exposition of 1893, some form of classicism had been the basis for most apartment (and hotel) designs.[86] Indeed, Club Six may have been planned to serve as an apartment building if its role as an Eleanor Club was not long lived.

Club Six was equipped with a roof garden and sleeping porches, but an even greater novelty was the fact that it was constructed to serve a second function. In addition to the provision of housing for working women and students, Club Six contained a series of rooms specifically designed to serve as a social center for the girls and young women of the neighborhood. Entered through a separate door on North Leavitt Street (see fig. 12.8), the Social Center was run by a permanent staff of directors and instructors, as well as volunteer teachers.[87]

While the previous buildings serving as Eleanor Clubs had brought residents into structures that already existed in established neighborhoods, this new purpose-built club was consciously constructed to bring the neighborhood into the club. It contained "class rooms, reading rooms, a gymnasium and stage" and served as "rallying-point for the neighborhood clubs for social improvement" by providing rooms for the meetings of organized clubs and by organizing "parties, entertainments, and community get-acquainted evenings for the members of the Center."[88] Educational opportunities included classes in art and art appreciation, piano, and dramatics. The Social Center operated a circulating library from its reading room and organized local sightseeing excursions called "See-Chicago Trips."[89]

Gymnasium classes included "regular gymnastic work, corrective exercises, and organized games, such as tennis, volley ball, base-ball," as well as classes in "social dancing" and tap dancing.[90] Furthermore, while the Social Center was intended to serve the needs of local girls and young women, from the start "there was no resisting the appeal of the boys," and the facilities of the building were soon opened to boys as well as girls aged seven and up.[91] Residents of Club Six were eligible to use the gymnasium "on the same terms as those offered to others living in the vicinity."[92] The fee was nominal—the cost of a year's membership was just one dollar in 1930.[93]

One of the speakers at the opening ceremonies of Club Six was Jane Addams, founder of Hull House, Chicago's highly influential settlement house.[94] Addams's presence at the club's opening highlighted the similarities between Ina Robertson's Eleanor Association work and her own work; the difference, of course, was that Addams's clientele was largely the immigrant poor, while Robertson and her association colleagues strove to serve, essentially, those of the working and lower-middle classes who found themselves in urban Chicago and (in the case of Eleanor Club residents) in service-sector, lower-middle-class employment.[95] Like settlement houses, though, Club Six blurred the line between residential and institutional architecture by combining housing for one group (young working women) and social and educational facilities for another (neighborhood children and adults) under one roof. The Social Center at Club Six was a success: attendance at its activities and use of its facilities numbered over 23,000 in 1916 and 90,000 in 1925.[96]

In 1916, the association itself financed the construction of a building specifically designed to be the permanent Eleanor Club One (fig. 12.9). Located on the Midway Plaisance in Hyde Park, virtually on the campus of the University of Chicago and near Jackson Park and Lake Michigan, this club was later described as "particularly pleasant in the summer time."[97] Designed in a more sedate classical style than

Club Six had been, Club One was the work of the Chicago architectural firm Schmidt, Garden and Martin. Carroll Westfall has noted that Schmidt, Garden and Martin was "one of the few Chicago firms able to do both innovative work allied with the Prairie School style and orthodox commercial buildings, as well as luxury flats and apartment buildings for investors resistant to innovation."[98] Their design for Club One demonstrates the more conservative side of their work, as well as their expertise in residential design. As noted in a 1916 *Architectural Record* article, Schmidt, Garden and Martin were adept at bringing large buildings down to a smaller and more domestic scale: "in spite of (the) repetition of equal elements on various floors and the handling of large surfaces"—the apartments built by the firm "are particularly commendable because of the distinct note of domesticity which they possess."[99]

Achieving this "note of domesticity" was no small feat at Club One, which measured 147 feet across the front. Club One was a steel-framed structure with floors and roof of reinforced concrete and brick exterior walls faced with wire-cut brick and limestone. Again, there was a roof garden.[100]

It seems that some fine tuning of the "Eleanor ideal" went on between the construction of Club Six and the permanent Club One. This second building had rooms for 115 residents, 35 fewer

Fig. 12.9. This 1916 photograph shows the newly built "permanent" Club One at 1442 East Fifty-ninth St., commissioned by the Eleanor Association and designed by Schmidt, Garden and Martin in 1916. Courtesy of the Eleanor Women's Foundation.

than the previously built club; a sacrifice in number of rooms was made in order to set the entrance back from the street. The U-shaped plan, which had not yet become ubiquitous for Chicago hotel and apartment architecture, separates this building from previous Eleanor Clubs.[101] Whereas hotel entrances tended to open right off the sidewalk to encourage passersby to come inside, this entrance was designed to keep unwanted visitors to a minimum (a lesson possibly learned from the experience of the previously commissioned club, which featured separate entrances to distinctly different parts of the building but did not distinguish architecturally between them). Here one would have to know what the building was and make a conscious decision to enter it; in addition, the large lawn area further domesticates this club. The deeply inset entrance, which placed those in front of the building in full view of residents behind the windows on three sides, might also have discouraged young women from loitering around the front of the building with their companions (not a "respectable" sight and therefore poor advertising for any Eleanor Club). The single main entrance ensured that no one could enter the building without first passing by the reception desk—again, a method of social control, but also a reassurance that the residents of the building would be "safe" and secure inside it. This guarantee of physical safety was important not only to the residents but also (perhaps even more so) to the parents of these young women, who often accompanied their daughters to the residences and desired assurance that they would be in good hands.[102] By restricting entrance to one artery, supervision over residents and visitors was maintained.

In her work on buildings designed for collective living, Elizabeth Cromley asks, "how should one enter a collective dwelling?" She notes that the solution used in many large apartment buildings was to "make more imposing architectural statements out of their front doors, handling them more like those of a public building, hotel or club."[103] Indeed, the focal point of the club building commissioned in 1916 is its grand entrance. Not only is the entrance set well back from the street, the doorway is inset into an elaborate masonry surround and further highlighted by stone quoins bordering either side of the entrance and continuing up to a large pediment above the third floor.

Public spaces inside this private building, however, indicate the dual purpose of maintaining security and fostering the atmosphere of the private home while, at the same time, developing the ideal of the surrogate family through the use of public spaces shared by all residents. Cromley explains that residents of apartment houses in this period needed to learn how to negotiate such public interior spaces as lobbies, reception rooms, dining rooms, hallways, and staircases. Were these spaces public or private? Where did the "privacy line" lie? Were hallways and staircases spaces for friendly greetings and discussion, or were they neutral terrain, more akin to the sidewalk outside? The Eleanor Clubs differed from apartment houses in this regard, because there was no question but that the goals of creating a family of residents and fostering intimacy meant that areas traversed or used in common were expressly intended to encourage sociability.

As seen in the ground-floor plan (fig. 12.10), steel-frame construction facilitated the creation of the large social spaces so important to Eleanor Club life. The dining area ("large enough to seat the entire family at one time") occupies most of the east wing (the right wing in the plan and photograph illustrated here).[104] The west wing contained a large ground-floor parlor, where residents were

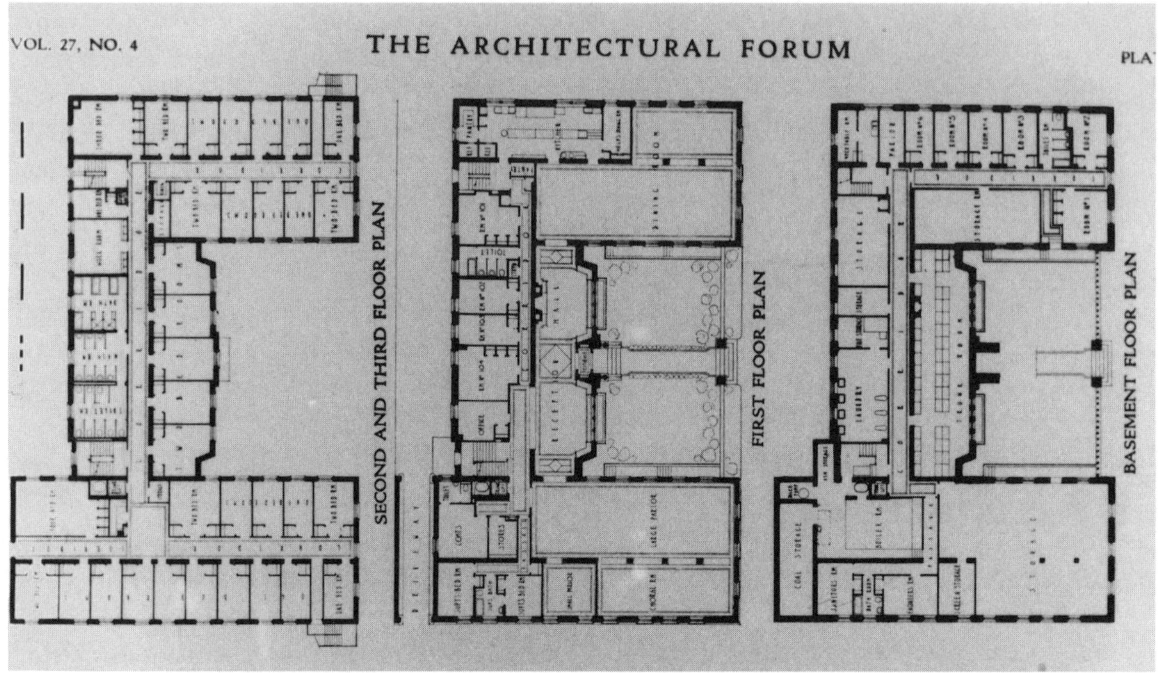

Fig. 12.10. Plans of Club One, 1442 East Fifty-ninth St. From *Architectural Forum* 27, no. 4 (Oct. 1917): plate 70.

free to entertain their male friends (no males were allowed above the ground floor in any Eleanor Club building). An entrance at the back of the parlor led to a "Choral Room" for dances, classes, and other communal activities. There was also a smaller, more private parlor behind the "Choral Room," entered into through the main parlor. This plan carefully delineates public from private space, gradually. For example, one must pass through the grand reception area (large enough to contain seating for friends and admirers waiting for their dates), before gaining access to the dining room at the right and the parlor at the left. While anyone might enter the building from the street, only those accompanied by an Eleanor girl would be allowed access to the "public" parlors and social room. A long corridor accessible only after passing by the monitor's desk affords access to the more private spaces: offices, the kitchen, the supervisor's private rooms, and the stairwells (only residents and their female visitors were allowed access to this corridor and thus to these yet more private spaces). Upstairs, bedrooms of various sizes flank the wing corridors and face the street, while the restrooms, bathrooms, and work rooms are located at the back (private) side of the building. The laundry room and series of storage rooms are located in the basement, along with janitorial offices in one wing and six more residents' bedrooms (and a parlor) in the other wing (see figs. 12.11–14).

The Eleanor Club building of 1916 closely resembles a women's dormitory, and, indeed, many of Robertson's concerns were mirrored by college administrators faced with the prospect of housing fe-

Fig. 12.11. Reception Hall at Club One, looking west to large parlor, through large parlor, and to small parlor, c. 1916. Courtesy of the Eleanor Women's Foundation.

Fig. 12.12. Large parlor at Club One, 1933. Furniture was informally arranged into groupings of various sizes to create a homelike atmosphere in a room spacious enough to accommodate many residents and their friends at one time. Courtesy of the Eleanor Women's Foundation.

male students. Some of the first women's colleges, such as Mount Holyoke, Vassar, and Wellesley, based their housing for women on the seminary system, with rooms for living and classrooms for learning all under the same roof. By closely supervising women in a single building, they created a "female world" which guarded female virtue and protected women from men. But eventually concern that this strictly female world did not prepare young women socially for life as wives and mothers, and, indeed, might result in too much female intimacy, led to other types of housing designs (such as Smith's individual cottages, each housing between thirty-two and fifty women separately from the buildings where education and organized social activities took place). Bryn Mawr, under the leadership of M. Carey Thomas at the end of the nineteenth century, borrowed the idea of collegiate Gothic quadrangles from Oxford and Cambridge, and this quickly became the favorite style of female dormitory buildings. While these structures emulated male dormitories on the exterior, inside the concern for women's security and safety continued to dictate design.[105] Women's dormitories invariably included matrons rooms and/or reception areas adjacent to the main entrances in order to monitor incoming and outgoing residents and their guests; in contrast, men's dormitories generally had no reception area, and the main entrances were flanked by study rooms, bedrooms, or, occasionally, a "recreation room."[106] Typically a women's dormitory grouped public rooms such as a common drawing room, a sitting room, and a dining room on the ground floor, while students' individual bedrooms, often linked into suites with a private or shared parlor, were located upstairs.

Even as Robertson and her Eleanor Association colleagues were developing their ideal home for working women, a home that would encourage the development of strong friendships among women, the ideal college dormitory was changing dramatically. Fears that cozy single-sex living arrangements promoted lesbianism led college dormitory planners to abandon suites and shared parlors upstairs, shifting instead to identical "study cubicles" on each side of a corridor. Social activities were moved downstairs, to grand parlors where residents could proudly receive male guests. Security continued to be maintained by channeling entrance through a main front door.[107] This transition to single rooms of identical size as the norm for college dormitories was effected by the 1920s.

The Eleanor Club of 1916 both harkens back to the ideal of innocent female intimacy and looks forward to the incoming standard of the single room and, in doing so, demonstrates the sensitivity of this building to its clientele. The design took into account the fact that women resided in Eleanor Clubs for different reasons and for different periods of time; some wished to retain the privacy afforded by a single room, while others came with one or more sisters or friends. Letters published in the *Eleanor Record,* the clubs' magazine, which began publication in 1915, attest to the fact that many pairs of sisters, and groups of friends from a hometown, often resided in an Eleanor Club and wished to share a room.[108] The 1916 building for Club One could accommodate a number of combinations: each of the two upper floors included twenty-one single rooms, eleven double rooms, one room intended for three occupants, and one room intended for four occupants. Furthermore, not all shared social activities were shifted to the lower floor in this plan: each upper floor housed a large "workroom" for its residents, and those living in the basement (where six single rooms were located) had the use of a shared parlor.

This club building is, therefore, a transitional form, embodying both earlier nineteenth-century desires for a "female world" of close female friendships[109] (as indicated by the shared rooms) while also bowing to the new ideal of individual privacy and more monitored public behavior. While encouraging female friendship, this plan also provides a number of social spaces on the ground floor where residents can entertain male visitors: the large parlor, the much smaller parlor, and the "social room" for dances and other entertainments.[110]

Fig. 12.13. Dining room at the newly completed Club One, large enough to seat "the entire family" at once, 1916. Courtesy of the Eleanor Women's Foundation.

In their quest to provide appropriate housing for young women making the transition from rural home life to urban business life, and from girlhood to womanhood, Robertson and her Eleanor Association colleagues faced the difficulty of balancing the individual freedom of residents with their safety and security. It was an especially daunting task to maintain the homelike atmosphere, as the size of the clubs grew ever larger. How does one create a domestic realm within an institutional structure? After eighteen years of trial and error, adapting existing buildings to the purpose of housing working women, Robertson and her fellow Eleanor Club officers believed they had created a new building type. While this "new" type bore similarities to women's college dormitory designs being developed at the same time, it did not completely mimic them.[111] It accommodated different combi-

Fig. 12.14. Single bedroom at Club One, 1933. The building also contained rooms for two, three, and four women to share. Courtesy of the Eleanor Women's Foundation.

nations of residents in differently sized rooms. And it provided "private" communal workrooms and a basement parlor, where working women could iron, mend their clothes, or simply relax in the company of other residents, but away from the ground floor public rooms where visitors from outside the home were allowed.

Life in an organized boarding home was not to every young woman's taste—hence the rise in popularity of rooming houses and furnished room districts in this period.[112] But it is just as clear that many young women welcomed the camaraderie and security of life in an Eleanor Club. The voices of these Eleanor residents are heard in the *Eleanor Record*. The December 1918 issue is particularly noteworthy: it celebrates the twentieth anniversary of the founding of the clubs and also details the activities of each club during the month of November, as World War I ends. Through these reports, a picture of life in the Eleanor Clubs emerges. Much excitement was felt as news of the armistice reached the residents on November 11—at Club Six "pandemonium broke loose," while the reporter from Club Three described how that club's residents paraded throughout the hallways of their building in the early morning hours before dressing and going out to join the rest of the city in celebration. Club Four's reporter stressed the Eleanor goal of service in her contribution: "We take pride in the fact that our Eleanor girls are exhibiting their patriotism as conditions demand. They have responded willingly with donations to aid the American war work." This reporter also hinted at the success of other Eleanor goals when she described the residents' recent move into their "new home" (previously a hotel) and noted that "our new cheerful surroundings have tended to strengthen the friendship among our girls." Also noted are the visits of numerous speakers at Sunday services, attendance at classes held in the clubs, contributions to charities, elections of club officers, and many parties. Club Five, for example, held a "get acquainted party" that month, complete with an all-female "mock wedding" and dancing.[113] A more somber note was cast in several of these club reports, which noted the deaths of more than one club resident from the influenza epidemic. Club Three's reporter gave special thanks to her club's "House Mother," who "has kept us all well while so many fatalities have resulted from the disease elsewhere, and we think this is worthy of comment."[114]

Ina Robertson's fortuitous inheritance, along with the instruction that she oversee expenditures for philanthropic and religious causes, allowed her to experiment with the provision of low-cost housing for working women. Certainly philanthropy was an acceptable occupation for a woman of means at the turn of the twentieth century. But Robertson's own experiences, as a teacher and principal, and then a graduate student living alone in a rented room, combined with her devoutly religious nature (she conducted Sunday religious services, taught Sunday school, and led a class of young Eleanor women training to be deaconesses) all contributed to the particular focus her philanthropy would take and, eventually, to the design of the "ideal" Eleanor Club. The purpose-built Eleanor Clubs incorporated into their design Robertson's goals of creating a "family" of "Eleanor girls" by encouraging camaraderie and friendship through communal meals in a large dining room, through shared spaces like parlors and workrooms, and also through the provision of shared bedrooms, at a time when college dormitories for young women were shifting completely to single cell-like rooms precisely to discourage female intimacy. At the same time, the design of the 1916 purpose-built Eleanor Club reveals the emphasis placed on maintaining security and protection for these young women.

Like Robertson herself, this building combined elements of modern urban reformism with nostalgia for an earlier era of female domesticity. It has been said that a purpose-built environment is "thought before it is built."[115] The history of the Eleanor Clubs provides an opportunity to witness the process of "thinking" a building through to its final execution.

As the Eleanor Clubs shifted to larger buildings, and as public perception of women living alone or in shared apartments changed, the smaller, more intimately scaled clubs were gradually closed. The first to do so, Club Two, was closed in 1922; Club Four closed in the early 1930s; two more clubs closed in the 1940s; and in the 1950s both the Eleanor Camp and Eleanor Club Three closed. Finally, in the 1960s the larger, purpose-built Club Six (along with its Social Center), and Club One were closed. However, in the 1950s, the Eleanor Association (now the Eleanor Women's Foundation) commissioned the firm of Childs and Smith to build a new housing club on the near North Side, at 1550 North Dearborn Pkwy. Strikingly similar in plan to Schmidt, Garden and Martin's 1916 Club One, the Eleanor Residence for Working Women and Students remains in operation today, continuing to fulfill Ina Robertson's mission of service to women.

Notes

I am grateful to the Eleanor Women's Foundation for giving me access to their many boxes of archival materials, and I particularly thank Susan Leinwohl and Lora York for their enthusiasm and assistance. The work of Joanne Meyerowitz on Chicago's independent, single working women has been invaluable to me in writing this article: *Women Adrift: Independent Wage Earners in Chicago, 1880–1930* (Chicago: Univ. of Chicago Press, 1988), and "Sexual Geography and Gender Economy: The Furnished Room Districts of Chicago, 1890–1930," *Gender and History* 2, no. 3 (autumn 1990): 274–96. In *Women Adrift*, Meyerowitz discusses the role organized boarding homes like the YWCA and the Eleanor Clubs played in creating domestic homes for women without family or relatives in Chicago. Lisa Fine's insightful discussion of the activities of Eleanor residents has also been very useful: *Souls of the Skyscraper: Female Clerical Workers in Chicago, 1870–1930* (Philadelphia: Temple Univ. Press, 1990), 151–65, and "Between Two Worlds: Business Women in a Chicago Boarding House 1900–1930," *Journal of Social History* 19 (spring 1986): 511–19.

1. One Eleanor club remains in operation today:

the Eleanor Residence for Working Women and Students at 1550 North Dearborn Parkway, designed by the firm of Childs and Smith in the 1950s.

2. John M. Coulter, "The Ideals of the Eleanor Work," in *Eleanor Record,* Dec. 1918, 4–5. A contemporary magazine article on the Eleanor Clubs described the "Eleanor Spirit": "service to others means kindling in them the desire to serve, as well as giving them physical comfort and intellectual companionship," Grace A Coulter, "The Eleanor Clubs in Chicago," *Forbes Magazine,* Apr. 20, 1918.
3. Jessie Veeder, "The Eleanor Association: Organization and Policy," pamphlet, Eleanor Association, June 1920, 6.
4. Anthony King, introduction to *Buildings and Society: Essays on the Social Development of the Built Environment,* ed. Anthony King (London: Routledge & Kegan Paul, 1980), 31.
5. The first buildings of the University of Chicago opened in 1892. Robertson is listed in the university's annual registers for 1895–96 and 1896–97. She left the Divinity School in 1897, returning in the summer of 1903 and autumn of 1904; Maxine Sullivan to J.C.L., Univ. of Chicago Registrar, Apr. 27, 1994.
6. Between 1880 and 1930, the female labor force in Chicago increased from 35,600 to 407,600—over 1,000 percent: *Tenth Census, 1880, Population,* vol. 1, 870; *Fifteenth Census, 1930, Population*, vol. 4, 440, quoted in Joanne Meyerowitz, *Women Adrift,* 5. Meyerowitz notes that this increase of the female labor force in Chicago was more than three times as great as the rate of increase of the female labor force for the nation as a whole. This period, 1880–1930, is also the era in which Chicago became an "apartment city," according to John Hancock, "The Apartment House in Urban America," in *Buildings and Society,* ed. Anthony King, 151–89, 172.
7. See Meyerowitz, *Women Adrift,* 1–20, for detailed statistics (including average age, nativity, race and ethnicity, and region of birth). For example, between 1880 and 1930, the total increase in population (both men and women) was 637,198 foreign-born; 248,623 black; and 953,433 increase in white population from elsewhere in the United States (13).
8. Joanne Meyerowitz notes that use of the phrase "women adrift" to describe wage-earning women living apart from relatives or employers was popularized by a federal report in 1910. See Meyerowitz, *Women Adrift,* xvii, 145 n. 3.
9. Robertson had met James Law and his sister, Eleanor, in the early 1890s on a fund-raising trip east for the Waitsburg Academy. By the late 1890s, James Law had designated Robertson, along with his sister Eleanor, trustees of his estate. In addition, James Law intended that Robertson would care for his elderly sister after his own death. Out of respect for James Law, Robertson took Law as her middle name and was known from then on as Ina Law Robertson. In 1899, James Law died, leaving his property jointly to his sister and Robertson. This information, as well as other facts related below, is contained in a 1922 biography of Ina Robertson by Dr. John Coulter, *The Power of an Ideal: The Story of the Life and Work of Ina Law Robertson, 1867–1916* (Chicago: Eleanor Association, 1977).
10. As noted above, Robertson did return to the University of Chicago, studying at the Divinity School in 1897 and again in the summer of 1903 and autumn of 1904.
11. Shaw was engaged to design and furnish the house, located at 6042 Kimbark Ave. (correspondence and bills from Shaw to Robertson, Dec. 15, 17, 1897, Eleanor Association).
12. Leonard Eaton, *Frank Lloyd Wright and Howard Van Doren Shaw: Two Chicago Architects and Their Clients* (Cambridge: MIT Press, 1969), 166.

13. J. Coulter, *The Power of an Ideal,* 23.
14. J. Coulter, *The Power of an Ideal,* 25–26. Early on, Robertson took over most, if not all, responsibility for these projects; the elderly Eleanor Law gradually fades from the historical record.
15. Jessie Veeder, "Organization of the Eleanor Work," *Eleanor Record,* Dec. 1918, 6; G. Coulter, "The Eleanor Clubs in Chicago."
16. At the time, the street was named Lexington Avenue, but by 1918 its name had been changed to University Avenue.
17. *Eleanor Record,* Dec. 1918, 8.
18. J. Coulter, *The Power of an Ideal,* 28.
19. Veeder, "Organization of the Eleanor Work," 6.
20. It should be noted that this movement was not limited to the United States: Martha Vicinus briefly discusses low-cost boardinghouses and "model homes" for working women in late-nineteenth-century London in *Independent Women: Work and Community for Single Women 1850–1920* (Chicago: Univ. of Chicago Press, 1985), 295–99.
21. On housing for working women, see Elizabeth Cromley, "Apartments and Collective Life in Nineteenth-Century New York," in *New Households: New Housing,* ed. Karen A. Franck and Sherry Ahrentzen (New York: Van Nostrand Reinhold, 1989), 35–38. M. Christine Boyer also discusses the Working Women's Hotel, designed in 1869 by John Kellum but not completed until 1878 (due to the depression of 1873) in *Manhattan Manners: Architecture and Style, 1850–1900* (New York: Rizzoli, 1985), 59–61.
22. Meyerowitz, 46; see also Ann Firor Scott, *Natural Allies: Women's Associations in American History* (Chicago: Univ. of Illinois Press, 1992, 104–10) on women's organizations and the origins of the YWCA, and Nina Mjagkij and Margaret Spratt, introduction to Mjagkij and Spratt, eds., *Men and Women Adrift: The YMCA and the YWCA in the City* (New York: New York Univ. Press, 1997).
23. See Meyerowitz's chapter on "Surrogate Families" in *Women Adrift,* 69–91.
24. Meyerowitz, *Women Adrift,* 70–72.
25. Ibid., 46.
26. A photograph of the Chicago YWCA of 1902 can be seen in Meyerowitz, *Women Adrift,* 51.
27. The Jane Club was almost entirely organized and run by its residents, a greater degree of self-government than was the case with the YWCA or, for that matter, the Eleanor Clubs. However, since the Jane Club received occasional support from Hull House, it was not entirely self-supporting; Meyerowitz, *Women Adrift,* 96–98, 101.
28. Martha Vicinus demonstrates the importance of the surrogate family ideal in England through her examination of nurses' housing, women's colleges, boarding schools, and settlement houses in *Independent Women.*
29. See Paul Groth on Progressive housing reform, *Living Downtown: The History of Residential Hotels in the United States* (Berkeley: Univ. of California Press, 1994), 202–8. See also Roy Lubove, *The Progressives and the Slums: Tenement House Reform in New York City, 1890–1917* (Pittsburgh: Univ. of Pittsburgh Press, 1962), Allen F. Davis, *Spearheads for Reform: The Social Settlements and the Progressive Movement, 1890–1914* (New York: Oxford Univ. Press, 1967), and Robert H. Wiebe, *Businessmen and Reform: A Study of the Progressive Movement* (Cambridge, Mass.: Harvard Univ. Press, 1962).
30. See Meyerowitz, *Women Adrift,* 52, 79; and Lisa Fine, *Souls,* 151–53.
31. Jane Addams, "Why Women Should Vote," *Ladies Home Journal* 27 (Jan. 1910): 21–22.
32. Quoted in Meyerowitz, *Women Adrift,* 52. Since this concept of women's role was so pervasive, it is no surprise that Ina Robertson

was described as "homemaker on a grand scale" in her 1916 *Chicago Daily Tribune* obituary.

33. J. Coulter, *The Power of an Ideal,* 46–47; *Eleanor Record,* May 1918, 7.
34. Veeder, "The Eleanor Association."
35. "Opening of Eleanor Club One" pamphlet, Eleanor Association, Jan. 6, 1917.
36. "The Eleanor Clubs and Camp," pamphlet, Eleanor Association, c. 1922, 11.
37. Joanne Meyerowitz discusses Chicago's shift from boarding homes to rooming houses in "Sexual Geography and Gender Economy" and also in *Women Adrift,* 73. Paul Groth notes that this switch had taken place by the turn of the century, in "'Marketplace' Vernacular Design: The Case of Downtown Rooming Houses," in *Perspectives in Vernacular Architecture II,* ed. Camille Wells (Columbia: Univ. of Missouri Press, 1986), 179–91. See also Harvey W. Zorbaugh, *The Gold Coast and the Slum* (Chicago: Univ. of Chicago Press, 1929), 69–86.
38. Meyerowitz, *Women Adrift,* 73.
39. Such wholesome social activities were thought to be sadly missing from the "cheap boarding-house existence" experienced by many young working women. J. Coulter, *The Power of an Ideal,* 20.
40. Indeed, the Eleanor Clubs were described as "veritable virtue-saving stations" by sociologist Annie Marion MacLean (a close friend of Robertson's) in the *Chicago Tribune,* May 16, 1914 (quoted in Meyerowitz, *Women Adrift,* 54). Gwendolyn Wright discusses criticisms of hotels and apartment houses between the 1880s and the 1920s in *Building the Dream: A Social History of Housing in America* (Cambridge, Mass.: MIT Press, 1981), 145–51.
41. Meyerowitz, *Women Adrift,* 101. Interestingly, Paul Groth notes that women in such relationships were referred to as "charity girls" in Living Downtown, 107.
42. J. Coulter, *The Power of an Ideal,* 29. Indeed, Robertson was so adamant that no charity be involved in the provision of Eleanor Club housing that she refused the persistent overtures of the United Presbyterian Church to sponsor the Eleanor Club work. Over this issue, Robertson left the United Presbyterian Church altogether and joined instead the Presbyterian Church in Chicago; typescript, history and chronology of the Eleanor work, Eleanor Association, n.d., 4.
43. J. Coulter, *The Power of an Ideal,* 44; Eleanor Club promotional pamphlets. See also Fine, Souls, 152.
44. Meyerowitz, *Women Adrift,* 86–89.
45. Sarah Cory Rippey, "Where the Sunshine Never Fails," *Continent,* Mar. 6, 1913. This writer continues: "Miss Robertson's longing is that the Christ spirit may be so thoroughly in and through and about the work that her girls may unconsciously grow into the image of that One who 'went about doing good.'"
46. Apparently a number of department store managers showed interest in the Hotel Eleanor and recommended it to their female employees. J. Coulter, *The Power of an Ideal,* 28.
47. J. Coulter, *The Power of an Ideal,* 30.
48. This building was very near Washington Park, an especially desirable location. J. Coulter, *The Power of an Ideal,* 30.
49. Within a few years, this negative attitude toward hotel living was summed up in a series of three articles that ran in the *Ladies' Home Journal* in 1909, all written by Maude Radford Warren: "The Child Who Lived in a Hotel" (Jan. 1909); "A Young Girl in a Hotel" (Feb. 1909); and "A Young Married Couple in a Hotel" (Apr. 1909). In each tale, the characters come into contact with "common people," stray from their moral compasses, pick up bad habits, and generally lower their standards

while residing in hotels. I am indebted to Molly Berger for referring me to these articles.

Paul Groth details the arguments against hotel living and reformers' attempts to provide and promote housing alternatives, in *Living Downtown,* 201–31. Eric Sandweiss discusses the perception of hotel living as necessarily "lonely" for those without families in "Building for Downtown Living: The Residential Architecture of San Francisco's Tenderloin," in *Perspectives in Vernacular Architecture, III,* ed. Thomas Carter and Bernard L. Herman (Columbia: Univ. of Missouri Press, 1989), 160–73. See also Wright, *Building the Dream,* 145–51.

It should be emphasized that the drawbacks and dangers of hotel life tended to be pointed out by moralists who did not live in hotels. They interpreted the freedoms of hotel life as threats to the traditional single-family home. Obviously, the vast majority of those living in hotels did not share these sentiments; many individuals embraced the freedom (from cooking, from chores) of hotel life.

50. The list of original stockholders has not been found; however, it is likely that Dr. John M. Coulter was among them. Coulter was a University of Chicago professor of botany; Robertson had known him at least since her coursework there. Coulter, his wife, and his daughter, Grace, were deeply involved with the Eleanor Association work: in 1917 Coulter was a member of the Eleanor Advisory Council, Mrs. Coulter a member of the Executive Committee, and Grace Coulter vice president of the Eleanor Association. Coulter produced his biography of Robertson, *The Power of an Ideal,* in 1922. See J. Coulter, *The Power of an Ideal,* ii, 37, and "Opening of Eleanor Club One" pamphlet, Eleanor Association, Jan. 6, 1917.
51. The pamphlet "Opening of Eleanor Club One" (Jan. 6, 1917) includes a list of Eleanor Association officers, directors, and trustees, along with executive committee and advisory council members. As described later, many of these individuals were "women of means"—they did not receive a salary for their Eleanor Association work ("Round Table Discussion on the Eleanor Association," typescript, 1942).
52. Veeder, "The Eleanor Association." According to Veeder, this initial loan was generally paid off within three years.
53. "Working girls" needed reasonable food at a cheap price, which the Eleanor Clubs provided. Moreover, since residents had already paid for their meals (along with their rent) they would be reluctant to spend their own money elsewhere to buy food. This policy had the effect of keeping residents safely inside the building as much as possible by ensuring that most of them would come home for dinner.
54. Veeder, "The Eleanor Association," 3.
55. Veeder, "The Organization of the Eleanor Work," 6–7. For information on wages, see Meyerowitz, *Women Adrift,* 33–38.
56. G. Coulter, "The Eleanor Clubs in Chicago."
57. Ibid.; J. Coulter, *The Power of an Ideal,* 33.
58. "Ina Law Robertson," obituary, *Chicago Daily Tribune,* Mar. 8, 1916.
59. *Eleanor Record,* 1916, 17.
60. J. Coulter, *The Power of an Ideal,* 27.
61. Ibid., 39.
62. Ibid., 42.
63. Harold M. Mayer and Richard C. Wade, *Chicago: Growth of a Metropolis* (Chicago: Univ. of Chicago Press, 1969), 56, and Homer Hoyt, *One Hundred Years of Land Values in Chicago* (New York: Arno Press, 1970), 93–94.
64. Mayer and Wade, *Chicago,* 209–10.
65. Groth describes the process of adapting a building, at first from a home into a boardinghouse, and then from the boardinghouse into a rooming house in "'Marketplace' Vernacular Design," 181–82.
66. See Cromley, "Apartments and Collective Life in Nineteenth-Century New York," 38–41, on

designs for "bachelor flats" at the turn of the century. These differed from women's housing in many ways and typically provided residents with suites consisting of parlor, bedroom, and bathroom, while entertainment and dining activities were expected to take place in such public spaces as clubs and restaurants (thus bachelor flats were kitchenless). Housing for men allowed for greater privacy and much less supervision than housing designed for women.

67. Sarah Cory Rippey, "Where the Sunshine Never Fails," *Continent* (Mar. 6, 1913).
68. Ibid.
69. "The Eleanor Clubs and Camp for Young Women," pamphlet, Eleanor Association, 1922, 6. The creation of a homelike residence through the provision of such shared social spaces as parlors and reception rooms was also important to the design of nurses' residences. See Annmarie Adams, "Rooms of Their Own: The Nurses' Residences at Montreal's Royal Victoria Hospital," *Material History Review* (fall 1994): 29–41; 33. See also Vicinus, *Independent Women*, 129.
70. Robertson's diary, Eleanor Women's Foundation.
71. Eleanor Clubs were located in Hyde Park, Washington Park, Kenwood, Douglas, the near South Side, and Grand Boulevard. For details on the evolution of these neighborhoods, see Glen E. Holt and Dominic A. Pacyga, *Chicago: A Historical Guide to the Neighborhoods: The Loop and South Side* (Chicago: Chicago Historical Society, 1979).
72. Letter, Martha Freeman Esmond to Julia Boyd of New York, June 5, 1909, reprinted in "When Chicago was Young," *Chicago Tribune* news clipping, no date, contained in scrapbook, Eleanor Women's Foundation.
73. Sanborn Fire Insurance Map, Chicago, vol. 4, 1912.
74. "The Evolution of Club Five," *Eleanor Record*, May 1926, 6. The author of the article notes that Club Five's occupancy of such a grand home owed much to urban reconfiguration: "There came a time when, as the city grew and pushed out and the foreigners were crowded nearer this neighborhood, the millionaires moved further away,—to Oak Park and other localities."
75. These buildings, as well most of the other buildings adapted for use as Eleanor Clubs, were constructed between 1872 and 1891; Chicago's architectural sources for this period are slim, especially for unremarkable buildings that are not located in a designated historic district. As a result, analysis of these buildings must be, to some degree, conjectural and based on sources that focus on specific building types. On the turn-of-the-century hotel, see C. W. Westfall, "From Homes to Towers: A Century of Chicago's Best Hotels and Tall Apartment Buildings," in *Chicago Architecture 1872–1922: Birth of a Metropolis,* ed. John Zukowsky (Munich: Prestel-Verlag, 1987), 267–89, Molly Winger Berger, "The Modern Hotel in America, 1829–1929" (Ph.D. diss., Case Western Univ., Ohio, 1997, and Paul Groth's chapter, "Midpriced Mansions for Middle Incomes," in *Living Downtown*, 56–89.
76. Hancock, "The Apartment House in Urban America," 172.
77. Unfortunately, the poor quality of these photographs prevents their reproduction here. They can be seen, however, in Lisa Fine, *The Souls of the Skyscraper*, illustrations 10 and 11.
78. Gwendolyn Wright notes that middle-class apartment buildings of the late-nineteenth century were often so cramped and the dimensions of the rooms so inconvenient that "sometimes the furnishings a family brought with them from their former house would not fit into the new quarters." Wright, *Building the Dream,* 142.

79. Thora Thorsmark, "Ole Club Three," *Eleanor Record,* Mar. 1926, 15.
80. Sanborn Fire Insurance Map, Chicago, vol. 4, 1912.
81. Ina Robertson, diary, Sept. 14, 1908.
82. Sanborn Fire Insurance Map, Chicago, vol. 3, 1911.
83. The plans and detailed description of the interior of this building have not yet been found. *Eleanor Record,* Dec. 1918, 17, and Oct. 1926.
84. J. Coulter, *The Power of an Ideal,* 41.
85. "Souvenir Program: Opening of Club Six," Eleanor Association, Apr. 18, 1914, 5.
86. Westfall, "From Homes to Towers," 285.
87. "Opening of Eleanor Club One," pamphlet, Eleanor Association, 1916, 6.
88. "Eleanor Social Center," pamphlet, Eleanor Association, c. 1930, 1.
89. Ibid., 2–3.
90. Ibid., 2.
91. *Eleanor Record,* Oct. 1926.
92. "The Eleanor Clubs and Camp," Eleanor Association, c. 1922, 9.
93. "Eleanor Social Center," 4.
94. "Souvenir Program: Opening of Club Six," 3.
95. Robertson perceived her work to be distinctly different from that of Jane Addams, noting in her diary on October 13, 1906: "Had meeting with Miss Jane Addams by appointment at Hull House. Talked over location of factory girls and plans for greater cooperation of all engaged in housing Chicago working girls." Robertson clearly saw her Eleanor Clubs as serving women of a different class from those helped through Hull House.
96. "Opening of Eleanor Club One," 5; *Eleanor Record*, Oct. 1926.
97. "The Eleanor Clubs and Camp for Young Women," 5.
98. C. W. Westfall, "From Homes to Towers," 286.
99. *Architectural Record* 39, no. 2 (Feb. 1916): 153.
100. *Architectural Forum* 27, no. 4 (Oct. 1917): 113.
101. Chicago's greatest apartment-building boom occurred in the 1920s, and it was then that the U-shaped plan became popular. See *Directory to Apartments of the Better Class along the North Side of Chicago* (Chicago: A. J. Pardridge & H. Bradley, c. 1917), and Carl W. Condit, *Chicago 1910–1929: Building, Planning, and Urban Technology* (Chicago: Univ. of Chicago Press, 1973), 162.
102. Fine, *Souls*, 153–54.
103. Cromley, "Apartments and Collective Life in Nineteenth-Century New York," 23.
104. Veeder, "The Eleanor Association."
105. Helen Lefkowitz Horowitz, *Alma Mater: Design and Experience in the Women's Colleges from Their Nineteenth-Century Beginnings to the 1930s* (New York: Alfred A. Knopf, 1984), 4–7.
106. For insight into the design development of women's college dormitories, especially as compared with those being designed for men, see the *Architectural Forum* 43, no. 6 (Dec. 1925), special issue on college architecture.
107. Lefkowitz Horowitz, *Alma Mater,* 311–14. Lefkowitz Horowitz notes that by the 1920s, "college planning manuals considered the single room of identical size the best arrangement in women's residence halls. While men's colleges set out consciously to foster male friendship in their living arrangements, female friendship was what the women's colleges, under attack for race suicide, feared the most" (314).
108. Fine, *Souls*, 160–61.
109. See Carroll Smith-Rosenberg, "The Female World of Love and Ritual: Relations between Women in Nineteenth-Century America," *Signs* 1, no. 1 (autumn 1975).
110. Interestingly, the design of the final purpose-

built Eleanor residence, constructed in the 1950s, is strikingly similar to this 1916 design.

111. See also Adams, "Rooms of Their Own," on nurses' residences being designed at this time.

112. Meyerowitz, *Women Adrift,* 73–74.

113. Lisa Fine analyzes the social activities such as "mock weddings" and "kid parties" that were popular in the Eleanor Clubs and argues that these activities helped ease the transition from girlhood to womanhood, noting that most of these young women were only temporarily urban wage earners. It was assumed that they would stop working when they married, thus leaving the Eleanor home for the home they would themselves make for their husbands and, eventually, children. Fine, *Souls,* 157–65.

114. All quotations from the Club "reporters" are in the *Eleanor Record,* Dec. 1918, 11–18.

115. Amos Rapoport, quoted in the introduction to King, *Buildings and Society,* 30.

CHAPTER 13

Marta Gutman

Inside the Institution: The Art and Craft of Settlement Work at the Oakland New Century Club, 1895–1923

When Eva Carlin discussed the condition of Oakland at the turn of the century, she presented her readers in *Overland Monthly,* the California journal of arts and letters, with a particular image of the western city. The schoolteacher and sometime essayist did not praise, as other writers did, the physical achievements of the city's builders and industrialists or call to her readers' attention material symbols of the city's progress, especially the growing display along the Oakland shoreline of wharves, factories, warehouses, and railroads. Instead, Carlin took pains to argue that the rapidly expanding city faced serious problems which, she asserted, were clearly expressed in certain neighborhoods of the industrializing urban landscape.[1]

Carlin made her case by focusing on an area in the western part of Oakland, near "the Point," as the district close to the western terminus of the transcontinental railroad was called. "It is hard," the reform-minded woman pointed out, for the affluent men and women who live "on the east side of Oakland to conceive" of the "limited and toilsome lives" of West Oakland's working-class residents and to understand the physical conditions under which they live, work, and play, near the Southern Pacific's railroad yards.[2] While Carlin recognized the economic and political causes of the inequalities she observed, her analysis did not stress either source. Rather, she emphasized the deleterious effects of specific buildings and urban settings on personal behavior, family life, and community experience in the ethnically diverse, racially integrated district. In Carlin's view, saloons, small and crowded wooden houses close to factories and the railroad, and a lack of churches and supervised open spaces for children's play made the Point "an unsavory spot in moral and material aspects." The district, she wrote, "gives weight to the statement that the modern city is a constant confession of social failure."[3]

Carlin's moralistic environmental determinism, common enough among socially concerned Americans at the turn of the century, led the progressive California woman to exaggerate the problematic physical state of West Oakland's landscape and to overemphasize the social problems that the residents faced.[4] Even Carlin argued that West Oakland was not really a "slum." It was, she admitted, just "a district of great ugliness," where "hard-working foreigners, with a fair sprinkling of Americans" lived, "attracted thither by the exigencies of their occupation" and "the cheapness of the rents."[5] Yet the essayist's suggestion that social improvement in modern cities depended on material and moral progress accurately described the sensibilities of many readers of *Overland Monthly*, including the women who ran the West Oakland Settlement, one of the ordinary social institutions that Carlin praised in the magazine.

The middle- and upper-class women who opened the settlement in 1895 did not question the broader order of industrial society, unlike other California women who joined movements for economic, social, or political reform.[6] Rather, the settlement's backers, more conservative in political inclination, adopted a different response to the material inequality and social upheaval so present in American cities during the 1890s: they formed a women's club to manage a small-scale charitable institution at the edge of their growing city. Inside the nonsectarian, racially integrated establishment, the club's members expected to assist the deserving poor, primarily working women and their children, and to present physical alternatives to the troublesome qualities of everyday life in the working-class neighborhood. The club also wanted to Americanize immigrants, to teach women and children needed skills, and to convince them of the value of frugal economic habits and conventional gender roles.[7]

Even though the settlement was torn down in the 1960s, the physical history of the socially significant charity, first directed by the West Oakland Settlement and later managed by its successor, the Oakland New Century Club, indicates the high value Progressive Era reformers placed on using architecture to shape working-class values and practices. In each phase of the settlement's incremental growth, the sponsors asserted the value of their moral materialism, turning first to interior design and facade alteration and later expanding their palette to include entire buildings and adjacent open spaces. At the same time, pragmatism and financial prudence affected their approach to urban institution building as much as ideological conviction did.

Initially inserted into an ordinary working-class house, the settlement became part of a bigger informally arranged complex by the turn of the century. Less intrusive and more economical than a larger purpose-built establishment, the altered everyday buildings in the complex depicted the advantages of orderly urban landscapes and, by inference, the problems of undisciplined ones. After the turn of the century, the settlement offered a more forthright presentation of elite architectural ideals, with the complex appearing in 1910 as if it were erected as a purpose-built institution. It contained a gymnasium, classrooms, and a seemingly new clubhouse. The latter building was, in fact, a renovated dwelling—the initial cottage rented for the settlement's use some fifteen years earlier by

Elizabeth Watt, the group's wealthy patron. In the 1920s, she convinced the city to open a playground in front of the gymnasium, thereby completing the physical elements of the setting.

With a few important exceptions, historians interested in the development of public buildings in modern American cities have not analyzed the physical histories of ordinary institutions like the New Century Club.[8] Focusing instead on more monumental structures, the studies, primarily of civic buildings, skyscrapers, and other grand edifices related to the City Beautiful movement, have tended to support the claims of other analysts, largely geographers and urban historians. They argue that a sharp break in the organization of American cities had occurred by 1910, resulting from successful political reforms, the spread of a corporate model of government, and the increasing rationalization of urban spaces and buildings.[9] That argument can explain the dramatic changes which occurred in the central business districts and civic centers during the Progressive Era. Yet, the model of rapid and abrupt modernization

Fig. 13.1. View of the West Oakland Settlement Complex, c. 1900. At the turn of the century, the two-story building on the far right, a renovated working-class cottage, was the main building of the settlement, containing meeting rooms and classrooms. The small house in the center was called the Little Housekeepers' Cottage, and the settlement used it for kitchen garden classes, where young girls learned domestic skills. The shedlike building, on the far left, a new building, contained a cooking school, later transformed into a library. From Oakland New Century Club, *Annual Greeting*, 1902, frontispiece. Courtesy of the Oakland History Room, Oakland Public Library.

Fig. 13.2. Home of the Oakland New Century Club, after 1907. The West Oakland Free Kindergarten is gathered in front of the settlement's main building, also known as the clubhouse. From Oakland New Century Club, *Annual Greeting*, 1910, frontispiece. Courtesy of the California History Room, California State Library, Sacramento, California.

does not account for the more varied patterns of continuity and change in less centralized urban areas. They developed, in part, from the expansion and contraction of the real estate market and, in part, from the complex effects of reform ideologies, social identity, and inequality on the fine grain of urban development.[10]

The Protestant women who joined with Elizabeth Watt to form the New Century Club straddled two worlds at the turn of the century, as did many other participants in the women's club movement and supporters of reform activities elsewhere in the United States. While the Oakland club women allied the settlement with Progressive Era causes (mostly in education and recreation), older attitudes toward morality and the purposes of charity influenced their thinking and shaped architectural decisions. In the sponsors' view, an artistic homelike establishment, run by women, mostly volunteers, made tangible the spatial practices working people needed to adopt and also nourished self-reliance, the work ethic, domesticity, and other important values. In the words of Eva Carlin, Oakland Point's working-class residents needed more "virtue"—which she defined as "industry, perseverance, patience, dexterity, economy, cleanliness, and thrift"—before their community's pressing problems could be resolved.[11] Fortunately, in Carlin's view, several organizations already at work in the Point could assist in the educational effort. They included a group which preceded the settlement, the West Oakland Free Kindergarten Association.

The First Ordinary Institution in Oakland Point

True to its name, the West Oakland Free Kindergarten Association offered financial and social support to a free kindergarten located in Oakland Point. In 1886, Elizabeth Betts, newly graduated from the California Kindergarten Training School in San Francisco, decided to open a free school for young children, placing it in the working-class community. Well schooled in Friedrich Froebel's teaching methods, the young teacher rented a "sunny room" on the first floor of a wood frame building, located on Peralta Street, scarcely a full block north of the railroad yards.[12] Since the building was purported to contain a former "liquor-saloon," the decision to rent the room and transform its use

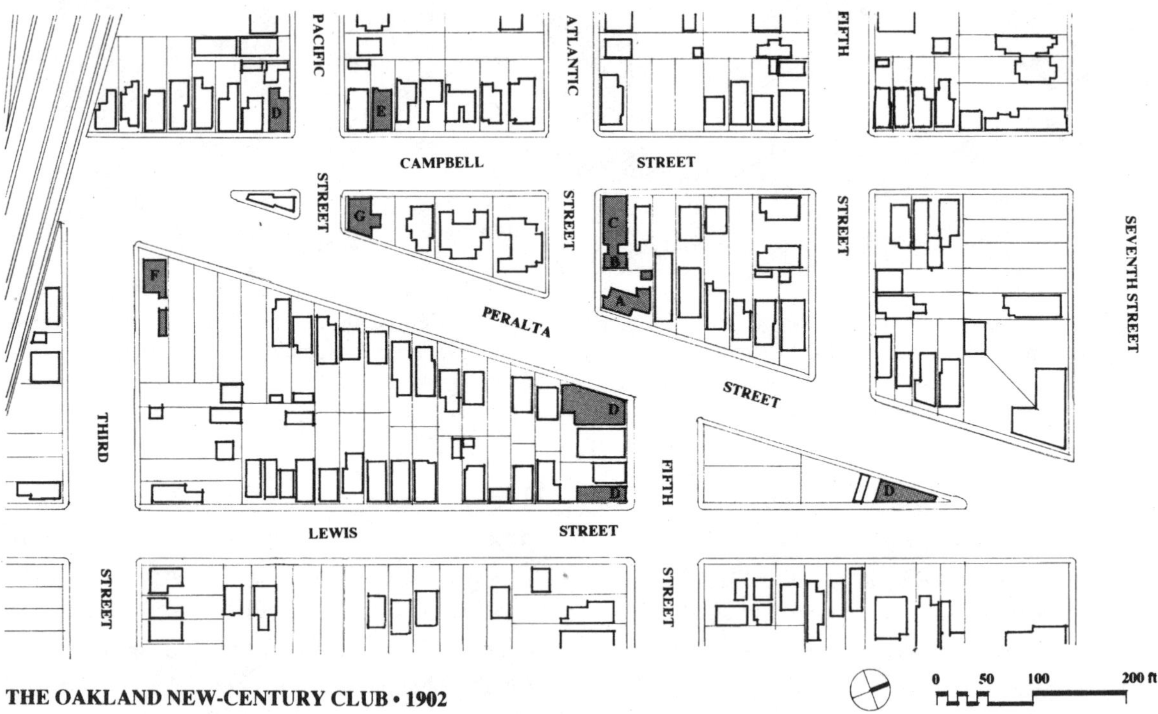

Fig. 13.3. Area Plan, Oakland New Century Club, 1902. Running a free kindergarten (at G) introduced female reformers to West Oakland in the late 1880s. As the school's program expanded, they decided to open a settlement in a rented house on Peralta Street (A) in 1895. The corner location, between the railroad yards and the commercial vitality of Seventh Street, lent some urban prominence to the building and presented it as an alternative to local saloons (D). Some rundown buildings (F) and another reform outpost—a church hall (E)—were close by. Between 1899 and 1900 the group opened a cooking school (C) and also rented the small cottage on Atlantic Street (B), used as an instructional space for the kitchen garden class. Drawn by Sibel Zandi-Sayek.

quickly attracted the attention of other reform-minded Oakland women. They formed a group which offered financial support to the new urban charity.[13]

Betts's choice of building method was not an unusual one, as much as the reputed prior use of the educational setting astonished her sponsors. The teacher had simply adopted the practice, often used in American cities, of locating charities inside standing buildings. Even though purpose-built institutions were quite evident in the nineteenth-century urban landscape, it was also common to adapt existing buildings to new functions, institutional purposes among them. Even in Oakland, a relatively new city where many empty lots awaited improvement in the 1880s and 1890s, private schools and voluntary societies, such as the Young Women's Christian Association, found renovated buildings to be fitting settings for their civic endeavors. Betts attached an ideological dimension to the institution-building method by renting a room in an everyday building near the heart of an industrializing neighborhood. Altering a space in that kind of urban setting best suited her purposes, not changing a grander home in a wealthier location. "There is little in heredity that can not be overcome by training and example," the New Century Club's mission statement would later declare, at once endorsing Betts's effort and linking Christian sentiment with a then-fashionable environmental determinism and social Darwinism. "Those who have given their time and means for the betterment of humanity are led to this one conclusion: we must reach the home life of those we would help upward."[14]

By the mid-1890s, the directors of the kindergarten association had started to broaden the focus of the free school, concerned about the effects of a national depression, alarmed by the Pullman strike, and inspired by the interests of the group's new president, Elizabeth Watt. Born in New England in 1844, Watt moved to California during the gold rush, married a wealthy Scottish immigrant, and had become by the 1890s a socially prominent Oakland resident.[15] Like other American women of her generation and social standing, Watt moved, with some ease, between the public and private spheres, often propelled by her charitable activities. But, Watt was not a feminist in the political sense, and she showed little interest in other ongoing movements for political and social change prevalent in California at that time. Different causes, more prudent in political intention, material in focus, and gendered in social construction, appealed to her, notably social settlements, kitchen gardens, and certain aspects of the movements for domestic reform and municipal housekeeping. As Karen Blair has pointed out, American club women, eager to merge moral and benevolent concerns with participation in the public sphere, often expressed interest in similar kinds of reforms.[16]

Under Watt's leadership, the kindergarten association made a concerted effort to diversify its constituency and programs during the mid-1890s, seeking first to engage the interest of older children and mothers, then young working adults and older men. Initially the new programs, which included sewing classes and a mothers' meeting, were located in the same building as the kindergarten, but Watt and her friends soon realized that those activities and other new programs needed more space and a separate organization to coordinate them. At first, the women did not formally separate the new group from the kindergarten's association. The women simply called the group a "settlement" or, at times, the West Oakland Settlement.[17]

In seeking a location for the new organization, Watt adopted a site selection strategy similar to the one Betts had employed a decade earlier. In 1895, she rented the first floor of a cottage dwelling just one block up Peralta Street from the kindergarten and across the street from another conspicuous local saloon.[18] A one-story building initially, the cottage was located on a corner lot and likely had a four-room plan, a layout often used in neighborhood houses. Although the settlement's backers did not live in the establishment, they held meetings and taught most of the programs and classes in the Oakland Point building, the dwelling which would soon become the core of a much larger institutional complex.

Making the Cottage into a Physical Setting, Suited to the Settlement's Social Work

In 1895, soon after Watt secured the lease for the Peralta Street cottage, the West Oakland Settlement took the next step in the incremental institution-building process. At first, the settlement did not inhabit a visually harmonious complex unified in stylistic or three-dimensional terms. Instead, with Watt in the lead, the women's group took a pragmatic approach to institution building, initially expressing didactic intentions with modest architectural alterations and interior renovations of the Peralta Street cottage (see fig. 13.1). Within the next few years, facade alterations smartened the appearance of the former dwelling; a new back porch and two sets of new exterior stairs were added; and three rooms on the first floor were combined into a larger multipurpose space used for sewing classes and the mothers' meeting. First this space and then several other rooms, used for members' meetings and other purposes, received a new decor. The relative simplicity of the decoration resembled in in-

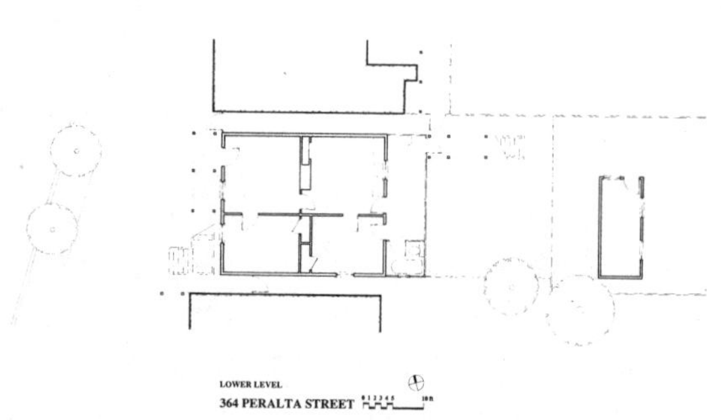

Fig. 13.4. 364 Peralta St., lower-level plan, initial construction c. 1875, drawn 1995. Probably the first floor plan of the settlement resembled the layout of this cottage, across Peralta Street from the settlement. Measured by Sibel Zandi-Sayek, Benjamin Chaqui, and the author. Drawn by Sibel Zandi-Sayek.

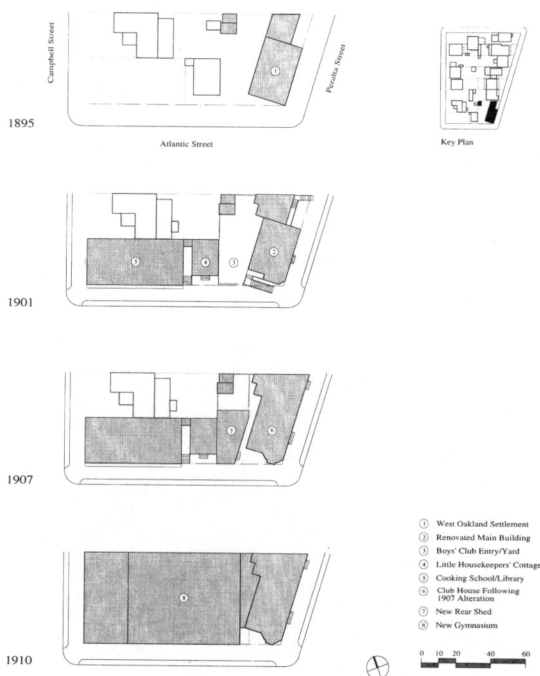

Fig. 13.5. Incremental building of the West Oakland/New Century Club Complex, 1895–1910. Drawn by A. Eugene Sparling.

tent, if not always in exact formal character, the approach taken inside other American settlements, and the disposition of interior spaces recalled the structure of a middle-class home. The builder is unknown, but Watt had a large hand in shaping the building's physical qualities, probably paying for the improvements as well.[19]

Watt approached the institution-building process with a businesslike financial caution, likely aware of the difficulty of erecting a new public building in a crowded urban setting. Certainly, a similar pragmatism affected the choices made by the leaders of settlements in other American cities, as Allen B. Pond, one of the designers of Hull House, pointed out in *The Brickbuilder.*[20] Pond questioned their incremental approach to institution building, arguing that purpose-built complexes more clearly expressed architectural intentions than ad-hoc settings did. Even so, the architect admitted, a nexus of factors caused his clients to take an additive approach to urban construction, among them, conditions of ownership, availability of sites in congested settings, and difficulty in raising funds. Still, as Pond suggested and as historians have also noted, the directors of American settlements often succeeded in giving physical substance to their multifaceted purposes and ideals.[21] As in Chicago, the Oakland women worked ably with rented buildings, commissioning meaningful alterations of them.

Turning the West Oakland cottage into an example of middle-class domesticity, the sponsors anticipated, would give the setting retreatlike quali-

Fig. 13.6. The sewing class, West Oakland Settlement, c. 1900. Sewing classes were held in this room, redecorated to suite the taste of the settlement's sponsors. The column and the beam indicate the position of the partition that previously divided the room into two smaller separate chambers. The photograph indicates that the sewing class was integrated, with the head teacher, likely Mrs. Watt, sitting next to an African American student. From *Domestic Science Monthly* 1 (Aug. 1900): 118.

ties and create a powerful example, one which would, they hoped, sway the social habits and spatial practices of working people. The new interior design, applied first to the multipurpose room and later to other spaces in the building, stressed the need for individual decorum through the orderly grouping of furniture and other fittings, emphasized the spatial expression of functional and social distinctions, and asserted the value of separate female and male spheres for working people, if not for the sponsors themselves. Indeed, as much as the sponsors wanted to encourage cross-class contact, they would soon begin to demarcate a distinct domain for themselves, inside the institution, by reserving specific rooms for their meetings.[22]

In selecting a decorative program, Watt and her associates avoided most of the fussiness found in older, more elaborate Victorian houses and turned to simpler motifs, with their taste swayed by the House Beautiful and Arts and Crafts movements and the Colonial Revival. Many decorative objects inside the building resembled artifacts found in up-to-date middle-class homes. The domestic qualities of the decoration evoked the gender of the patrons, and, as at Hull House, the simplified imagery hinted at the more inclusive and progressive inclinations of the group, especially the interest in affirming the value of health, art, openness in family life, and neighborliness in the socially diverse working-class district.[23]

The interior design also responded to less noble aspects of turn-of-the-century cultural politics. Prejudices against charity and fears of pauperization encouraged the settlement's sponsors to adopt, at least initially, relatively frugal means for executing architectural change. Used furniture and inexpensive ornamental objects, prime among them flowers and prints, appeared in the small rooms, with new wallpaper covering the imperfections of the plaster walls. Imbued with sentiment and a veneration of the work ethic, domesticity, and handicraft, the imagery of the interior spaces presented a conservative message to working people, one based on "the assimilation of unruly workers," as T. Jackson Lears has written.[24] Material culture also likely affected the content of the group's Americanization programs, with Windsor chairs, spinning wheels, and other accouterments of the Colonial Revival manifest in the rooms (and later publications) of the establishment. In many settlements, such items were taken to be important tools, useful in teaching immigrants the value of an "American" culture.[25]

Thus the institution's interior decor projected a paternalist vision of American democracy in which the Progressive managers of society tolerated racial, ethnic, and religious heterogeneity, so long as a shared commitment to elite political values, art, and culture repressed labor conflict and subsumed acute expressions of social difference. In certain instances, the actual uses of the settlement followed through on the benevolent promise of social inclusion—although always under the watchful eye and tutelage of the sponsors. Under Watt's leadership the settlement was integrated, at a time when American charities often ran segregated establishments. "This Club has ever tried to keep free from a spirit of prejudice," Watt wrote. "Children of all races and religions are received into the classes, while the colored woman and her children are . . . made welcome as those of fairer skin."[26] However, condescending stereotypes ran through the settlement's texts, and although the group had an Asian American staff member, few seem to have used the services.[27]

Other spatial practices reinforced social distinctions and endorsed strict discipline, especially in regard to children. The settlement, following the example of the kindergarten down the street, expected to make working-class children "useful" members of society by teaching them new habits, stressing the value of home life, and offering lessons in practical skills—sewing being one of the most popular courses offered. As in local public schools, classes met at regular hours, in specific rooms, and children were separated, for the most part, by age and sex. The settlement directed sewing lessons at girls; boys learned handicrafts and manual skills to ready them for factory jobs (although a few enrolled in the girls' classes, too). And, to challenge the allure of city streets, the group opened clubs for older boys and working girls. The initial location of the clubs in the Peralta Street building—girls upstairs, boys downstairs—confirmed the value of clean, orderly, and separate settings for men and women.[28]

The Working Girls' Recreation Club met in two tidy rooms, rented expressly for the purpose. Modeled on the "house beautiful," the appearance of the sitting room and the lounge asserted the merits of domesticity to older girls who lived in the area, worked in varied trades, and often did not earn enough to support themselves as independent wage earners.[29] "They are clerks or cash-girls in candy-stores and printing-offices; they work in cotton-mills and shoddy-mills. There are girls who make things, girls who sew things, and girls who sell things . . . They dress in 'the style,' following its extreme vagaries, and generally boast of a 'steady' to escort them to the cheap theaters and the frequent dances held in town."[30] As in other aspects of the settlement's work, the club's setting and programs emphasized the need for better behavior, not economic or political change. The settlement expected that girls, tucked safely away upstairs in artistic and commodious rooms, would improve themselves with quiet activities intended to develop them into moral guardians of art and culture, assist in Americanization, and provide a substitute for drinking, dancing, and other even more questionable practices, such as "treating."[31] In the eyes of the reformers, the free club, filled with examples of early American furniture and educationally sound entertainment, offered a substantive and economical alternative to immoral activities. "Here they find a teacher of fancy sewing, books, magazines, rest and comfort . . . and enjoy 'personally conducted travel evenings' as well as those devoted to music and social enjoyment."[32] The club closed within a few years, a victim of the sponsors' moralistic expectations, and the settlement took the rooms for their club's own use.[33]

Boys entered their ground-floor club from the street, moving into the building through the small backyard, where appliances for cleaning up were plainly stationed. Inside the gentlemanly parlor, the West Oakland Settlement tried to combat the allure of saloons and unregulated play on the neighborhood's streets and empty lots with "delicate blue and white" furnishings, "good strong" portraits of George Washington and Phillips Brooks (a popular preacher), and activities directed at male tastes—specific kinds of arts and crafts projects, games, and military drills. The activities were a component of other settlement programs in the area, and both they and the physical setting were expected to Americanize the club's cleaned-up members and encourage refinement, sanitary practices, and respect for authority.[34]

In 1900 Carlin reported that the boys' club had almost seventy members, taking the quantity as certain evidence of the program's success. Her account also suggested that the boys needed more physical activity and manly guidance, and she urged the settlement to address the issue by making specific changes: teaching woodworking, building a gymnasium, and hiring a male teacher who needed to be, Carlin stressed, a fatherlike figure, "a man of strength and

Fig. 13.7. The Working Girls' Recreation Club, c. 1900. From *Domestic Science Monthly* 1 (May 1900): 30.

Fig. 13.8. The Boys' Club, c. 1900. From *Domestic Science Monthly* 1 (Aug. 1900): 119.

truth."[35] The boys required such an exemplary figure because they were, Carlin acknowledged, often difficult to reach and initially ungrateful of the settlement's efforts to send them along the admittedly difficult route to self-improvement. Eventually a male volunteer would participate in the boys' club; the group would adopt the latest approach to carpentry instruction; and it would construct a modern gym. The latter two activities were predicated on training the mind through disciplining the eye, the hand, and the body to paraphrase Carlin, and they would reinforce habits precious to industrial employers—organization, synchronization, and discipline. For the time being, however, another pressing issue took precedence—the situation of West Oakland's working women.

The Next Step: Adding a Cottage for Little Housekeepers and a New Cooking School

The skepticism some local children expressed about programs at the West Oakland Settlement does not seem to have slowed either the group's desire to widen its agenda or expand its physical plant. Between 1898 and 1900, the settlement decided to offer several new classes in housework and cooking and open a salvage bureau. Watt continued to absorb the costs of the complex's incremental expansion: she rented another cottage, a tiny, two-room building on Atlantic Street, which the settlement used for classes in housekeeping and laundry, and she paid for the construction of an adjacent, and much larger, new building on the corner of Atlantic and Campbell Streets.[36] The new structure, an unassuming shedlike building, was founded as a cooking school, and it instigated a debate among members of the West Oakland Settlement and the Oakland Club about the purposes of charity and the best way to respond to technocratic approaches to household organization, then appearing on the national scene, specifically domestic science.[37] The Oakland Club, another women's society, was also active in West Oakland's charities; it co-sponsored the cooking school and there was overlap in the clubs' membership, including Watt.[38]

Seemingly, little debate accompanied the decision to aim the new programs at mothers, young women, and girls. The gendered direction of the classes did not indicate a loss of interest in boys and men; rather the focus expressed the settlement's concern with working women and what reformers euphemistically called "the servant problem."[39] The fact that industrial employment had started to reduce the ranks of servants by the turn of the century distressed middle- and upper-class women—who, of course, relied on them to take care of their homes. "The girls of the neighborhood are not 'in service,'" Eva Carlin complained. They "all seem to have a feeling of self-satisfaction at escaping from the monotonous drudgery of the home."[40] The situation troubled Oakland's charity workers, who, like other socially concerned American women, worried about the effects of long working hours and child labor on family life, health, and the often criticized "moral laxity" in working-class neighborhoods.[41]

The West Oakland Settlement responded to the multiple demands on working mothers' time—and their daughters' lack of interest in domestic service—by proposing to alleviate the drudgery of housework. The organization adopted a multifaceted educational program, modeled on curricula developed in specialized kindergartens and other kinds of educational institutions. In 1898 or 1899, the settlement placed in the small cottage on Atlantic Street one well-known program of instruction for young girls, developed by Emily Huntington in New York City during the 1870s. Called the kitchen-garden method, instructors used children's songs, games, and plays to attract girls, as young as five, to domestic service and teach them housekeeping skills.[42] In seeking to convince the children (and their mothers) of the value of the educational proposal, the West Oakland Settlement tried to reconcile older understandings of charity and domesticity, which emphasized the links between material and moral culture, with newer approaches to philanthropy and domestic reform, which stressed the importance of professionalism and science. Inside the tiny house, renovated interiors introduced the future servants, called "Little Housekeepers," to the design and care of middle- and upper-class dwellings. One room in the cottage was "charmingly fitted up" to teach housekeeping. The "green and white" color scheme appeared "in the curtains, cushions, and dishes"; the wallpaper's "design of medallions" illustrated the "various phases of child's life."[43] The other room was turned into an educational laundry, complete with modern appliances including a new washing machine.

In arranging the cottage for the "Little Housekeepers," the West Oakland Settlement adopted a relatively cautious attitude toward new household technologies, endorsing the labor-saving potential of the appliances, all the while embedding the machines in a cultivated and artistic setting evocative of older domestic buildings. When the new cooking school opened later in 1899, the settlement and its co-sponsor, the Oakland Club, embraced an altogether different aesthetic strategy which more directly endorsed the new inventions. In contrast to the renovated cottage next door, the brand-new school showed the value of professionally run, purpose-built institutional settings and also promoted domestic science, a new approach to cooking. Inspired by the growing interest in applying industrial efficiency, business management practices, and scientific practices in the home, the technocratic approach to cooking (and other forms of housework) started to sweep through American reform movements at the beginning of the century and shape the curriculum and affiliated instructional spaces in settlements, public schools, and other sorts of institutions. In West Oakland, Watt hired a professional teacher to run the cooking school's austere model kitchen. Fitted out with new stoves and other modern appliances, the space looked more like a laboratory than a kitchen in an older home.[44]

The two sponsoring organizations anticipated that the cooking school would increase the appeal of domestic service among young working women by defusing the differences between household work and factory labor. An education, based on the scientific method, would turn students into skilled workers who followed predictable routines in their workplaces and, hence, enjoyed the better salaries and higher social status of factory employees, or so the Oakland Club argued in *Domestic Science Monthly,* that group's new journal.[45] But, in fact, live-in servants usually earned as much as their counterparts employed in factories, laundries, and canneries, and the educational program in the Oakland school did not address other common complaints about domestic service—grueling work, long hours, condescending employers, and demands for sexual favors. Indeed, in Oakland, as in training schools in other American cities, the domestic focus of the curriculum further emphasized already obvious class distinctions. The women who organized classes in cooking, cleaning, laundry, and other household skills for West Oakland's working women and children urged them to remain in the domestic sphere, working either as mothers or as servants, at the same time as the elite patrons left their own homes to run charitable institutions and educational establishments.[46]

Fig. 13.9. A practice class in the Oakland cooking school, c. 1900. From *Domestic Science Monthly* 1 (Apr. 1900): 2.

Apparently, soon after the cooking school opened, the two sponsoring organizations began to quarrel about their philanthropy's larger purposes. Watt and other members of the settlement, it seems, wanted the educational effort to be largely a charitable one, directed at local residents. The Oakland Club expected that teaching cooking "in the most practical and scientific way" would benefit "all classes" and help "all girls" prepare for "what will be the life work of the great majority of them, the making and keeping of a home." While the club invited all women "of whatever age and station" to attend cooking classes, the expectation that elite women would actually come to school in a working-class neighborhood defied standard practice. In addition, as much as the Oakland Club intended to make instruction in domestic science accessible to all of the city's female workforce, the school's cofounder insisted the educational facility be self-sustaining, not a charity. The group wanted to charge for classes, expecting employers would pay for servants to attend. In the eyes of this club's directors, the city was "overburdened" with charities and did not need any more of them, although the elite women's group promised to offer scholarships and one or two free classes—should an adequate endowment be formed to pay for them.[47]

Watt's decision to augment the educational effort with a salvage bureau must have fueled the antagonisms developing between the two groups. Opened once weekly during the mothers' meeting in the Peralta Street building, the salvage bureau offered, at nominal prices, secondhand and cast-off items, collected from the settlement's supporters and other Oakland residents. Watt ran the weekly meetings herself "to come into closer personal relations with the limited and toilsome lives of the mothers." With babies and young children in tow, women came for a free cup of tea and to purchase shoes, clothes, kitchen equipment, carpets, and bedding.[48] The settlement used the proceeds to offset operating costs, and the sales procedure emphasized to clientele the need to adopt thrifty practices and personal restraint. "Every article," Carlin insisted, "is neatly wrapped up and tied, so that the transactions assume the dignity of store purchases."[49] The decision to meet pressing community needs by selling recycled consumer products inside a modestly redesigned house also helped donors grasp the apparent ease with which meaningful and economical improvements could be achieved in the neighborhood. "Who," one appeal queried, "would not be willing to aid in this beautiful alchemy—the turning of waste material into schools, libraries, gardens, baths, clubs and other helpful agencies? May we send you a bag [to collect old clothes and other items]?"[50]

The Oakland Club apparently had little interest in the old-fashioned approach to charity, and the different sensibilities of the two groups soon exploded into polite but forthright conflict. Tensions were evident in April 1900 when the Oakland Club insisted in the first issue of *Domestic Science Monthly* that the school was the club's own project, distinct from the settlement's work (although the club admitted that the educational endeavor was linked historically with the West Oakland Free Kindergarten). "It is the [club's] ultimate intention," emphasized the lead article in the new journal, "to have a 'Home' established up town, as soon as public interest is sufficiently aroused to admit of the increased expenditure of money."[51] By November, the Oakland Club had gathered enough money to put the cooking school on an independent footing—at least free of Watt's financial support. Phoebe Hearst, among others, had made a donation to the club and the new magazine was selling well, making enough profit to support the school. Proudly declaring the cooking school had "lost its characteristic" as Watt's "individual enterprise," the Oakland Club moved the model kitchen to a more prestigious location, near the society's "uptown" meeting place.[52]

Early the next month Watt and a few good friends signed the New Century Club's incorporation papers, and just after the new year they issued the association's first *Annual Greeting*.[53] The statement of purpose endorsed domestic science but included no overt reference to the Oakland Club or the cooking school: the two groups had irrevocably parted ways. Although there were elements of personal disagreements and a battle over turf in the dispute—the Oakland Club operated a vacation school at a nearby public school—the different practices the clubs endorsed and the different imagery they used to represent themselves gives some indication that their dispute had more profound ideological dimensions.

The New Century Club shared with the Oakland Club an interest in making working people "self-supporting and useful members of society."[54] Watt also recognized the value of institutional affiliations and had interest in domestic science and the efficiency movement. But Watt and her friends took exception to the Oakland Club's more distanced approach to philanthropy and, perhaps, its alliance with the city's Associated Charities, an umbrella organization modeled on groups in other American cities. In the November issue of *Domestic Science Monthly,* the issue in which the Oakland Club announced the move uptown, the group also published its decision to work with the larger organization. "Relations" between the club's philanthropic department and the Associated Charities, the statement stressed, stood as "a fair example of the impersonal character of the highest philanthropic work."[55]

Watt had little faith in dispensing charity impersonally or at any distance from people in need of help. In her view, effective charities needed to be placed within working peoples' communities, located in homelike settings, and run by women who personally demonstrated correct practices to the poor. "We, of this Club," she insisted in the mission statement, "believe that teaching by precept or proverb is not sufficient, there must be illustration—the power of example."[56] The New Century Club also prided itself on running a multiethnic and integrated establishment in a city where economic and cultural antagonisms often shaped relations between social groups. The Oakland Club, too, came down squarely on the side of civil rights, but the Associated Charities supported segregated institutions, and Watt did not approve of that approach.[57]

Transforming the Clubhouse: "My, How Alive and Progressive You Are!"

The quiet, clean, and decisive break between the two groups—women of similar social standing who frequently lived in the same Oakland neighborhoods and shared many ideals and practices—provided an incentive to expand the former settlement's programs and make the West Oakland setting into a more compelling physical representation of the new club's objectives. So too did a self-conscious interest in linking the new group with Progressive Era political causes and the burgeoning women's club movement in California. Other women's groups in Oakland became more active in urban affairs and constructed more elaborate institutional settings during the first decade of the twentieth century, a time of rapid urban growth and economic expansion in northern California. In this period the New Century Club asserted—and tried to represent properly—its position within the expanding network of the state's women's organizations.[58] The club, with Watt as president and chair of the House and Home Committee, took on an ambitious building program between 1901 and 1911, first transforming the cooking school into a free library, then further altering the interior and exterior of the initial building, and finally constructing a new gymnasium on the former sites of the Little Housekeepers' Cottage and the cooking school/library.

The members of the New Century Club declined to meet at an uptown location or endorse outright the virtues of professionalization, in contrast to the Oakland Club and other local women's groups. Watt certainly could have afforded to offset the cost of a relocation, but the group selected a familiar structure for a clubhouse, the building at the corner of Peralta and Atlantic (which Watt had rented for the settlement five years earlier). Economic considerations likely influenced the decision to continue to invest in the West Oakland property, as did issues of representation and ideology, especially the desire to make clear the activist position of the new group.[59] "The Oakland New Century Club has no attractive social features to offer its members, neither does it at its monthly meetings tax their time with long papers," Watt wrote in the *Second Annual Greeting,* calling into question the practices of other women's clubs in Oakland. Instead, "it invites them to come in and help in doing good to others, by developing and making most effective: Cooking Classes for young women, Sewing Schools for beginners, and Garment Makers, Boys' Clubs, Mothers' Meetings, and Working Girls' Clubs. It is work worth doing and absorbingly interesting."[60] Although the club hired some professional instructors, members continued to volunteer and directed most of the classes and programs. Women (and men) often endorsed professionalism at the turn of the century—as Abigail Van Slyck has shown, almost always at the eventual expense of the autonomy of volunteers. The New Century Club, like the settlement before, took a very cautious approach to the process, seeking to locate trained professionals within a domesticated institutional setting run for the most part by female volunteers.[61]

The similarities in management practices, site, and program established important continuities between the New Century Club and the West Oakland Settlement which were matched by the use of familiar physical tools to upgrade the institution's landscape. The group set out first to redress the problems caused by the removal of the Oakland Club's School of Domestic Science. The West Oakland group started an independent cooking class, which was placed on the second floor of the clubhouse, and opened a free library in the building on the corner of Atlantic and Campbell (the location of the former cooking school). The reading room also doubled as a space for the mothers' meeting and sewing classes, and large celebrations were held in it, including annual Christmas parties.

In a move that must have been intended as a stinging rebuke to the Oakland Club, the design of the newest program spaces tempered the earlier outspoken endorsement of impersonal professionalism, so evident in the rationalized design of the first cooking school. Modern kitchen equipment, including gas stoves and ranges, was placed within the new model kitchen, a highly decorated room reminiscent of the Little Housekeepers' Cottage. But, scientific practices continued to influence the curriculum even though the aesthetic sensibilities expressed in the renovated space evoked artistic and domestic associations similar to the older rooms in the complex. Again, a teacher professionally trained in domestic science ran the classes, which were seen in this setting also to serve the purposes of Americanization, increasingly a matter of public concern in Oakland. Watt insisted the club's pioneering work in cooking instruction established the curricular standards later adopted by public schools—where efforts to Americanize immigrants continued well into the 1920s.[62]

The appearance of the new library made no allusion to the laboratory aesthetic that informed the design of the first cooking school, the former occupant of the reading room's space. Here, too, the new interior design incorporated decorative sensibilities used elsewhere in the complex, but with important modifications in the spatial ideology. The reading room contained examples of early American furniture and secondhand decorative objects, further indications of a continued preoccupation with Americanization and the "evils" of pauperization. Yet, the library also included linoleum floors, natural finishes, and clinker brick—simpler and more cautiously modern materials than had been used previously in the establishment. "A klinker-brick [sic] fire-place was built . . . and box seats extending all around the room were finally made satisfactory as well as attractive. The interior of the building was painted throughout a soft green shade. The box-seats were left a natural redwood finish. Linoleum of a cheerful design was then laid down upon floors . . . pictures were hung . . . plate racks fastened up, and a perfect treasure of an old clock . . . found in a second-hand store . . . set in place on the klinker fire-place."[63] Ongoing stylistic shifts in American design likely influenced the emphasis on craft in the reading room, the understated modernity of the space, and the simplifications in the room's decorative program.[64] Probably, the stylistic shift was also intended to neutralize the affiliation of the library with any gender or generation. Although one of the club's female members directed the reading room, the club expected, or at least wanted, both men and women and boys and girls to use the new facility.[65]

The New Century Club never explained why it decided to open a free library in West Oakland when the city had rented space in nearby halls for reading rooms since the 1870s. But, concerns about the public facility's location, the ever-present need for more space, and tensions about the planning process of Oakland's first Carnegie Library may have affected the club's decision. Just prior to the opening of the private reading room, the Ebell Society, another women's group, had successfully directed a drive to purchase a substantial site for the library's new main branch but had been abruptly disfranchised from participating further in the building process, with gender cited as the reason by the library's board.[66] Also, at about the same time, the city decided to move the local library into Alcatraz Hall, a new Masonic lodge, located on Peralta Street, only a few blocks north of the club's facility. The proximity of the new site to saloons, which often occupied the ground floor of West Oakland's lodges and public halls, probably added to the New Century Club's resolve, as did a desire to make the group's establishment more appealing to a broader spectrum of the West Oakland community.

Since the settlement's inception, Watt and other sponsors had calculated that the appearance of the establishment would help cross class, gender, and generational divisions, in addition to overriding ethnic and racial ones. The group expected that the cultivated setting would act as a magnet, drawing first women and young children, then teenagers, and young adults and men following close behind. Although the institution-building strategy did not work as fully intended, mothers and children do seem to have responded to the settlement's and the club's

Fig. 13.10. The Free Library, 1902. From Oakland New Century Club, *Annual Greeting*, 1912, 28.

programs, if not the spatial ideologies. Both Eva Carlin's articles and the club's publications suggest, however, that young adults and working men had little interest in the group's campaign to convince them of the value of art and culture—and coffee and tea—and exhibited some discomfort with the building's aestheticized qualities. The overtly female character of the club, and, as at Hull House, the feminized and domestic cast of much of the interior space may have added to the lack of interest, in addition to the club's support of temperance. Thus the neutral cast of the library's decoration may have been a deliberate attempt to overcome male antipathy, anticipating the approach taken a few years later in the gymnasium.[67]

Still, even as the club made the gesture in the library toward overcoming social divisions, the group proceeded to establish in the former house on Peralta Street larger and fitting meeting places for members—virtually all of whom were middle- and upper-class women who lived outside of the neighborhood. By 1902, the club had claimed about half of the space in the main building. Membership had also grown from the core of six women (who initially ran the settlement) to more than thirty people. Indeed, in spite of Watt's insistence that the New Century Club "had no attractive social features to offer its members," the group used three rooms in the building—one for monthly luncheons, another for committee meetings, and a third served as simply the club's "room." The renovation strategy made no concession to gender neutrality, in contrast to the experiment in the library. Rather in the dining and meeting rooms the group returned to the artistic, feminized approach, formerly used in the settlement, although more elaborate fittings and furnishings decorated the club's new spaces. The third room, formerly the Working Girls' Lounge, had already been remodeled and needed no further alteration to suit the taste of the new occupants. A caretaker also moved into the Peralta Street building. She lived in two rear rooms on the upper story, near the model kitchen.[68]

The renovation of the clubhouse and accompanying shifts in use did not, by any means, remove working people from the main building; such a move would have contradicted the club's class-bridging intentions. Yet, in the United States, the designs of different kinds of charitable and reform organizations, including settlements, often reinforced social differences with spatial distinctions, making palpable the economic gulf that usually existed between sponsors and clientele. Such a strategy had informed in a modest way the interior organization of the West Oakland Settlement. The New Century Club resuscitated this approach, applying it in a more emphatic manner. The relative isolation of the cooking classes and the caretaker's apartment from the club's new rooms gave tangible presence to power relations inside the institution at the same time as the richer decoration of the club rooms, the leisurely uses of the spaces, and their distribution in the building (toward the angled corner on Peralta and Atlantic Streets), marked a portion of the former house as the club's own domain.

The architectural moves added social significance to the two-story corner structure, but they did not endow the rented building with enough material distinction to suit the club's ambitions. Finally, the group needed to confront the question of property ownership, as the club sought to exteriorize its heretofore largely internal representational strategy.[69] Thus when the interior renovation of the clubhouse was complete, the House and Home Committee turned to even larger tasks: raising funds to buy all of the rented properties and making plans for a new gymnasium and playground. "Our chief ambition for the coming year is the purchase of the lot on which our commodious building is located," Anna Sangster, the club's recording secretary, wrote in 1902. "The owner is willing to sell at a reasonable figure, and it is of the greatest importance that we should own the property. We are not what would be termed a rich corporation, so it will be necessary to appeal to our friends for aid."[70] Sangster's oblique reference to "friends" was likely meant to inspire further generosity on the part of the club's president, although Watt did not immediately dispense all of the needed financial assistance (and all of the properties were not for sale). It seems, however, that some funds were forthcoming, probably given by Watt and her acquaintances, because within the year, the group bought the Little Housekeepers' Cottage and the plot on which the cooking school/library had been constructed. The group waited, however, until 1905 to purchase the clubhouse site and then held off, for the moment, further alterations.[71]

In her memoir, Watt does not offer any explanation of the delay, directing her attention instead to far more momentous events which took place between 1906 and 1907—her move to San Francisco, a week before the great 1906 earthquake and fire, the subsequent devastation of the city and her new home, and her husband's death, several months later. While Watt recuperated from her loss, the Ebell Society built in downtown Oakland a "magnificent" new clubhouse, "one of the handsomest structures in the city," according to the *Oakland Tribune*.[72] The rival club's construction project and the overall frenetic pace of rebuilding in the San Francisco Bay Area likely contributed to the New Century Club's resolve to improve its meeting place. By 1907 the former cottage on Peralta Street had been transformed into a seemingly new building and a long one-story shed constructed along the western edge of the lot. The outside of the older building was totally remodeled: the exterior stairs were removed; new shingles sheathed both street facades; new windows and a roof were installed; and a new fireplace, exterior chimney, and upper-story porch were added on. Even the oddly bent corner on the front of the building was fully integrated into the new massing; and Watt also donated a new flagpole and American flag, prominently displayed above a new canopy and the graciously recessed new front door.[73] The service entry remained, appropriately located in the portion of the building set back from Peralta Street.

The freshly shingled exterior of the New Century Club's meeting place shared significant representational features with the Ebell Society's new building and other purpose-built charities in San Francisco. In West Oakland, the display of the American flag, the club's new sign, the emphasized main entry on the front facade, and other expressive elements intensified the civic status of the renovated dwelling and suggested that the quasi-domestic, cautiously modern, Arts and Crafts setting was a didactic institution, as well as the private outpost of a group of wealthy and enlightened California women. In fact, the additive method of building the West Oakland establishment heightened the assimilationist messages, affiliated with arts and crafts ideology. Inside, the clubhouse retained most of the spatial character from earlier alterations. Presenting a facade that now matched the spirit of the interior design, the clubhouse gave little hint of the institution's modest origins in working-class housing. Users of the complex in later generations would believe it to have been constructed at one time and as a purpose-built establishment, albeit one with a domestic cast.[74]

Completing the Complex with a Gymnasium and a Playground

The addition of architectural distinction to the clubhouse enhanced the institution's presence in the West Oakland neighborhood and created a setting fully appropriate for the club's meetings. The landscape represented, inside and out, the complications of intention and ambiguities of motivation in the sponsoring organization. But, however splendid the appearance of the main building, the complex lacked architectural cohesion and other desired civic elements, among them a gymnasium and a playground.[75] Nevertheless, the women's club put off further expansion, although the group was still interested in adding programs for male children in the West Oakland community. By 1909, the attic in the clubhouse contained rooms and equipment for new classes in woodworking and gymnastics, two elements that Eva Carlin had urged the group to adopt for boys a decade earlier.[76] These spaces must have proved to be inadequate because, soon after, the club revived the gymnasium project, thus beginning the final phase of the institution's incremental physical expansion.

Once again, a constellation of factors—personal motivations, responses to reform ideologies, ongoing changes in the civic arena, and perhaps even continued interclub competition—contributed to the decision to expand the New Century Club's public face. Watt returned from a lengthy European trip at about the same time as Oakland's mayor established the city's first Playground Commission (in 1909), with the intention of launching an ambitious playground construction project and garnering support for the allocation of public funds to the recreation program. Three members of the Oakland Club sat on the commission: the women's group had been an important early player in the movement for organized play in Oakland.[77] In the early twentieth century, private groups often pressed city officials to develop facilities for organized children's play, asserting that supervised, orderly games on dedicated sites developed moral fortitude; produced healthier, more uniform youthful bodies; aided Americanization; assimilated future workers to industrial routines; and helped avoid delinquency. In fact, the New Century Club tried, unsuccessfully, to purchase a block near the clubhouse for a playground and also urged the city to do the same. The group probably timed the gymnasium's construction project to add clout to that request and to situate the club more firmly in the rapidly emerging new arena for Oakland reformers—organized urban recreation.[78]

Thus in 1910 the organization moved ahead with plans to build the new edifice, having gained control of requisite sites, secured a loan for just over three thousand dollars, and hired a promi-

Fig. 13.11. Temporary Gymnasium at the New Century Club, c. 1910. From Oakland New Century Club, *Annual Greeting*, 1910, 20. Courtesy of the California History Room, California State Library, Sacramento, California.

nent local builder.[79] For unexplained reasons, the group decided to demolish the Little Housekeepers' Cottage and the library/former cooking school and build the gymnasium on the club's Atlantic Street properties. The strategy required the purchase of only one additional site, a small dwelling, on Campbell Street (directly behind the club's meeting place); allowed the new facility to be directly connected to the clubhouse; and resulted in the transformation of the entire complex into an impressive, uniform civic setting, architecturally coordinated with the exterior of the club's meeting place. The new "big shingled building," according to a report in a local newspaper, was "fitted with everything dear to the heart of a boy—acting bars, dumb bells," and even "hot and cold shower baths." A smaller new structure, attached to the gym's western end, contained rooms for girls' classes and club meetings.[80]

After the purpose-built structure opened in early 1911, the club pointed to the success of its achievement in the next year's *Annual Greeting*. While both boys and girls would use the new structure, the recording secretary's report stressed the gymnasium's importance in the moral, physical, and social education of young men, the people who had taken little interest in the club's earlier, more decorous approach to urban recreation. "And this year we find the new bed planted last year growing, in a bed not of frail blossoms, but sturdy oaks, growing upward, their branches spreading in many directions. One cannot help but feel when they realize the change a year of proper direction and training has made in these boys, that were being blown and tossed by every wave that came . . . We look with pride at the new gymnasium, which means so much to the boys."[81] Familiar themes reverberated in the sentimental praise of the modern facility—importantly, in this case, the association of physical culture with moralism, environmental determinism, and manly discipline. Similar ideas were often discussed in contemporary literature and influenced the practices Progressive Era reformers used in other recreational complexes. But, in emphasizing the generational and gendered appeal of the West Oakland gym, the New Century Club also reiterated its earlier, often stated desire to run an inclusive establishment, one with programs of interest to all members of the West Oakland community. Indeed, to some degree, the club's commitment to an inclusive mandate can be measured by the fact that the group was willing, for the first time, to incur debt for a construction project. Clearly, the loan troubled some members; in 1910 the club continued to run the salvage bureau and preach the virtues of thrift to the West Oakland community. "What if it [the gym] is not all paid for?" the recording secretary queried, after praising the new building. "We have faith, we have trust, and are not afraid to work so that in due time it will all be ours." Watt paid off the loan.[82]

Some curricular shifts followed the physical changes: the group became interested in "folk culture," and recreation programs began to take center stage in the club's facility, as occurred in most American settlements during the early twentieth century. Yet many older programs—sewing classes, the mothers' meeting, the Salvage Bureau, and the Boys' Club—remained part of the institution even after the club donated the entire complex to the city's new Department of Recreation in 1923. The private group, which reserved a right to meet in the now public building, had finally convinced the department to open a playground in front of the complex and expected the city to turn the clubhouse into a community center and field house for the public play area. Occupying a full urban block, the city equipped the new playground with "all of the latest play apparatus," including a baseball diamond and sandboxes. Two years later, the Board of Education opened a new school nearby that shared the recreational facilities.[83]

The construction of the large playground completed the setting envisioned by Watt and her friends. With seemingly little change in the physical components, the formerly private institution worked well as a public community center until the complex was demolished in the late 1960s to make way for a large mail sorting facility.[84] As a prescient, if ultimately ineffective, action, the club had stipulated in the 1923 deed that the property would revert to the original owners should any change of use occur. But even if civic authorities had wanted to honor the restrictions of the deed, the club had long since disbanded. The New Century Club Recreation Center was bulldozed, and the site was buried under an asphalt parking lot.[85]

Ideology, Identity, and Reform at the Oakland New Century Club

None of the buildings or open spaces associated with the New Century Club still stand in West Oakland; all are casualties of urban renewal programs. Still, the history of this ordinary urban institution substantiates the arguments made by scholars, largely from outside architectural history, that a crucial transfer and exchange of ideologies and practices took place in the United States at the century's turn. In regard to the development of the welfare state, a diverse group of thinkers has examined the intellectual exchanges that helped shape the purposes of modern American philanthropic institutions. Without doubt, as these scholars have argued and the West Oakland case study confirms, middle- and upper-class women took an active role in forging the character and the practices inside those institutions.[86] The intersecting histories of the West Oakland Settlement, the New Century Club, and the New Century Club Recreation Center also point to the *physical* overlaps that connected the privately built charitable settings, developed by women, with the more abstract and rationalized public landscapes of the welfare state. The current focus of scholarly literature on social, not material, issues leaves little analyzed of the significance of the physical settings that women established in the nineteenth century, either in terms of ideologies presented, affiliations with everyday building practices, representations of power relations, and links with changes in the larger urban landscape.

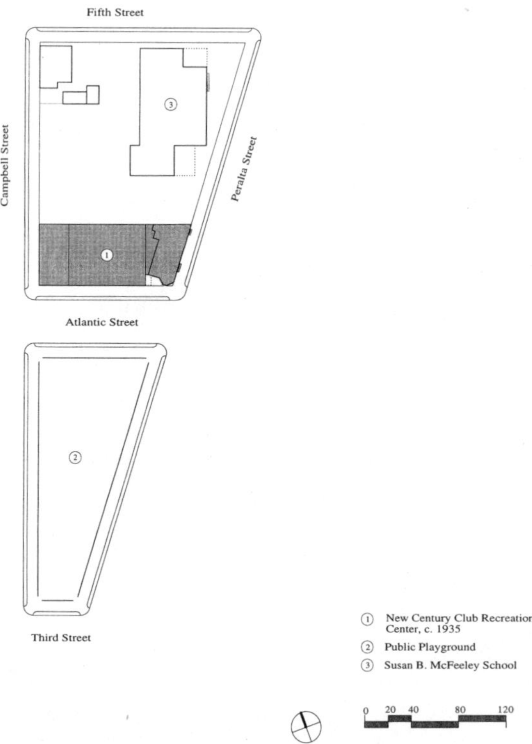

Fig. 13.12. Site Plan, New Century Club Recreation Center, 1935. Drawn by A. Eugene Sparling.

Many reform-minded women infused philanthropic settings with ideological intent because their aspirations were deeply rooted in the moralistic environmental determinism, long a factor in the Anglo-American charitable tradition.[87] In the nineteenth century, philanthropists often elected to erect purpose-built institutions, asserting that social problems demanded the construction of substantial, often physically isolated complexes. But, middle- and upper-class women also opened charitable institutions in less formidable settings—inserting them in ordinary urban buildings, sited in everyday working-class neighborhoods. In West Oakland, the sponsors' reasons for site selection were symbolic and practical; and the female institution builders adopted common patterns of urban construction in altering the setting incrementally, using interior renovations, architectural alterations, and additions to standing buildings.

The expectation that rectified personal virtue and a more orderly urban landscape would assure the community's well-being fueled the New Century Club's incremental building campaign. Yet the ambitious architectural program endowed West Oakland with an ambiguous setting. Often an interest in amelioration and a proclivity toward caution shaped the political aspirations of activists in the women's club movement in the United States, and the sponsors of the second-tier charitable establishments were usually more conservative than their more well-known counterparts in larger American cities.[88] Thus, it is not surprising that in West Oakland, California's club women failed to press for the kinds of political, economic, and social transformations that were necessary for broader, more substantive changes in working people's lives. Although other women pressed for those kinds of reforms at the turn of the century, the uses and designs of rooms and buildings in the West Oakland complex projected, quite clearly, the aspirations and also the limitations of the sponsors' reform intentions.

The club opened the charitable establishment to a diverse clientele, expecting to re-create inside the institution a microcosm of the neighborhood's social fabric. Notwithstanding the laudable qualities of the proposition, a geographic limit instantly bounded the experiment in inclusion, and the institution's patrons tolerated social difference only to a degree. The West Oakland establishment ended up sustaining traditional class relations and conventional gender roles—in some degree for club members and in large measure for the group's racially and ethnically diverse clientele. The club extended the inclusive dictate only to the West Oakland context and did not, for example, expect to apply the mandate in the members' own houses or residential neighborhoods. And, as much as the patrons voiced an interest in running a heterogeneous establishment, they wanted their clientele to assimilate elite practices and norms, as occurred in many other Progressive Era institutions. In the clubhouse, where an artful new facade wrapped a renovated residential core, room uses, locations, and decoration expressed existing social divisions, power relations, and the belief that the domestic realm constituted the appropriate milieu for working women, no matter how much the sponsors' own activism belied such conclusions. In the cooking school, a progressive veneer of science, rationality, and professionalism overlaid another expression of the cult of domesticity. And, the orderly routines of the recreational programs in the new gymnasium, largely directed at a male clientele, asserted that the growth of manly virtue would help form a cohesive, healthy, and obedient workforce, suitable for employment in Oakland's industries.

Clearly, the West Oakland reformers did not instantaneously fabricate domesticated and Americanized subjects, despite the reformers' great faith in the didactic power of their charitable establishment. Cultural authorities "always aim at installing an order," as Roger Chartier, the historian, has commented; yet invariably order is "multifaceted" and never as "all-powerful" as authorities anticipate.[89] While it is very difficult to document the response of working people to either the spaces or the programs of the New Century Club, the group's annual reports, oral histories, and newspaper articles hint at a complex pattern of acceptance and rejection, suggesting that women and children appreciated the facility and used programs selectively, on an as-need basis and without absorbing all of the prescriptive messages. Indeed, oral histories especially emphasize the fact that this and other charities addressed very real needs in the working-class community—offering after-school programs, space for recreation, even a bath, some clothing, a cup of tea, or a glass of milk.[90] The more casual exterior photographs of children and women involved with the New Century Club also imply that humanitarian impulses and

Fig. 13.13. Women distributing milk, near the New Century Club, c. 1912. Courtesy of the Oakland History Room, Oakland Public Library.

practical exigencies may have tempered authoritarian tendencies and moralistic intentions—just as the incremental building program met multiple needs, purposes, and ideals.

Certainly, the current condition of the neighborhood brings into sharp relief the earlier achievements of female reformers, especially their ability to navigate the worlds of social difference and produce built results. The relations between a setting and larger worlds are not fixed at the time of construction, and the New Century Club established a credible public setting and physical framework for later municipal interventions, so long as they remained at a finer-grain scale. West Oakland became a majority African American community in the 1930s and 1940s, and, as might be expected, significant local protest and repeated court challenges greeted the federal government's decision to build the enormous mail sorting facility in the neighborhood. The post office was just one of the many large-scale postwar urban renewal projects that radically transformed the physical fabric of West Oakland; it, alone, required clearing twelve urban blocks of houses, stores, small factories, and a public school, in addition to the New Century Club Recreation Center and playground. In the course of the legal battles, led by African American homeowners, many of them women, civic authorities agreed to replace quickly the aging public building with a new and modern facility.[91]

Thirty years later, the center remains unbuilt. In a startling evocation of past practices, journalists from local newspapers have returned to West Oakland, writing investigative reports about the Oakland Point area, by and large a poor African American and Hispanic working-class neighborhood.[92] As Eva Carlin's essays did nearly a century ago, the contemporary articles document, among other issues, the deleterious effects of social and environmental conditions on local children and argue that the community needs more municipal services, including a recreation center. This time, parents and children agree—but no group, public or private, has come to fill the gap.

Notes

This paper is part of my dissertation, "On the Ground in Oakland, Women and Institution Building in an Industrial City." In this essay I expand on arguments made in "Domesticating Institutions: Progressive Women and Environmental Activism in West Oakland," an earlier version of this paper published in *Sites and Sounds: Essays in Celebration of West Oakland,* ed. Suzanne Stewart and Mary Praetzellis (Rohnert Park and Oakland, Calif.: Anthropological Studies Center, Sonoma State Univ., and CALTRANS, District 4, 1997). For comments on this version I am grateful to Dell Upton, Paul Groth, Abigail Van Slyck, the editors, and the 1996–97 fellowship group at the Doreen B. Townsend Center for the Humanities, University of California, Berkeley. Gray Brechin, Betty Marvin, and Aicha Woods graciously made research materials available, and ongoing discussions with Jim Buckley, Elaine Jackson-Retondo, and Bill Littmann have sharpened my critical thinking. Thanks, too, to Sibel Zandi-Sayek for assistance with drawings and to Gene Sparling, who has helped in countless ways to keep my thinking and writing on track.

1. Carlin published two articles, "California's First Vacation School: An Oakland Experiment," *Overland Monthly,* n.s., 35 (May 1900): 425–34, and "A Salvage Bureau," *Overland Monthly,* n.s., 36 (Sept. 1900): 246–55.
2. Carlin, "Salvage Bureau," 256.
3. Ibid., 247.
4. Kathryn Kish Sklar calls the attitude "moral

materialism" in *Florence Kelley and the Nation's Work: The Rise of Women's Political Culture, 1830–1900* (New Haven: Yale Univ. Press, 1995), xii ff.

5. Carlin, "California's First Vacation School," 425.
6. For a good overview of elite women's activities in Oakland, see Joseph T. Baker, ed., *Past and Present of Alameda County, California* (Chicago: S. J. Clarke Publishing Co., 1914), chap. 13. For further discussion of women's involvement in Oakland's temperance, suffrage, and labor movements, see Aicha Woods, "The Women's Domestic Reform Movement in Oakland, 1880–1910," in West Oakland: *"A Place to Start From,"* ed. Mary Praetzellis (Oakland and Rohnert Park, Calif.: Anthropological Studies Center, Sonoma State Univ., and CALTRANS, District 4, 1994), 176–84.
7. The programs of the West Oakland Settlement resembled those found in many other "second tier" social service establishments. See Ruth Hutchinson Crocker, *Social Work and Social Order: The Settlement Movement in Two Industrial Cities, 1889–1930* (Urbana: Univ. of Illinois Press, 1992), 28–34, 75–78, 118–22.
8. The exceptions include studies of settlements, almost always of Hull House. See Helen Lefkowitz Horowitz's "Hull-House as Women's Space," *Chicago History* 12 (winter 1983–84): 40–55; Guy Szuberla's "Three Chicago Settlements: Their Architectural Form and Social Meaning," *Journal of the Illinois State Historical Society* 70 (May 1977): 114–29; Dolores Hayden, *The Grand Domestic Revolution: A History of Feminist Designs for American Homes, Neighborhoods, and Cities* (Cambridge, Mass.: MIT Press, 1981), 162–70, and Sklar, *Florence Kelley and the Nation's Work*, chap. 8. Other useful works include Abigail A. Van Slyck's *Free to All: Carnegie Libraries and American Culture, 1890–1920* (Chicago: Univ. of Chicago Press, 1995) and Deborah E. B. Weiner, *Architecture and Social Reform in Late-Victorian London* (Manchester and New York: Manchester Univ. Press and St. Martin's Press, 1994).
9. For examples, see David Ward and Olivier Zunz, eds., *The Landscape of Modernity: Essays on New York City, 1900–1940* (New York: Russell Sage Foundation, 1992); Robin Einhorn, *Property Rules: Political Economy in Chicago, 1833–1872* (Chicago: Univ. of Chicago Press, 1991); and Daniel Bluestone, *Constructing Chicago* (New Haven: Yale Univ. Press, 1991). Gwendolyn Wright touches on similar themes in *Moralism and the Model Home: Domestic Architecture and Cultural Conflict in Chicago, 1873–1913* (Chicago: Univ. of Chicago Press, 1980).
10. For discussion of patterns of continuity and change in West Oakland's housing, see Paul Groth and Marta Gutman, "Workers' Houses in West Oakland," in *Sites and Sounds: Essays in Celebration of West Oakland,* ed. Suzanne Stewart and Mary Praetzellis (Oakland and Rohnert Park, Calif.: Anthropological Studies Center, Sonoma State Univ., and CALTRANS, District 4, 1997).
11. Carlin, "Salvage Bureau," 428.
12. "West Oakland Kindergarten: A Little of Its History and Also Its Coming Benefit," *Oakland Enquirer,* Apr. 13, 1891.
13. Carlin, "Salvage Bureau," 148. There is no record of the free kindergarten's initial building having been used as a saloon, except in the later recollection of reformers. For an excellent analysis of the antipathy of the middle and upper classes for saloons, see Roy Rosenzweig, *Eight Hours for What We Will: Workers and Leisure in an Industrial City, 1870–1920* (New York: Cambridge Univ. Press, 1983), chap. 4.
14. "The Mission of the New-Century Club," in *Oakland New-Century Club, A New Century*

Greeting (Oakland: Oakland New-Century Club, 1901), unpaginated.

15. Watt tracks her interests in charity, women's clubs, and reform in her memoir, "My Long Life," MS, 1925, on file in The Bancroft Library, Univ. of California, Berkeley.
16. See Blair's *The Clubwoman as Feminist: True Womanhood Redefined, 1868–1914* (New York: Holmes and Meier Publishers, 1980). Watt's political prudence resembles attitudes taken by elite male reformers, the latter discussed in George E. Mowry, *The California Progressives* (Berkeley: Univ. of California Press, 1951) and *California Progressivism Revisited,* ed. William Deverell and Thomas Sitton (Berkeley: Univ. of California Press, 1994).
17. In *Social Work and Social Order,* Crocker argues that second-tier social service institutions often adopted less formal organizational strategies than better-known charities.
18. Carlin hoped, naively, that the West Oakland Settlement would prove "a barrier to the establishment of any more saloons in the neighborhood." See "Salvage Bureau," 257.
19. "Good Work of a Quiet Social Settlement in Oakland," *San Francisco Call*, May 18, 1900. Just before the group moved in, the cottage had been raised to two stories and an addition extended into the side yard.
20. Allen B. Pond, "The 'Settlement House' III," *Brickbuilder* 11 (Sept. 1902): 183, 184.
21. See Horowitz, "Hull-House as Women's Space," 42–52; and Szuberla, "Three Chicago Settlements," 118–26.
22. The first two annual greetings of the New Century Club emphasize, repeatedly, the group's desire to express middle-class domestic ideals in the institution's interior spaces, an interest typical of many settlements, as Wright points out in *Moralism and the Model Home,* 115. Hull House, of course, contained separate settings for residents and clientele, although paths crossed inside the establishment, much to the annoyance of some visitors, including Beatrice Webb. See Horowitz, "Hull-House as Women's Space," 51, 52.
23. Horowitz, "Hull-House as Women's Space," 40, 47, and Eileen Boris, *Art and Labor: Ruskin, Morris, and the Craftsman Ideal in America* (Philadelphia: Temple Univ. Press, 1986), 62.
24. T. Jackson Lears, *No Place of Grace: Antimodernism and the Transformation of American Culture, 1880–1920* (Chicago: Univ. of Chicago Press, 1981), 91; also Boris, *Art and Labor*, 61–62, 77–78, and Wright, *Moralism and the Model Home*, 128.
25. William B. Rhoads, "The Colonial Revival and the Americanization of Immigrants," in The Colonial Revival in America, ed. Alan Axelrod (New York: W. W. Norton, 1985), 344–47.
26. Elizabeth Watt, "Report," in Oakland New Century Club's *Second Annual Greeting of the Oakland New Century Club* (Oakland: Press of the *Oakland Enquirer*, 1902), 8. For discussion of racial prejudice in the settlement movement, see Crocker, *Social Work and Social Order, and Elizabeth Lasch-Quinn, Black Neighbors: Race and the Limits of Reform in the American Settlement House Movement, 1890–1945* (Chapel Hill: Univ. of North Carolina Press, 1993).
27. Carlin describes the different social groups who lived in West Oakland and presumably attended the settlement in "Vacation School," 425–26. She does not mention Chinese or Japanese Americans.
28. I indebted to Abigail Van Slyck for suggestions about my analysis of the settlement's clubs for boys and girls. For an excellent discussion of working girls' clubs, see Kathy Peiss, *Cheap Amusements: Working Women and Leisure in Turn-of-the-Century New York* (Philadelphia: Temple Univ. Press, 1986), 168–71.

29. Peiss, *Cheap Amusements,* 51–52.
30. Carlin, "Vacation School," 426.
31. For discussion of treating, see Peiss, *Cheap Amusements,* 52–55, 108–14.
32. Carlin, "Salvage Bureau," 250.
33. Working girls often resented patronizing attitudes in the clubs, and the organizations simply could not compete with the appeal of commercial culture. See Peiss, *Cheap Amusements,* 171–78; Sklar, *Florence Kelley and the Nation's Work,* 145.
34. Carlin, "Salvage Bureau," 251–52. The College Settlement in West Berkeley, supported by Phoebe Hearst, ran similar programs. See the *Annual Report for 1900–1901*, 10ff.
35. Carlin, "Salvage Bureau," 252.
36. According to property tax records, the school and the Little Housekeepers' Cottage were located on the same lot, owned by the Bruning family. The cooking school was constructed on rented property, with Watt owning the building independently of the ground beneath, unusual in American building practice.
37. The term "domestic science" has several meanings, referring to changes in housework, household organization, and design, as well as to programs in cooking instruction. See Wright, *Moralism and the Model Home,* chap. 5, 8, 9; Hayden, *Grand Domestic Revolution*, chap, 9, 10; David M. Katzman, *Seven Days a Week: Women and Domestic Service in Industrializing America* (New York: Oxford Univ. Press, 1978), 244–45ff.
38. See news item in *Domestic Science Monthly* 1 (May 1900): 36. Watt chaired the domestic science department at the Oakland Club.
39. For an excellent discussion of the "servant problem," see *Seven Days a Week,* chap. 6. According to Katzman, the West Coast experienced a boom in the servant population between the 1880s and 1900, due to increased immigration (55–58). However, anxiety about the decreasing popularity of domestic service was present in Oakland by the late 1890s.
40. Carlin, "Vacation School," 426.
41. "The Oakland New Century Club," in Oakland New Century Club, *Annual Greeting* (1912), 5.
42. Matilda E. Barber, "The Origin of the Kitchen Garden in Oakland," *Domestic Science Monthly* 1 (May 1900): 28; Elizabeth Dewy Watt, "Kitchen Garden, or Teaching Housework with Toys," *Domestic Science Monthly* 1 (June 1900): 57–61. For discussions of Huntington's curriculum, see Hayden, *Grand Domestic Revolution*, 125–26 and Wright, *Moralism and the Model Home*, 320 n. 2.
43. Carlin, "Salvage Bureau," 255.
44. A. B., "Women's Clubs and What They Are Doing," *Domestic Science Monthly* 1 (Nov. 1900): 219.
45. "The Oakland School of Domestic Science," *Domestic Science Monthly* 1 (Apr. 1900): 1.
46. For the widespread antipathy of working women to domestic service, see Katzman, *Seven Days a Week,* chap. 6, and Sklar, *Florence Kelley and the Nation's Work,* 210.
47. The quotations in this paragraph are taken from "Oakland School of Domestic Science," 1, 3, 4. Katzman discusses class differentiation in training programs in *Seven Days a Week,* 244–45.
48. Carlin, "Salvage Bureau," 256. She reported the bureau was based on similar groups run by the Salvation Army and a project initiated by the People's Church of St. Paul during the 1894 depression.
49. Carlin, "Salvage Bureau," 256.
50. The quote is taken from a pamphlet published by the New Century Club in 1912, and it is a paraphrase of a statement that Eva Carlin used to describe the salvage bureau in 1900. The reuse of clothing and other items was quite common in working-class communities at the

turn of the century, as Nancy Page Fernandez points out in "'If a woman had taste . . .': Home Sewing and the Making of Fashion, 1850–1910" (Ph.D. diss., Univ. of California, Irvine, 1987), 9–10, 105, 114–21.

51. "Oakland School of Domestic Science," 4.
52. A. B., "Women's Clubs," 219.
53. Watt makes no mention in her memoir of the source of the Oakland New Century Club's name. It may have been the New Century Club in Philadelphia, an eminent women's organization founded in 1877. See Sklar, *Florence Kelley and the Nation's Work*, 73–74. Initially, "New Century" was hyphenated, emphasizing the connection of club's formation with turn of the century, but the group dropped the hyphen after 1901.
54. "The Oakland New-Century Club," *A New Century Greeting*, unpaginated.
55. A. B., "Women's Clubs," 219.
56. "Mission of the New-Century Club," *A New Century Greeting*, unpaginated.
57. Mrs. John Bakewell, "Women's Clubs and What They Are Doing," *Domestic Science Monthly* 2 (July 1901): 111.
58. For an overview of California women's clubs, see Hattie Elliott Crane, "Woman's Place in the Government and Conduct of Society: As Illustrated by the Splendid Achievements of California Women," *Overland Monthly*, n.s., 59 (Apr. 1912): 359–65.
59. Christine Rosen discusses the persistence of plot in American city-building practices in *The Limits of Power: Great Fires and the Process of City Growth in America* (New York: Cambridge Univ. Press, 1986).
60. Watt, "Report," 8.
61. The club maintained the strategy until the mid-1920s, when the establishment became city run. Even then, female volunteers continued to assume important positions within the organization. I suspect similar processes occurred in other women's groups, although the displacement of volunteers by professionals in the early twentieth century has been well documented by historians. For excellent discussions in regard to women, see Abigail Van Slyck, *Free to All,* 133–34, and Daniel J. Walkowitz, "The Making of a Feminine Professional Identity: Social Workers in the 1920s," *American Historical Review* 95 (Oct. 1990): 1051–75.
62. "The Oakland New Century Club," *Annual Greeting* (1912), 5; "Retrospection," *Annual Greeting* (1914/15), 11.
63. Elizabeth Watt, "House and Home," in *Second Annual Greeting,* 14.
64. Gwen Wright offers an excellent discussion of the "new aesthetics of simplification" in *Moralism and the Model Home,* 240–46.
65. See Mary Olney's report on the library in the *Second Annual Greeting,* 16.
66. Local newspapers reported in detail the success of the Ebell Society's fund-raising campaign and the subsequent, quite arbitrary removal of the club from further decisions about the building. The decision infuriated the club, and the library's board made one concession: granting the club control over the design of the Children's Reading Room. See scrapbooks pertaining to the history of the Oakland Public Library in the Oakland History Room (at the Oakland Public Library), esp. volumes for 1899–1900, 1901–7.
67. There are no attendance records for the West Oakland Settlement or the New Century Club, independent of reform accounts. I am drawing my conclusions from oral histories, cited below in note 90, and scattered references in published accounts; for example: Carlin, "Salvage Bureau," 256–57; "New Century Greeting," *A New Century Greeting*, unpaginated. Horowitz reports that the elegant Arts and Crafts interior of the coffee house at

Hull House "intimidated" intended clients and the space was redesigned. See her "Hull-House as Women's Space," 47–48, citing Dorothea Moore's account of "A Day at Hull-House" in the *American Journal of Sociology* (1897).

68. Watt, "House and Home," 14. By 1914 a full-time house mother and resident worker lived in the clubhouse in a part of the building that had been added on to the structure before Watt rented it. See discussion in the Oakland New Century Club's *Annual Greeting* (1914/15), 7.
69. The parallels to the development of Hull House are obvious.
70. Anna Sangster, "Recording Secretary's Report" in *Second Annual Greeting,* 10.
71. The data come from city directories and property tax records.
72. "Ladies to Have New Home" *Oakland Tribune,* Apr. 14, 1906, 1; "Magnificent New Home of the Ebell Society, To Open Soon," *Oakland Tribune,* Feb. 9, 1907, 14.
73. Watt gave the flag in honor of George Washington's birthday; the subsequent flag-raising ceremony celebrated her benevolence as much as it did the holiday. E. Marwedel, "Report of Civic Committee" in *Annual Greeting* (194/1915), 23.
74. In the 1940s and 1950s, the interior decor resembled photographs of the spaces taken in the first decade of the twentieth century, according to a neighborhood resident. Arthur Patterson, informal conversation with author, Oakland, Calif., May 25, 1995, and taped interview by author and Sibel Zandi-Sayek for the Cypress Freeway Replacement Project, June 8, 1995, MS, 35–38. The typed transcript is on file at the Anthropological Studies Center, Sonoma State University, Rohnert Park, California.
75. Watt, "My Long Life," 153–54. Watt also expressed an interest in building a public bath, a bandstand, pools, and public gardens.
76. Mrs. L. V. Shaw, "Superintendent's Report, Boys' Club," in *Annual Greeting* (1910), 21.
77. After her husband's death, Watt left Oakland and traveled to Europe. For the Oakland Club's involvement with the recreation movement, see Crane, "Woman's Place," 362–63, and Dewitt Jones, ed., "Oakland Parks and Playgrounds," Oakland, MS, 1936, 201, 203–6. On file, Oakland History Room, Oakland Public Library. The club raised all the funds necessary for the construction and maintenance of the first two public playgrounds in the city, located in West Oakland.
78. "Activities," New Century Club, *Annual Greeting* (1912), 5. By the end of the nineteenth century, reformers, "child-savers," and psychologists realized that play was an instrumental part in child development; the insight shaped the content of the playground movement. See Rosenzweig, *Eight Hours for What We Will,* 140–48, and Galen Cranz, *Politics of Park Design* (Cambridge, Mass.: MIT Press, 1982), chap. 2.
79. Charles Ingerson, an Oakland builder and carpenter, filed for a building permit for the gymnasium's construction on Sept. 7, 1910. See City of Oakland, Permit Ledger 7 (June 14, 1910, to June 13, 1911).
80. Gladys Adams, "Oakland Women Build Fine New Gymnasium for West Oakland Youngsters," *Oakland Enquirer,* Nov. 28, 1910, 12; Lillian Stratton, "Recording Secretary's Report" in Oakland New Century Club, *Annual Greeting* (1912), 8; Mrs. William T. Blackburn, "Treasurer's Report," ibid., 10–11.
81. Stratton, "Recording Secretary's Report," 8.
82. Blackburn, "Treasurer's Report," 11, and "Support the Settlement," *Oakland Observer* 1 (Sept. 30, 1911): 8–9.
83. The New Century Club gave the complex—valued at about $25,000—to the city free of charge. "Clubhouse Given to Oakland for

Recreation Use," *Oakland Tribune,* Jan. 15, 1923; "Fine Playground for Children of Oakland Opened," *Oakland Tribune,* Mar. 16, 1923.

84. In 1934, the City of Oakland ran three community centers, two located in West Oakland; annual attendance at all three was greater than 100,000 people. See Jones, "Oakland Parks and Playgrounds," 215–16. Jones's report stressed the diversity of programs in the New Century facility and argued the "arrangements" of the community houses made them "attractive" to individuals and to families. Also see Patterson, informal conversation with author and taped interview, 14, 16, 35, 38.
85. "Clubhouse Given to Oakland," *Oakland Tribune,* Jan. 15, 1923; "New Century Club Will Disband at Lunch Meet," *Oakland Tribune,* Feb. 3, 1954; "12 Blocks Cleared for Postal Center," *Oakland Tribune,* Nov. 30, 1960.
86. Theda Skocpol, *Protecting Soldiers and Mothers: The Political Origins of Social Policy in the United States* (Cambridge, Mass.: Harvard Univ. Press, 1992), Michael B. Katz, *In the Shadow of the Poorhouse: A Social History of Welfare in America,* rev. ed. (New York: Basic Books, 1996), and Sklar, *Florence Kelley and the Nation's Work.*
87. Historians often criticize the environmental determinism of charity workers and social reformers but rarely examine the relationships of the ideas to actual spatial practices. Recent studies of prisons offer welcome alternatives—among them, Michel Foucault, *Discipline and Punish: The Birth of the Prison,* trans. Alan Sheridan (New York: Pantheon Books, 1975, 1977); Michael Ignatieff, *A Just Measure of Pain: The Penitentiary in the Industrial Revolution, 1750–1850* (New York: Pantheon Books, 1978); and Robin Evans, *The Fabrication of Virtue: English Prison Architecture, 1750–1840* (New York: Cambridge Univ. Press, 1982).
88. See Blair, *Clubwoman as Feminist* and *Crocker, Social Work and Social Order.*
89. Roger Chartier, *The Order of Books,* trans. Lydia D. Cochrane (Stanford: Stanford Univ. Press, 1994), viii.
90. Crocker makes similar points in *Social Work and Social Order,* 224. Local residents recall a helpful agency, friendly teachers, and useful programs. See scattered references in the *West of Market Boys' Journal,* Greg Kosmos, taped interview by Karana Hattersley-Drayton for the Cypress Freeway Replacement Project, Mar. 6, 1995, MS, 14, and Bernyce Rydman, taped interview by Pamela Morton for the Oakland Neighborhood History Project, Sept. 7, 1981, MS, 11. The typed transcripts are on file at the Anthropological Studies Center, Sonoma State University, Rohnert Park, California.
91. Patterson, taped interview, 1995, 50–51; Elaine-Maryse Solari, "Project Gateway," unpublished paper, 1995, 10.
92. Annie Nakao, "Out of the Shadows," *San Francisco Examiner,* Nov. 19, 1995, A-1, A-14.

Select Bibliography

Barrows, Robert. "Beyond the Tenement: Patterns of American Urban Housing, 1870–1930." *Journal of Urban Housing* 9, no. 4 (Aug. 1983): 395–420.

Brown, Kenneth. *Holy Ground: A Study of the American Camp Meeting*. New York: Garland, 1992.

Bushman, Richard L. *The Refinement of America: Persons, Houses, Cities*. New York: Knopf, 1992.

Carson, Cary, Ron Hoffman, and Peter J. Alberts, eds. *Of Consuming Desires: The Style of Life in the Eighteenth Century.* Charlottesville: Univ. Press of Virginia, 1996.

Cromley, Elizabeth. "Apartments and Collective Life in Nineteenth-Century New York." *In New Households: New Housing,* ed. Karen A. Franck and Sherry Ahrentzen, 35–38. New York: Van Nostrand Reinhold, 1989.

Crowley, John E. "In Happier Mansions, Warm and Dry: The Invention of the Cottage as the Comfortable Anglo-American House." *Winterthur Portfolio* 32, no. 2/3 (1997): 169–88.

Fine, Lisa. "Between Two Worlds: Business Women in a Chicago Boarding House, 1900–1930." *Journal of Social History* 19 (spring 1986): 511–19.

———. *Souls of the Skyscraper: Female Clerical Workers in Chicago, 1870–1930*. Philadelphia: Temple Univ. Press, 1990.

Foucault, Michel, *Discipline and Punish : The Birth of the Prison*. Translated from the French by Alan Sheridan. New York: Vintage Books, 1979.

Giedion, Sigfried. *Space, Time, and Architecture.* Cambridge: Harvard Univ. Press, 1941.

Gottfried, Herbert. "The Machine and the Cottage: Building, Technology, and the Single-Family House, 1870–1910." *Journal of the Society for Industrial Archaeology* 21, no. 2 (1995).

Groth, Paul. *Living Downtown: The History of Residential Hotels in the United States.* Berkeley: Univ. of California Press, 1994.

Hayden, Dolores. *The Grand Domestic Revolution: A History of Feminist Designs for American Homes, Neighborhoods, and Cities.* Cambridge: MIT Press, 1981.

Hilton, George W., and John F. Due. *The Electric Interurban Railways in America.* Stanford: Stanford Univ. Press, 1964.

Hoagland, Alison K. *Buildings of Alaska.* New York: Oxford Univ. Press, 1993.

Horowitz, Helen Lefkowitz. "Hull-House as Women's Space." *Chicago History* 12 (winter 1983–84), 40–55.

Jakle, John, with Keith Sculle and Jefferson Rogers. *The Motel in America.* Baltimore: Johns Hopkins Univ. Press, 1996.

Jandl, H. Ward. *Technology of Historic American Buildings.* Washington, D.C.: Foundation for the Preservation of Technology and Association for Preservation Technology, 1983.

King, Anthony, ed. *Buildings and Society: Essays on the Social Development of the Built Environment.* London: Routledge & Kegan Paul, 1980.

Liebs, Chester. *Main Street to Miracle Mile: American Roadside Architecture.* Boston: Little, Brown & Co., 1985.

Martin, Ann Smart. "Makers, Buyers, and Users: Consumerism as a Material Culture Framework." *Winterthur Portfolio* 28, no. 2/3 (summer–autumn 1993): 141–57.

Marx, Leo. *The Machine in the Garden: Technology and the Pastoral Ideal in America.* New York: Oxford Univ. Press, 1964.

McKendrick, Neil, John Brewer, and J. H. Plumb. *The Birth of Consumer Society: The Commercialization of Eighteenth-Century England.* Bloomington: Indiana Univ. Press, 1982.

Meyerowitz, Joanne. "Sexual Geography and Gender Economy: The Furnished Room Districts of Chicago, 1890–1930." *Gender and History* 2, no. 3 (autumn 1990): 274–96.

———. *Women Adrift: Independent Wage Earners in Chicago, 1880–1930.* Chicago: Univ. of Chicago Press, 1988.

Miller, Orlando W. *The Frontier in Alaska and the Matanuska Colony.* New Haven: Yale Univ. Press, 1975.

Moore, Charles W. *Home Sweet Home: American Vernacular Architecture.* Los Angeles: Craft and Folk Art Museum, 1983.

Mosher, Anne, and Deryck Holdsworth. "The Meaning of Alley-Housing: Examples from Late-Nineteenth and Early-Twentieth-Century Pennsylvania." *Journal of Historical Geography* 18, no. 2 (1992), 174–89.

Pevsner, Nikolaus. "Johannesburg: The Development of a Contemporary Vernacular in the Transvaal." *Architectural Review* 113, no. 679 (June 1953): 361–82.

Rothman, David. *The Discovery of the Asylum.* Boston: Little, Brown & Co., 1971.

Sears, John. *Sacred Places: American Tourist Attractions in the Nineteenth Century.* New York: Oxford Univ. Press, 1989.

Stilgoe, John. *Metropolitan Corridor: Railroads and the American Scene.* New Haven: Yale Univ. Press, 1983.

Szuberla, Guy. "Three Chicago Settlements: Their Architectural Form and Social Meaning." *Journal of the Illinois State Historical Society* 70 (May 1977): 114–29.

Upton, Dell. "Toward a Performance Theory of Vernacular Architecture: Early Tidewater Virginia as a Case Study." *Folklore Forum* (1979): 173–96.

———. "Traditional Timber Framing." In *Mate-*

rial Culture of the Wooden Age, ed. Brooke Hindle. Tarrytown, N.Y.: Sleepy Hollow Press, 1981.

———. *Holy Things and Profane: Anglican Parish Churches in Colonial Virginia.* New York: Architectural History Foundation, 1986.

Van Slyck, Abigail. *Free to All: Carnegie Libraries and American Culture, 1890–1920.* Chicago: Univ. of Chicago Press, 1995.

Vicinus, Martha. *Independent Women: Work and Community for Single Women, 1850–1920.* Chicago: Univ. of Chicago Press, 1985.

Walther, Susan Danly, ed. *The Railroad in the American Landscape.* Wellesley: Wellesley College Museum, 1981.

Ward, David. *Poverty, Ethnicity, and the American City, 1840–1925: Changing Conceptions of the Slum and the Ghetto.* Cambridge: Cambridge Univ. Press, 1989.

Weiner, Deborah E. B. *Architecture and Social Reform in Late-Victorian London.* Manchester: Manchester Univ. Press, 1994.

Weiss, Ellen. *City in the Woods: The Life and Design of an American Camp Meeting on Martha's Vineyard.* New York and Oxford: Oxford Univ. Press, 1987.

Wells, Camille. "The Planter's Prospect: Houses, Outbuildings, and Rural Landscapes in Eighteenth-Century Virginia." *Winterthur Portfolio* 28, no. 1 (spring 1993): 1–31.

Williams, Michael Ann. "Pride and Prejudice: The Appalachian Boxed House in Southwestern North Carolina." *Winterthur Portfolio* 25, no. 4 (winter 1990): 217–30.

Wright, Gwendolyn. *Building the Dream: A Social History of Housing in America.* New York: Pantheon, 1981.

Contributors

ANNMARIE ADAMS is associate professor at the School of Architecture, McGill University, Montreal, Quebec, where she teaches courses in architectural history, material culture, and housing research. She is the author of *Architecture in the Family Way: Doctors, Houses, and Women, 1870–1900.*

ARNOLD R. ALANEN, who has a B.A. in architectural studies and a Ph.D. in geography from the University of Minnesota, has been the recipient of both a Fulbright Graduate Fellowship to Finland and a W. K. Kellogg Foundation National Fellowship. For the past quarter century, he has been a professor of landscape architecture at the University of Wisconsin–Madison. The author of scores of publications on landscape and settlement history and cultural resource preservation, he is the co-author of *Main Street Ready-Made: The New Deal Community of Greendale, Wisconsin,* and co-editor of the forthcoming *Preserving Cultural Landscapes in America.*

ANNA VEMER ANDRZEJEWSKI is currently completing her Ph.D. in architectural history at the University of Delaware. Her work on camp meetings developed out of her dissertation, "Architecture and the Ideology of Surveillance in Modern America, 1870–1945." She has recently held fellowships at the Center for the History of Business, Technology and Society at the Hagley Museum and Library and at the Winterthur Museum, Garden and Library, and serves on the VAF board of directors.

REBECCA GINSBURG is a doctoral candidate in the architecture department at the University of California, Berkeley. She received a B.A. in English from Loyola Marymount University and a J.D. from the University of Michigan Law School before moving to Johannesburg in the mid-1980s to do anti-apartheid work. She is currently writing her dissertation on the cultural landscape of suburban Johannesburg during apartheid.

MARTA GUTMAN, an architect, is currently a Ph.D. candidate in architectural history at the University of California, Berkeley.

THOMAS C. HUBKA is a professor of architecture at the University of Wisconsin–Milwaukee. He is currently writing a book on the wooden synagogues of Eastern Europe.

ELAINE JACKSON-RETONDO grew up in Johnstown, Pennsylvania, and completed undergraduate studies at the University of Notre Dame, where she received a Bachelor of Architecture. She worked for three years in prison and jail design at Quinn Associates, Architects in New Britain, Connecticut. More recently she has worked for an architectural firm in San Francisco as a researcher and programmer. She holds a Master of Architecture degree from the University of California–Berkeley and is now completing a Ph.D at Berkeley in architectural history.

JUDITH T. KENNY is an associate professor of geography at the University of Wisconsin–Milwaukee. She maintains a research project on housing and urban reform issues in early-twentieth-century Milwaukee and is completing a book on colonial urban planning and the hill stations of British India.

ZEYNEP KEZER is a postdoctoral fellow in architecture and geography at the University of British Columbia. She has recently completed her dissertation, entitled "The Making of a Nationalist Capital: Ideology and Socio-Spatial Practices in Early Republican Ankara," in the department of architecture at the University of California–Berkeley.

JEANNE CATHERINE LAWRENCE is a doctoral candidate in American studies at Yale University. Her dissertation is titled "Merchandising Class: The Department Store and Urban Social Relations in Turn-of-the-Century Chicago and Glasgow." She holds an M.Sc. in the history of modern architecture from the Bartlett School of Architecture, University of London, and an M.A. in history from the University of California at Riverside, where she studied anthropology and English literature as an undergraduate. She currently teaches history, American studies, and the humanities at California State University, Chico.

ANN SMART MARTIN holds a B.A. in history and anthropology from Duke University and a doctorate in early American history from the College of William and Mary. In the fall of 1998 she became the first Chipstone Professor of American Decorative Arts in the art history department of the University of Wisconsin–Madison. Her previous positions have included assistant professor in the Winterthur Program of Early American History and Culture, acting director of the Advanced Studies Department at Winterthur Museum, and research historian at the Colonial Williamsburg Foundation. Her publications include a special material culture issue of the *William and Mary Quarterly* and the co-edited volume *American Material Culture: The Shape of the Field.*

TRAVIS C. MCDONALD JR. is an architectural historian who has been director of architectural restoration at Thomas Jefferson's Poplar Forest since 1989. He holds a graduate degree from the University of

Virginia and has formerly worked at Colonial Williamsburg and the National Park Service.

Sally McMurry holds a Ph.D. in history from Cornell University. Currently she is professor of history at the Pennsylvania State University, where she teaches a variety of courses in U.S. history. Her research interests include nineteenth-century rural history, women's history, and cultural history. Her publications include *Families and Farmhouses in Nineteenth-Century America: Vernacular Design and Social Change and Transforming Rural Life: Dairying Families and Agricultural Change.* She has served as a VAF board member.

Larry Morrisey is the Heritage Program director at the Mississippi Arts Commission in Jackson. He holds an M.A. in folk studies from Western Kentucky University and has worked on several folklife projects in that region.

Fred W. Peterson was born in Chicago in 1932. He received the Ph.D degree in art history from the University of Minnesota in 1961. Since that year he has been on the faculty of the University of Minnesota, Morris, where he initiated the studio arts and art history programs. A descendant of more than five generations of Swedish carpenters and a long-time resident of the rural upper Midwest, he began research and fieldwork in vernacular architecture in 1974. In addition to numerous articles on farmhouses in the region, he is the author of *Homes in the Heartland: Balloon Frame Farmhouses in the Upper Midwest, 1850–1920* and *Building Community, Keeping the Faith: German Catholic Vernacular Architecture in a Rural Minnesota Parish.*

William B. Rhoads is a professor of art history at the State University of New York at New Paltz. His publications include studies of the Colonial Revival, Franklin Roosevelt's sponsorship of art and architecture, and the architecture of the Hudson Valley. In 1958, he and his family acquired a Philadelphia streetcar built in 1926. It remains an operating trolley in a picturesque landscape in Lancaster County, Pennsylvania.

Michael Ann Williams, a professor of folk studies at Western Kentucky University, is former editor of the Vernacular Architecture Newsletter and is author of *Homeplace: The Social Use and Meaning of the Folk Dwelling in Southwestern North Carolina,* a winner of the Abbott Lowell Cummings Award.

Index

Page number notations in **boldface** refer to illustrations in the text.

People, Power, Places was designed and typeset on a Macintosh computer system using PageMaker software. The text and chapter openings are set Sabon. This book was designed and typeset by Angela Stanton-Anderson and manufactured by Thomson-Shore, Inc. The recycled paper used in this book is designed for an effective life of at least three hundred years.